Public Speaking for College and Career

SECOND EDITION

Public Speaking for College and Career

HAMILTON GREGORY

Asheville-Buncombe Technical Community College

McGRAW-HILL PUBLISHING COMPANY
New York   St. Louis   San Francisco   Auckland   Bogotá   Caracas   Hamburg
Lisbon   London   Madrid   Mexico   Milan   Montreal   New Delhi   Oklahoma City
Paris   San Juan   São Paulo   Singapore   Sydney   Tokyo   Toronto

To my mother
Rachel Smith Gregory

4 5 6 7 8 9 0 DOC DOC   9 4 3 2 1

ISBN   0-07-024666-1

This book was set in ITC Garamond Light by Ruttle, Shaw & Wetherill, Inc.
The editors were Hilary Jackson, Kathleen Domenig, and Jeannine Ciliotta;
the designer was Leon Bolognese;
the production supervisor was Valerie A. Sawyer.
R. R. Donnelley & Sons Company was printer and binder.

COVER PHOTOS: *Top left,* Michael Hayman/Stock, Boston; *right,* Comstock; *bottom left,* Steve Payne, Charleston, WV.

CHAPTER-OPENER CREDITS:

Chapter 1 McGraw-Hill photo by Mary Schoenthaler, courtesy Pace University Speech & Drama Department
Chapter 2 Hazel Hankin
Chapter 3 Steve Payne
Chapter 4 Richard Wood/Taurus
Chapter 5 Steve Payne
Chapter 6 Steve Payne
Chapter 7 Ron Cooper/EKM-Nepenthe
Chapter 8 Kathy Sloan
Chapter 9 Frank Siteman/The Picture Cube
Chapter 10 Deborah Kahn/Stock, Boston
Chapter 11 Frank Siteman/EKM-Nepenthe
Chapter 12 McGraw-Hill photo by Safra Nimrod, courtesy Pace University Speech & Drama Department
Chapter 13 Ulrike Welsch
Chapter 14 Steve Payne
Chapter 15 Lionel Delevingne/Picture Group
Chapter 16 Nancy Ploeger/Monkmeyer
Chapter 17 David Powers/Stock, Boston

Library of Congress Cataloging-in-Publication Data

Gregory, Hamilton.
    Public speaking for college and career / Hamilton Gregory.—2nd ed.
        p.   cm.
    Includes bibliographical references.
    ISBN 0-07-024666-1
    1. Public speaking.   I. Title.
PN4121.G716   1990
808.5′1—dc20   89-13045

Contents

PART FOUR   Presenting the Speech   231

PART FIVE   Types of Public Speaking   275

Preface

Those of us who teach public speaking are faced with two important challenges: How can we show our students the basic principles of speech communication? And how can we teach them to apply those principles to the speeches they must give in the classroom, in their careers, and in their communities?

In this new edition of *Public Speaking for College and Career,* as in the first, I have tried to meet these challenges. While presenting thorough coverage of basic principles, drawn from contemporary research and from the accumulated wisdom of over 2,000 years of rhetorical theory, I have endeavored to show students the real-life applicability of those principles by providing copious examples from classroom, career, and community contexts, and by presenting models of good speeches.

I have prepared this revised edition in order to respond to instructors who used the first edition and made suggestions on how it could be improved. I have expanded and clarified a number of key points and also updated many examples. I have maintained the career orientation of the first edition by providing over 100 examples from business and professional contexts. Some of these examples come from a survey I conducted of 34 professional speakers, including such national figures as Dr. Henry Heimlich, the Ohio surgeon who invented the Heimlich Maneuver for aiding persons who are choking. (I refer to the speakers as "professional" because all of them, having achieved success in business or professional life, now make their living by speaking at conventions, workshops, and professional meetings.) Their suggestions and experiences are sprinkled throughout the chapters and in Tips for Your Career, a special feature that appears at the end of each chapter.

I also interviewed business and professional leaders to find out what communication skills they considered important on the job. Not surprisingly, their views reinforce the basic concepts public speaking instructors have been teaching for years. I discovered, for example, that they all dislike hearing speeches read from a prepared manuscript and consider outlining a vital part of preparation. In addition, I drew from my own experiences in giving speeches to civic clubs, professional organizations, college forums, and parent-teacher associations on such topics as "How Mentally Retarded Citizens Can Be Integrated into the Work Force," "How to Help Refugees Learn English and Get Jobs," and "How Parents Can Help Their Children Develop Effective Study Skills."

The major themes of this book are the same ones most public speaking instructors stress in the classroom. For example, audience-centered communication is emphasized throughout the book: how to analyze the listeners; how to be sensitive to their needs and interests; and how to talk *to* and *with* them, not *at* them. Students are urged to communicate ideas to real people, rather than merely stand up and go through the motions of "giving a speech."

A rule of thumb in American seminaries is that ministers should spend an hour in the study for each minute in the pulpit. Since this ratio is a good one for any speaker, I devote 10 chapters to showing students how to go through the preliminary stages systematically—analyzing the audience, selecting a topic and specific purpose, devising a central idea, finding verbal and visual support material, organizing the material into a coherent outline, and practicing effectively.

At every stage of preparation and delivery, students are encouraged to engage in critical analysis, to ask themselves such questions as these: "What are the attitudes and interests of my audience?" "How can I adapt my subject to their special needs and concerns?" "How can I make my ideas understandable and persuasive?" By the time students finish this book, they will have been trained not only in public speaking, but in critical thinking as well. These skills will be useful to them in the future as tools for their own speeches, and as a means for analyzing the persuasive appeals of politicians and advertisers.

Because many students are troubled by a lack of self-confidence, I have tried to show how speakers can possess and project confidence in themselves and in their ideas. Chapter 3 provides a reassuring discussion of nervousness, and shows students how to turn their nervousness into an assest by using it as constructive energy.

New Features

I and a number of other instructors who used the first edition have noticed that some students need extra help in planning and organizing their speeches. Consequently, in this new edition I have expanded and improved explanations in the following chapters: The last section of Chapter 5 has been rewritten to better explain why a speech needs a central idea and how to create one. Chapter 9 (The Body of the Speech) has been revised to show students how to create main points and distinguish them from supporting points. Chapter 11 (Outlining the Speech) has been revamped to include both *topic* and *complete-sentence* outlines and to show students how to test an outline to see if it is well-organized, logical, and sufficient. Chapter 11 has also been strengthened by two new graphics that help students understand the outlining process and the contents of an outline. A sample process (how-to) speech has been added to the end of Chapter 11.

In Chapter 14 (Speaking to Inform) a new section, "Make Information Interesting," has been added. In Chapter 15 (Speaking to Persuade), the section on appealing to motivations has been expanded with additional discussion and examples. In Chapter 16 (Special Types of Speeches), a section on presentation speeches has been inserted.

To update *Public Speaking for College and Career,* I have substituted many new examples, anecdotes, and sample speeches. There are two new Tips for Your Career (the tips they replace have been transferred to the instructor's manual for those teachers who want to reproduce them and use them in the classroom). For greater clarity and readability, I have rewritten and polished many paragraphs throughout the book.

Overview of the Book

Most instructors have their own ways of organizing and presenting information for this course. I have tried to make each chapter as self-contained as possible so that it can be adapted to any instructor's syllabus.

Part I, Foundations of Effective Communication, contains basic introductory material. Chapter 1 describes the benefits of a public speaking course, including advantages in the job market. It also explains the speech communication process and discusses speakers' responsibilities toward their audience.

Chapter 2 guides students in improving their effectiveness as listeners and discusses the listener's responsibilities toward the speaker.

Chapter 3 is a comprehensive treatment of nervousness, with suggestions on how speakers can convert nervous tension into positive energy. Students should find reassurance in the examples of famous people who suffer from stage fright. For the second edition, a new section has been added on the need for speakers to regard their task as communication, not performance.

Part II, Preliminary Stages, guides the students through the difficult but crucial tasks of choosing and refining a topic and gathering materials. Chapter 4 emphasizes a major theme of the book—the need to focus on the listeners at every stage of preparation and delivery. Students are shown how to analyze the audience and how to adapt their remarks accordingly.

Chapter 5 is a practical guide to selecting a topic and narrowing it to manageable proportions. For students who have trouble finding topics, two worksheets—one for exploring personal interests, the other for brainstorming—are explained and illustrated. After students refine their topics, they are shown how to devise a general purpose, a specific purpose, and a central idea. For the second edition, I have strengthened the section on the central idea.

Chapter 6 explains how to research a topic using several sources, including personal experiences, libraries, computer databases, and interviews. It also discusses taking notes and finding the right materials quickly and efficiently.

Chapter 7 discusses verbal materials that can be used to support ideas: definitions, descriptions, examples, narratives, comparison and contrast, testimony, and statistics. Special attention is given to the use and misuse of statistics.

Chapter 8 examines visual supports for ideas. Various types of visual aids—graphs, charts, drawings, photographs, computer graphics, objects, and models—are discussed, along with media for visual aids: chalkboards, posters, flip charts, handouts, overhead transparencies, slides, films, and videotapes. Also included are nine guidelines for using visual aids effectively. For the second edition, I have inserted some surprising new research on the use of handouts, and I have also clarified how one may use handouts during a presentation.

Part III, Organizing the Speech, explains time-tested methods for arranging materials for a speech. Chapter 9 deals with the body of the speech—how to select main points and organize them in a logical pattern. This edition includes a new section, "Developing Material," to help students who get lost in their notes and can't distinguish main points from subpoints. Attention is also drawn to using transitions to carry the listener from one part of a speech to another.

Chapter 10 focuses on introductions and conclusions. Introductions are explained as a two-part process: first, capturing attention and interest, and second, preparing the audience for the body of the speech. In the section on conclusions, the emphasis is on reinforcing the central idea.

Chapter 11, which has been revised and expanded in this edition, provides a step-by-step guide for developing an outline and then preparing speaking notes based on the outline. Included in the chapter is a full-length sample of a student's outline and speaking notes, followed by a transcript of the speech as it was delivered.

Part IV, Presenting the Speech, examines verbal and nonverbal dimensions of speechmaking. Chapter 12 deals with the need for speakers to use language that is appropriate, accurate, clear, and vivid. One section also shows the differences between oral and written language.

Chapter 13 is a comprehensive treatment of delivery, including how to practice. It also discusses how to handle question-and-answer periods.

Part V, Types of Public Speaking, focuses on the major kinds of speeches that students are likely to give in the classroom and in their careers. Chapter 14 provides guidelines on informative speaking. A sample informative speech, with commentary, is included at the end of the chapter. A section called "Make Information Interesting" has been added in this edition.

Chapter 15 is devoted to persuasive speaking. Two popular types of persuasive speeches—the speech to influence thinking and the speech to motivate action—are examined, followed by a discussion of the elements of persuasion. A sample persuasive speech, with commentary, is featured at the end of the chapter. For this edition, the section on appealing to motivations was revised to provide more examples and explanation.

Chapter 16 covers special types of speeches. At the suggestion of several instructors, I have added a new speech to this chapter—the speech of presentation. From the first edition, I have retained the entertaining (or after-dinner) address, as well as speeches of introduction, acceptance, tribute, and inspiration.

Chapter 17 deals with group discussions, with special emphasis on the reflective-thinking method for solving problems, and team presentations (symposiums and panels).

Appendix A gives pointers on how to speak in front of the camera. In many college courses, students produce or participate in videotaped demonstrations or discussions. More and more businesses and professions are using videotapes for instructions, sales pitches, and in-house communications.

Appendix B is a selection of sample speeches that illustrate and reinforce concepts taught in the text.

Resources for Instructors

Ancillary materials for the text include *Supplementary Readings* in the form of photocopy masters. These handouts provide valuable extensions to the text and can be reproduced and distributed to students at appropriate points during the course. A handout on speech phobia, for example, gives tips for self-therapy to those students whose fear goes far beyond the normal range discussed in Chapter 3. This handout has proved valuable in many colleges and universities in encouraging phobic students not to drop out of public speaking class. Other handout titles include "Quick Guide to Public Speaking" (to help students with their early speeches), "Self-Introduction Speech," "Evaluating Speeches," "Using a Personal Computer for Research," "Oral Interpretation of Literature," "Handling Job Interviews," and "Voice Production." A new handout for this edition is called "Public Speaking Tips for ESL Students."

The instructor's manual provides dozens of worksheets and forms for use in the classroom, including two handouts that list over 100 topics for informative and persuasive speeches, worksheets for discovering library materials, and exercises to practice outlining. The manual also gives tips on how instructors can videotape student speeches and suggestions on how student speeches can be evaluated. A reproducible transcript of Martin Luther King's famous "I Have a Dream" speech is reprinted in the manual for instructors who would like to use it as a model for students.

The second edition of the manual contains a number of new or revised forms and worksheets, including an outline "skeleton" on which students can create their own outlines. This form has been field-tested and refined in several classes, with instructors reporting significant improvements in the quality of student outlines. At the suggestion of several instructors, I have created—and field-tested—a new short evaluation form that students can use to evaluate each other's speeches.

Acknowledgments

In preparing this edition, I received valuable suggestions from the following people who reviewed the book: Lew S. Akin, Abraham Baldwin Agricultural College; Robert L. Huber, Monmouth College; Maria B. Miller, Jefferson Community College; Robert Payne, East Central University; Pamela Perkins, Bunker Hill Community College; E. George Sutter, Joliet Junior College; and Michael A. Weatherson, Southeast Missouri State University.

A note of thanks is also due to a number of first edition users who provided helpful feedback: Barry Alexander, Findlay College; Melvin H. Berry, Nicholls State University; John S. Cease, University of Wisconsin—Whitewater; Robert L. Dey, Colorado Northwestern Community College; Betty Dvorson, City College of San

Francisco; Dr. L. A. Gavés, Queensborough Community College; Alan Ginsburg, State University of New York at Cobleskill; Dr. Robert Greene, Cazenovia College; Connie Gremore, College of St. Thomas; Margaret E. Griffin, Rockingham Community College; Anne Grissom, Mountain View College; Ann Harrell, McLennan Community College; Richard P. Haven, University of Wisconsin—Whitewater; D. E. Jukes, Community College of Allegheny County; Oliver Land, Darton College; Eugenia McAvoy, St. Xavier College; Phil McFarland, New Mexico State University; Carol Messing, Northwood Institute; Carlos Morton, Laredo Junior College; Caroline Parker, Hudson County Community College; Debra Pittman, Guilford Technical Community College; Steven A. Rollman, James Madison University; Natalie S. Rubin, Hudson County Community College; Evelyn T. Silliman, Alice Lloyd College; Mark H. Sterner, Valley City State University; David Svaldi, Adams State College; Patricia Townsend, University of Wisconsin—Whitewater; Eleanor Tucker, Grossmont Community College; Kathleen B. Watters, College of St. Catherine and College of St. Thomas; Sandra Waugh, City College of San Francisco; and James Wilde, Kentucky State University.

I would like to express my continuing appreciation to reviewers of the first edition manuscript: Martha Bergeron, Vance-Granville Community College; Vincent L. Bloom, California State University, Fresno; Marjorie Brody, Bucks County Community College; Steve Collins, Modesto Junior College; Jeanne W. Creech, Dekalb Community College; Sandra F. Davis, Pikes Peak Community College; Fran Franklin, University of Arkansas at Monticello; Marion Gans, University of Connecticut; G. Jack Gravlee, Colorado State University; Anne Grissom, Mountain View College; Charlene Handford, Louisiana State University, Shreveport; Jim Hasenauer, California State University, Northridge; Harry P. Kerr, University of Maine at Farmington; Anne Marcus, Edison Community College; Marjorie McGregor, Central State University; Martha W. Moore, Murray State University; C. R. Newman, Parkland College; Jon F. Nussbaum, The University of Oklahoma; David Payne, The University of Texas at Austin; William R. Rambin, Northeast Louisiana University; Lloyd Rohler, University of North Carolina at Wilmington; Bob G. Sampson, Central Piedmont Community College; Monika Sutherland, Edgecombe Community College; Jim Towns, Stephen F. Austin State University; Forrest D. Tucker, The University of Southern Mississippi; and Gretchen E. Wheeler, Chadron State College.

In the movies, behind-the-scenes people like producers and directors get top billing in the screen credits, along with the screenwriter. It's a shame that books don't have the same tradition because if they did, the name of my principal editor, Kathleen Domenig, could be emblazoned in big letters on the cover of this book. Such tribute would be fitting: without her astute editing, wise counsel, and unflagging sense of humor, this book could not have been written. I also wish to acknowledge, with gratitude, the valuable assistance of my other editors: Roth Wilkofsky, Hilary Jackson, Jeannine Ciliotta, Kathy Bendo, Leon Bolognese, and Mary Farrell.

I am also grateful to the following individuals: Dr. Olin Wood, for urging me to write this book; Tom Gaffigan and Dr. Celia Miles, for giving me encouragement and support; Emily Gean Bergere, Sandy Cagle, and David Holcombe, for supplying ideas on teaching public speaking; Billie Dalton, Maretta Hensley, Terry Holt, and

Peggy Kyle, for ordering research materials for me; Randy Barnett, for lending me a wealth of Toastmasters' publications; Richard Babb, Alan Wilcox, C. L. Satterfield, and Jim Cavener, for providing ideas in the early stages of the book; D. Michael Frank, past president of the National Speakers Association, for giving me an entrée to most of the professional speakers who contributed to this book; Attorney Paul Rifkin, for putting me in touch with Mr. Frank; Nido Qubein of Creative Services, Inc., for supplying me with back issues of his newletter; Bob Sampson of Central Piedmont Community College, for contributing two of his class handouts to the instructor's manual; Dr. G. Michael Shehi, formerly of Highland Hospital, for providing me with information on speech phobia; Larry Schnoor, executive director of the Interstate Oratorical Association, for giving permission to reprint speeches from *Winning Orations.*

I am indebted to the hundreds of students in my public speaking classes over the years who have made teaching this course a pleasant and rewarding task. From them I have drawn most of the examples of classroom speeches.

And for their support and patience, special thanks to my wife Merrell and to my children, Jess, Jim, and June.

Hamilton Gregory

PART ONE

Foundations

of

Effective

Communication

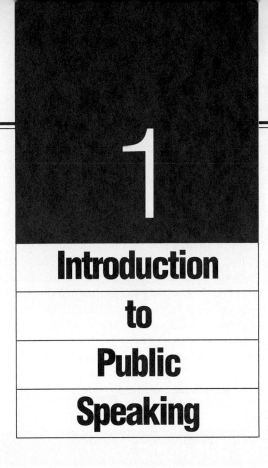

1

Introduction to Public Speaking

Benefits of a Public Speaking Course

The Speech Communication Process

The Speaker's Responsibilities

Lee Iacocca, chairman of Chrysler Corporation, is considered by many people to be one of the most dynamic and successful communicators in America. He took command of Chrysler when the Detroit automobile firm was nearly bankrupt; a few years later the corporation was rolling up record profits, thanks in large part to Iacocca's communication skills: he inspired Chrysler employees to work hard and put out reliable products, and he persuaded American consumers (via TV commercials) to buy his cars.

Iacocca is much in demand as a public speaker. He receives over 3000 speaking invitations each year and accepts about 45 of them. "He devotes enormous energy" to each speech, says *Time* magazine. "At the 1983 University of Michigan graduation exercises, the audience was not hot for him at first." The seniors seemed to be expecting just another dull, stodgy commencement speech. But Iacocca set his audience on fire. "When he finished with the graduates 45 minutes later," reported *Time*, "some 14,000 people were on their feet, cheering and stomping."[1]

How did Iacocca learn to be such an effective communicator? He attributes his success to a public speaking course he took at age 25. Before that, he says, he was a "terrible" speechmaker.[2]

This book and the public speaking course that you are embarking upon may not turn you into an Iacocca, but they are designed with one goal in mind: to help you deliver effective speeches with confidence and vigor—not only in college but in your career as well.

Benefits of a Public Speaking Course

After leaving school, many college graduates look back upon all the courses they took in college and say that public speaking was one of the most valuable.[3] Here are some of the reasons why this course is considered so important:

1. *You learn how to speak to a public audience.* Knowing how to stand up and give a talk to a group of people is a rewarding skill to have for the rest of your life. For example, imagine yourself in the following public speaking scenarios:

☐ In court you explain to a jury why a particular traffic accident was not your fault.
☐ At the monthly meeting of your club, you give a treasurer's report.
☐ You talk to a gathering of neighbors about your ideas for curbing crime in the neighborhood.
☐ You teach softball techniques to thirty boys and girls on the team you coach.

Throughout your life you will encounter many such occasions that require public speaking ability.

2. *You learn skills that apply to one-on-one communication.* Though the emphasis of this course is upon speaking to groups, the principles that you learn also apply to communication with individuals.[4] Throughout your lifetime you will be obliged to talk in situations such as these:

☐ In a job interview, the personnel manager says, "We've got fifty applicants for this job. Why should we hire *you*?" If you know how to give a reply that is brief, interesting, and convincing, you obviously improve your chances of getting the job (assuming, of course, that your qualifications are as good as those of the other forty-nine applicants). In a public speaking course, you learn how to organize and present such a persuasive message.

☐ You sit down in front of a bank executive to ask for a loan so that you can buy a new car. The skills of nonverbal communication (eye contact, facial expression, etc.) that you learn in a public speaking class should help you convey to the executive that you are a trustworthy and reliable person who can be counted upon to repay the loan.

After taking a public speaking course, many students report that their new skills help them as much in talking to one person as in addressing a large audience.

3. *You develop the oral communication skills that are prized in the job market.* Employers are looking for people who can analyze and understand audiences, develop and support ideas, organize information coherently, deliver a talk with confidence and power, and listen intelligently. These are the skills that a public speaking class develops and sharpens.

When you go out to seek a job, which of the following factors is most likely to influence the employer when he or she decides whether to hire you?

☐ The reputation of your school
☐ Your grade-point average
☐ Your letters of reference
☐ Your technical knowledge of the field you are entering
☐ Your oral communication skills—speaking and listening
☐ Your written communication skills—reading and writing

Research shows that "oral communication skills" is the correct answer.[5] Employers generally rank the ability to speak well and listen intelligently as the most highly prized of all skills when it comes to hiring—and promoting—employees.

The answer to the above question is surprising to many students. Surely "technical knowledge of the field" is the most important factor for jobs in science and technology, isn't it? Not according to employers. Take engineering, for example: engineers work mainly with numbers, designs, and materials, so one might assume that communication skills would be less important than technical skills. But according to a survey by *Engineering Education* magazine, 500 leaders in engineering said that the most important capability for civil and electrical engineers was communication skills. *All the technical skills were ranked second in importance.*[6]

In the same survey, the leaders evaluated the recent engineering graduates and rated 59 percent of them as "inferior" in communication skills.[7] This means that the most highly prized skill for engineers—communicating effectively—is lacking in the majority of engineering graduates. Thus, if you are a competent engineer who also possesses good communication skills, you have a big advantage over many other engineers in getting a good job and in gaining promotions.

The same holds true for most other professions as well. For example, alumni of the University of Minnesota Business School ranked oral communication at the top of a list of skills needed for job success.[8]

While being a good communicator can help you get a job or a promotion, the opposite is also true: being a *poor* communicator can block you from being hired or promoted. When 170 business and industrial firms were asked to list the most common reasons for rejecting job applicants, the most frequent replies were "inability to communicate" and "poor communication skills."[9]

Why are communication skills so highly regarded? From an employer's point of view, good communication prevents costly mistakes, improves employee morale, and raises productivity. Consider the case of a General Motors automotive plant that provided classes for its 6000 employees on how to improve their communication skills. As a result of the classes, the plant showed an improvement in employee morale, a decline in absenteeism, and a decrease in production errors. In a two-year period, the program netted a savings for the company of $7 million.[10]

"No one who aspires to success in any profession," says Jack Valenti, president of the Motion Picture Association of America, "can neglect the art of communica-

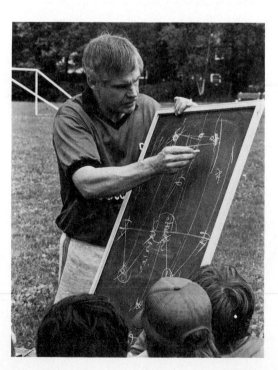

The skills you learn in your public speaking course may be valuable to you in many community and career situations. *(Alan Carey/ The Image Works)*

tion. The role of communicator has become dominant in the careers of business [executives], professors, union [leaders], politicians—of anyone who must try to convince others of a point of view. . . . It is not enough to be intellectual, gorged with facts, smart, competent in administration or in designing strategy. You must be able to speak reasonably, believably, engagingly."[11]

4. *You practice and gain experience in an ideal laboratory.* Effective communicators say that they became adept at communicating by learning certain skills and then practicing them—the way carpenters become masters of their trade by learning woodworking skills and then practicing them. The classroom is an ideal laboratory for practicing your skills because (1) it is an unthreatening setting—no one will deny you a job or a raise based on the way you perform in class and (2) your audience is friendly and sympathetic—made up of students who must go through the same experience.

Extremely valuable to you are the critiques given by your instructor (and, in some cases, by fellow students). If, for example, you say "er" or "uh" between every sentence, you can get help in breaking yourself of this habit. If you have difficulty organizing your thoughts, you can learn strategies for constructing ideas logically.

5. *You gain self-confidence.* One of the greatest benefits of this course is in helping you gain confidence in yourself and in your speechmaking ability. Giving a public speech is one of the most difficult tasks in life; so if you learn to do it well, you gain an extraordinary amount of self-confidence. It is similar to Outward Bound, the program that teaches urban citizens to climb mountains and survive in the wilderness. "After Outward Bound," one graduate of the program told me, "I can take on any challenge." Many students have the same feeling of pride and self-worth after completing a public speaking class.

The Speech Communication Process

A mistake made by some speakers is to think that when they have given a speech, communication has necessarily taken place. It often does take place, of course, but it sometimes does not, for this reason: *Speaking and communicating are not the same thing.* You can speak to a listener, but if the listener does not understand your message in the way you meant it to be understood, you have failed to communicate.[12] Here's an example:

At one hospital's fitness clinic for persons recovering from heart attacks, Brenda Shapiro, a staff nurse, gave a speech on cholesterol. "To decrease your cholesterol level," she told the audience, "you should stop eating red meat."

A couple of months later, when she checked the cholesterol levels of the participants, she discovered that one man's cholesterol level had failed to drop. In fact, it had gone up slightly.

"Did you stop eating red meat?" Shapiro asked.

"Yes," said the patient. "I used to eat my steaks medium-rare, but now I cook them until they are brown through and through."

Shapiro could easily see the problem. Most people know that *red meat* refers to meats such as beef and mutton that are red before they are cooked. The term is a simple way to distinguish between these meats, which are high in cholesterol, and other meats, such as poultry and fish, which are low in cholesterol. This patient, however, had the mistaken notion that when a steak was cooked until it was brown, it was no longer considered red meat. Thus he continued to eat the kind of meat he was supposed to eliminate from his diet.

This incident illustrates that speaking and communicating are not synonymous. The nurse (in the role of speaker) gave instructions, but true, effective communication failed to take place because the patient (the listener) interpreted the message incorrectly.

Let us examine how speech communication works, using Figure 1.1 as our guide.

Speaker

When you are a *speaker*, you are the source, or originator, of a message that is transmitted to a listener. Whether you are speaking to one individual or to an audience of 500, you bear a great responsibility for the success of the communication. The key question that you must constantly ask yourself is not "Am I giving out good information?" or "Am I performing well?" but rather "Am I getting through to my listeners?"

Listener

The *listener* is the recipient of the message sent by the speaker. As we saw in the red meat incident, the true test of communication is not whether a message is delivered by the speaker, but whether it is accurately received by the listener. Professional speaker David W. Richardson says, "A speech takes place in the minds of the audience."[13] In other words, no matter how eloquent the speaker, no matter how dynamic the speaker's delivery, if the listeners' minds do not receive and interpret the message correctly, the desired communication has failed to take place.

Who is to blame for such failure—the speaker or the listener? Depending on the situation, the blame could be placed on either, or both. While speakers share part of the responsibility for communication, listeners also must bear some of the burden. They must try hard to pay attention to the speaker, fighting off the temptation to daydream or think about personal concerns. They must listen with an open mind, avoiding the tendency to prejudge the speaker or discount a speaker's views without a fair hearing.

Message

The *message* is whatever the speaker communicates to the listeners. The message is sent in the form of *symbols*, either *verbal* or *nonverbal*.

Verbal symbols are words. It is important for you to recognize that words are not things; they are *symbols* of things. If you give me an apple, you transfer a solid object from your hand to mine. But if you're making a speech and you mention the word *apple*, you are no longer transferring a concrete thing. You are transferring a symbol, which may be interpreted by your listeners in ways that are quite

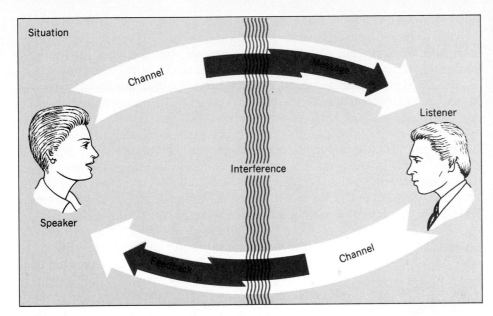

Figure 1.1
A model of the speech communication process. In the context of a particular *situation*, the *speaker* sends a *message* via a *channel* to the *listener*, who in turn gives *feedback* via a *channel* to the *speaker*. *Interference* is whatever impedes the flow back and forth.

different from what you had in your mind. Thus, when you say *apple*, one listener may think of a small green fruit, while another conjures an image of a big red fruit. One listener might think of crisp tartness, while another thinks of juicy sweetness.

Nonverbal symbols are what you convey with your tone of voice, eyes, facial expression, gestures, posture, and appearance.

Everything that you express in a message is in the form of symbols. For example, if you want to tell me about your headache, you cannot transfer the ache and pain from your head to mine. You must transmit a symbolic description of it. The symbols you use might be verbal ("My head feels as if it's splitting apart") and nonverbal (a grimace).

When listeners receive messages, they must interpret the symbols—that is, make sense out of the speaker's verbal and nonverbal symbols. This can cause misunderstanding and confusion because symbols are only an approximation of reality. The listener who hears of your headache might interpret the words "My head feels as if it's splitting apart" in a way that you did not intend. For example, listeners who have never had a headache (there are a few such lucky people in the world) might have trouble imagining the pain. Some listeners might misinterpret the symbols *splitting apart* and think that you had a psychotic break with reality.

As a speaker, you should strive to use symbols that will cause the listener to arrive at a meaning that is as close as possible to the one in your mind. For example, do not say, "Smoking may cause you a lot of trouble." The vague verbal symbols at the end of the sentence—*a lot of trouble*—might be interpreted by some listeners to mean "coughing," by others to mean "stained teeth," or by still others to mean "cancer." Be specific: "Smoking may cause lung cancer."

When you use abstract words like *socialism, feminism,* and *censorship,* you must be especially careful to define precisely what you mean because listeners often have their own widely varying interpretations of such verbal symbols. The term *censorship*, for example, might mean "stamping out filth" to some listeners, or "total government control of the press" to others.

Ideally, the two types of symbols, verbal and nonverbal, are harmonious, but if they are not, the listeners receive a mixed message. For example, suppose you say to an audience, "I'm delighted to be here tonight," but as you say these words, your face has a mournful expression and your tone of voice is regretful. The listeners are getting a mixed message. Which will they believe, your words or your nonverbal behavior? In most instances of mixed messages, listeners accept the nonverbal behavior as the true message. In this case, they will believe that you are not delighted to be there. This is an example of how your intended message is not always the same as the actual message received by listeners.

The solution to this problem is to make sure the nonverbal part of your message reinforces, rather than diminishes, the verbal part. In other words, smile and use a friendly tone of voice when you say, "I appreciate the opportunity to speak to you tonight."

Channel

The *channel* is the medium used to communicate the message. A speech can reach you by means of a variety of channels: radio, television, a public address system, or direct voice communication.

For public speaking in the classroom, you have the best channel of all—direct face-to-face contact. For some speeches in the community, you may have a public address system. This can be a very effective channel (if the system works well and the acoustics in the room are good) because you can speak in an easy, conversational style without having to raise your voice.

Feedback

Feedback is the response that the listeners give the speaker. Sometimes it is verbal, as when a listener asks questions or makes comments during a lecture. In most public speeches, and certainly in the ones you will give in the classroom, listeners refrain from giving verbal feedback until the question-and-answer period at the end of the speech.

Listeners also give nonverbal feedback. If they are smiling and nodding their heads, they are obviously in agreement with your remarks. If, on the other hand, they are yawning and looking at you with a glazed expression, they are probably bored or weary. ("A yawn," wrote English author G. K. Chesterton, "is a silent shout.")

As a speaker, you should be especially sensitive to negative feedback and try to help the listeners. If, for example, you are explaining a concept, but some of your listeners are shaking their heads and giving you looks that seem to say "I don't understand," you should try again, using different words, to make your ideas clear.

While some audience feedback, such as a bewildered look, is easy to understand, there are times when audience behavior is difficult to decipher. If a couple of listeners are sleeping through your speech, it does not necessarily mean that

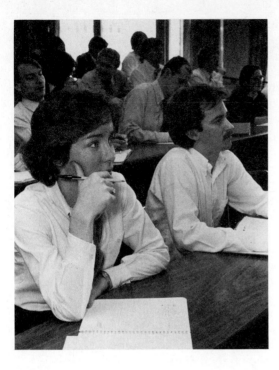

Most feedback during a speech is nonverbal. As a speaker, you should be sensitive to listener responses and adapt to them. *(Frank Siteman/EKM-Nepenthe)*

your speech is boring. It could mean that they stayed out all night at a party and are physically exhausted.

Interference

Interference is anything that blocks or hinders the communication of a message. It could be horns honking outside the classroom or someone coughing loudly inside the room. It could be static and snow on a TV screen that makes it hard to view a videotape. It could be an air-conditioning breakdown that leaves the listeners hot and sticky and preoccupied with their discomfort.

Sometimes listeners will fight to overcome interference—for example, straining to hear the speaker's words despite a truck roaring down the street outside the room. At other times, however, some listeners will fail to make the extra effort, and no communication takes place.

Sometimes interference is "internal"—that is, it comes from within the listeners: some of them might be daydreaming or worrying about a test in their next class. They may be tired or sleepy or hungry—and therefore disinclined to expend mental energy on listening. One of the worst forms of internal interference is jumping to conclusions: listeners block out what the speaker is actually saying because they are sure they already know what the message or conclusion will be. As a speaker, you can help listeners overcome internal distractions by making your speech so lively and interesting that the audience feels compelled to listen to you. In the rest of this book we will look at ways in which you can prepare and deliver lively, interesting speeches.

On other occasions, the speaker might be the cause of interference because he or she uses words that are unfamiliar to the audience or uses words that are interpreted in a way that the speaker did not intend. If the speaker wears bizarre clothing, some listeners might scrutinize the attire instead of concentrating on the speech.

When you are a speaker, you should watch for any signs of interference and if possible take steps to overcome the problem. For example, if a plane roars in the sky and you see your listeners leaning forward to hear your words, you can either speak louder or pause until the plane's noise has subsided.

Situation

The _situation_ is the context—the time and place—in which communication occurs. Different situations call for different behaviors on the part of both speaker and listener. For example, one who delivers a eulogy in the stately hush of a cathedral does not crack jokes. Similarly, in such a setting the audience would not respond to the speaker's remarks with boisterous joy. Jokes and laughter, however, would be quite appropriate for an entertaining after-dinner speech at a convention.

Time of day plays a part in how receptive an audience is. Many listeners, for example, tend to be sluggish and sleepy between 3 and 5 P.M.; if you gave a speech during that period, you would need to have an especially lively presentation, perhaps using colorful visual aids to "jazz" up your speech. If your speech is a long one, you might invite the listeners to stand up and stretch at the midpoint of your speech so that they could shake off their sleepiness.

When you prepare a speech, it is important for you to find out as much as possible about the situation: Where will the speech be given, indoors or outdoors? What is the nature of the occasion? How many people are likely to be present? By assessing these variables in advance, you can adapt your speech to make it appropriate to the situation.

The Speech Communication Process in Action

The speech communication process is a dynamic process in which speaker and listener constantly interact, depending upon each other to keep the process going. In the following story, you can see how the variables of the speech communication process interact in a successful speaking situation. Refer to Figure 1.1 as you study the variables.

Carl Braun* (_speaker_), a counselor for a drug-abuse hotline, was asked to speak at a workshop on drug abuse (_situation_) for about 200 high school students (_listeners_) from throughout his city. When it was his turn to speak, it was midafternoon, the room was hot and stuffy, and the audience was already weary from having heard an hour's worth of public speaking (_situation_). As Braun began his talk (_message_), speaking into a microphone hooked up to a public address system (_channel_), he noticed the drooping eyelids of many of his listeners (_feedback_), so he said (_responding to the feedback_), "You've been sitting a long time. I'd like to ask everyone to stand up and shake hands

* Except in cases where written permission has been given, the names of community and student speakers cited in examples in this book have been changed to protect privacy.

with four different people." The audience responded with gratitude; the novelty of shaking hands instead of just stretching created a mood of good humor. After the audience had sat back down, Braun continued with his speech. Soon, however, he noticed from the listeners' expressions that many of them had once again become sluggish (*feedback*), so he abandoned the microphone and walked out into the midst of the audience (*new channel*). His close presence and his occasional strolls from one part of the room to another (*responding to feedback*) seemed to increase the alertness of most of the listeners. As he continued, however, he noticed that three students were smirking and whispering among themselves (*interference*). Looking directly at them (*confronting interference*), Braun said, "I know what some of you are thinking: What does this old guy know about drugs? Why should we listen to him?" By the look of embarrassment and surprise that flashed across the three students' faces, Braun figured that he had correctly guessed the nature of their reaction. Without denigrating the three, Braun said in a gentle, good-natured way, "I don't blame you for having that attitude. Indeed, how can I claim to know anything at all about the world of teenage drug use?" He then went on to explain what he had learned as a counselor for the drug-abuse hotline (*message*). For the rest of the speech, Braun continued to interact dynamically with his audience. For example, he "revved" them up by throwing out questions and then asking for volunteers to answer the questions (*feedback*). Braun's speech was a success because he had overcome formidable problems—an audience that was already weary of speeches, a room that was too hot, and a time of day (midafternoon) that was more conducive to drowsiness than to mental alertness—and had managed to reach the audience with information that was delivered with energy and genuine concern.

The Speaker's Responsibilities

A speaker who stands before an audience has certain personal and ethical responsibilities which an honest person should accept. Here are some suggestions which I hope will help you develop an awareness of these responsibilities.

Respect Your Audience

As a speaker, you should respect your listeners, no matter who they are or why they have come to listen to you.

A speaker who failed to respect an audience wrote the following account of his fiasco for the benefit of readers of this book:

When I was a senior in college, I was older than most of my fellow students and had already spent five years as a full-time journalist. When I was asked to take the job of managing editor of the school paper, I agreed, even though it meant that I was stepping down from the glamorous arena of daily journalism into the lowly (as I saw it) world of college reporting. But I thought it would be fun to teach these college "kids" the hard realities of the cold, cruel world beyond the hallowed halls of ivy. At the first staff meeting, I played the role of the hard-boiled newsman, haranguing the fledgling reporters on what they could and could not do. I told them that I was a veteran writer who would not tolerate lateness and that I would ruthlessly edit poorly written articles. Then, with a parting admonition to work hard, I gruffly dismissed them. A few hours later, the editor-in-chief approached me sheepishly and informed me that every single one of the twenty reporters had resigned. I was without a staff, and I had to step aside to make way for a new managing editor. I had utterly failed to consider the sensitivities of my audience. I had failed to give them the respect that should be given to *any* group of people. Deep down I had thought of them as wet-behind-the-ears dunces and they had correctly picked up on my attitude. The slap in the face they gave me by resigning *en masse* was a painful slap that I richly deserved.

This anecdote provides a valuable lesson: as a speaker, you should always respect your listeners. A sour, negative attitude not only alienates your audience, it also diminishes you. It deprives you of meaningful communication with your fellow human beings.

You should never patronize your listeners or talk down to them. If you say, "I know I won't change anybody's mind today, but . . . ," it is almost the same as saying, "I know you idiots are all close-minded and won't listen to me intelligently." You are insulting your audience. One professor used to close each of his lectures by gathering up his notes and declaring, "Well, I've finished casting my pearls." The statement was clearly an insult, since it was an allusion to the Biblical verse, "Neither cast ye your pearls before swine." When you insult or antagonize listeners, you do more than make them angry or defensive; you reduce the possibilities of reaching them with your ideas.

Michelle Cuomo, a student speaker, tried to persuade her audience that smoking should be banned in restaurants. Since she knew that some of her listeners smoked, she could have given them a stern tongue-lashing: "Don't you smokers have any common decency? How do you think the rest of us feel when you blow your foul smoke into the air that we must breathe?" If she had berated her audience in this fashion, how do you think the smokers would have reacted? With anger and defensiveness, of course. Wisely, Michelle used a more respectful approach. She said, "I know that some of you smoke, and I know that when you go out to eat at a restaurant with your friends, it's very enjoyable to have a cigarette at the end of the meal. I normally would not want to do anything to take away from your enjoyment, except that I have asthma, and I'd like to explain what smoke does to me." Notice how friendly and reasonable Michelle was. She refrained from attacking the intelligence or morals of the smokers; she merely presented her case in a respectful, but assertive manner that should have prevented any listener from getting angry or defensive. And who knows? She might have convinced some smokers to accept her views.

Take Every Speech Seriously

Contrary to what some students think, your classroom speeches are as important as any speeches that you may give in your career, and they deserve to be taken seriously. Here is why: (1) Speech class is an ideal place to practice, and as with any endeavor in life, you get the maximum benefit from practice if you exert yourself to the fullest. High jumpers who win gold medals in the Olympics do so by trying as hard in practice as they do in Olympic competition. (2) While the classroom is a laboratory for speechmaking, the speeches are not artificial. They deal with real human issues, and they are given by real human beings. As a teacher, I look forward to classroom speeches, not only because they are interesting, but also because they are highly instructive. I learn a great deal from them. To cite just a few examples from recent years: I have learned how to save the life of a person choking on food, I have learned the correct way to cut down some decaying trees in my backyard, and I have modified my views on gun control because of the persuasive talents of several students.

Some speakers think that if an audience is small, or a great deal smaller than they expected, they need not put forth their best effort. This is a mistake; you should try as hard to communicate with an audience of five as you would with an audience of five-hundred. At conventions, there are usually a number of speakers scheduled at the same time in different meeting rooms. I have seen some speakers get so angry at seeing only a handful of people show up for their talk (while hundreds are crowding in to hear the speaker across the hall) that they let their disappointment color their speech. They give their speech in a peevish mood. Isn't it ironic? They are irritated because of the people who did not come, but their negative "vibrations" go out to the people who honored them by attending. They impatiently hurry through their presentation; their attitude seems to be: why should I take pains with just a handful of people?

Now contrast that kind of speaker with Nido R. Qubein, a professional speaker who was scheduled to give a talk at a convention of the Associated General Contractors of America. Because of some last-minute scheduling changes, he found that his competition was none other than the President of the United States! Instead of having an audience of hundreds, he found himself with only about thirty listeners. "It would have been easy for me to assume that . . . it was a hopeless situation," he said. "But I realized that those people who came really wanted to hear my message, and I tried twice as hard to please them. I called them up to the front of the room, seated them around a large table, and we had a group discussion. They got so involved that it was hard to break it off at the appointed time."[14]

Professional speakers have learned to take every audience seriously, even if it is an audience of only one. James "Doc" Blakely, a professional speaker, tells of a colleague who traveled to a small town in the Canadian province of Saskatchewan to give a speech, but found that only one person had showed up to hear him. He gave the lone listener his best efforts, and later that listener started a national movement based upon the speaker's ideas.[15]

Be Ethical

Being ethical means being honest and straightforward with your listeners, avoiding all methods and goals that are deceitful, unscrupulous, or unfair.[16]

As an ethical speaker, you should follow two important principles:

1. *Be as well-informed as you possibly can.* You should speak on a subject only after you have thoroughly investigated it, finding out as much as possible. If, for example, you are planning to speak on the incidence and causes of airplane crashes, you should carefully collect data and analyze the statements of the experts—both inside the air-traffic industry and outside it. Sometimes, of course, there will be gaps in your knowledge of a subject; you should be willing to admit this to the audience (for example, "I couldn't find a figure on the number of crashes so far this year, but I do have the figure for last year. . .").

2. *Be honest with facts and figures.* Do not fabricate information to prove a point. Refrain from distorting data to fit an argument. But, you might ask, isn't it all right to bend the facts if one's cause is noble and good? No, for the honest speaker, the ends never justify the means. It is unethical to be dishonest in the service of a good goal. For example, let's say that you sincerely believe that the controversial drug Laetrile is the miracle cure for cancer that the world has long awaited. You come across an article that reports that twelve out of the sixteen doctors interviewed by the authors favored legalization of the drug on an experimental basis even though they all predicted that the medicine would prove to be worthless. Would it be ethical to say in your speech, "Three out of four doctors surveyed support legalization of Laetrile"? This would of course be an outrageous distortion of statistics. Your statement would make it sound as if three-fourths of all doctors in America favor legalization, when in fact only sixteen doctors were involved in the poll. Furthermore, you would be withholding a vital piece of information from your audience: the fact that all the doctors predicted that the drug would prove to be worthless. Even if you could get away with this kind of dishonest reporting (that is, not being challenged by anyone in the audience), it would be unethical to pursue it, regardless of how admirable you think your goal is.

Summary

A public speaking course helps you develop the key oral communication skills (speaking well and listening intelligently) that are highly prized in business, technical, and professional careers. You gain both confidence and experience as you practice these skills in an ideal speechmaking laboratory—the classroom—where your audience is friendly and supportive.

The speech communication process consists of seven elements: speaker, listener, message, channel, feedback, interference, and situation. Communication does not take place just because a speaker transmits a message; the message must be accurately received by the listener. When the speaker sends a message, he or she must make sure that the two components of a message—verbal and nonverbal—do not contradict each other.

As a speaker, you should hold your listeners in high esteem. You should respect them and treat them courteously, no matter who they are or how large the audience is. In every aspect of your speech, you should maintain high ethical standards, making sure that you are as well-informed as possible and that you are honest with your facts and figures.

Review Questions

1. Why are communication skills important to your career?
2. Name five personal benefits of a public speaking course.
3. What are the seven elements of the speech communication process?
4. Why is speaking not necessarily the same thing as communicating?
5. If there is a contradiction between the verbal and nonverbal components of a speaker's message, which component is a listener likely to accept as the true message?
6. What are the three major responsibilities of a speaker, as discussed in this chapter?

Tips FOR YOUR CAREER

Tip 1: Avoid the Five Biggest Mistakes Made by Speakers

In a survey of thirty-four professional speakers, I asked what they considered to be the most common mistakes made by public speakers in America today. Here are the mistakes that were most often cited:

1. Failing to tailor one's speech to the needs and interests of the audience
"The most common mistake of speechmakers," says professional speaker Philip D. Steffen of Marietta, Georgia, "is failure to educate yourself about the specifics of the audience to which you will be speaking, [such as] age, gender, the essential points of their business, what problems they are facing, challenges they face, what they do well, where they and their business are going, and objectives of the overall meeting."[17]

Steffen gives over 125 talks to American corporations each year on management, sales, marketing, and production. Before each presentation, he finds out everything

he can about the company that he will address. He interviews company officials and gets his name put on the organization's mailing list. "Most of my presentations are booked months in advance," he says. "I keep a file folder on each client. When I run across something I feel might be appropriate for the group, I put it in the file. Thus I am constantly preparing for them."[18]

Most good speakers are like Steffen—they center themselves and their messages on the listeners, finding out as much as possible about them and then striving to meet their needs and interests.

2. Being poorly prepared Some speakers give mediocre talks because they have failed to devote enough time to researching their topic, organizing their material, and rehearsing their speech.

A good speech does not just "happen"—it requires a big investment of time and energy. Jock Elliott, chairman emeritus of

Ogilvy & Mather advertising agency, spends about 28 hours preparing each of his speeches.[19] Roy Fenstermaker of Lakewood, California, who won the 1983 Toastmasters' International Speech Contest championship with a rousing address entitled "Retirement, Never!" started working on his speech two years before it was delivered. To gather ideas, he tapped his own experience as a retired person, read about fifteen books on retirement, and culled through his personal notebook of favorite quotations. He wrote twenty drafts of his outline before deciding upon the final version. Then he practiced his speech many times, making sure that he stayed within the contest's strict time limits (4½ to 7½ minutes).[20]

3.   Trying to cover too much in one speech   Some speakers are so enthusiastic and knowledgeable about their topic that they want to tell you everything they can. So they try to cram a huge amount of material into a short speech. As professional speaker Arnold "Nick" Carter puts it: "They try to put ten pounds of information in a one-pound bag."[21]

Covering too much material causes the listeners to suffer from "information overload." They simply cannot absorb huge quantities of information in one sitting. A wiser approach is to give the listeners one big idea with a few main points to back it up.

4.   Failing to maintain good eye contact   Listeners tend to distrust speakers who do not look them in the eye. Yet some speakers spend most of their time looking at their notes or at the floor or at the back wall.

One good way to maintain eye contact with your listeners is to think of your speech as a conversation with them. Hope Mihalap, a professional speaker from Norfolk, Virginia, says that she tries to "make the audience feel that we're all sitting together in a living room, having a warm, one-on-one conversation."[22] Treating a speech as if it were conversation helps your eye contact because, in the words of another professional speaker, Rosita Perez of Brandon, Florida, "you tune in to the audience instead of to yourself."[23]

5.   Being dull   A dull speech can be caused by poor content or by poor delivery. To avoid being dull, you should (1) choose a subject about which you are enthusiastic, (2) prepare interesting material, (3) have a strong desire to communicate your message to the audience, and (4) let your enthusiasm shine forth during your delivery of the speech.

2

Listening

How to Listen Effectively

The Listener's Responsibilities

Because of some misunderstandings, a secretary who worked for an extremely busy executive began to suspect that her boss was so preoccupied with paperwork that he never truly listened to her. To verify her suspicion, she arrived late for work one morning, entered the boss's office, and said, "I'm sorry I'm late but I had to pick up my ticket to Brazil. You see, I've been embezzling company funds and now that I've reached my goal, I'm off to Rio."

The harried executive glanced up from the mound of papers on his desk and said, "Well, at least you're here. Can you get me the notes on the Thompson proposal?"[1]

This story illustrates the difference between hearing and listening. *Hearing* occurs when your ears pick up sound waves being transmitted by a speaker. *Listening* involves making sense out of what is being transmitted. The boss heard the secretary's voice, but he failed to listen to everything that she said. He apparently paid attention to the words, "I'm sorry I'm late" but let his brain tune out the rest of her remarks.

We may snicker at the boss's gaffe, but most of us are just as ineffective at listening as the boss was.[2] According to Dr. Lyman K. Steil of the University of Minnesota in St. Paul, "Tests have shown that immediately after listening to a 10-minute oral presentation, the average listener has heard, understood, properly evaluated and retained approximately half of what was said. And within 48 hours, that drops off another 50% to a final 25% level of effectiveness. In other words, we quite often comprehend and retain only one-quarter of what is said."[3]

Society pays a heavy price for our poor listening, Dr. Steil says, "With more than 100 million workers in this country, a simple $10 mistake by each of them, as a result of poor listening, would add up to a cost of a billion dollars. And most people make numerous listening mistakes every week. Letters have to be retyped, appointments rescheduled, shipments rerouted. Productivity is affected and profits suffer."[4]

Poor listening also hurts us at home. Many marriages, for example, are weakened by the absence of real listening. "Most couples never truly listen to each other," says Dr. M. Scott Peck, a psychiatrist and author of several best-selling books on mental health. "When couples come to us for counseling or therapy, a major task we must accomplish . . . is to teach them how to listen."[5]

Effective listening is taught not only by marriage counselors but by many American businesses as well. To boost productivity and sales, giant corporations such as 3M, AT&T, and General Electric routinely send employees to special listening-skills classes. One of New England Telephone Co.'s divisions was losing $874,800 a year because 20 percent of its operater-assisted calls were delayed by listening problems. After the company developed a program to teach effective listening, it recovered about $500,000 of its annual loss.[6]

If you know how to listen effectively, you enhance your chances of getting a job. A survey of California business leaders conducted by one university asked what skills they looked for in hiring employees. A majority of the executives felt that listening was *the most important skill* for a potential employee.[7]

Once you have a job, good listening can help you get ahead. "In most companies," one executive told me, "men and women who are good listeners are so rare that no matter what their job—blue collar or white collar—they are usually the ones who win promotions and raises. A company doesn't want to see them hired away by somebody else."

How to Listen Effectively

If you are reading a book, you can put it aside when you become weary or distracted, and then come back to it later. If the book contains complicated material, you can reread passages until you extract the meaning.

While the printed page is stable and enduring, a speech is transitory and short-lived—"written on the wind," as someone once said. That is why listening is more difficult than reading. If you listen to a speech and you fail to get the message the first time around, there is usually no way to go back and retrieve it.[8]

Though listening is a difficult task, there are some skills that you can develop to maximize your understanding and retention of material. These skills are presented in the following discussion.

Don't Fake Attention

If you are like most people, you have indulged in fake listening many times. You go to history class, say, and sit in the third row and look squarely at the instructor as she speaks. But your mind is far away, floating in the clouds of a pleasant daydream. Occasionally you come back to earth: the instructor writes an important term on the chalkboard, and you dutifully copy it in your notebook. Every once in a while the instructor makes a witty remark, causing others in the class to laugh. You smile politely, pretending that you heard the remark and found it mildly humorous. You have a vague sense of guilt that you are not paying close attention, but you tell yourself that you can pick up the material from the textbook or from a friend's notes. Besides, the instructor is talking about road construction in ancient Rome and nothing could be more boring. So, back you go to your private little world.

You should never fake attention, for two main reasons: (1) you miss a lot of information, and (2) you can botch a personal or business relationship. Writer Margaret Lane relates an embarrassing instance of such fakery:

> Years ago, fresh out of college and being interviewed for a job on a smalltown newspaper, I learned the hard way . . . [that] the ability to listen and respond can make all the difference in any relationship. . . . My interview had been going well, and the editor, in an expansive mood, began telling me about his winter ski trip. Eager to make a big impression with a tale of my own about backpacking in the same mountains, I tuned him out and started planning *my* story. "Well," he asked suddenly, "what do you think of that?" Not having heard a word, I babbled foolishly, "Sounds like a marvelous holiday—great fun!" For a long moment he stared at me. "Fun?" he asked in an icy tone.

"How could it be fun? I've just told you I spent most of it hospitalized with a broken leg."[9]

If you fake listening, you will rarely be so painfully exposed, but this does not mean that you can get away with deception most of the time. Many speakers are sensitive to facial cues and can tell if you are merely pretending to listen. Your blank expression, your unblinking gaze, and the faraway look in your eyes are the cues that betray your inattentiveness.

Even if you are not exposed, there is another reason for not faking attention: it is easy for this behavior to become a habit. For some people, the habit is so deeply ingrained that they automatically start daydreaming the moment a speaker begins talking on a subject that seems complex or uninteresting. Such a habit cuts them off from valuable communication with others and causes them to miss a lot of interesting and valuable information.

Be Willing to Expend Energy

When you listen to a comedian cracking jokes on TV, do you have to work hard to pay attention? No, of course not. You simply sit back in a comfortable chair and enjoy the humor. It is easy, effortless, relaxing.

If you are like many listeners, you assume that when you go into a room for a lecture or a speech on a difficult subject, you should be able to sit back and absorb the content just as easily as you do in listening to a comedian's jokes. This is a major misconception because the two situations are actually quite different. Listening to light, entertaining material requires only a modest amount of mental effort, while listening effectively to difficult, complex material requires arduous work. You must be alert and energetic, giving total concentration to the speech, with your eyes on the speaker, your ears tuned in to the speaker's words, and your mind geared to receive the message.

The more complicated the material, the more raw energy you must put forth. Dr. M. Scott Peck tells of attending a lecture by a man who spoke on some interesting, but highly abstract theories of psychology. "Throughout the hour and a half he talked, sweat was literally dripping down my face in the air-conditioned auditorium. By the time he was finished, I had a throbbing headache, the muscles in my neck were rigid from my effort at concentration, and I felt completely drained and exhausted." Was the effort worth it? Yes, concluded Dr. Peck, because the speaker rewarded his concentration by giving him "a large number of brilliant insights."[10]

Fortunately, most speeches do not leave us in such an exhausted state, but Dr. Peck's experience illustrates the strenuous nature of active listening. As Dr. Ralph G. Nichols, who did pioneering work on listening skills at the University of Minnesota, put it, "Listening is hard work. It is characterized by faster heart action, quicker circulation of the blood, and a small rise in body temperature."[11]

If you tend to drift away mentally whenever a speaker begins to talk about unfamiliar or difficult material, try to break yourself of the habit. Vow to put as much energy as necessary into paying attention.

Prepare Yourself

Since listening to difficult material is hard work, you must prepare yourself as thoroughly as a runner prepares for a race.

Prepare yourself *physically.* Get plenty of sleep the night before. If necessary, exercise right before the speech or lecture. If, for example, you will be sitting in a warm room in midafternoon (and therefore likely to become drowsy and lethargic), you might want to take a brisk walk before entering the room to make yourself alert and keen-minded.

Prepare yourself *intellectually.* If the subject matter of the speech is new or complex, do research or background reading beforehand. In this way, the speech will be much easier to understand. As the American philosopher Henry David Thoreau once said, "We hear and apprehend only what we already half know." The truth of this statement is shown in the way one student prepared for listening:

> Margaret Edney, a student nurse, planned to attend a lecture by an expert on Alzheimer's disease, a crippling disorder affecting many elderly persons. Margaret realized that unless she did some background reading, the lecture would probably be too difficult to understand because of the unfamiliar medical terms that would be used. So she went to the library and found two recent articles on the disease. As she read the articles, she looked up definitions of some of the more important clinical terms associated with the disease—*cholinesterase, acetylcholine, physostigmine,* etc. Later, when she went to the lecture, she was able to make sense out of the expert's remarks—thanks to her advance research.

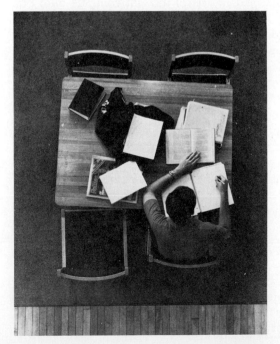

Researching the topic before you hear a speech can help you understand new or complex material more easily. *(Peter Vandermark/ Stock, Boston)*

This technique is of course what all good students do in perparing for their classes. They read the relevant textbook pages before attending a lecture so that they can gain maximum understanding of the instructor's remarks.

Resist Distractions

Concentrating on a speech is always hard work, but the task is made even more difficult by distractions of all sorts. There are auditory distractions: a fly buzzing near your ear, an air conditioner that creates a racket, people coughing or whispering. There are visual distractions: cryptic comments on the chalkboard (from a previous meeting), a nearby listener who is intriguing to look at, birds landing on a windowsill. There are also physical distractions: headaches or stuffy noses, seats that are too hard, rooms that are too hot or too cold.

On top of all these distractions, we are plagued by mental distractions such as daydreams, worries, and preoccupations. We think about tomorrow or evaluate yesterday when we should be paying attention to the present moment. Mental distractions are often caused by our minds running faster than the speaker's words. In most speeches, we as listeners can process information at about 500 words per minute, while most speakers talk at 125 to 150 words a minute. This means that our brain works three or four times faster than the speed needed for listening to a speech. This creates a lot of mental spare time. Dr. Nichols says, "What do we do with our excess thinking time while someone is speaking? If we are poor listeners, we soon become impatient with the slow progress the speaker seems to be making. So our thoughts run to something else for a moment, then dart back to the speaker. These brief side excursions of thought continue until our mind tarries too long on some enticing but irrelevant subject. Then, when our thoughts return to the person talking, we find he is far ahead of us. Now it is harder to follow him and increasingly easy to take off on side excursions. Finally we give up; the person is still talking, but our mind is in another world."[12]

How can you keep your mind from wandering? Only by using rigorous self-discipline. Shortly before a speech, prepare yourself for active listening by arriving in the room a few minutes early and getting yourself situated. Find a seat that is free from such distractions as blinding sunlight or friends who might want to whisper to you. Make yourself comfortable, lay out paper and pencil for taking notes, and clear your mind of personal matters. When the speech begins, concentrate all your mental energies on the speaker's message. There are two things you can do to aid your concentration—listen analytically and take notes. We will discuss both of these techniques in the following sections.

Listen Analytically

You should analyze a speech as it is being presented, both to help you concentrate and to help you understand and remember the speaker's message. There are two elements that you should examine analytically: the main points and the support materials. Let's examine each in turn.

Focus on Main Ideas

Some listeners make the mistake of treating all of a speaker's utterances as being equal in importance. This causes them to "miss the forest for the trees," that is, to spend so much time looking at individual sentences that they fail to see the "big picture," or larger meaning.

As you listen to a speech, try to distinguish the speaker's primary ideas from the secondary material—such as facts, figures, and stories—that are used to explain or prove the primary ideas. If a speaker tells an interesting story, for example, ask yourself, "Why is the speaker telling me this? What main idea is the speaker trying to get across to me by telling this story?"

In the following passage, taken from a classroom speech by Rick Ballard, see if you can identify the main idea:

> Cocaine can kill you. Without warning, it can cause a fatal reaction at any time with any kind of user. Not just heavy users; also light, so-called recreational users who snort only at weekend parties and ingest only a small amount of cocaine during any given evening. Two years ago, one of these recreational users, a 20-year-old woman in Miami, went to a disco party, drank some wine, snorted some cocaine, and then told friends she needed to lie down. A few moments later she experienced a violent seizure—caused by cocaine, not by epilepsy. The seizure was so strong that it threw her off the bed. An ambulance was called, but before it arrived, she was dead. She had used cocaine on previous occasions; for some reason her body—without warning—had suddenly developed an intolerance for the drug. Drug-abuse experts say that there is no way of predicting who will die from cocaine—it could be a regular user or a first-time user. Miami, Florida, has two cocaine deaths each month. Washington, D.C., had 88 last year. We should all remember that cocaine is a poison; cocaine used pharmaceutically in hospitals has the familiar poison warning—a skull and crossbones—on the bottles.

After hearing the above passage in a speech, some unskilled listeners might remember only that cocaine bottles in hospitals have a skull and crossbones on them or that a young woman in Florida died after using cocaine. But these items are *not* the main idea of the passage. A careful listener would concentrate on, and try to remember, one idea above all else: cocaine can randomly kill any user—light or heavy—without warning.

Evaluate Support Materials

Most speakers use support materials such as stories, statistics, and quotations to explain, illustrate, or prove their main points. As a listener, you should evaluate each support as it is being presented: Is it accurate? Are objective sources used? Is enough support given? Am I getting an accurate picture of reality or a distorted one?

As an example of how to evaluate support materials, let's suppose that a speaker tries to persuade us that all states should revoke the drivers' licenses of motorists over 75 who cannot pass a comprehensive vision and safety test every year. Let's evaluate the evidence as the speaker gives it to us:

Elderly drivers are sometimes a menace on our highways. According to *USA Today*, an 84-year-old Hesperia, California, man climbed into his station wagon last January and headed down the San Bernardino Freeway—going the wrong way. Police stopped him, drove him back to his house, and started paperwork aimed at lifting his license. The next day, the man got into his station wagon again and headed down the freeway—again driving the wrong way. This time he was stopped by a head-on collision with a car filled with teen-agers. The man and a 16-year-old girl were killed.

This story is tragic, but does it prove the speaker's point—that drivers over 75 should be rigorously tested every year? No, this could be just an isolated case that proves nothing about elderly drivers in general. We need more evidence.

Though people age at different rates, most people at about age 75 experience a dramatic drop-off in their visual acuity, reflex quickness, and muscular coordination.

This is interesting but a bit vague. If such a drop-off does exist, does it really affect one's driving all that much? We still need more evidence.

According to the National Safety Council's analysis of traffic fatalities, there are 55 fatalities for every 100,000 drivers over 75. That's more than twice the rate for middle-aged motorists.

Now we have some solid evidence, from a prestigious source, that drivers over 75 are a high-risk group. But will stringent annual testing of this age group cut down on accidents?

Two states—Hawaii and Iowa—have instituted comprehensive test requirements for the very old. Both states have reported a decline in the rate of traffic accidents by drivers over 75.

This last piece of evidence is quite compelling. The speaker's plan has been tried out in two states, and apparently it works. Unless we come across information that refutes these arguments, we will have to concede that the speaker has marshaled some very convincing support for the main point.

Take Notes

I strongly urge you to take notes whenever you listen to a speech for the following reasons:

1. *Note taking gives you a record of the speaker's most important points.* Unless you have superhuman powers of memory, there is no way you can remember all of a speaker's key ideas unless you take notes.

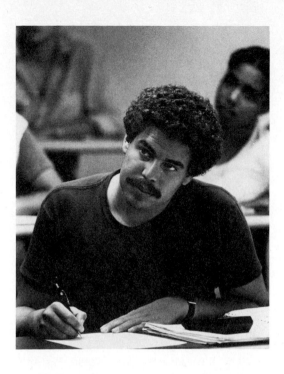

Taking notes during a lecture or speech can help you focus on the speaker's ideas. *(Susan Lapides/Design Conceptions)*

2. *Note taking sharpens and strengthens your ability to listen analytically.* When you take notes, you force your mind to scan a speech like radar, looking for main points and evidence. You end up being a better listener than if you did not take any notes at all.[13]

3. *Note taking is a good way to keep your attention on the speaker and not let your mind wander.* This is why I recommend taking notes on *all* speeches—not just on important lectures at school. A colleague explains why he takes notes at every meeting he attends, even though he usually throws them away soon afterward:

> I take notes at any talk I go to, whether it's a business briefing, a professional seminar, or an inspirational speech. I usually review the notes right after the meeting to solidify the key points in my mind. Afterwards, I may save the notes for my files or for some sort of follow-up, but usually I drop them in a trash can on my way out of the room. This doesn't mean that I had wasted my time by taking notes. The act of writing them helped me to listen actively and analytically. It also—I must confess—kept me from daydreaming.

When taking notes, don't try to write down the speaker's exact words because you could easily fall into the habit of transcribing without evaluating. As much as possible, put the speaker's ideas into your own words, so that you make sure that you understand what is being said.

There are many different ways of taking notes, and you may have already developed a method that suits you. Whatever system you use, your notes should include major points, with pertinent data or support materials that back up those points. You may also want to leave space for comments to yourself or questions that might need to be asked. One effective method for taking notes is to list your main ideas in one column, support materials in a second column, and listener responses in a third column. Here's a sample of the top of a sheet as it would look at the beginning of a speech:

Main Ideas   **Support Material**   **Response**

Using this method, let's examine a passage from a classroom speech by Stella Baldwin:

Why do some men physically abuse their wives? There are many contributing factors, but the two most frequent causes are, first of all, stress in the man's life and secondly, abuse of alcohol or other drugs. Let's talk about stress for a moment: things go wrong in some area of his life. It's often his job. For example, he's involved in an ongoing dispute with his boss. He can't punch the boss (which is what he'd like to do) because he would lose his job. So what does he do? He comes home, full of rage, and takes it out on his wife. If he loses his job and can't find work, the stress is even worse. His self-esteem is badly damaged. Unemployment is probably the biggest stressor in our society today. Figures compiled by Helpmate, an agency that assists battered women, show that as unemployment goes up, so does the incidence of wife beating. After a General Motors plant was closed in Fremont, California, a few years ago, a task force appointed to study the effects of the closing on workers found a dramatic increase in the number of phone calls to the police because of violence in the home.

Abuse of alcohol and other drugs often goes hand in hand with stress. Frustrated by problems in their own lives, some men turn to alcohol or some other substance for relief. The problem is that these chemicals often rip away their inhibitions, and men who would normally never strike their wives (or their children) suddenly become violent. Nancy Presson, drug abuse coordinator for San Francisco County, says that alcohol and other drugs play a part in 60 to 80 percent of wife-beating cases.

Now let's examine some notes based on the above passage:

Main Ideas	**Support Material**	**Response**
Two main reasons for wife beating:		
1. Stress in the man's life	Anger on the job—takes it out on his wife Unemployment a major stressor	Why can't these men learn to release anger in less destructive ways?

| 2. Alcohol/drug abuse | "Chemical" relief for stress
Takes away normal inhibitions
One county—60–80% of wife beating involved alcohol/drugs | Does our county have same situation? |

The response column is designed to help you interact with the speaker and ask questions that arise in your mind during the speech. When the question-and-answer period begins, you can scan the response column and ask questions. If a question that you jotted down gets answered later in the speech itself, no harm has been done; having raised the question will cause you to listen to the explanation with extra-special interest. The response column also enables you to plan follow-up research (for example, a response note for a classroom lecture might be a reminder to yourself: "Look up additional info in library").

If you have taken notes on a class lecture or some other complex presentation, review your notes soon afterward and expand them if necessary while the speaker's words are still fresh in your mind. If any parts of your notes are vague or confusing, seek help from another listener (or the speaker, if available).

Avoid Prejudgments

Prejudging a speaker is an unfortunate tendency that many listeners have. Some people reject a speaker even before he or she stands up to speak. They dislike the speaker's looks or clothes or the organization the speaker represents. Let's say, for example, that a Catholic priest speaks on marriage; some people in the audience might say to themselves, "Why should I listen to him? What does a priest, who is celibate, know about marriage?" What is unfortunate about this reaction is that such listeners cut themselves off from gaining skills and insights. A priest might offer some excellent advice based on years of counseling couples.

Do not reject speakers because their delivery is ragged or because they seem shaky and lacking in confidence. Their ideas might be worth paying attention to. Professor Wayne Austin Shrope gives a good example of the value of concentrating on the message rather than on delivery:

When I was in college I took a history class from an instructor who was generally considered a very dull lecturer. He sat behind his desk and read his notes in a dull monotone. The other students I knew approached the lectures with the attitude that they would be bored by his dull delivery, and that they would learn nothing. This turned out to be a self-fulfilling prophecy: they *were* bored, and they *did* learn nothing. I, on the other hand, approached the lectures determined to get something from them—perhaps because I found that if I listened carefully I didn't have to read the text. At any rate, I found the lectures to be the best organized I have ever heard, and I thought the examples, details, facts, and language were fascinating. I liked the course better than any history course I ever took. I learned a great deal about history and particularly the people who made it. My classmates, who apparently listened only to the monotone and nothing else, were amazed at how well I did in the course despite little time spent studying, just by listening well in class.[14]

When you listen to a speech, try to concentrate on the message rather than on a speaker's looks, dress, or delivery. Give every speaker a fair chance.

Don't Mentally Argue with the Speaker

Some people avoid prejudging a speaker, but as soon as he or she starts talking about a controversial topic, such as sex education or gun control, they immediately have a powerful emotional reaction that seems to cut off intelligent listening for the rest of the speech. Instead of paying attention to the speaker's words, they "argue" with the speaker inside their heads or think of ways to retaliate during the question-and-answer period. They often jump to conclusions, convincing themselves that the speaker is saying something that he or she really is not. Here is an example:

> John Rafferty, a veteran and a businessman, gave a speech to a group on why he was opposed to the military draft. His main argument was that conscription weakens our armed forces because it brings in some people who are unmotivated and unsuited for military service. "The best military forces," he argued, "are those made up of volunteers who have high morale and a strong commitment to their training. I am against the draft because it would place unmotivated people into the ranks; it would weaken the morale of our armed forces. I want a strong military, and a volunteer system is the best way to achieve this goal." In the question-and-answer period at the end of the speech, some members of the audience accused Rafferty of wanting to weaken the armed forces and of being antimilitary. These people had failed to listen to what Rafferty said; if they had listened, they would have known that he was opposed to the draft not because he was antimilitary, but because he was promilitary. "Most of the audience heard me correctly," Rafferty reminisced, "but those people who didn't understand—they just floored me. I felt like saying, 'Are you deaf or retarded, or what?'"

When you are listening to speakers who seem to be arguing against some of your ideas or beliefs, make sure you understand exactly what they are saying. Hear them out, and *then* prepare your counterarguments.

The Listener's Responsibilities

As we discussed in Chapter 1, the speaker who is honest and fair has ethical and moral obligations to his or her listeners.

The converse is also true: the honest and fair listener has ethical and moral obligations to the speaker. Let's examine three of the listener's primary responsibilities.

Avoid Rudeness

If you were engaged in conversation with a friend, how would you feel if your friend yawned and went to sleep? Or started reading a book? Or looked at the floor the entire time? You would be upset by your friend's rudeness, wouldn't you?

There are many people who would never dream of being so rude to a friend in conversation, yet when they sit in an audience, they are terribly rude to the speaker. They fall asleep or read a newspaper or study for a test or carry on a whispered conversation with their friends. Fortunately, a public speaking class cures some people of their rudeness. As one student put it:

> I had been sitting in classrooms for 12 years and until now, I never realized how much a speaker sees. I always thought a listener is hidden and anonymous out there in a sea of faces. Now that I've been a speaker, I realize that when you look out at an audience, you are well aware of the least little thing somebody does. I am ashamed now at how I used to carry on conversations in the back of class. I was very rude, and I didn't even know it.

If you are seated in the audience and you turn to whisper to a friend, your movement is as noticeable as a red flag waving in front of the speaker's eyes. If you do more than whisper—if you snicker or grin—you can damage the morale and confidence of inexperienced speakers, for they may think that you are laughing at them.

You should think of a speech as nothing more than enlarged conversation, and therefore you should show the speaker the same politeness you would show your best friend during a chat.

Provide Encouragement

A good philosophy to follow is summed up in the Golden Rule of listening: "Listen unto others as you would have others listen unto you." When you are a speaker, you want an audience that listens attentively, courteously, and enthusiastically. So when you are a listener, you should provide the same response.

Support the speaker with as much encouragement as possible. You can do this by giving your full attention, taking notes, leaning slightly forward instead of slouching back in your seat, looking directly at the speaker instead of at the floor, and letting your face show interest and animation. If the speaker says something you particularly like, nod in agreement or smile approvingly. (If the speaker says something that offends you or puzzles you, obviously you should not give positive feedback; I am not recommending hypocrisy.)

The more encouragement a speaker receives, the better he or she is able to speak. Most entertainers and professional speakers say that if an audience is lively and enthusiastic, they do a much better job than if the audience is sullen or apathetic. From my own experience, I feel that I always do better in giving a speech if I get encouragement. Maybe it is just a few people who are displaying lively interest, but their nods and smiles and eager eyes inspire me and energize me.

If we as listeners cause a speaker to give a good speech, we are doing more than an act of kindness; we are creating a payoff for us: the better the speaker is, the easier it is for us to listen. And the easier it is to listen, the better we will understand and remember. That's why, if for no other reason but self-interest, we should try to give encouragement to help the speaker do a good job.

Listeners exert a tremendous power over the speaker. At one college, some psychology majors conducted an experiment to prove that professors can be as easily manipulated as laboratory rats by means of positive reinforcement. In one political science class, if the professor walked to the left side of the classroom during his lecture, the students would give him approving looks, nod their heads in agreement, and enthusiastically scribble notes in their notebooks. But when he stayed in the middle or walked to the right side of the class, they would lay down their pencils and look away from the professor with glum expressions on their faces. Before long the professor spent the entire hour standing on the left side of the room. Carrying their experiment a step further, the students "rewarded" the professor with encouraging looks and nods only if he stood on the left side next to the window and absent-mindedly played with the lift cord of the venetian blinds. Soon the professor was spending all his lecture time holding the lift cord, blithely unaware that he was the "guinea pig" in a behavior-modification experiment.

I tell this story not to suggest that you manipulate a speaker, but to show the power that you as a listener exert. Use that power wisely. Use it to encourage and uplift the speaker.

Find Value in Every Speech

There will be times when you are forced to hear a speech you feel is boring and worthless. Instead of tuning the speaker out and retreating into your private world of daydreams, try to exploit the speech for something worthwhile. Make a game of it: see how many diamonds can be extracted from the mud. Is there any new information that might be useful to you in the future? Is the speaker using techniques of delivery that are worth noting and emulating?

What if a speech is complicated and over your head? Listen anyway, and try to broaden your knowledge. Dr. Steil gives some good advice on this point:

> The listener who responds to complex material by "tuning out" can be missing a great opportunity to learn, to discover, to broaden himself. We have all had the experience of mastering a body of information, and then—when the material has become entirely familiar—using it as a foundation for understanding additional, even more complex information. It is a heady feeling—one of the joys of learning. And it can only be felt if we as listeners greet the arrival of complex information with anticipation. Not with anxiety.[15]

If a speech is so bad that you honestly cannot find anything worthwhile in it, you can always look for a how-not-to-do-it lesson. Ask yourself, "What can I learn from this speaker's mistakes?" Here is an example of how one business executive profited from a poor speaker:

> At a convention recently I found myself in an extremely boring seminar (on listening, ironically enough). After spending the first half-hour wishing I had never signed up, I decided to take advantage of the situation. I turned my thought, "This guy isn't teaching me how to run a seminar on listening," into a question: "What is he teaching me about how *not* to run a seminar?" While providing a negative example was not the presenter's goal, I got a useful lesson.[16]

"Turn your lemons into lemonade," some wise person once advised. If you look for value or a how-not-to-do-it lesson in every poor speech, you will find that the sourest oratorical lemon can be turned into lemonade. "Know how to listen," the Greek writer Plutarch said twenty centuries ago, "and you will profit even from those who talk badly."

Summary

Listening effectively is often a difficult task, but it can be rewarding for the person who is willing to make the effort. The guidelines for effective listening include the following: (1) Avoid fakery. Do not pretend to be listening when in fact your mind is wandering; this kind of behavior can settle into a hard-to-break habit. (2) Be willing to put forth energy. Since listening is hard work, especially if the material is new or difficult, you must have a strong desire to listen actively and intelligently. (3) Prepare yourself for the act of listening. Do whatever background reading or research that is necessary for gaining maximum understanding of the speech. (4) Resist distractions, both external and internal. Use rigorous self-discipline to keep your mind concentrated on the speaker's remarks. (5) Listen analytically, focusing on main ideas and evaluating support materials. (6) Take notes, not only for a record of key points but as a way of keeping your mind from wandering. (7) Avoid prejudgments. Do not dismiss a speaker before he or she even starts the speech. (8) Do not mentally argue with a speaker, or you may think that the speaker is saying something that he or she really is not.

As a listener you have three important obligations to a speaker: to avoid all forms of rudeness, to provide encouragement, and to find value in every speech. The more support you give a speaker, the better the speech will be and the more you will profit from it.

Review Questions

1. What is the difference between *hearing* and *listening*?
2. Why is listening to complex material in a speech more difficult than reading the same material in a book?

3. List several ways in which you can prepare yourself both physically and intellectually to listen to a speech.
4. List five possible distractions that can keep a listener from concentrating on a speech.
5. What are the advantages of taking notes during a speech?
6. When you are a listener, how can you encourage a speaker?

Tips

FOR YOUR CAREER

Tip 2: Take Notes in Important Conversations and Small-Group Meetings

In any job that you may hold, take notes while your superiors and colleagues talk to you (either one-on-one or in a group meeting) about work-related matters. This not only enhances your listening ability, as we discussed earlier, but it also gains favorable attention for yourself. By taking notes, you show that you are a good listener who values the advice and opinions of the speaker. It is a nonverbal way of saying, "Your ideas are important to me—so important that I want to make sure I get them down correctly." Contrary to what some may think, taking notes does *not* signify to others that you have a poor memory.

One of the most common gripes of employees is that "the boss never listens to what we say." So, if you are ever in a supervisory position, take notes whenever one of your subordinates comes to you with a suggestion or a complaint. It shows that you are taking the employee's comments seriously and that you are preparing yourself to take action if necessary. Even if you are unable to take action, the employee's morale is boosted because you have shown you truly listen and truly care.

3

Controlling
Nervousness

Reasons for Nervousness

The Value of Fear

Guidelines for Controlling Nervousness

Hollywood actor George C. Scott, famous for his fierce, bulldog demeanor, has played such gruff characters as General Patton, the dictator Mussolini, and Charles Dickens's Scrooge. He is also known as a blunt, irascible person in real life; he has admitted that his nose has been broken five times in brawls.[1] When actress Maureen Stapleton once complained to her director, Mike Nichols, that she was afraid of her co-star Scott, Nichols replied: "Don't worry. The whole world's afraid of George Scott."[2]

Yet, for all his intimidating ferocity, Scott confessed to a magazine reporter that "it's terrible when I have to make a speech. I really suffer. I'm a nervous wreck. When I get up, I shake all over like a dog shaking the water off." When Scott was asked why he was able to speak so effectively in films, he replied that while acting, he could "hide behind" whatever character he was playing but in giving a speech "there's nothing to hide behind."[3]

George C. Scott is not the only person terrified of speaking in public. When researchers ask Americans to name their greatest fears, the fear of speaking to a group of strangers is usually at the top of the list. It is cited more often than fear of snakes, insects, lightning, deep water, heights, or flying in airplanes.[4]

Reasons for Nervousness

Is it foolish to be afraid to give a speech? Is this fear as groundless as a child's fear of the boogeyman? I used to think so, back in the days when I first began making speeches. Like Scott, I was a nervous wreck, and I would often chide myself by saying, "Come on, relax, it's just a little speech. There's no good reason to be scared." But I was wrong. There *is* good reason to be scared; in fact, there are *four* good reasons:

1. *Fear of being stared at.* In the animal world, a stare is a hostile act. Dogs, baboons, and other animals sometimes defend their territory by staring. Their hostile gaze alone is enough to turn away an intruder. We human beings have similar reactions; it is part of our biological makeup to be upset by stares. Imagine that you are riding in a crowded elevator with a group of strangers. Suddenly you realize that the other people are staring directly at you. Not just glancing. *Staring*. You probably would be unnerved and frightened because a stare can be as threatening as a clenched fist—especially if it comes from people you do not know. That is why public speaking can be so frightening. You have a pack of total strangers "attacking" you with unrelenting stares, while you are obliged to stand alone, exposed and vulnerable—a goldfish in a bowl, subject to constant scrutiny. As George C. Scott suggested, there's nothing to hide behind.

2. *Fear of failure.* Most speakers worry about botching their speech: What if I make a fool of myself? What if my mind goes blank and I forget everything I was planning to say? What if I stumble or stammer? Any normal person, especially if he or she is an inexperienced speaker, is apt to have this fear. Indeed, a person who never has self-doubts is probably foolish and vain.

3. *Fear of rejection.* What if we do our best, what if we deliver a polished speech, but the audience still does not like us? It would be quite a blow to our ego because we want to be liked and, yes, even loved. We want people to admire us, to consider us wise and intelligent, and to accept our ideas and opinions. We do not want people to dislike us, reject us, or worst of all, consider us a fool.

The most terrifying speaking situation of my life occurred in high school when I decided to telephone a girl to invite her to a dance. I was attending an all-boys' school, I was shy around girls, and it was my first date. Before I called her, I was afraid that I would fail to think of clever things to say, so I made note cards with sentences written out in full—things like "What is your favorite subject in school?" and "What kind of music do you like?" Even with these cue cards, I was choked with fear when I finally gathered enough courage to call her; my heart was thumping so furiously that it leaped up into my throat, and I could barely get my words out. She did say yes, but when I hung up the phone, I realized that I was now faced with a fresh terror: I would have to talk to her on our date, and I would have no cue cards to guide me through. What made this event so excruciating, of course, was my fear of rejection.

4. *Fear of the unknown.* Throughout our lives we are apprehensive about doing new things, such as going to school for the first time, riding a bus without our parents, or going out on our first date. We cannot put a finger on exactly what we are afraid of because our fear is vague and diffused. What we really fear is the unknown; we worry that some unpredictable disaster might occur. When we stand up to give a speech, we are sometimes assailed by this same fear of the unknown because we cannot predict the outcome of our speech. Fortunately, this fear usually disappears as we become experienced in giving speeches—we have enough confidence to know that nothing terrible will befall us, just as our childhood fear of riding in a bus by ourselves vanished after two or three trips.

All four of these fears are as real and as understandable as the fear of lightning. There is no reason why you should be ashamed of having them.

The Value of Fear

Because the fears engendered by public speaking are real and understandable, does this mean that it is impossible to get rid of nervousness (which is also called butterflies, the jitters, or the shakes)? If you are like many of the students who come into my public speaking class, this is your primary concern: to completely eliminate all traces of nervousness. My response may surprise you as much as it surprises my students: *You should not try to banish all your fear and nervousness. You need a certain amount of fear to give a good speech.*

You *need* fear? Yes, fear energizes you; it makes you think more rapidly; it helps you speak with vitality and enthusiasm. Here is why: when you stand up to give a speech and fear hits you, your body goes on "red alert," the same biological mechanism that saved our cave-dwelling ancestors when they were faced with a hungry lion or a human foe and had to fight or flee in order to survive. Though not as crucial to us as it was to our ancestors, this system is still nice to have for emergencies: if you were walking down a deserted street one night and someone tried to attack you, your body would release a burst of adrenalin into your bloodstream, causing fresh blood and oxygen to rush to your muscles, and you would be able to fight ferociously or run faster than you have ever run in your life. The benefit of adrenalin can be seen in competitive sports: athletes *must* get their adrenalin flowing before a game begins. There is one high school football coach who looks at his players' hands before the kickoff. Any player without sweaty palms is benched; he is obviously not fired up enough to play well. The great home-run slugger Reggie Jackson said during his heyday, "I have butterflies in my stomach almost every time I step up to the plate. When I don't have them, I get worried because it means I won't hit the ball very well."[5]

Public speakers often have the same attitude. Don Beveridge, a professional speaker, says, "I've been speaking professionally for 15 years. I have given speeches to [audiences consisting of] 4,000 Burger King franchisees, 3,000 AT&T managers, and 5,000 Century 21 salespeople. I've taught classes of 15 people at the University of Wisconsin and communicated one-on-one. No matter what the speaking situation, my hands sweat before each and every presentation, and frankly that's what makes me a good speaker. . . . The day my palms stop sweating, I'll quit!"[6]

In public speaking, adrenalin infuses you with energy; it causes extra blood and oxygen to rush not only to your muscles but to your brain as well, thus enabling you to think with greater clarity and quickness. It makes you come across to your audience as someone who is alive and vibrant. Elayne Snyder, a speech teacher, uses the term *positive nervousness*, which she describes in this way: "It's a zesty, enthusiastic, lively feeling with a slight edge to it. Positive nervousness is the state you'll achieve by converting your anxiety into constructive energy. . . . It's still nervousness, but you're no longer victimized by it; instead you're vitalized by it."[7]

If you want proof that nervousness is beneficial, observe speakers who have absolutely no butterflies at all. Because they are 100 percent relaxed and cool, they give speeches that are dull and flat, with no energy, no zest. There is an old saying popular with some speechmakers: "Speakers who say they are as cool as a cucumber usually give speeches about as interesting as a cucumber." Most good speakers report that if they do not have butterflies before a public appearance, their delivery is poor. One speaker, the novelist I. A. R. Wylie, said, "I rarely rise to my feet without a throat constricted with terror and a furiously thumping heart. When, for some reason, I am cool and self-assured, the speech is always a failure. I need fear to spur me on."[8] In sports, we all know of champion teams that got smashed by puny underdogs. Why? Because the champs were too relaxed and confident, while the underdogs were supercharged with strong emotions. This is why coaches get apprehensive if their teams have a perfect season going into their final game. The players may lose that vital nervous energy they need to win.

There is another danger in being totally devoid of nervousness. Some years ago, before I learned the value of controlled nervousness, I tried to talk myself into being completely relaxed for a speech. I told myself, "There's nothing to be afraid of. Be calm, play it cool." On one particular occasion it worked—for a while. I was an after-dinner speaker at a banquet. For once, I was able to eat food before a speech without having it taste like cardboard. I congratulated myself on being completely relaxed as I sat at the head table and listened to the master of cere- monies introduce me. There was not a single butterfly in my stomach. I got up

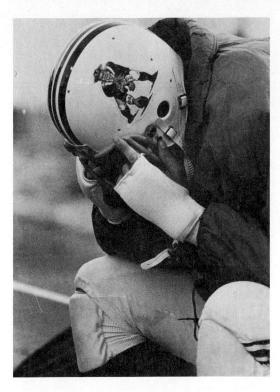

Before a game, football players are often gripped by nervous tension. When they are actually sent in, they concentrate on the plays, and their tension recedes into the background. Public speakers too may be filled with anxiety before a speech, but if they concentrate on communicating with their audience, their anxiety will move to a back burner, where it can provide energy for the task. *(Peter Southwick/Stock, Boston)*

confidently, strode to the lectern, looked out at my audience, and then—WHAM!— I was suddenly struck by a lightning bolt of panic. I got a huge lump in my throat, my heart pounded, and I had so much trouble breathing that every word had to be wrestled from my suffocating larynx and forced out of my mouth. My face turned red and I started sweating heavily. It was a nightmare. Somehow I got through the speech and sat down, humiliated and angry at myself. But I learned a lesson I would never forget: to avoid last-minute panic, I must be "psyched up." Nowadays I never go into a speech without encouraging my butterflies to flutter around inside, so that I can be poised and alert. Other speakers have come to the same conclusion: if they aren't "pumped up" for a speech, they either suffer the kind of panic that hit me or else they give boring speeches that have no fizz and sparkle.

Guidelines for Controlling Nervousness

We have just discussed how a complete lack of nervousness is undesirable. What about the other extreme? Is *too much* nervousness bad for you? Of course it is, especially if you are so frightened that you forget what you were planning to say or if your breathing is so labored that you cannot get your words out. What you want to do is keep your nervousness under control, so that you have just the right amount—enough to energize you, but not enough to cripple you. How can you do this? Here are some ideas that have helped my students.

In the Days and Weeks Before Your Speech

Choose a Topic You Like and Know a Great Deal About

Nothing will get you more rattled than speaking on a subject about which you know little. If you are asked to talk on a topic you are not comfortable with, decline the invitation (unless, of course, it is an assignment from a boss who gives you no choice in the matter). Speaking on a topic you know a lot about will give you enormous self-confidence; if something terrible happens (for example, if you lose your notes on the way to the meeting), you can always improvise because your head is filled with information about the subject. Also, you will be able to handle yourself well in the question-and-answer period after the speech.

Prepare Yourself Thoroughly

Here is a piece of advice that is given by many experienced speakers: *The very best precaution against excessive stage fright is thorough, careful preparation.*[9] You have heard the expression, "I came unglued." In public speaking, the best "glue" to hold you together is good, solid preparation. Professional speaker Joel Weldon (who quips that he used to be so frightened of audiences that he was "unable to lead a church group in silent prayer") gives his personal formula for controlling fear: "I prepare and then prepare, and then when I think I'm ready, I prepare some more."[10] Weldon recommends 5 to 8 hours of preparation for each hour in front of an audience.[11] That ratio is not unusual. Most good speakers will

Practicing with a friend or relative can help you deliver a speech more smoothly and confidently. (Sitting informally is all right for early practice sessions, but in later sessions you should stand just as you will in the speech itself.) *(Rae Russel)*

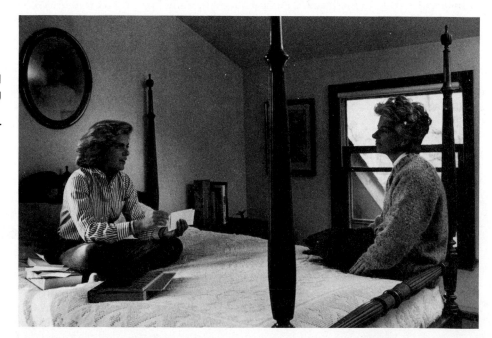

tell you that 75 to 90 percent of their total effort goes into getting ready for the actual delivery.

Preparation means gathering ideas and information, organizing them into a coherent outline, writing note cards, and then practicing delivery of the speech. If you put time and energy into your preparation, you will become the master of your material and will know it thoroughly. This will give you self-confidence.

Be sure to leave plenty of time for practicing your delivery. Do not just look over your notes—actually stand up and deliver your talk in whatever way suits you: in front of a mirror, into a tape recorder, before a family member or friend. Do not rehearse just once; run through your entire speech at least four times. If you "give" your speech four times at home, you will find that your fifth delivery— before a live audience—will be smoother and more self-assured than if you had not practiced at all.

Do Not Read or Memorize Your Speech

Never write out a speech in its entirety and then read it. This is the perfect way to put an audience to sleep.

Another undesirable method is to memorize a speech, for this courts disaster. As a young man, Winston Churchill—considered one of the greatest orators of modern times—used to write out and memorize his speeches. Then one day, while giving a memorized talk to Parliament, he suddenly stopped. His mind went blank. He began his sentence all over. Again his mind went blank. He sat down in embarrassment and shame. Never again did Churchill try to memorize a speech. This same thing has happened to many others who have tried to commit a speech to memory. Everything goes smoothly until they get derailed, and then they are hopelessly off the track.

Even if you do not get derailed, there is another reason for not memorizing: you will probably sound mechanical, like a robot with a tape recorder in its mouth. In addition to considering you dull and boring, your audience will sense that you are speaking from your memory and not from your heart, and they will question your sincerity.

Regard Your Task as Communication, Not Performance

Try to think of speechmaking as *communication* rather than *performance*. Dr. Michael T. Motley of the University of California, Davis, says that speakers who suffer from excessively high levels of anxiety make the mistake of thinking they are performing for listeners, whom they see as hostile evaluators. Such people say, " 'The audience will ridicule me if I make a mistake. I'll be embarrassed to death.' " But in fact, says Dr. Motley, audiences are more interested in hearing what you have to say "than in analyzing or criticizing how [you] say it." Audiences "usually ignore errors and awkwardness as long as they get something out of a speech."[12]

When speakers stop worrying about "How well am I performing?" and start thinking about "How can I share my ideas with these people?" two things usually happen: (1) their anxiety level comes down to a manageable level, and (2) their delivery improves dramatically. By treating speechmaking as more like one-on-one communication than as a stage exhibition, they tend to talk *with* people, instead of orate *at* them; they tend to speak conversationally rather than in a stiff, unnatural way.

When one of my students, Maxine Jones, began her first classroom speech, her voice sounded artificial and cold, but after she got into her talk, she sounded animated and warm, as if she were carrying on a lively conversation. This caused her to become more interesting and easier to follow. Later she explained her transformation: "At first I was scared to death, but then I noticed that everyone in the room was looking at me with curiosity in their eyes, and I could tell that they really wanted to hear what I was saying. I told myself, 'They really *care* about this information—I can't let them down.' So I settled down and talked to them as if they were my friends. I got so involved with explaining things to them that I didn't worry too much about being scared."

Maxine's transformation came about because she stopped focusing on herself as a performer, and started seeing herself as a communicator with good ideas that deserved to be shared with her audience.

If you stop thinking of a speech as a performance, you can rid yourself of the idea that you *must* give a perfect, polished speech. Such a notion puts enormous—and unnecessary—pressure on you, and it causes you to concentrate your energies on yourself instead of on what should be your real target—your listeners. Remember that they do not care whether your delivery is perfect; they simply hope that your words will enlighten or entertain them. Think of yourself as merely a telegram messenger; the audience is interested in the telegram, not in how well you hand it over.

Imagine Yourself Giving a Good, Strong Speech

Let yourself daydream a bit: picture yourself going up to the lectern, nervous but in control of yourself, then giving a forceful talk to an appreciative audience. Does this sound silly? It is a technique that has worked for many speakers and it might work for you. Whatever you do, do not let yourself imagine the opposite—a bad speech or poor delivery. Negative daydreams will add unnecessary fear to your life in the days before your speech, and sap you of creative energy—energy that you need for preparing and practicing. Actress Ali McGraw says, "We have only so much energy, and the more we direct toward the project itself, the less is left to pour into wondering 'Will I fail?' "[13]

Notice that the daydream I am suggesting includes nervousness. You need to have a realistic image in your mind: picture yourself as nervous, but nevertheless in command of the situation and capable of delivering a strong, effective speech.

In addition to picturing yourself as confident and in control, you need to imagine yourself reaching out to your audience. Try to focus as much *positive* mental energy as possible on the people who will be listening to your message. One professional speaker, James "Doc" Blakely, has an effective, audience-centered technique that he uses before each speech: "I learn everything I can about the organization I'm going to address as far in advance of the speaking date as possible.

Then at least four hours prior to the actual speaking engagement, I review all the facts I know about the group, go over the points I want to make with them, and then concentrate on pouring positive thoughts into my mind about the group. I visualize them as accepting me as a friend, of being wildly enthusiastic about what I have to say to them, and I block out every negative emotion in my mind. . . . Concentrating totally on the needs and concerns of your listeners is great therapy for a speaker."[14]

Some speakers have trouble imagining success because deep down they do not really believe that they are capable of success. These speakers are often shy individuals who think that their shyness blocks them from becoming good speakers. Actor and speechmaker Steve Allen says it is a mistake for shy people to disqualify themselves from public speaking. "I tend toward shyness, particularly in the presence of strangers in small social gatherings," he says, noting that other Hollywood figures such as Johnny Carson and Dick Cavett are also shy and introverted, and yet are excellent speakers.[15] "Like stutterers who have no trouble singing, we shy introverts often blossom when placed on stage, in front of a camera, or next to a microphone," he says. "So whether you personally are a life-of-the-party type or are inclined to sit and listen to others means little so far as . . . public speaking is concerned."[16] (To Allen's list of shy introverts in show business can be added Carol Burnett, Barbara Walters, Garrison Keillor, and Michael Jackson.[17])

The truth of Allen's remark is demonstrated by Joe W. Boyd of Bellingham, Washington. "I used to stammer," says Boyd, "and I used to be petrified at the thought of speaking before a group of any size." Despite his shyness, Boyd joined a Toastmasters club to develop his speaking skills. Two years later, in 1984, he won the Toastmasters International Public Speaking Contest by giving a superb speech to an audience of over 2000 listeners.[18]

Remember: It Is Not Abnormal to Have Stage Fright

When you get the jitters, it should console you to know that you are not reacting in an abnormal way. Most great public speakers have suffered from stage fright before or during their speeches. When Churchill was prime minister of Great Britain, he said that every time he had to give a speech, he had a block of ice, nine inches by nine inches, in the pit of his stomach. Philosopher Bertrand Russell said he was so afraid of giving speeches that every time he had to leave home to deliver a speech, he hoped he would break a leg so that he would not have to give his talk. General U. S. Grant played a major part in the Union victory over the Confederates in the Civil War, but he said giving a speech was more terrifying to him than leading troops into battle.

During Your Speech

Deal Rationally with Your Body's Turmoil

If you are a typical beginning speaker, you will suffer from some or all of the following symptoms when you begin your talk:

☐ Pounding heart
☐ Trembling hands
☐ Shaky knees
☐ Dry, constricted throat
☐ Difficulty in breathing
☐ Quivering voice
☐ Flushed face

You usually suffer the greatest discomfort during the first few minutes of your speech, but then things get better. If, however, your symptoms get worse as you go along, it might be because your mind has taken the wrong path (see Figure 3.1).

If you take route A, you are trapped in a vicious cycle. Your mind tells your body that disaster is upon you, and your body responds by getting worse. This, in turn, increases your brain's perception of disaster. If you take route B, however, your mind will help your body stay in control. You can remind yourself that your symptoms, rather than being a prelude to disaster, are evidence that you are keyed up enough to give a good speech.

Concentrate on Getting Your Ideas Across

Before the kickoff, football players are nervous and tense—most are filled with butterflies. But what happens when the game actually starts? Though nervousness is still present, it recedes into the background as the players concentrate on catching the ball or making a tackle.

Public speaking is similar. You may experience terrible anxiety at the beginning, but once you get into your speech, if you focus all your attention on communicating your ideas to your listeners, your nervousness will recede into the background. It does not go away, of course; it simply simmers on a back burner, where it can remain an ongoing source of energy.

When you concentrate on getting your message across to your listeners, you do more than quell your butterflies; you also give a better speech than you would if you were self-absorbed. Hugh Downs, television commentator for ABC News, learned this lesson in dealing with his own nervousness problem. "Somehow when you give full attention to subject matter and audience," he said, "you wind up looking and sounding better than when you're focused on yourself."[19]

Remember: Most Bodily Reactions Are Not Seen

Some speakers get rattled because they think the audience is keenly aware of their thumping heart and quaking hands. You, of course, are painfully aware of these symptoms, but believe it or not, your audience is usually oblivious to your body's distress. Remember that people are sitting out there wanting to hear your ideas. They are not saying to themselves, "Let's see, what signs of nervousness is this person displaying?" I have had students tell me after a speech that they were ashamed or embarrassed about their jittery performance, yet I and the other listeners in the class saw no signs of nervousness. We were listening to the ideas and failed to notice the speaker's discomfort. Various studies have found the same

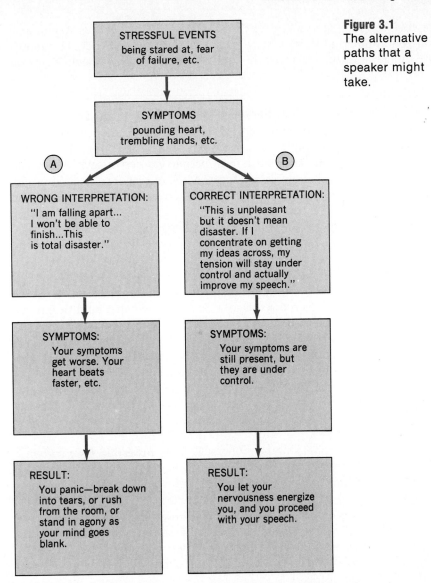

Figure 3.1
The alternative
paths that a
speaker might
take.

thing to be true: audiences simply are unaware of signs that the speakers think are embarrassingly obvious.[20] In other words, you are probably the only one who knows that your knees are shaking and that your heart is pounding.

Speaking of his own problems with nervousness, TV talk show host Dick Cavett says that stage fright on TV "varies from night to night. The best thing to do is tell yourself it doesn't show one-eighth as much as you feel. If you're a little nervous, you don't look nervous at all. If you're very nervous, you look slightly nervous. And if you're totally out of control, you look troubled. It scales down on the screen. Anybody who appears on a talk show should always remind himself that everything he's doing *looks* better than it *feels*. . . . Your nervous system may be giving you a thousand shocks, but the viewer can only see a few of them."[21] The same thing holds true for a speech: during delivery, you look better than you feel.

Never Call Attention to Your Nervousness or Apologize for It

Despite what I said above, there may be times when an audience does notice your nervousness—for example, if your hands are shaking as you hold your note cards. But so what? Everyone knows that most people get nervous when they talk in public, so why mention it or apologize for it? Whether or not your nervousness is noticeable, you should never make comments about it because of two big dangers.

First of all, you might get yourself more rattled than you were to begin with. I remember listening to a teacher who was giving a talk to a PTA meeting one night. In the middle of her remarks she suddenly blurted out, "Oh my god, I knew I would fall apart." Up to that time, I had not been aware of any discomfort or nervousness. She tried to continue her talk, but she was too flustered. She gave up the effort and sat down with a red face. I do not know what kind of internal distress she was suffering, of course, but I am certain that if she had said nothing about her nervousness, she could have dragged herself through the speech. When she sat down, I felt irritated and disappointed because I had been keenly interested in her remarks. How selfish of her, I thought, to deprive me of the second half of her speech simply because she was nervous. I know that my reaction sounds insensitive, but I wanted to share it with you so that I can underscore an important point: your listeners do not care about your emotional distress; they only want to hear your ideas.

The second risk you run if you mention your symptoms is this: your audience might have been unaware of your nervousness before you brought it up, but now you have distracted them from your speech, and they are watching the very thing you do not want them to scrutinize—your body's behavior. If you say, for example, "I'm sorry about my voice being so rough, but my throat is very dry," what do you think the audience will play close attention to—at least for the next few minutes? Your voice, of course, instead of your speech. Keep your audience's attention focused on your ideas, and they probably will pay little or no attention to your emotional and physical distress.

Do Not Let Your Audience Upset You

Some inexperienced speakers get rattled when they look out at the audience and observe that most listeners are poker-faced and unsmiling. Does this mean they are displeased with your speech? No, their solemn faces have nothing to do with your performance. This is just one of those peculiarities of human nature: in a conversation, people will smile and nod and encourage you, but when listening to a speech in an audience, the same people will wear (most of the time) a blank mask. The way to handle those stony faces is to remind yourself that your listeners want you to succeed; they hope that you will give them a worthwhile message. If you are lucky, you will notice two or three listeners who are obviously loving your speech; they are nodding in agreement or giving you looks of appreciation. Let your eyes go to them frequently, for they will give you courage and confidence.

If you are an inexperienced speaker, you may get upset if you see members of an audience whispering to one another. You may wonder, "Are these people making negative comments about me?" If the listeners are smiling, it's even worse: You ask yourself, "Did I say something foolish? Is there something wrong with my clothes?" If this happens to you, try to keep in mind that your rude listeners are probably talking about something other than the quality of your speech or your personal appearance. Most likely, they are just sharing some personal gossip. If by chance they *are* whispering about something you've said, it's not necessarily negative. The following story, told to me by an experienced speaker, illustrates this point.

> I was speaking to a group in El Paso, Texas, on why I, as a Vietnam veteran, was opposed to the [then-raging] war in Vietnam. It was a highly emotional issue, and I knew that many people in El Paso were staunch supporters of the war. So, even before I started my speech, I was apprehensive and defensive because I feared that my ideas would provoke anger and disagreement among some of my listeners. I began my talk and had said no more than three sentences when I saw a man in the back row turn to his companion and grin and whisper something. I was sure that he was making some snide, derisive comment about me. I got very annoyed and I had trouble maintaining my composure. At the end of the speech, however, the man came up to me and said, "I was glad to hear you say you were from Chattanooga, Tennessee. I am, too." It turned out that we had grown up in the same part of town and had friends in common. His grin and his whispers during the speech had not been negative feedback, after all, but rather a positive reaction to the discovery that I was a fellow Chattanoogan.

If you ever see whisperers in your audience, your best approach is to assume that they are friendly rather than negative or hostile. After all, they may be whispering that they agree with you 100 percent.

Additional Hints

Use visual aids. Many speakers find that they can keep their nervousness under control if they use such visual aids as slides or charts or a chalkboard. Visual aids can help you in two ways: (1) you shift the audience's stares from you personally to your illustrations, and (2) you walk about and move your hands and arms, thereby siphoning off some of your excess nervous energy.

Whatever illustrations you decide to use, make sure they are understandable and appropriate. There is nothing better than a visual aid that is right on target ("One picture is worth more than ten thousand words"), but there is nothing worse than a visual aid that does not make sense or is completely inappropriate.

Check arrangements in advance. Long before you give your speech, inspect the place where the speech is to be delivered and anticipate any problems. For example: Is there an extension cord for the slide projector? Do the windows have curtains so that the room can be darkened for your slide presentation? Is there a chalkboard? Some talks have been ruined and some speakers turned into nervous wrecks because at the last moment they discover that the entire building lacks an extension cord.

Arrive early on the day of your speech and reinspect every aspect of the arrangements. Has the extension cord been laid out for you? Is there chalk in the chalkboard tray? Is there an eraser for the chalkboard? If you are using equipment for visual aids, set it up to make sure it is working. If there is a public-address system, test your voice on it before the audience arrives so that you can feel at ease with it.

Devote extra practice time to your introduction. The beginning of your speech is the time when you are apt to suffer the greatest amount of distress, so you should spend a lot of time practicing your introduction.

Most speakers, actors, and musicians report that if they can survive the first minute or two, their nervousness moves to the background and the rest of the speech is relatively easy. Madame Schumann-Heink, the famous singer, said, "I grow so nervous before a performance, I become sick. I want to go home. But after I have been on the stage for a few minutes, I am so happy that nobody can drag me off." Perhaps happiness is too strong a word for what you will feel, but if you are a typical speaker, you will find the rest of your speech smooth sailing once you have weathered the first few minutes of turbulent waters. So practice your introduction until you can stand up and give it with confidence.

Get acclimated to your audience and setting. It can be frightening to arrive at the meeting place at the last moment and confront a sea of strange faces waiting to hear your talk. It is a good idea to arrive early so you can get acclimated to the setting and, if possible, chat with people as they come into the room. In this way, you will see them not as a hostile pack of strangers, but as ordinary people who wish you well.

Dr. Henry Heimlich, a popular lecturer and creator of the famed Heimlich Maneuver for rescuing people who are choking, says, "I am always a little nervous wondering how a particular audience will accept me and my thoughts. It is good to meet some of the audience socially before lecturing to them, in order to relate to their cultural and intellectual backgrounds. You are then their 'friend.' "[22]

Another professional speaker, Danielle Kennedy, says that when she began speaking 10 years ago, she was so nervous she would hide out in a bathroom until it was time for her to speak. Now, she says, she mingles with the listeners as they arrive and engages them in conversation. "This reminds me that they are just nice people like anyone else who wants to be informed. I also give myself pleasant thoughts. Things like: 'Can you imagine these people drove 100 miles just to hear me. I am so lucky. These people are wonderful.' I get real warm thoughts going by the time I get up there."[23]

Breathe deeply or do exercises to release tension. To drain off excessive tension, try taking a couple of deep breaths right before a speech. Inhale slowly and exhale slowly. Or try doing some exercises that can be performed quietly, without calling attention to yourself, while you are waiting to speak. Here are some examples: (1) Tighten and then relax your leg muscles. (2) Push your arm or hand muscles against a hard object (such as a desk top or chair) for a few moments, then release the pressure. (3) Squeeze your hands together in the same way: tension, release . . . tension, release. . . .

Act poised. To develop courage when you face an audience, you should act as if you already are courageous. Why? Because playing the role of the confident speaker can often transform you into a speaker who is genuinely confident and poised. In various wars, soldiers have reported that they were terrified before going into combat, but nevertheless they acted brave in front of their buddies. During the battle, to their surprise, what started off as a pretense became a reality. Instead of pretending to be courageous, they actually became so. The same thing often happens to public speakers.

Pause a few moments before starting your speech. All good speakers pause a few moments before they begin their talk. This silence is effective because (1) it is dramatic, building up the audience's interest and curiosity, (2) it makes you look poised and in control, (3) it calms you, and (4) it gives you a chance to spread out your note cards and get your first two or three sentences firmly in mind.

Many tense, inexperienced speakers rush up to the lectern and start their speech at once, thus getting off to a frenzied, flustered start. In the back of their mind they have the notion that silence is a terrible thing, a shameful void that must be filled up immediately. To the contrary, silence is a good "breathing space" or punctuation device between what went before and what comes next. It helps the audience tune in to the speaker and tune out extraneous thoughts.

Look directly at the audience as much as possible. If you are frightened of your audience, it is tempting to stare at your notes or the back wall or the window, but this will only add to your nervousness rather than reduce it.

Force yourself to establish eye contact, especially at the beginning of your speech. Good eye contact means more than just a quick, furtive glance at various faces in front of you; it means "locking" your eyes with a listener's for a couple of seconds. Locking may sound frightening, but it actually helps to calm you. In an article about a public speaking course that she took, writer Maggie Paley said, "When you make contact with one other set of eyes, it's a connection; you can relax and concentrate. The first time I did it, I calmed down 90 percent, and spoke . . . fluently."[24]

Get audience action early in the speech. I said earlier that it's a bit unnerving to see your listeners' expressionless faces. In some speeches, you can change those faces from blank to animated by asking a question. (Tips on how to ask questions will be discussed in Chapter 10.) When the listeners respond with answers or a show of hands, they show themselves to be friendly and cooperative, and this obviously reduces your apprehension. When they loosen up, you loosen up.

Use bodily actions to dissipate some of your nervous energy. I mentioned earlier that adrenalin is a good thing, providing athletes and public speakers with wonderful bursts of energy. There is, however, a bad side to adrenalin. When your body goes on red alert, you get pumped up and ready for action, but you also get trembling hands and jittery knees. If you are an athlete, this is no problem, because you will soon be engaged in vigorous physical activity that will enable you to drain off your excess nervous energy. But the public speaker lacks such easy outlets for these unpleasant symptoms.

Nevertheless, there are two tension releasers that you can try: (1) Let your hands make gestures. You will not have any trouble making gestures if you simply allow your hands to be free. Some speakers clutch their note cards or thrust their shaking hands into their pockets or grip the lectern until their knuckles turn white. If you let your hands hang by your side or rest on the lectern, you will find that they will automatically make gestures. You will not have to think about it at all. (2) Walk about. Though you obviously should not pace back and forth like a caged animal, you can walk a little bit. You can speak at the lectern for a while, then step to one side for a few moments, then return to the lectern. If you have visual aids, you can easily move about as part of your presentation.

Gestures and movement will not only siphon off excessive tension, but they will also make you a more exciting and interesting speaker than someone who stands frozen in one spot.

Do not be afraid to make mistakes. If you give many speeches in your life, you are bound to make a few mistakes along the way. Do not worry; it happens to everyone. Even Prince Charles and Princess Diana, the future king and queen of England, got flustered during their wedding ceremony and made some (literally) royal goofs. The bride called her groom "Philip Charles Arthur George" instead of "Charles Philip Arthur George." When he, in turn, was supposed to pledge to share all his worldly goods with her, he forgot to say "worldly."[25]

If you completely flub a sentence or mangle an idea, you might say something like, "No, wait. That's not the way I wanted to explain this. Let me try again." If you momentarily forget what you were planning to say, do not let it defeat you. Pause a few moments to regain your composure and find your place in your notes. There is no need to apologize. In conversation, you pause and correct yourself all the time; to do so in a speech makes you sound spontaneous and natural.

If you make a mistake that causes your audience to snicker or laugh, try to join in. If you can laugh at yourself, your audience will love you—they will see that you are no "stuffed shirt." Some comedians deliberately plan "mistakes" as a technique for gaining rapport with their audience.

Most audiences are very generous. They will forgive any amount of bumbling if they are convinced that you are sincere. Sincerity is more important in a speech than all the polished oratorical skills put together. The late Senator Robert Kennedy often stumbled badly in his speeches and had an embarrassing stammer at times, but audiences admired him because his earnestness and sincerity shone through.

Welcome experience. If you are an inexperienced speaker, please know that you will learn to control your nervousness as you get more and more practice in pubic speaking, both in your speech class and in your career. You should welcome this experience as a way to further your personal and professional growth.

One student told her public speaking instructor at the beginning of the course that she just *knew* she would drop out of the class right before her first speech. She stayed, though, and developed into a fine speaker. She later got a promotion in her company partly because of her speaking ability. "I never thought I'd say this," she commented, "but the experience of giving speeches—plus learning how to handle nervousness—helped me enormously. Before I took the course, I used to panic whenever I started off a talk. I had this enormous lump in my throat, and I thought I was doing terrible. I would hurry through my talk just to get it over with." But as a result of the course, she said, "I learned to control my nervousness and use it to my advantage. Now I'm as nervous as ever when I give a speech, but I make the nervousness work *for* me instead of *against* me."

In your career, rather than shying away from speaking opportunities, seek them out. As the old saying goes, experience is the best teacher.

Summary

The nervousness engendered by stage fright is a normal, understandable emotion experienced by most public speakers. Instead of trying to eliminate nervousness, you should welcome it as a source of energy. Properly channeled, it can help you give a better speech than if you were completely relaxed.

The best way to avoid excessive, crippling nervousness is to pour time and energy into preparing and practicing your speech. Then, when you stand up to speak, deal rationally with your nervous symptoms (such as trembling knees and dry throat); remind yourself that the symptoms are not a prelude to disaster, but instead are evidence that you are keyed up enough to give a good speech. Never call attention to your nervousness and never apologize for it; the listeners do not care about your emotional state—they just want to hear your message. Concentrate on getting your ideas across to the audience; this will get your mind where it belongs—on your listeners and not on yourself—and it will help you move your nervousness to a back burner, where it can still simmer and energize you without hindering your effectiveness.

Review Questions

1. Why are fear and nervousness beneficial to the public speaker?
2. Why does extensive preparation help a speaker to keep nervousness within bounds?
3. Why is delivering a speech from memory a bad method?
4. Why should you never call attention to your nervousness?
5. Does an audience detect most of a speaker's nervous symptoms? Explain your answer.

Tip 3: Don't Speak Too Fast

Because of nervous tension and/or a desire to "get it over with," many speakers race through their speech. "Take it slow and easy," advises Dr. Michael T. Motley of the University of California, Davis. "People in an audience have a tremendous job of information processing to do. They need your help. Slow down, pause, and guide the audience through your talk by delineating major and minor points carefully. Remember that your objective is to help the audience understand what you are saying, not to present your information in record time."[26]

To help yourself slow down, rehearse your speech in front of friends or relatives and ask them to raise their hands whenever you talk too rapidly. For the actual delivery of the speech, write yourself reminders in large letters on your notes (such as "SLOW DOWN"). While you are speaking, look at your listeners and talk directly to them in the same calm, patient, deliberate manner you would use if you were explaining an idea to a friend.

PART TWO

Preliminary
Stages

4

Reaching the Audience: Analysis and Adaptation

Do you want your audience to respect you and consider your speech a success? All of us, of course, would answer yes to this question. Yet some speakers make it hard for audiences to respect them. Three types of such speakers I call robots, fountains of knowledge, and boors.

Robots are lifeless speakers who have no energy, no desire to reach the audience. They prepare dull, uninteresting speeches, which they deliver without a trace of enthusiasm. They often read in a monotone from a manuscript and scarcely glance at their listeners, who are half asleep with boredom.

Fountains of Knowledge, who are enthusiastic and knowledgeable about their subject, expect the audience to absorb their ideas as easily as a sponge soaking up water. So they pour out a huge amount of information quickly. They seem unaware that listeners need help in processing information—a slow, patient delivery with plenty of explanations and examples.

Boors are thoughtless speakers who wrongly assume that listeners share their prejudices or their notions of what is funny. A few years ago a network anchor (for *CBS Morning News*) gave a talk to the San Francisco Press Club on acquired immune deficiency syndrome (AIDS). He made a crude joke about AIDS that angered and upset some listeners, especially those who had witnessed and written about the agonies of persons dying from AIDS. In another speech, a male speaker began his answer to a female questioner with, "Well, honey . . ." His condescending response caused some members of the audience to turn against him.[1]

What these speakers have in common is a low sensitivity to their audience—a failure to understand and reach the people sitting in front of them.

When you stand up in front of an audience, what is your goal? To deliver a good speech and then sit down? If your focus is upon yourself or upon your speech, you will never be an effective speaker. Your goal should be to reach your listeners and change them, so that they walk away with new information or new opinions or with a warm feeling in their hearts.

All good speakers are audience-centered. They truly want to make contact with their listeners—to inform, persuade, entertain, or inspire them. Carol Conrad, a student in one of my classes, typified this kind of speaker. In evaluating one of her speeches, another student said, "I had the feeling she was talking to me personally." How did Carol achieve this success? She composed her speeches carefully, selecting items that she knew would greatly interest her particular audience. And when she delivered a speech, she displayed a strong desire to communicate with her audience—she would look her listeners in the eye and speak directly to them. Her tone of voice and facial expression carried a clear message to the listeners: "I care about you and I want you to understand and accept my message."

In this chapter we will look at how you, too, can become an audience-centered speaker.

The Importance of Analyzing and Adapting

To be an audience-centered speaker, you need to carry out two important tasks: (1) *Analyze* the listeners to find out exactly who they are and what they know. (2)

Adapt your speech to their particular needs and interests. Analyzing and adapting should be done at every step of your preparation—when you choose your topic, when you gather your materials, and so on.

When I was a freshman in college, I signed up for Introduction to Astronomy. At the beginning of the course I was very excited because I wanted to learn some basic facts about the universe, and this particular class was to be taught by a visiting professor, a highly regarded astronomer from a leading observatory. My enthusiasm soon dissipated, however, when I sat through the first lecture. The professor was brilliant—no doubt about that—but he came into class and spent an hour discussing complex ideas that only a graduate student in astronomy could have understood. We freshmen were hopelessly lost. Though his ideas were brilliant, the professor had failed in the most important task of any speaker: to communicate ideas in a way that can be understood by the listeners. He had concentrated on himself and his ideas rather than on his audience. He had wasted his time—and ours.

Now let's look at another astronomer, Dr. Carl Sagan, professor of astronomy and space sciences at Cornell University and host of the television series, *Cosmos,* which has been viewed by 140 million people throughout the world. In one of the programs, Sagan is shown visiting an elementary school where he explains a few facts of astronomy to a class of sixth-graders. He speaks in language the children can understand. For example, he draws an analogy that is beautifully clear but not insultingly simplistic: "A handful of sand contains about 10,000 grains, more than the number of stars we can see with the naked eye on a clear night. But the number of stars we can *see* is only the tiniest fraction of the number of stars that *are*. . . . The total number of stars in the universe is greater than all the grains of sand on all the beaches of the planet Earth."[2]

Notice the big difference in how these two astronomers handled analysis and adaptation. The first failed to analyze the audience to find out who we were, and he failed to adapt his ideas to our level of understanding. Dr. Sagan, on the other hand, shrewdly sized up his audience. He knew that to show sixth-graders the richness of the universe, he would have to devise an analogy based on their own experience: every child has a good knowledge of a handful of sand, the size of a grain, and the vastness of beaches. Notice how he avoided the extremes of overestimating and underestimating his audience. In other words, he did not talk over their heads, nor did he talk down to them as if they were kindergartners. He pitched his remarks to their level.

Adapting does not mean being insincere or compromising one's principles. Suppose that you are strongly opposed to the use of all illegal drugs and you have been invited to talk on drug abuse to a class of eighth-graders. Should you use the current slang of eighth-graders to show that you are one of the gang? No, that is not what is meant by adapting. That would be phony, and the students would resent your chummy approach. Should you water down your beliefs, dropping your opposition to marijuana in order to win audience support for your stand against cocaine? No, that is not what is meant by adapting, either. Such a tactic would be foolish; you would lose respect for yourself, and weaken your credibility with the audience (if you are perceived as inconsistent). How, then, can you adapt your ideas to the eighth-graders without being a phony? In the first place, use terms and concepts that all eighth-graders can understand; for example, say "pep pills" instead of "amphetamines." Second, relate your ideas to their lives and interests; for example, "I know that sometimes you feel down in the dumps. Maybe you're making bad grades in one of your classes, or you're afraid that a certain person no longer likes you, or you're having constant hassles with your parents. In times like these, it's easy to be tempted by little pills that someone tells you will make you feel good."

When you carefully tailor your speech to a particular audience, you are showing your listeners a lot of respect. You are saying, in effect, "I care about you." One of my students gave a speech about her trip to the Middle East. While showing slides of the pyramids in Egypt, she said, "I know some of you are engineering students, so I thought you'd like to hear the latest theory about how the ancient Egyptians were able to construct the pyramids without sophisticated machinery." I am sure the engineering students were flattered and pleased by her acknowledgment of them and of their interests.

Some speakers shy away from analysis and adaptation because they think the whole thing smacks of manipulation. Though an unethical speaker could indeed use these techniques for devious purposes, the ethical speaker uses them for honorable ends. For example, one of the most honorable goals you can have is to avoid wasting your listeners' time. Most people are very busy, and they consider time as a precious asset. If you make a careful analysis of your audience, you can give them a speech that means time well spent, and they will love you for it. But if you waste their time, they will regret having listened to you. Not long ago, I was required to stay after work for two hours to hear a man speak on how to manage stress. When I went into the room, I was a bit negative. Was this man making me stay overtime for nothing? Was he planning to tell me stuff I already knew? As it turned out, his speech was very helpful. Though he was from out of town, he had arrived early and had interviewed some of my colleagues to get information on our particular problems; then he aimed his remarks at helping us overcome them. He had not wasted my time after all.

Let us now look at the ways in which you can analyze your listeners and then adapt your speeches to their special needs.

Attitudes

Attitudes are the emotional baggage—the favorable or unfavorable predispositions—that the listeners bring to your speech. Here are some questions that will help you understand and adapt to the audience's attitudes.

What Are the Listeners' Attitudes toward the Topic?

Are your listeners negative, neutral, or positive toward your ideas? If they are negative toward your ideas, you should design your speech with their opposing arguments in mind. Suppose, for example, that you want certain industries to stop spewing toxic wastes into the atmosphere. You advocate the passage of laws that would force the plants to clean up their emissions. As you prepare your speech, you anticipate that your listeners will say, "But won't the cost of cleaning up the emissions be so great that the plants will go out of business, throwing thousands of people out of work?" To counter this argument, you find information showing that similar plants in other states were forced to stop polluting, without causing economic harm to the companies.

Do not become disheartened if you fail to win the support of an audience that is negative toward your ideas. Sometimes your ideas may be so far removed from what the audience believes that you have no realistic chance of persuading all the listeners. In such cases, the best you can hope for is to soften their opposition. You give a speech, for example, in favor of raising the speed limit on interstate highways to 75 miles per hour. Everyone in the audience disagrees with you, but by the end of the speech many of the listeners admit that your argument has merit and that they will have to reassess their own position. In this instance, a "limited" victory might be the best you can realistically hope to achieve.

If your listeners are apathetic or neutral, try to involve them in the issue, and then win them to your side. For example, during times of peace, when there is no military draft, most listeners are neutral and apathetic about whether the country should bring back conscription. To win an audience to one side or the other, a speaker would have to paint a picture of imminent war and say something like, "Six months from now, all of you—male and female alike—could be standing in the ranks of the United States Army." Such a picture, if believed by the audience, could move them from neutrality and apathy toward the position you espouse. What you are trying to do, of course, is show that the issue is not a faraway abstraction but a real possibility that could affect their own lives.

If your audience is favorably disposed toward your ideas, your task is to reinforce their positive views and perhaps even motivate them to take action. For example, you give a pep talk to members of a political party in your community, urging them to campaign on behalf of the party's candidate in an upcoming election.

What Are the Listeners' Attitudes toward the Speaker?

Sometimes audiences will have a negative attitude toward you because they think you are unqualified to speak on a particular subject. You can sometimes overcome this attitude by establishing your credibility at the beginning of your speech. Bob Monroe, one of my students, gave a speech on CPR (cardiopulmonary resuscitation). Even though he was just out of high school, he proved his expertise (and gained the audience's confidence) by telling us of the lives he had saved using CPR as volunteer firefighter/rescue worker in a rural community. This sort of reporting is not bragging; it is a way of saying, "You can trust me to give you reliable information because I've used this knowledge myself with good results."

If you are not an expert on a subject, you can sometimes enhance your credibility by explaining how you got your information. Francine DuBois, a 19-year-old single woman, gave a classroom talk on the secrets of a happy, successful marriage. She knew that some of her listeners might say to themselves, "What does a young single woman know about this?" So she said, "I realize that some of you may be wondering how I can claim to know anything about marriage. To prepare for this speech, I read four books and a dozen magazine articles on the subject, and I interviewed some people I know who have good, solid marriages. I don't claim to be an expert, but I have done a lot of research and I'd like to share what I've come up with." By telling of her preparation, Francine bolstered her personal credibility with the audience.

What Are the Listeners' Expectations?

Is the audience expecting to be instructed, inspired, or amused? If you fail to act as expected, you may disappoint or anger them. For an after-dinner speech, for example, your audience would expect you to give a light, diverting talk. If instead you gave a tedious, highly technical speech, they would groan inwardly and tune you out.

Audiences also get upset if you talk about something completely different from what they were expecting. A well-known science writer was invited to speak at a large university a few years ago. Most of the people in the audience expected him to speak on science; when he talked instead on a controversial political issue, the audience was outraged. There were mutterings of discontent throughout the speech, and some people even walked out in disgust.

Interest Level

As you choose and develop a topic, you need to ask yourself how much interest your listeners will have in your material. Consider the following example:

> A student whom I'll call Calvin had an unusual hobby: collecting and firing muzzle-loading rifles, the kind used in George Washington's day. He gave a speech on how to clean such rifles. It was terribly boring; no one in the audience cared about technical things like patches and cleaning oil and ramrods. During the question-and-answer period, however, there was lively interests in the rifles: Why would anyone in the modern world want to fire antique rifles? Are they dangerous? Are they accurate? How quickly can you reload? It was clear that if Calvin had spoken on the rifles themselves, he would have had an interesting topic. He should have saved his "how to clean" speech for his fellow gun-club members, who would have loved all the technical lore.

Now contrast Calvin's failure with a successful speech:

> Ray Dillingham, a student speaker, knew how to train horses, and he planned to give a speech on how to train the Tennessee Walking Horse for competition. As he analyzed his audience, however, he realized that such a specialized talk would be uninteresting to anyone but a horse trainer, so he switched his focus

to horses in general. He spoke on the different breeds of horses, showing color slides to demonstrate their variety and beauty. The speech was well received by the listeners, who found it very interesting.

These two examples show that whenever you prepare a speech, you should ask yourself what aspect of your topic would be most interesting to your particular audience. In some cases, if your audience is not very interested in a topic before you speak, you can *generate* interest. Here is how one speaker generated interest by using a provocative introduction:

Student speaker Maxine Fletcher chose tattoos as her topic. The speech might have failed to stir much interest if she had not done something very dramatic during her introduction: she pulled up the sleeve of her sweater to reveal a large, colorful tattoo on her upper arm. It was the first time most of the students had ever seen a tattoo on a woman, and they became very interested, asking many questions at the end of the talk.

A good way to gain interest is to figure out which aspect of your topic would be most relevant to the personal lives of the listeners. Think back to your own experiences as a member of an audience. If you are like most people, you wanted to know, "What's in it for me?" In other words, did the speaker have anything to say that you considered useful in your own life? People like to hear speeches that will help them reach their personal goals. They want to be healthy, feel secure, have friends, make money, solve problems, enjoy life, and learn interesting things. If you can talk about such things in an appealing way, people will listen to you with great interest. Here is an example of how one student related her topic to her audience.

Brenda Gudger wanted to convince her audience to use bargaining techniques in buying a used car. She knew that many of her listeners might find the subject boring and unrelated to their own lives, so she began by saying: "A lot of people don't like to haggle over buying a car. They'd rather pay the sticker price than bargain with the salesperson. Well, a couple of months ago, I haggled over a used car, and I was able to get $500 knocked off the price of the car. Today I'd like to tell you how you can save yourself a lot of money by bargaining with salespeople."

By appealing to everyone's desire to save money, Brenda increased the audience's interest in her speech.

Knowledge

As you analyze your listeners, find out what they already know about the topic. Do they know a lot? A moderate amount? Nothing at all? Here are some tips on handling the different kinds of audiences.

Audiences that know a lot about the topic. Your audience will be bored and resentful if you give information that everyone already knows. Suppose that you have been asked to talk on computers. Is your audience a group of business executives who already own personal computers? If so, you do not need to define such basic terms as *default* and *booting up*. What you should do is give them new ideas and concepts.

Audiences that know little or nothing about the topic. Here are some hints on how to handle the audience that does not know much about your topic:

☐ Carefully limit the number of new ideas you discuss. People cannot absorb large amounts of new information in a short period of time. If you overwhelm them with too many concepts, they will lose interest and tune you out.
☐ Whenever possible, use visual aids to help the listeners grasp the more complicated concepts.
☐ Use down-to-earth language; avoid technical jargon. If you feel that you must use a specialized word, be sure to explain it.
☐ Repeat key ideas, using different language each time.
☐ Give vivid examples.

Mixed audiences. What should you do if some listeners know a lot about your subject and others know nothing? Whenever possible, the solution is to start off at a simple level and add complexity as you go along. Suppose you are speaking on computers; you ascertain that some listeners know very little and some know a great deal. You can say something like this: "I hope the computer buffs here will bear with me, but I know that some people in the audience will be confused unless I spend a few moments explaining what a disk drive is." The computer buffs will not be upset, because you have acknowledged their presence and their expertise, and they will not mind a little review session (they might even pick up something new). The computer novices, meanwhile, will love you for being sensitive to their inexperience.

Demographic Variables

Making a demographic analysis of your audience will give you many clues to the items we have just discussed—attitudes, interest, and knowledge. Now let us take a look at the basic questions you should ask.

What Are the Listeners' Ages?

If you have a variety of ages represented in your audience (as is often the case in college classes today), you should be sensitive to the interests, attitudes, and knowledge of all your listeners, giving explanations or background whenever necessary. For example, if you are talking about a musician who is popular only with young people, you may need to give some information about his music and lifestyle for the benefit of older members of the audience.

A demographic analysis can help the speaker adapt to an audience's knowledge, interests, and attitudes. *(Ulrike Welsch)*

Here is an example of insensitivity to the ages of listeners:

> At the graduation exercises of a state university, the commencement speaker told the graduates, "Your parents are proud of you. . . . You are now entering full citizenship. . . . You will soon enter the work force. . . . You will settle down and raise a family." The speaker was treating all of the graduates as if they were in their early twenties—a big mistake because one-fourth of the graduates in front of him were over 30 and had been in the work force for years. Many of them had already raised a family. One middle-aged graduate said later, "I lost all respect for the speaker. Couldn't he just look at us and see that we were mature adults?"

This story illustrates that you need to find out the ages of your listeners ahead of time, and then adapt your remarks accordingly. Now let's turn to an example of effective adaptation:

> William Edwards, a minister, was well known in his community for conducting a special service on Sunday mornings for families with small children. His sermon was usually in the form of a parable—a simple story with an easily grasped moral, such as the story of the Good Samaritan. He would tell the story in a dramatic fashion so that the children were captivated by the narrative; in the meantime he would subtly point out the deeper allegorical meanings to the adult listeners. Thus, Edwards succeeded in adapting his sermon to the wide age span of the audience; he reached the 4-year-old and the 44-year-old, without talking down to anyone, without boring anyone. People of all ages went away satisfied.

Are Both Sexes Represented in the Audience?

The sex of your audience will give you some clues about their background knowledge. If, for example, you are talking on sex discrimination to an all-female audience, you might need to provide little or no explanation of what you mean by sex discrimination. They already know—some from firsthand experience—what you are talking about. If there are males in the audience, however, you might need to elaborate by giving anecdotes about the subtle ways in which women are sometimes treated unfairly.

Both male and female listeners become irritated when a speaker seems to exclude them because of their gender. Some male nurses, for example, say they are peeved when a supervisor uses the pronoun *she* in talking about the typical nurse; they feel as if they are being viewed as unwanted intruders in the nursing profession. And female executives have good reason to be annoyed at situations like the one described by Janet Elliott of Los Angeles: "A speaker at a seminar for men and women insurance agents turned off a portion of his audience when he began by saying, 'As you look at your face in the mirror each morning when you shave . . .' He did not choose his words carefully to avoid offending by exclusion all those in his audience who have never shaved their faces."[3]

What Is the Educational Background?

Always consider the educational background of your listeners. Avoid talking over their heads, using concepts or language that they cannot understand. Likewise, avoid the other extreme: do not talk down to your listeners. Find the happy medium. Albert Einstein, considered by many to be the most brilliant scientist of the twentieth century, could present his incredibly complex theories to his scientific peers in language that was appropriately sophisticated for their level of understanding, yet he could also adjust his speech for the benefit of the 99.9 percent of us who cannot begin to comprehend his theories. For example, he once made part of his theory of relativity understandable to the average person by using this analogy: "Time is relative. If you sit on a park bench with your girl friend for an hour, it seems like a minute. But if you sit on a hot stove for a minute, it seems like an hour." Thus did Einstein humorously and simply illustrate part of his theory—that time seems to slow down in relation to other events.[4]

Define terms whenever you think that someone in the audience does not know what you are talking about. Fred Ebel, past president of a Toastmasters club in Orlando, Florida, says that to one audience, "I told a joke which referred to an insect called a praying mantis. I thought everyone knew what a praying mantis was. But I was greeted by silence that would have made the dropping of a pin sound like a thunderclap. Several listeners came up to me and asked, 'What is a praying mantis?' It came as a shock to me until I realized that not everyone had taken a course in biology."[5]

What Are the Occupations?

Adapt your speeches to the occupational backgrounds of your listeners. The best examples of this kind of adaptation can be found near election time when politicians size up the needs and interests of each audience they face. With steelworkers, for example, the typical politician may discuss competition from Japanese industries; with farmers, soil erosion; with truck drivers, highway speed limits; and with bankers, credit regulations. None of this is necessarily manipulative or unethical; it is simply good audience analysis and adaptation: steelworkers do not want to hear about soil erosion, and farmers do not want to hear about Japanese steel imports.

What Are the Racial and Ethnic Backgrounds?

Find out the racial and ethnic backgrounds of your listeners so that you can adapt your remarks to their needs and interests. For example, in many college classrooms (and in other audiences as well), you will find a sprinkling of foreigners. As much as possible, you should try to include them in your adaptation. One student speaker, Mark Hopkins, was planning a speech on "hot rod" automobiles. While conducting informal interviews with members of his speech class, he discovered that some of the foreign students did not know what a hot rod was. So he prepared a drawing of a hot rod on a large piece of poster board, and then displayed it at the beginning of his speech.

Most important of all, you should avoid material that might offend any racial or ethnic group. In this connection, a note of warning: some people think that if there are no members of a particular race or ethnic group present, it is all right to make insulting jokes. It is never all right. Such slurs are offensive and un-funny to many men and women who don't happen to belong to the group being ridiculed, and they will automatically lose respect for the speaker.

What Are the Religious Backgrounds?

Knowing the religious affiliations of your audience will give you some good clues about their beliefs and attitudes. Most Seventh-Day Adventists, for example, are very knowledgeable about nutrition because of the strong emphasis the denomination places on health; many Adventists are vegetarians and nondrinkers. If you were asked to speak to an Adventist group on a health-related issue, you could assume that the audience had a higher level of background knowledge on the subject than the average audience has; you would therefore avoid going over basic information they already know.

While religious background can give you clues about your audience, you have to be cautious. You cannot assume that all members of a religious group subscribe to the official doctrines. A denomination's hierarchy, for example, may call for a stop to the production of nuclear weapons, while the majority of the members of that denomination may not agree with their leaders' views.

What Is the Economic and Social Status of the Audience?

You need to be sensitive to the economic and social backgrounds of your listeners so that you can adapt your speech accordingly. Suppose you are going to speak in favor of food stamps for the poor. If your listeners have low incomes, most of them will probably be favorably disposed to your ideas before you even begin. You might therefore want to aim your speech at encouraging them to support political candidates who will protect the food-stamp program. If they are upper-middle-class, however, many of them will be opposed to your ideas and you will have to aim your speech at winning them over to your way of thinking.

The Occasion

Find out as much as you can about the occasion and the setting of your speech, especially when you are giving a speech in your community or at a career-related meeting. Here are some questions to ask; pay special attention to the first one.

What Is Your Time Limit?

It is important that you find out how much time has been allotted for your speech, and then abide by the time restriction. I have seen several public occasions marred by long-winded speakers who droned on and on, oblivious to the lateness of the hour and the restlessness of the audience. Once I attended a banquet where a half-dozen speakers had been asked to speak for only 5 minutes apiece but four of the six exceeded the time limit by 30 to 45 minutes each. By midnight, most of the people at the tables were yawning and looking at each other in weary disbelief.

If you are a speaker in such a situation, you may want to pare your speech down, if at all possible. Your audience will love you for it. When I am invited to speak at events where there are several speakers, I have learned to prepare two versions of my speech—a full-length one to use if the other speakers respect their time limits, and a shorter version if the situation dictates that I trim my remarks. You might want to consider doing the same thing for occasions that are loaded with many speakers and activities.

Though many audiences will suffer through an interminable speech without being rude to the speaker, some will not. One speaker found this out the hard way when he gave a speech to a civic-club luncheon. At the hour when the meeting was supposed to be over, even though the speaker was still holding forth, the club members got up and walked out. It was explained later that all the members had to get back to their jobs by a certain time.

Some speakers have absolutely no concept of time. For a 5-minute speech, some of my students talk for 20 minutes and then swear later that they could not possibly have talked for more than 5—something must have been wrong with my stopwatch. As we will see later, practicing your speech at home will help you keep within time limits.

People who give long-winded speeches might desist from this terrible vice if they knew what misery they cause their audiences. The poor listeners are forced to undergo an agony of boredom, as they squirm and fidget, stifle their yawns, and yearn for release from this windbag who tortures them for what seems like an eternity. If you tend to be a garrulous speaker, you should follow the wise speechmaking formula of President Franklin D. Roosevelt:

☐ Be sincere
☐ Be brief
☐ Be seated

What Is the Purpose of the Occasion?

A leading television commentator, widely known for his probing questions during live TV interviews, was paid $25,000 to lead a panel discussion at a national computer show in Atlanta. His task, according to *PC Week* magazine, was to extract "pithy and provocative insights" from major computer industry leaders. He failed to carry out this assignment, however, because he "evidently misunderstood the show's business orientation." Instead of asking probing questions about how businesses can use computers, he "repeatedly hammered on the subject of home computing, to the apparent confusion and irritation of the panelists."[6]

Avoid this commentator's mistake by finding out in advance the purpose of the meeting. Suppose you are an authority on the life and music of the late singer John Lennon, a member of the Beatles who was murdered by a deranged fan, and you are asked to give a talk at a club meeting. To prepare your speech, it would be crucial for you to know the purpose of the occasion. Is the club meeting devoted to remembering Lennon's tragic death? If so, you would obviously want to prepare a somber eulogy to Lennon. Or is the meeting devoted to a celebration of the Beatles' music? In this case, you might want to give an upbeat talk on Lennon's personality, interlaced with tape-recorded playings of his music.

What Other Events Will Be on the Program?

It is important to find out about all the other events on a program. Are there other speakers on the agenda? If so, what will they speak on? It would be disconcerting to prepare a speech on the life of Martin Luther King and then discover during the ceremony that the speaker ahead of you is talking on the same subject.

Even more disconcerting is to come to a meeting and find out that you are debating someone on your topic. Obviously you need to know such information in advance so that you can anticipate what the other speaker will argue and prepare your rebuttal accordingly.

How Many People Will Be Present?

It can be unsettling to walk into a room expecting an audience of twenty, but instead finding two hundred. Knowing the size of your audience ahead of time will not only help you to prepare yourself psychologically but it will also help you to plan your presentation. Will you need extra-large visual aids? Will you need a microphone?

Where your listeners sit in relationship to others can be important. If you have fifteen people scattered about in a large hall, it will be easier to make contact with them if you first have them move to seats at the front and center. Nightclub comedians are very sensitive to seating arrangements; they make sure tables are pushed close together because they know that patrons are more likely to laugh if they are jammed together in warm coziness. Some comedians would never dare tell jokes to an audience widely scattered in a large room; people feel isolated, and they are afraid that if they laugh, they will be conspicuous. (Have you ever noticed that funny movies are funnier if you see them in a packed theater than if you see them in a sparsely attended theater?)

Will There Be a Question-and-Answer Period?

If there is a question-and-answer period, who will moderate it, you or the program chairperson? How long will it be? Will it come after each speech or after all the speeches?

In most speeches, the questions from the audience should come after the speech is finished. If they were to come during the speech, they could spoil the carefully organized flow of your remarks. Some questions could get you side-tracked onto issues that are not directly relevant to your subject. And of course some questions might be premature, bringing up points that you have not covered yet.

In classroom speeches, your instructor will establish rules for asking questions. In talks that you give out in the community, you might want to establish guidelines for your audience in the early part of your speech. For example, you could say, "If you have any questions during my talk today, please hold them until the end and I'll be happy to try to answer them."

A question-and-answer session at the end of a speech may help a speaker respond to an audience's needs more directly. *(Laimute E. Druskis/Taurus)*

Getting Information about the Audience

Where can you get information about your audience? For classroom speeches, there are several ways to gain information. If your class has speeches in which students introduce themselves, you can make notes regarding their backgrounds, interests, and other features. Also, you can interview your fellow students directly.

For speeches in the community, your best source is usually the program director (or whoever invited you to speak). Using the suggestions in this chapter, find out all that you can about the audience and the occasion. In addition, here are some open-ended questions you can ask:

☐ Is there anything special about this group or this meeting that would help me prepare my speech?

☐ Does the group want me to speak on a particular topic? If I choose my own topic, has the group heard a speech recently on what I'm planning to talk about? What are some of the recent topics of other speakers who have spoken to the group?

☐ What facilities will be available (microphones, audiovisual equipment, chalkboards, lectern, etc.)? Are there any peculiarities about the meeting place that I should be aware of (poor acoustics, loud noises from adjoining rooms, etc.)?

☐ Could I have the names and phone numbers of some of the members of the group so that I can interview them on their background knowledge, attitudes, etc.?

☐ Could I have the names and phone numbers of a few previous speakers so I can interview them on what worked and what didn't work with this group?

If time permits, you may want to use a questionnaire to poll your future listeners on their knowledge, interests, and attitudes. If, for example, you were planning to argue against corporal punishment in schools, you could devise a statement like this—"Schools should not be permitted to spank children"—and ask your listeners to circle one of these responses: "Strongly agree," "Mildly agree," "No opinion," "Mildly disagree," "Strongly disagree." If most of your future listeners strongly disagree, you obviously should devote much of your speech to trying to change their minds. Another example: If you were planning to speak on computer viruses, you could devise a simple true-false quiz to determine how much accurate information the listeners already have.

Adapting during the Speech

Adapting to your audience, so important during the preparation stages, must also take place during the actual delivery of the speech. You must be sensitive to their moods and reactions, and then make the necessary adjustments, if possible. Here is an example:

Using a portable chef's stove, Lester Petchenik, a student speaker, was demonstrating how to cook green beans *amandine.* At one point, he sprinkled a large amount of salt into his pan—an action that caused several members of the audience to glance at each other with looks of surprise. Noticing this reaction, Lester ad-libbed, "I know it looks like I put too much salt in, but remember that I've got three pounds of green beans in this pan. In just a moment, when you taste this, you'll see that it's not too salty." (He was right.)

Reading the mood of your audience is really no different from what you do every day with your friends. You tell them about the new "framas" that you've just bought; they say "Huh?" and give you a quizzical look. You then explain what a framas is. In like fashion, if you see people in your audience frowning when you mention a technical term, you need to add a definition.

Try to overcome any barriers to communication. John Naber, a professional speaker and former Olympic gold medalist in swimming, says that he once gave a speech in a room with poor acoustics. Realizing the audience would have trouble understanding him if he stayed at the lectern, he said, "I moved into the middle of the group and walked among them as I spoke."[7]

You should be especially sensitive to the mood of the listeners. Are they bored, drowsy, or restless? Sometimes they are listless not because your speech is boring but because of circumstances beyond your control. It is 8 o'clock in the morning, for example, and you have to explain a technical process to a group of conventioneers who have stayed up partying half the night.

If you ever need to "wake up" a listless audience, here are some techniques you can use: (1) Invite audience participation (by asking for examples of what you are talking about, or by asking for a show of hands of those who agree with you). (2) "Rev up" your delivery (by moving about, by speaking slightly louder at certain points, or by speaking occasionally in a more dramatic tone). (3) Use visual aids.

Sometimes it is easy to "read" audience behavior. If listeners are drumming their fingers on their desks and glancing at their watches, you know they are impatient and eager to leave the meeting. If their eyes are glazed over and they are slouching in their chairs and occasionally stifling yawns, you know they are weary or bored.

In other cases, however, it is hard to interpret your listeners' faces. That man in the third row with a sour face—is he displeased with your speech? Before you jump to conclusions, pay heed to the astute observation of the well-known inspirational lecturer, Earl Nightingale:

I've seen people in my audiences many times who appeared to be outright hostile to what I was saying, who seemed to be trying to tell me by their expressions that I was a blithering idiot, yet I have learned over the years that it's often these same people who come up to the head table afterwards with the most profusive compliments and expressions of gratitude. They just happen to look like that. They wear customary frowns and their mouths turn down at the corners as though they had just bitten into a dill pickle. That's the way they look.[8]

What if the frowns do mean disapproval? Should you alter your speech to make everyone in the audience happy? No, of course not. While trying to be sensitive to the mood of the audience, you should never compromise your principles or violate your personal integrity simply to win approval. Your goal in public speaking is not to have the audience like you, but to communicate your ideas to them as clearly and as effectively as possible.

Summary

To be an effective speaker, you must concentrate your attention and energies on your audience, and have a strong desire to communicate your message to them. You must analyze the listeners beforehand and adapt your materials and presentation to their needs and interests.

You should analyze the listeners' attitudes toward you and your topic, their level of interest in your subject matter, and their degree of knowledge about your material. You should take into consideration a variety of demographic factors: age, sex, educational levels, occupations, racial and ethnic backgrounds, religious affiliations, and economic and social status. You should also analyze the occasion to gather details about the time limit, the purpose of the meeting, other events on the program, the number of people who will attend, and whether or not there will be a question-and-answer period.

Be prepared to adapt to the needs of the listeners during the speech itself. Try to be sensitive to the cues that indicate boredom, restlessness, or lack of understanding.

Review Questions

1. How should you deal with listeners who think you are unqualified to speak on a particular subject?
2. Why are listeners' expectations important?
3. What guidelines should be followed for a speech to an audience that knows little or nothing about your topic?
4. What demographic factors should you consider in analyzing an audience?
5. What aspects of the speech occasion should you examine before giving your talk?

Tip 4: Develop a Positive Attitude toward Each Audience

There is an old comedy routine you have probably seen at least once on TV in one form or another. It goes something like this: a nervous young man is waiting for a blind date to appear at a prearranged spot. As he waits, he fantasizes how she will react to him. The TV camera captures the fantasies: when she approaches him, she looks at him with disappointment bordering on disgust. When he introduces himself, she laughs at his name and says it is stupid. When he suggests that they go to a particular restaurant for dinner, she ridicules his idea of good food. When he tries to make small talk, she laughs at his accent. The fantasy goes on and on, from one humiliation to another. Finally, the fantasies fade away as the real, live date appears on the scene. By now, however, the young man is so outraged that he screams at the date, "Well, I didn't want to go out with you, either!" and storms away, as the startled date stands alone, blinking her eyes in confusion.

In like fashion, some speakers indulge in fantasies of audience rejection and when they actually stand up to speak, they act very defensive, as if they *know* that everyone in the audience is going to reject them and their ideas. Their "body language"—tone of voice, facial expression, posture—is defensive, sometimes even angry and sullen. I saw one such speaker argue in favor of the sport of hunting animals. He knew that some members of the audience were

opposed to hunting. From start to finish, he acted as if the audience had just insulted him. "We are not sadistic people who enjoy watching animals suffer," he said angrily. Who said he was sadistic? Who said he enjoyed watching animals suffer? Like the young man waiting for his blind date, this speaker had worked himself into an unnecessary rage.

Do not prejudge your audience. Most listeners are kind and sympathetic to speakers. Even if they reject your ideas, they usually are respectful of you the speaker, as long as you are respectful of them.

Instead of nurturing gloomy fantasies, try to develop a positive attitude toward every audience you address. Professional speaker Rosita Perez of Brandon, Florida, attributes her success as a public speaker to her love and respect for her audiences. "The key to giving a good speech," she says, "is remembering that the audience is the single most important element there. When we tune in to them, and set aside our ego needs, some magical things happen because they *feel* our commitment."[9]

It helps to think of the audience not as an impersonal mass, but as a collection of individuals who are basically no different from you and your friends. "When I speak," says Perez, "I communicate to the audience in the most personal way I am able to. In an auditorium of 3,000, I speak as if to one."[10]

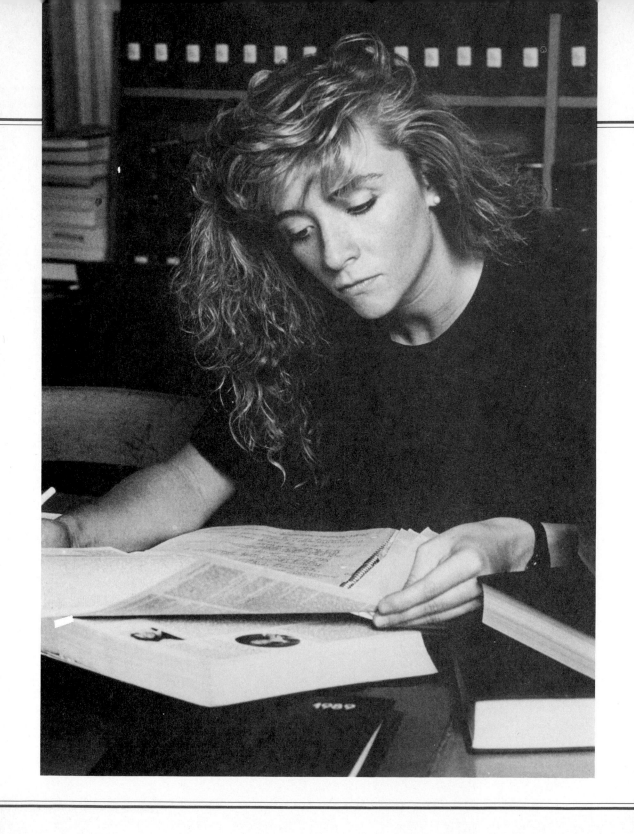

5

Selecting Topic, Purpose, and Central Idea

The best way to write a love letter, the Swiss-French philosopher Jean Jacques Rousseau once said, is to begin without knowing what you are going to say. Such a formula might be effective for the ecstatic outpouring of a love letter, but if applied to speechmaking, it is a recipe for failure. Yet I know a few foolhardy individuals who insist that they do not have more than a vague idea of what they are going to say to an audience until they stand up and "go with the mood of the moment" (as one of them expressed it). A couple of these people, I have to admit, are effective speakers, but most of them range from mediocre to devastatingly boring. Because their own minds are unfocused, their speeches are fuzzy. They ramble, fail to clarify ideas, and get bogged down in irrelevant matters.

The best speeches I have heard were given by men and women who sounded as if they were speaking spontaneously but who had in fact spent hours and days in careful preparation. In this chapter we will examine some of the most important steps in preparing a speech—selecting a topic, a general purpose, a specific purpose, and a central idea.

Selecting a Topic

For many of the speeches that you will give during your lifetime, your topic will be chosen by someone else. Your boss, for example, tells you to give a talk to your fellow employees on a new product. Or you are asked to speak to the Rotary Club on safe driving skills because you are known in the community as an expert on the subject.

In most public speaking classes, on the other hand, students are permitted to choose their own topic, a freedom that causes some students a lot of grief. They spend days walking around with a dark cloud over their heads, moaning to friends, "I have to give a speech next week and I can't think of a *thing* to speak on." Do not let yourself get stuck at this stage. Choose your topic as far ahead of your speech date as possible because you will need to spend a great deal of time and energy on other important tasks, such as researching, outlining, and practicing. If you spend days and days stewing over which topic to select, you may find yourself without enough time to adequately prepare the speech.

As you read this chapter, keep a note pad handy and jot down ideas for topics as they come to you so that you will have a stockpile to draw from throughout the course. In the weeks ahead you can add to your list as you get more ideas.

Here are some important points to bear in mind as you look for a topic.

Select a Topic That You Care About

Have you ever had something happen to you that was so exciting, you could hardly wait to tell your friends? That is the way you should feel about your speech topic. It should be something you care about, something you are eager to communicate to others. Are you angry over the air pollution in your town? Speak on air pollution. Are you excited about the wizardry of your personal computer?

Speak on computers. Are you having so much fun baking pastries that you try a new recipe every week? Speak on how to bake pastries.

Enthusiasm is contagious; if you are excited, some of your excitement will infect your listeners. If, on the other hand, you are unexcited about your topic, you are apt to do a lackluster job in preparing the speech, and when you deliver it, you will probably come across as dull and unconvincing.

Here are two examples that illustrate how enthusiasm, or the lack of it, can make the difference between a good speech and a poor one:

A student whom I'll call Bob had trouble coming up with a topic for his speech class. So at the last moment he grabbed a magazine article and used it as the basis for a talk on gun control. His speech was poorly constructed and tedious. Worst of all, he seemed to have no real emotion about his subject. Normally, when a student talks on gun control, there is a lively response from the audience during the question-and-answer period, but Bob's listeners seemed as listless as he was; they had no questions or comments for him.

Theresa Schmidt gave a talk on doll collecting and brought along some of the dolls from her own collection. I was afraid that her talk would be boring to an audience of grownups, but she started off by telling why she, as an adult, still collected dolls. Then she related fascinating stories about how she got some of them from foreign countries and told of particular dolls' names and personalities. Her speech was a success, not just because of her well-told stories and colorful visual aids, but because she herself displayed a consuming, passionate interest in her subject. While she was speaking, I glanced around at the students in the class; their animated faces showed that they were fascinated.

Now look at these two speakers. Gun control is one of the most highly emotional subjects in our society today, as likely as any topic you can name to capture an audience's interest. But Bob succeeded in making it dull because he had a ho-hum-I-don't-really-care attitude. Theresa, on the other hand, took a subject unlikely (at first glance) to appeal to adults, and made it into a wonderful speech, mainly because she was imbued with a contagious enthusiasm. She *cared* about her subject.

Select a Topic That You Know a Lot About (or Can Learn About)

Make things easy for yourself. Speak on something you are already thoroughly familiar with—or can learn about through research. If your listeners realize they know more about the subject than you do, they lose confidence in you. This can be especially painful if your speech is followed by a question-and-answer period. When I was in college, I was asked to give an oral report on a particular issue in a sociology class; I had no interest in the subject and did little research. After I gave my report, a student in the class (who knew a great deal about the subject) ridiculed my omissions and errors. I felt like an absolute fool. But I learned an important lesson: a person should *never* give a speech unless he or she knows the subject matter extremely well.

Here are several ways to probe for topics that you know a lot about (or can learn about).

Personal Experiences

If you are permitted to choose your own topic (rather than have one assigned to you), my advice is to start your search with the subject on which you are the world's foremost expert—your own life.

"But my life isn't very interesting or exciting," you might say. You are wrong. Maybe you are not an international celebrity, but there are dozens of aspects of your life that could make fascinating speeches. Let me give you some examples, all of them involving students:

Mike Gronowski gave a speech about the only job he had held in his life—bagger at a supermarket. At first glance this sounds like a dull job and a boring speech. But Mike made it fascinating: he told about the fashionably dressed woman who tried to hide T-bone steaks in her overcoat, the surprisingly large number of customers who could not find their cars in the parking lot, and the fact that if a bagger got bitten by a dog while loading groceries into a car, the attacker was more likely to be a snippy little dog than a huge snarling Doberman pinscher.

Susan Peterson went to her first rock concert and discovered that the rock fans were as interesting as the band. She gave a speech about the different types of fans she observed, using vivid descriptions that amused and fascinated her audience.

Carlos Gomez loved to jog every afternoon to dissipate the tensions of the day. He gave a speech on the mental and physical benefits of jogging, showing his listeners how they, too, could feel better if they took up this form of exercise.

Mitzi Stevens worked as a waitress in a restaurant. She gave a talk on the way customers treat waitresses, with some fascinating insights. She reported, for example, that the most generous tippers are parents of small children, who apparently feel guilty for the fuss and mess their kids create.

These four students were *ordinary* people who chose to speak on *ordinary* aspects of their lives, but their speeches turned out the way all good speeches should turn out—interesting. So when you are trying to come up with a topic, start with yourself and look for the interesting things in your own life. Figure 5.1 is an inventory that you can fill in to help you identify topics.

After you have filled in the inventory, go back and analyze the list for possible speech topics. If you are not sure which items would make good speeches, ask your friends for advice or consult your instructor. Figure 5.2 is an example of how one student, Karin Johansson, filled in the inventory.

In Karin's inventory, which items could make a good speech? All of them are

Figure 5.1
This personal inventory can help you pinpoint speech topics from your own life.

Name:

Personal Inventory

Jot down as much information about yourself as you can in the categories below:

Work experience (past and present)

Special skills or knowledge

Pastimes (hobbies, sports, recreation)

Travel

Unusual experiences

School interests (academic and extracurricular)

Concerns or beliefs (politics, society, family, etc.)

potentially good speech topics. Which would be the best? That would depend on Karin's current state of enthusiasm; her rafting trip on the Colorado River through the Grand Canyon sounds exciting, for example, but if it turned out to be a disappointing trip and Karin is tired of telling about it, this would obviously be a poor topic for her.

Exploring Interests

What if the personal inventory fails to yield a topic that you are happy with? Or what if you simply dislike talking about yourself? Do not despair. There are

Figure 5.2
Personal inventory,
as filled in by one
student.

Name: Karin Johansson

Personal Inventory

Work experience (past and present)

   Emergency medical technician (paramedic)
   Ambulance driver
   Volunteer firefighter
   Waitress

Special skills or knowledge

   Cardiopulmonary resuscitation
   Rescue from burning buildings
   First aid

Pastimes (hobbies, sports, recreation)

   Water skiing
   Swimming
   Cooking Chinese food
   Restoring antiques

Travel

   Quebec
   Mexico
   Colorado River (rafting)

Unusual experiences

   Rescuing two children from a burning house
   Rafting through the Grand Canyon

School interests (academic and extracurricular)

   Nursing courses
   Biology
   Drama Club

Concerns or beliefs (politics, society, family, etc.)

   We need to stop child abuse
   Learning CPR should be a prerequisite for
      getting a driver's license
   Curtail sale of handguns (but not rifles)

plenty of topics outside your personal life that can captivate your audience. Choose one that you have always wanted to know more about—something that intrigues you. The following case illustrates what I am talking about:

A few months before she enrolled in a public speaking class, Julia Lavagetto saw a television documentary on unidentified flying objects (UFOs). This whetted her curiosity, and she yearned to read some books and articles on UFOs, but unfortunately she was too busy with her schoolwork. When she took the public speaking course, Julia realized that she now had the opportunity to meet her speech assignment and satisfy her intellectual craving at the same time. She read books and magazine articles on UFOs, and gave an interesting speech.

Some students use their speech assignment as a vehicle for gaining vital information for their own lives. Here is an example:

Lloyd Feinberg still mourned the suicide of a close friend in high school. He deeply regretted that he had been unable to dissuade his friend from taking an overdose of pills. For his classroom speech, he decided to do research on suicide. He read books and magazine articles, and interviewed a suicide-prevention counselor. He ended up giving his talk on "How to counsel a person who threatens to commit suicide," a topic he chose because he wanted to know how to handle such a situation if it ever happened again. During his research he found tips and insights that were valuable not only for his audience, but for himself as well.

In the two cases just cited, the main point of this section—select a topic you know a lot about—still applies. If you do not know a great deal about the subject now, you can do some research and make yourself knowledgeable. Perhaps you will not qualify as an expert, but you will at least know more about the subject than most of your listeners.

Brainstorming

If the suggestions already discussed do not yield a topic, try brainstorming (so called because it is supposed to create a lot of intellectual thunder and lightning). In *brainstorming*, you write down whatever pops into your mind. For example, if you start off with the word *school*, the next word that floats into your mind might be *homework* and then the next word might be *algebra,* and so on. Do not censor any words. Do not apply any critical evaluation. Simply write whatever comes into your mind. Nothing is too silly or bizarre to put down.

Using a sheet of paper or the guide in Figure 5.3, jot down words as they come to your mind.

When you finish brainstorming, analyze your list for possible topics. Do not discard any possibility until you have a chosen a topic. Here is an example of how brainstorming might work: Under the heading "Things," let's say you write *cars*. Then you might think of the following: car payments . . . trips . . . highways . . . accidents . . . drunk drivers. . . . When you analyze the list, perhaps the word *trips* leads you to choose a trip to Mexico as your topic. Or the term *drunk drivers* causes you to realize that you feel strongly about the need for stronger laws against driving while intoxicated, so you choose drunk driving as your topic.

Figure 5.4 is a sample of one student's brainstorming notes. Under most categories the student's brainstorming was fairly straightforward. It is easy to see his train of thought. But under "Places," he made some interesting jumps (which is okay; writing down whatever comes to mind is the way the "game" is played). He started with a place, the gym, which reminded him of the gym's swimming pool. This made him think of the laps he liked to swim every day, and this led him to think of the backstroke. Then his mind leaped to some Olympics trials he had seen on TV, and this made him think of East German prowess in swimming

Figure 5.3
A brainstorming guide can be helpful in finding topics.

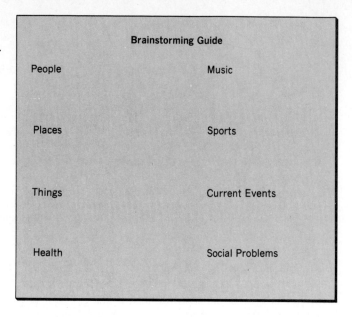

competition. As it ended up, the list gave him a lot of choices for topics: swimming for exercise, competitive swimming, Olympic competition, East German participation, etc.

Based on his brainstorming under "Current Events," this student chose to give a speech on Israel's vulnerability to an atomic bomb ("Israel is only one bomb wide," he said) and what that nation can do to protect itself. He could have easily picked another topic from his list: "Paranoia in Islamic countries" could have led to a speech on why some Islamic fundamentalists view the United States as a bastion of evil.

The other categories could have also yielded many topics. His brainstorming under "Sports," for example, could have led to a talk on the good-versus-bad symbolism of professional wrestling on TV. He also could have made speeches on other items suggested by the list: boxing, hockey, violence in sports, etc.

You may be wondering why you should put all this down on paper. Why not just let all these ideas float around in your mind? The advantage of writing items down is that you end up with a document that can be analyzed. It helps you focus your thinking.

Library Search

If the techniques previously discussed fail to yield a topic, there is another method you can use: go to the library and look through magazines or an encyclopedia or the *Reader's Guide to Periodical Literature* until you find something that appeals to you and should also appeal to your audience. Here is an example:

Roosevelt Evans went to the library and picked up the most recent copies of several popular magazines. As he leafed through the magazines, he spotted

Figure 5.4
One student's en-
tries on a brain-
storming guide.

Brainstorming Guide

People
  Dad
  fishing
  weekend trips
  camping
  great fun, no fish
  excuses—fishermen

Music
  guitar
  how to play
  country music
  records
  bluegrass bands

Places
  gym
  swimming pool
  laps
  backstroke
  Olympics
  East Germans

Sports
  hockey
  violence
  boxing
  wrestling
  'rasslin'
  villains
  good guys

Things
  money
  greed
  rat race
  power
  high finance
  Wall Street

Current Events
  nuclear war
  disarmament
  Russians
  Russian paranoia
  Paranoia in Islamic
    countries
  Iran
  Middle East
  Israel
  Atomic attack on
    Israel

Health
  vitamins
  nutrition
  vegetables
  vegetarians
  red meat

Social Problems
  pollution
  crime
  juvenile delinquency
  drunk driving
  legal age for drinking
  age for voting
  age for military duty

an article on the foods one should eat in order to avoid cancer. This subject was so interesting to him that he read other articles on the same topic and decided to give his speech on it.

Choose a Topic That Interests the Audience

Some students are unsure of their ability to determine whether a topic is worthwhile. "I'm excited about a topic," they say, "but how do I know whether it will be interesting to the audience?" Here are some ways of assessing the interest level of a topic:

☐ Analyze the audience as thoroughly as you can, as suggested in Chapter 4. This should enable you to make good, educated guesses about the topics that would be ideal for your audience.
☐ Consult your instructor for suggestions.
☐ Ask your friends how much interest they would have in the subject if they were part of the audience.
☐ Several weeks beforehand, distribute a questionnaire to members of the audience to find out how interested they would be in several potential speech topics. For each topic have a rating scale, such as "very interesting," "moderately interesting," and "not very interesting."

Narrow the Topic

Once you find a topic, you often need to narrow it. Suppose you want to give a speech on crime in America; 5 minutes—or 20—is not enough time to adequately cover such a broad topic. How about limiting yourself to crimes of violence? Again, 5 minutes would be too short to do justice to the topic. How about one type of violent crime—rape? This subject perhaps could be handled in a 5-minute speech, but it would be advisable to narrow the topic down even more—to one aspect of the subject: How to fight off a rapist. Or: Why some men rape.

Here are some examples of topics that can be narrowed:

Too broad: Politics in America
Better: My stint as a volunteer campaign worker in a congressional election

Too broad: Relations between parents and children
Better: How some parents unwittingly display higher expectations for sons than for daughters

The most important way to narrow your topic is to formulate a specific purpose, which will be discussed later in this chapter. But first, let's take a look at your general purpose.

The General Purpose

Once you have a topic, your next step is to decide your general purpose in giving the speech. Most speeches have one of the following purposes:

☐ To inform
☐ To persuade

There are other purposes—to entertain, to inspire, to stimulate, to introduce, to create goodwill, and so on—but the two above are the most common. Let's take a closer look at them.

Informative Speech

In the informative speech, you are concerned about giving new information to your listeners, not with winning them to your way of thinking. The informative speech can take a variety of forms, such as defining a concept (feminism, for example), explaining a situation (why TV soap operas are so popular), or demonstrating a process (the correct way to ski cross-country).

You main concern in this kind of speech is to have your audience learn and remember new information. You are in effect a teacher—not a preacher, not a salesperson, not a debater. Here is a sampling of informative topics:

- ☐ How to complain—and get results—when you receive poor products or service in a store
- ☐ The use of computers in the home
- ☐ Soccer—the world's most popular sport
- ☐ The life of Martin Luther King
- ☐ How to design and create a leather belt

Persuasive Speech

Your aim in the persuasive speech is to convince the listeners to come over to your side, to adopt your point of view. You want to *change* your listeners in one or both of these ways: (1) to change their minds (for example, persuade them to believe that the nuclear arms race should be ended), and/or (2) to change their behavior—get them to *start* doing something they normally do not do (such as using seat belts) or get them to *stop* doing something they normally do (such as sprinkling salt on their food).

Here are some examples of persuasive topics:

- ☐ Colleges should abolish letter grades and give only "pass" or "fail."
- ☐ Married couples should not go into debt on anything except a home.
- ☐ Every person should travel to a foreign country at least once in his or her lifetime.
- ☐ Congress ought to cut off all military aid to repressive dictatorships.
- ☐ The summer Olympic games should be held at a permanent site in Greece from now on.

The Specific Purpose

After you have chosen a topic and determined your general purpose, your next step is to formulate a *specific* purpose, stating exactly what you want to accomplish in your speech. Here is an example:

> *Topic:* Life on other planets
> *General Purpose:* To inform
> *Specific Purpose:* To inform my listeners of the three main reasons why some astronomers believe that life exists on other planets

The specific purpose serves two important functions: (1) it helps you narrow your topic to something that can be covered comfortably and effectively in the time allotted, and (2) it forces you to put your ideas into sharp focus.

If you chose a topic such as television, and then did nothing to bring it into sharp focus, you might make the mistake of talking about a lot of different things on TV. To target one specific idea concerning TV, you would need a statement such as this:

> *Topic:* Television
> *General Purpose:* To inform
> *Specific Purpose:* To explain to my audience the reasons for the popularity of TV soap operas

Now you have a sharp focus for your speech. You have limited yourself to something that can be covered adequately in a short speech.

Here are some guidelines for writing a specific-purpose statement.

Begin the Statement with an Infinitive

An infinitive is a verb preceded by the word *to*—for example, *to write, to read.* By beginning your purpose statement with an infinitive, you clearly state your intent.

> *Poor:* Hiking in the mountains
> *Better:* To inform the audience of the health and recreational benefits of hiking in mountain terrain

For informative speeches, your purpose statement can start with such infinitives as "to explain," "to show," "to demonstrate." For persuasion speeches, your purpose statement can start with infinitives such as "to convince," "to prove," and "to get the audience to believe."

Include a Reference to Your Audience

Your specific purpose should include references to your audience, by means of such phrases as "to my listeners" or "to the audience." This may seem like a minor matter, but it is important for you to keep your listeners in mind at every stage of your speech preparation. Writing them into the specific purpose helps remind you that your goal is not to stand up and talk, but rather to communicate your ideas to real flesh-and-blood human beings.

> *Poor:* To explain how fast-food restaurants use colors and music to stimulate sales
> *Better:* To explain to my listeners how fast-food restaurants use colors and music to stimulate sales

Limit the Statement to One Major Idea

Avoid the temptation to try to cover several big ideas in a single speech. Limit yourself to only one.

> *Poor:* To convince the audience that scenes of explicit sex and violence in prime-time television shows should be censored and that local TV stations should be encouraged to expand their local coverage
>
> *Better:* To convince the audience that scenes of explicit sex and violence in prime-time television shows should be censored

In the first example, the speaker tries to cover two major ideas in one speech. While it is true that censorship and local news both pertain to TV, they are not closely related and should be handled in separate speeches.

> *Poor:* To demonstrate to my audience how to take care of their cars by changing the oil and oil filter, tuning the engine, adjusting the carburetor, flushing out the radiator, and properly inflating the tires
>
> *Better:* To demonstrate to the audience how to change the oil and oil filter in a car

The first example covers too much territory. If you tried to compress all that information into a 5-minute speech, you would have to race through so fast that your listeners would be unable to keep up with you.

Make Your Statement As Precise As Possible

You should strive to have a statement that is clear and precise.

> *Poor:* To help my audience brighten their relationships

This statement is fuzzy and unfocused. What is meant by "to help"? What is meant by "brighten"? And what kind of relationships are to be discussed—marital, social, business? Here is one possible improvement:

> *Better:* To explain to my listeners four techniques people can use to communicate more effectively with loved ones

Make Sure You Can Achieve Your Objective in the Time Allotted

Do not try to cover too much in one speech. It is better to choose a small area of knowledge that can be developed adequately than to select a huge area that can only be covered sketchily.

> *Poor:* To tell my audience about cancer

This statement is much too broad for a speech; you would need hours and hours to cover the subject. Here is one way to improve the statement:

Better: To tell my audience about the six warning signals for cancer

Now the focus has been narrowed so that you can adequately cover one aspect of the topic in a short speech.

Do Not Be Too Technical

You have probably sat through a speech or lecture that was too technical or complicated for you to understand. Do not repeat this mistake when you stand at the lectern.

Poor: To explain to my listeners the different types of golf clubs and their uses

This is too technical for the average classroom audience. Some listeners have never played golf and probably never will. The speaker should shift to some aspect of golf that will appeal to *all* listeners. Here is one possibility:

Better: To tell my audience why golf is an enjoyable sport for millions of Americans.

If you are speaking on a topic on which you are an expert, you may need to take particular care to avoid making the speech too technical for your audience. *(Rae Russel)*

The Central Idea

"When we ministers preach a sermon," a clergyman friend told me, "we like to think everyone in the congregation understands everything we're saying. And we like to think that when they leave the church, they carry our eloquent words with them in their hearts and in their minds." But unfortunately, he confessed, it does not always work out that way. "They remember our human-interest stories, but they either don't understand the point behind the stories or they soon forget it. It's always disappointing to have someone shake your hand after the service and say, 'Just what *were* you driving at this morning?'"

If people ask this question after you have given a speech, you have failed to accomplish your most important task—to communicate your central idea. The *central idea* is the basic message of your speech expressed in one sentence. It is the same thing as the *thesis sentence* or *controlling statement*, terms you may have encountered in English composition courses. If you were forced to boil your entire speech down to one sentence, what would you say? *That* is your central idea. If, a month after you have given your speech, the audience remembers only one thing, what should it be? *That* is your central idea.

As we will see in later chapters, the central idea is a vital ingredient in your outline for a speech. In fact, it *controls* your entire speech—that is, everything you say in your speech should develop, explain, illustrate, or prove the central idea. Everything? Yes, everything—all your facts, anecdotes, statistics, and quotations.

Let's imagine that you decide to give a speech on the incompetence of some teachers. You plan to cite cases of certain elementary school teachers who cannot write coherent sentences and some high school math teachers who cannot solve algebra problems. You bring up these cases because you believe that teachers should not be employed in the public schools unless they can pass a competency test. The specific-purpose statement of your speech might look like this:

> *Specific Purpose:* To persuade my audience to support mandatory testing of all teachers in grades K through 12

Next, you develop your central idea by asking yourself, "What is the key idea I want my audience to retain if they forget everything else?" Your central idea might look like this:

> *Central Idea:* All teachers in grades K through 12 should be required to pass a competency test on basic reading, writing, and math skills before being allowed to teach in public schools.

Now you have the controlling statement for your entire speech. Your task in preparing the rest of the speech will be to find materials—such as examples, statistics, and quotations—to explain and prove your central idea.

Because the specific purpose and the central idea are similar, you may be asking whether there is any significant difference between them. The answer is yes. The specific purpose is written partially from your point of view—it is what *you* set out to accomplish. The central idea is written entirely from the listeners' point of view—it is the message *they* go away with.

In planning your speech, the specific-purpose statement should be written first—before you start gathering material. In many cases, you will be able to write the central idea immediately afterward but not always. In some cases you may need to postpone formulating the central idea until you have completed your research.

Imagine, for example, that you are preparing a speech on the use of steroids by athletes and bodybuilders. From watching news on television, you know that coaches and health experts are warning people not to use steroids, and you feel certain that your investigation in the matter will confirm this view. So you start off with a specific-purpose statement like this:

Specific Purpose: To inform my audience of the health risks of using steroids for developing muscles

You haven't done any research yet, so you can't really write a central idea. But after you spend a few days in the library, studying articles on steroids, you are able to put your central idea at the top of your outline:

Central Idea: Persons who chronically use steroids run the risk of suffering kidney and liver damage and of developing serious mental disorders.

Now that you have a clear statement of the key idea of your speech, your task will be to show the audience that what you say about steroids is true by citing statistics, case studies, and the testimony of experts.

Every speech should have only one central idea. Why not two? Or three? Because you are doing well if you can fully illuminate one big idea in a speech. If you try to handle more than one, you run the risk of overwhelming the listeners with more information than they can comfortably absorb.

Devising a central idea keeps you from rambling in your speech. It prevents you from being the kind of speaker who never quite gets to the point. CBS news correspondent Charles Osgood, who gives many speeches throughout America, says that if you lack a central idea, your speech will be unfocused and scattered "all over the place." Worst of all "your audience will sit there with your message going in one ear and out the other."[1]

It is important that you actually write down your central idea—at the top of your outline—rather than have some vague notion floating around in your mind. Writing it down gives you a path to follow and a clearly defined destination. As you prepare your outline, you can evaluate every potential item in light of the central idea. Does fact A help explain the central idea? If yes, keep it. If no, throw it out. Does statistic B help prove the central idea? If yes, keep it. If no, throw it out.

Let's assume that you want to give a talk on the following topic and general purpose:

Topic: The metric system
General Purpose: To persuade

Next you write down what you want to accomplish with your audience:

Specific Purpose: To convince my audience that the metric system should be adopted by the United States

To carry out your specific purpose, you need to plant an idea in the minds of his listeners—one key idea:

Central Idea: Using the metric system gives a nation economic benefits in world trade.

Now you have your speech in a nutshell. As you decide what to put in the speech, you should let the central idea control the process. Let's say, for example, that you find an interesting story about how our present system of measurements got started—a *foot* was originally the length of an average person's foot, and so on. Fascinating information, but does it relate directly to your central idea about the value of the metric system? No, so discard it. Next you come across an estimate by the Secretary of Commerce that U.S. firms lose $4 billion a year in export trade because their nonmetric products are excluded from some international trade markets. This, of course, is a powerful argument for your central idea, so use it.

Here are some additional examples. Study them carefully, noting the difference between the specific purpose and the central idea in each case.

Topic: Crash diets
General Purpose: To persuade
Specific Purpose: To persuade my listeners never to go on a crash diet
Central Idea: Crash diets should be avoided because they endanger one's health.

Topic: Esperanto
General Purpose: To inform
Specific Purpose: To inform my audience of the basic characteristics of Esperanto
Central Idea: Esperanto is a 100-year-old artificial language designed to give all human beings a universal second tongue.

Topic: Photo-radar equipment
General Purpose: To persuade
Specific Purpose: To convince my audience that computer-driven photographic radar devices should be used by police to catch speeding drivers

Central Idea: If police are allowed to use devices that photograph over-the-speed-limit cars and their license plates, speeding on highways will be reduced and lives will be saved.

The time you spend formulating the items discussed in this chapter—general purpose, specific purpose, and central idea—may seem like an extra burden of time and energy, but in reality these items are shortcuts. Because they channel your thinking, they prevent you from scattering your efforts across too wide a field. They end up saving you time. More importantly, they help you give a better speech than you otherwise might give.

Summary

In choosing a topic for your speech, think of subjects that (1) you care a great deal about, (2) you know a lot about (either now or after you complete your research), and (3) your audience will find interesting.

After you choose a topic, decide upon your general purpose in speaking (such as to inform or to persuade) and then formulate your specific purpose—exactly what you hope to accomplish in the speech. Next, write out your central idea: the one big idea that you want your audience to remember if they forget everything else in the speech.

Though they may seem time-consuming, these preliminary steps will actually save time in the long run, and they will help you organize your ideas in a coherent, understandable form.

Review Questions

1. When a speaker is enthusiastic about his or her ideas, how do listeners usually react?
2. How does one go about brainstorming ideas?
3. List three *general* purposes for speeches.
4. List the six criteria discussed in this chapter for writing a specific-purpose statement.
5. What is the central idea of a speech?
6. What is the difference between the specific purpose and the central idea?

Tips

FOR YOUR CAREER

Tip 5: Be Yourself

It is ethical to study other speakers and borrow some of their ideas and methods, but you make a big mistake if you try to imitate them—if you try to make yourself over in their image.

Be yourself. Do not try to be someone else. I once knew a man who, whenever he gave a speech, tried to sound exactly like the famous evangelist Billy Graham. He succeeded in reaching his goal: if you closed your eyes, you would swear that Billy Graham himself was addressing the audience. But people considered this imitator an insincere fool and laughed at him behind his back. There is only one Billy Graham and there is only one you. This is not to say that you should not try to improve your speaking style. Just make sure the finished product is a polished you, not a polished imitation of someone else.

"You should always try to be *you*," advises professional speaker Arnold "Nick" Carter. "You should express how *you* think, feel, and believe. Imitation is suicide in public speaking."[2]

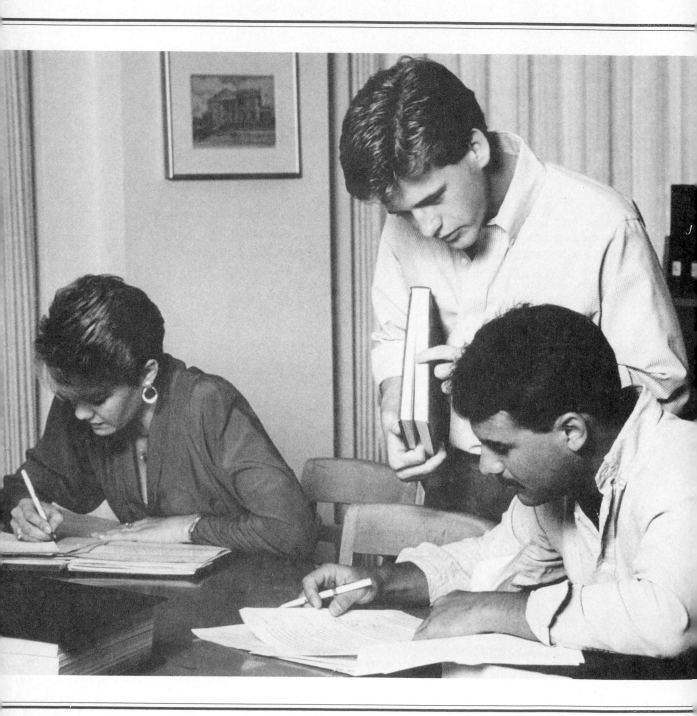

6

Finding
Materials

At a textile plant hiring over 1000 people, many employees asked the company to provide in-plant day care for their preschool children. The company responded by assigning Gloria Lopez, the personnel manager, to study the request and make specific recommendations to the board of directors.

To prepare for her presentation, Lopez drew from her own experiences as a working mother. She went to a nearby university library and checked out books on day care. With the help of her company's research department, she tapped into a computer database and extracted 14 recent articles from magazines and *The Wall Street Journal* on corporations that have instituted day care centers. She interviewed over a dozen workers to find out exactly what kind of day care they needed, and she sent questionnaires to all employees to determine how many needed this service and at what hours. Traveling to three different states, she observed the workings of day care centers that other corporations had already established, and she quizzed her fellow executives: How much money were they spending on day care? Did employee morale and productivity improve? Would they recommend that her company establish a day care center? Finally, she interviewed employees at these other plants to find out whether they were satisfied with the quality of the day care they had.

By the time Lopez finished her investigation, she had accumulated a wealth of information, and it was easy for her to prepare a proposal that was thorough, well-substantiated, and persuasive. When she stood before the board of directors, she gave an authoritative presentation on the need for an in-plant day care center, and she asked the board for its approval. After a brief discussion, the directors approved the proposal.

Lopez was successful because she had researched her topic thoroughly. A good speech should not be a collection of vague ideas and unsupported opinions; rather, it should be like Lopez's—an interesting package containing a rich variety of solid, up-to-date information. In this chapter we will discuss where and how to find materials for your speeches.

Personal Experiences and Investigations

In gathering materials for a speech, some speakers overlook their personal experiences, which can be a gold mine of good material. If it is relevant, a story from your own life can be the most interesting part of a speech. Your personal experiences can be especially useful when they are used to amplify information you have gleaned from books or magazine articles, as in the case below:

> Student speaker David Rhodes gave tips on how to buy a good car at the lowest possible price. He presented information from *Consumer Reports*, supplementing it with firsthand knowledge he had gained in his job as a car salesperson the previous summer. An example of his "insider's" knowledge: "When the car salesperson gives you the price on a car," David advised, "say that you'll think about it and maybe call back the next day. Start to walk away. Before you leave the lot, the salesperson will give you a lower price—anything so you don't get away."

You can also undertake personal investigations to gather material for a speech. For a speech on acid rain, for example, you can visit a mountaintop that has been ravaged by pollutants, making observations and perhaps even taking color slides. For a speech on prison conditions, you can visit a county jail or state prison and then tell your audience what you have seen. For a speech on animal overpopulation, you can tour a local animal shelter and interview the director.

Another type of investigation is to conduct public opinion surveys. One student polled her classmates on their views concerning the death penalty. This survey not only helped her analyze and adapt to her audience, but it also provided interesting data to include in the speech itself.

Library Resources

A library is a wonderful treasury of resources for your speeches. Your campus library is the best place to begin, but do not forget that there are many other kinds of libraries. Your local newspaper has a *morgue*, a library of old news stories that are clipped and filed by subject matter. These clippings are usually limited to local and state affairs; no effort is made to collect national and international news articles. Most newspapers allow researchers to look at the files and photocopy any items they want. There are also specialized libraries maintained by historical societies, museums, professional associations, law firms, medical societies, and large businesses. To find the location of these libraries in your community, consult the *American Library Directory* (in the reference section of your college library), or ask people who are knowledgeable about the particular field.

Getting Help from Librarians

Rather than wandering inside a library hoping to stumble upon good information for your speech, seek help from the librarians. Contrary to what some students think, a librarian's work is not limited to ordering, shelving, and checking out books. An important part of a librarian's job is helping patrons find materials, so don't be shy about asking for help.

When you start your research, introduce yourself to a member of the library staff and explain the nature of your project. A librarian will be designated to help you; in large libraries, there is usually a reference librarian whose sole job is to help people like you track down information.

One of the most helpful services that librarians provide is interlibrary loan. This means that if your library does not have the book or magazine article you need, the librarians can make a search (often very quick and computerized) of other libraries in your state until they find it and borrow it for you. It often takes less than a week to get the book. (You should not count on its coming quickly, however; some books are hard to locate and mail delivery can be slow.) Most libraries have this service; ask your librarian for details.

Consulting Reference Works

The reference section of the library, with its encyclopedias, dictionaries, yearbooks, and other aids, is an important resource. In most libraries, reference books cannot be checked out, so you need to allow yourself ample library time when you delve into these books.

General encyclopedias. For some research projects, encyclopedias are a good place to begin because they can give you an overview of your subject—a general idea of the basic concepts and issues. They also list books and articles on your subject, saving you the time it would take to compile such a list on your own. If the library carries several editions of a particular encyclopedia, look for the most recent edition. Following is a list of some of the most popular encyclopedias:

☐ *The New Columbia Encyclopedia*
☐ *The New Encyclopaedia Britannica*
☐ *Random House Encyclopedia*
☐ *World Book Encyclopedia*

Specialized encyclopedias. Many specialized encyclopedias offer technical information written in language that a nonspecialist can understand. One of the best and most popular of these is the *McGraw-Hill Encyclopedia of Science and Technology*, a fifteen-volume set that includes an index. Here is a sampling from among the dozens of other specialized encyclopedias:

☐ *Encyclopedia of Advertising*
☐ *Encyclopedia of American History*
☐ *Encyclopedia of Athletics*
☐ *Encyclopedia of Psychology*
☐ *Encyclopedia of Superstitions*
☐ *Encyclopedia of World Art*

Dictionaries. For definitions of currently used words in the English language, consult dictionaries such as *The American Heritage Dictionary, The Random House Dictionary,* or *Webster's Third International Dictionary*. For the history of a word, look at *The Oxford English Dictionary*. Also available are specialized dictionaries such as the following:

☐ *Dictionary of American Slang*
☐ *Dictionary of Scientific and Technical Terms*
☐ *Dorland's Illustrated Medical Dictionary*
☐ *Sports Dictionary*

Almanacs and yearbooks. Because they are published annually, almanacs and yearbooks provide a great amount of updated facts and statistics. A few of the more popular are:

☐ *Facts on File*
☐ *Information Please Almanac*

☐ *Statistical Abstract of the United States*
☐ *The World Almanac and Book of Facts*

Atlases and gazetteers. Atlases contain maps and other geographical information; gazetteers are geographical dictionaries. Here are some of the most widely used:

☐ *Britannica Atlas*
☐ *Rand McNally Cosmopolitan Atlas*
☐ *Times Atlas of the World*
☐ *Webster's New Geographical Dictionary*

Biographical sources. Most libraries have many different biographical references, giving you information about the lives and careers of famous people, living or dead. Here is a sampling:

☐ *Current Biography*
☐ *Dictionary of American Biography*
☐ *Notable American Women*
☐ *Who's Who in America*
☐ *Who's Who of American Women*

Collections of quotations. If it is appropriate and interesting, a quotation can enrich a speech. Here are some sourcebooks:

☐ *Bartlett's Familiar Quotations*
☐ *Dictionary of Quotations*
☐ *Peter's Quotations*
☐ *The Quotable Woman*

Finding Books

To find a book in the library, you have two major resources—the librarians and the card catalog (sometimes called the public catalog), which tells you which books the library owns. It was once available only in the form of index cards in filing drawers, but now some libraries display the cards on microfiche, microfilm, or computer monitors.

The catalog lists books alphabetically by (1) author's last name (2) title, and (3) subject. (In some libraries, name and title cards are housed separately from subject cards.) Which type of card should you consult? It depends on your situation. If you do not know much about your topic, the subject cards are very helpful. For example, if you want to do research on lasers but you do not already know the titles of any books in that field, begin by looking under the subject heading "lasers." If, on the other hand, you know the name of an author in the field, you may want to go directly to that name in the "author" section and write down a list of his or her books. For example, if you know that Stanley Leinwoll is an expert on lasers, look under the author's last name, "Leinwoll." Finally, if you know of a book called *Laser Handbook* but you cannot recall the author's name, look for the title under "L" in the "title" section of the catalog.

Sample cards are shown in Figure 6.1. The most important item on a card is the call number in the upper left corner, for this tells you where to find the book in the library's stacks. The call number is usually derived from either the Dewey Decimal System or the Library of Congress System.

Most libraries have a chart or map showing how to locate books in the stacks. Or you can ask a librarian for help.

Finding Articles

Sometimes magazine and newspaper articles are better sources than books because they are more up-to-date and may even contain information that will

Figure 6.1
Subject, title, and author cards of a typical library book.

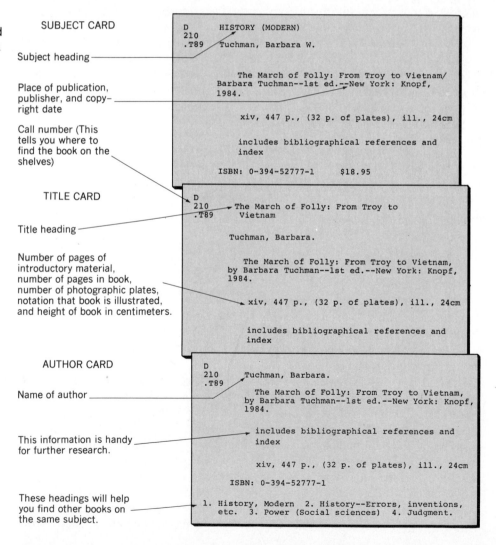

SUBJECT CARD

Subject heading

Place of publication, publisher, and copyright date

Call number (This tells you where to find the book on the shelves)

```
D          HISTORY (MODERN)
210
.T89    Tuchman, Barbara W.


           The March of Folly: From Troy to Vietnam/
        Barbara Tuchman--1st ed.--New York: Knopf,
        1984.

           xiv, 447 p., (32 p. of plates), ill., 24cm

           includes bibliographical references and
           index

        ISBN: 0-394-52777-1     $18.95
```

TITLE CARD

Title heading

Number of pages of introductory material, number of pages in book, number of photographic plates, notation that book is illustrated, and height of book in centimeters.

```
D
210      The March of Folly: From Troy to
.T89       Vietnam

         Tuchman, Barbara.

           The March of Folly: From Troy to Vietnam,
        by Barbara Tuchman--1st ed.--New York: Knopf,
        1984.

           xiv, 447 p., (32 p. of plates), ill., 24cm


           includes bibliographical references and
           index
```

AUTHOR CARD

Name of author

This information is handy for further research.

These headings will help you find other books on the same subject.

```
D
210      Tuchman, Barbara.
.T89
           The March of Folly: From Troy to Vietnam,
        by Barbara Tuchman--1st ed.--New York: Knopf,
        1984.

           includes bibliographical references and
           index

           xiv, 447 p., (32 p. of plates), ill., 24cm

        ISBN: 0-394-52777-1

     1. History, Modern  2. History--Errors, inventions,
        etc.  3. Power (Social sciences)  4. Judgment.
```

never appear in book form. What is the best way to find magazine articles? If, for example, you want to find articles on modern aircraft carriers of the U.S. Navy, should you get a bunch of back issues of *Armed Forces Journal* and browse through until you find an article on aircraft carriers? No, this would be a waste of time. Go instead to one of many indexes that are available in most libraries.

Readers' Guide to Periodical Literature. Your library is certain to have the *Readers' Guide to Periodical Literature*, a general index of over 170 popular magazines published since 1900. Articles are listed alphabetically by author and subject. Each entry gives you all the information you need in order to track down the article. (If you do not understand any of the abbreviations, consult the key in the front of each *Readers' Guide*).

Figure 6.2 illustrates what you would find in the *Readers' Guide* if you wanted to look up an article on videotapes.

The Magazine Index. *The Magazine Index*, which is on microfilm, covers over 400 magazines (far more than the *Readers' Guide*). It provides coverage of the last 5 years; as a new month is added, the corresponding month 5 years ago is deleted. If you wanted to go back earlier than 5 years, you would have to consult a special file containing the deletions (see your librarian for help). *The Magazine Index* also provides "Hot Topics," a monthly supplement (in printed form and kept in a looseleaf notebook) of current articles on such timely issues

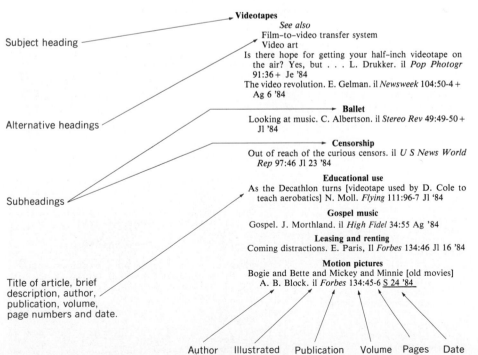

Figure 6.2
Sample entry from *Readers' Guide to Periodical Literature.*

as gun control, the arms race, and family violence. Some libraries have the *Magazine Collection*, a retrieval system that contains the full text of selected articles from *The Magazine Index*. To be able to identify which articles are available in this form, see the explanation of a typical entry in Figure 6.3.

Newspaper indexes. Your library may have back issues of several newspapers on microfilm. Some newspapers are indexed, others are not; check with your librarian to find out what is available. If your library has only one newspaper on microfilm, it is likely to be *The New York Times* because of that publication's broad coverage of national and international events. *The New York Times Index* is a valuable resource because each entry contains a brief abstract of the story; if you are looking for a single fact, you can sometimes find it in the *Index* without having to go to the issue cited. Another good resource is *The Newspaper Index*, which indexes *The Wall Street Journal, The New York Times, The Christian Science Monitor, The Los Angeles Times*, and *The Washington Post*.

Special indexes. If you need information from specialized publications that are not covered by the above indexes, there are a number of other indexes you can consult:

- ☐ *Applied Arts Index*
- ☐ *Applied Science and Technology Index*
- ☐ *Art Index*
- ☐ *Biological Abstracts*
- ☐ *Biological and Agricultural Index*
- ☐ *Business Index*
- ☐ *Business Periodicals Index*
- ☐ *Cumulative Index to Nursing and Allied Health Literature*
- ☐ *Education Index*
- ☐ *Engineering Index*
- ☐ *Environment Index*

Figure 6.3
An example from *The Magazine Index*.

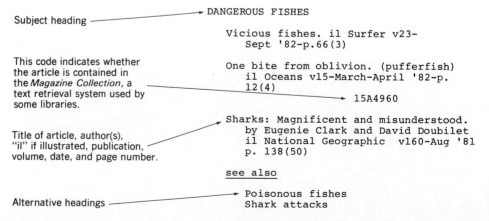

Subject heading ⟶ DANGEROUS FISHES

Vicious fishes. il Surfer v23- Sept '82-p.66(3)

This code indicates whether the article is contained in the *Magazine Collection*, a text retrieval system used by some libraries.

One bite from oblivion. (pufferfish) il Oceans v15-March-April '82-p. 12(4)
⟶ 15A4960

Title of article, author(s), "il" if illustrated, publication, volume, date, and page number.

Sharks: Magnificent and misunderstood. by Eugenie Clark and David Doubilet il National Geographic v160-Aug '81 p. 138(50)

see also

Alternative headings ⟶ Poisonous fishes
Shark attacks

☐ *General Science Index*
☐ *Hospital Literature Index*
☐ *Humanities Index*
☐ *Index Medicus*
☐ *Psychological Abstracts*
☐ *Social Sciences Index*

Finding Audiovisual Materials

Most libraries have audiovisual materials that can be checked out or played in the library. These materials include videotapes, 16-mm films, audiotapes, phonograph records, filmstrips, and slides. These items may be listed in the card catalog or in a separate catalog. Ask your librarian for help.

Sometimes audiovisual materials that help in your research can be incorporated as aids into your speech (see Chapter 8).

Computer Databases

Computer databases are vast storehouses of information. Some of them duplicate what is already in libraries—complete encyclopedias, periodical indexes, and reference works—while others offer information not available elsewhere. Your college library (or one in your community) might have computers that can tap into one of the more than 2000 databases currently available in the United States. Even if your library has no computers, it might be able to order a computerized search by an outside source on your behalf.

Computers offer these advantages as research tools: (1) They provide the fastest search available. In minutes computers can find and compile information that might take several days of diligent labor in the library to locate. (2) Databases are updated more frequently than reference books; many receive new information daily. In some subjects, printed encyclopedias are out of date within 2 years of publication; their electronic versions are much fresher; the *Academic American Encyclopedia*, for example, is revised twice a year. (3) Databases provide access to more magazines and technical journals than most libraries could possibly afford to subscribe to. For example, *Biosis Previews*—just one out of the 200 databases offered by Dialog Information Services—provides research information about the life sciences from 9000 medical and scientific journals published in the United States and abroad.

There are, however, a few disadvantages: (1) Making a computer search can be expensive (though not necessarily so; check with your library concering fees because some libraries charge only a modest amount). (2) You usually get words only—no photos, drawings, or diagrams, which are often an important element in understanding an article. (3) Most databases go back no earlier than the 1970s. For most speeches this is not a problem because you want the most recent information available; but if you need to read articles written before the seventies (for example, if you want to find contemporary articles on hippies of the sixties), databases will offer no help.

Many libraries offer computerized re- search facilities, from computerized ''card catalogs'' to databases. *(David E. Kennedy/TexaStock)*

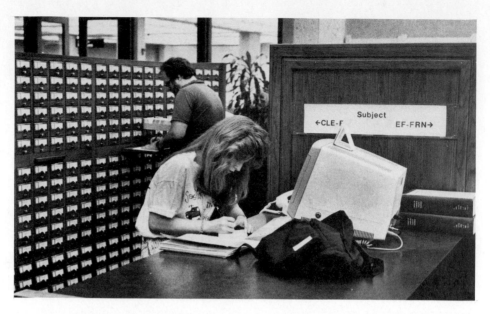

Databases provide information in three forms (some databases offer only one of these types; some offer all three):

1. *Citations.* This is a basic bibliographic reference, which usually gives the name of the article, the author(s), the name of the magazine, volume number, issue number, page numbers, and date.

2. *Abstracts (or brief summaries) of an article.* An abstract is designed to give you enough information to decide whether you want to see the complete text of an article. Sometimes, however, the abstract itself gives you as much information as you need. For example, let's say you want to know if Laetrile can cure cancer; you see the abstract of an article in *The New England Journal of Medicine* which examines 10 years of research on Laetrile and finds no efficacy in Laetrile. Without reading the entire article, you can say in your speech, "According to a recent article in *The New England Journal of Medicine*, Laetrile has been found to be ineffective in the treatment of cancer."

3. *Complete texts.* A few databases offer complete texts of articles. You usually have three options: (1) You can read the text on the screen, making notes on paper as necessary; (2) you can print out the text on a computer-linked printer; or (3) you can pay the database owner to print out the text for you and mail it to you.

To give you an idea of the incredible wealth of information at your fingertips, here is a sampling of what databases can do:

☐ If you are speaking on arms negotiations between the United States and the Soviet Union, you can get the latest United Press International news reports from The Source or the latest Associated Press dispatches from CompuServe.

☐ If you are interested in the ethical problems raised by genetic engineering, Georgetown University in Washington, D.C., has a database on bioethics issues that you can get free of charge.

☐ If you want to find articles related to financially troubled computer companies, you can type the words *bankrupt* and *computer* on the Dow Jones News/ Retrieval database and retrieve articles about bankrupt computer companies from the pages of *The Wall Street Journal, Barron's,* and the *Dow Jones News Service*, dating back as far as June 1979.

Many college and local libraries are hooked up to the 80 databases offered by BRS (Bibliographic Retrieval Services) of Latham, New York. These databases cover such subjects as mathematics, robotics, pollution, engineering, physics, drug abuse, alcoholism, psychology, religion, sociology, education, and marriage.

How can you find out what is available? Check with librarians not only at your college library but at public and specialized libraries as well. Or find a copy of *Online Database Search Services Directory* (Detroit: Gale Research Company, revised annually). This directory not only describes databases but lists those organizations, such as libraries, that will conduct information searches for the general public.

If you cannot find a library that offers computerized searches, there are other possibilities. If you own a personal computer or if you can borrow time on a friend's computer, you might want to tap the databases directly. All you need is a modem (telephone hookup) and telecommunications software. Some databases can be used free of charge; others charge a fee, ranging from modest to exorbitant. Many database services charge a much smaller fee if you make your search in the evenings or on weekends.

Once you start doing research on a computer, you may become so dazzled by the quickness and thoroughness of the process that you will never want to use any other technique. As the *Whole Earth Software Catalog* puts it, "you may never look at a card catalog again."[1]

Interviews

While the library is an important source, do not overlook the possibility of conducting interviews with people who are knowledgeable about your subject. These individuals can often give your current information that is not yet available in magazines or books. In the world of computers, for example, change occurs so rapidly that a magazine article published 3 months ago on a particular kind of software can be hopelessly outdated today.

Who can you find to interview? The obvious place to start is your own college; some faculty members may have expertise in your area of interest. In the larger community beyond the campus you may find experts in many different fields. If you are speaking on snakebites, for example, and there is a nationally recognized herpetologist living in your community, you could obviously learn a lot from an interview. In some cases, you may want to interview fellow students. If you are preparing a speech on communication problems between males and females, for instance, you might want to collect the ideas, experiences, and observations of other students.

If you are lucky, there can sometimes be a wonderful bonus from an interview: you might develop a professional contact or personal friendship that will prove useful to you in later years. Consuela Martinez, an accounting major in one of my classes several years ago, interviewed an official at a local bank to get information for a speech. The official was so impressed with Consuela that when she graduated and returned to the bank to seek a job, he hired her. Another student, Skyler MacPherson, interviewed a well-known poet in his community; after the interview, the poet asked Skyler to come to his house for dinner, and a long-term friendship began, with the poet helping Skyler to get some of his own poems published.

Do not let fear of rejection deter you from asking for an interview. Some students have the idea that the knowledgeable persons they want to interview are so important and so busy, they will certainly have no time for questions from a "lowly" student. This is a mistaken notion. I have sent hundreds of students out for research interviews, and I have found that virtually everyone in the community loves to be interviewed. Does this surprise you? Think about yourself for a moment: when a friend asks you for advice (on such things as how to bake a cake or how to solve an algebra problem), don't you enjoy holding forth as an "expert"? The same thing is true of knowledgeable people in your community—they are flattered to be interviewed by a student.

Should an individual be interviewed in person or over the telephone? If you have only two or three short, easily answered questions, you could conduct your interview over the telephone, but if you want detailed answers to many different questions, you are more likely to get good responses if you conduct your interview in person. People tend to speak more freely and in greater detail during face-to-face encounters than they do on the telephone. There is also a greater chance of warmth and trust developing between you. Here are some guidelines for planning and conducting interviews.

Preparing for the Interview

There are a few things you should be sure to do before you interview a person.

Telephone Interviewee in Advance for an Appointment

Arrange a time that is convenient for the person you want to interview by telephoning beforehand. Do not just drop by and expect the person to agree to an interview on the spot; you may catch the person off-guard or during a hectic time of day. When you call to line up the appointment, explain briefly what you are trying to find out and why you think he or she can help you. Such an explanation gives the person time to get his or her thoughts together before talking to you.

Conduct Research before Interview

You need to read up on your subject *before* you go to an interview. Here is why: first of all, you need to know enough about the subject to ask intelligent questions. Suppose you are planning to interview a psychiatrist about schizophrenia. If you read articles and books on the mental disorder beforehand, you will know enough about the subject to ask an important question, such as "Do researchers feel that they are close to discovering a cure?" In addition to helping you ask intelligent questions, research will also help you avoid asking embarrassing questions like "How does the split in personality occur?" Such a question would be embarrassing because it would reveal your ignorance of what the term *schizophrenia* means. (It means a psychotic break with reality, not a Jekyll-and-Hyde split in personality.)

Second, if you find something in your reading that you do not understand, the interviewee might be able to explain it. Suppose that while you are doing your library research on schizophrenia, you come across the term *folie à deux*. You look up the term in a dictionary but cannot make sense out of the formal definition. In your interview with a psychiatrist, you ask for a plain-English explanation of what the term means (it is a psychotic delusion that one person persuades another person to share).

Finally, if you fail to find vital information in your library research, you can often get it from the interviewee. Suppose that you are investigating the effectiveness of automobile air bags in traffic accidents. You want to know, "Will air bags save a motorist's life if he or she is driving at 55 miles per hour and has a head-on collision with a car traveling at the same speed?" Your weekend spent in the library sifting through government studies failed to turn up the answer, but 5 minutes with a traffic-safety expert may give you the information.

Prepare Questions in Advance

Decide ahead of time exactly what questions you want to ask, and write them down on a piece of paper, putting the most important ones first in case you run out of time.

Decide How to Record Interview

It is a mistake to think that you can conduct an interview without a pencil or a tape recorder and then remember all the key information later when you are organizing your speech. Since human memory is highly fallible, you need to have a system for recording the interview. Most interviewers use either or both of the following methods:

Writing down key ideas. Use a pencil or pen and a notepad. Jot down key ideas only; if you try to write down every word the person is saying, you will be completely absorbed in transcribing sentences instead of making sense out of what is being said. It is far more important to comprehend the interviewee's ideas than to get the exact words on paper.

Using video or audio tape. A videocassette camcorder (on a tripod) or an audio tape recorder can be ideal when it is important to get a word-for-word record of the interview—you need not worry about forgetting key points or misquoting your source. Some interviewees, knowing they are being recorded, may try extra hard to be precise and accurate in giving information. In some cases, you can use some of your videotape in your actual speech (as did one speaker, who interviewed an engineer at the construction site of a bridge).

There are some disadvantages in using recorders, however, according to Thomas Hunter, public relations director for Union Camp Corporation. "Recorders are mechanical beasts subject to malfunctions. And they can bog you down in hours of replay and transcription."[2]

If you want to use a recorder, you should seek permission from the interviewee beforehand. Most people will permit recording, but occasionally a person will refuse. You should of course respect his or her wishes.

Important note: If you use a video or audio tape recorder, you should also take notes. At first glance it may seem silly to take notes while getting everything down on tape, but I recommend it for these reasons: (1) a mechanical foul-up might cause you to lose your entire tape; having notes would give you a backup record of the interview. (2) The act of making notes forces you to concentrate on the key ideas of your interviewee, thereby making you more alert in your questioning.

If you plan to take notes and make a recording simultaneously, you may want to have a friend accompany you to help with the recording. This frees you of all worry about operating the equipment.

Conducting the Interview

Here are some tips on how to conduct the interview.

Start interview in a friendly, relaxed manner. Before you begin your questions, you need to establish rapport with the interviewee. You can do so by making a statement of appreciation (for example, "Thanks for letting me come by to talk to you today") and by engaging in small talk on obvious topics (the weather, the beautiful painting on the wall, etc.). Small talk is an important lubricant in conversation, especially at the beginning of a dialogue, so you need not feel that it is a waste of time. You should also repeat the purpose of the interview; the person may have forgotten exactly what you are seeking. While these preliminary remarks are being made, you can set up your recorder (if you have previously received permission to use one).

Get biographical information about interviewee. The person you are interviewing is one of your sources, so you need to be able to tell your audience later why he or she is an authority on your subject. If you have not been able to get background information in advance, the early part of the interview is a good time to get it because it continues the building of rapport. You could say, for example, "Where did you get your doctorate?" Or "How long have you been working on this problem?"

Ask both prepared and spontaneous questions. Earlier we noted that you should decide ahead of time exactly what questions you want to ask. Make these questions as specific as possible. It would be ludicrous to walk into the office of an expert on robots and say, "Tell me what you know about robots." Such a question would probably draw a laugh and a comment like, "Have you got two months to listen?" A better, more specific question would be something like this: "Will robots someday replace all automobile assembly-line workers?"

There are two types of questions that can be prepared in advance:

1. *Closed* questions require only "yes" or "no" responses or short, factual answers. Examples: "Do Democrats outnumber Republicans in this state?" "What percentage of registered voters actually voted in the last presidential election?" Closed questions are effective in getting specific data.
2. *Open* questions give the interviewee a wide latitude for responding. For example, "How do you feel about the nuclear arms race?" The advantage of such a broad question is that the interviewee can choose the points he or she wishes to emphasize—points that it may not have occurred to you to ask about. The disadvantage is that sometimes an interviewee can wander off the subject into irrelevant side issues.

There are two other types of questions that cannot be prepared in advance but may need to be asked spontaneously during the interview:

1. *Clarifying* questions are used when you are confused about what the person means. Do not write down a murky response and say to yourself, "I'll study this in my notes later and try to figure it out." If you cannot make sense out of it during the interview, there is not much chance you will succeed later. Ask a question like this: "Could you explain that a little more?" Or: "Correct me if I'm wrong, but I understand you to say that. . . ." Some students shy away from asking clarifying questions because they are afraid to show their ignorance. This is illogical. You are there to interview the person precisely because you are "ignorant" in his or her area of expertise. So ask about any point that you don't understand.
2. *Follow-up* questions are designed to encourage the interviewee to elaborate on what he or she has been saying—to continue a story or to add to a comment. Here are some examples: "What happened next?" "Were you upset about what happened?" "Could you give me some examples of what you're talking about?"

Make the interview more like a relaxed chat than an interrogation. Be natural and spontaneous, and follow the flow of conversation. In other words, don't act as if you must plow through your list of questions item by item. The flow of conversation might lead to questions being answered "out of order." Simply check off the questions as they are answered. Toward the end of the interview, ask those questions that still have not been answered. Also, the person may bring up surprising aspects of your topic that you have not thought about; this should inspire you to ask spontaneous follow-up questions.

When the interviewee mentions things that are not on your checklist, write them down, even if they seem inconsequential at the time, because you may find a use for them later. This advice would not apply if the person goes off on a tangent, telling you things that are totally unrelated to the subject. In such a case, you should steer the conversation back toward the pertinent topic.

Ask interviewee about other sources and visual aids. Interviewees may know of library resources that you are unaware of. They may have a pamphlet or a book that they are willing to lend you. In some cases, they may even lend you a map or chart or some other kind of visual aid that you can use in your speech.

Near the end, ask if you have omitted any questions. When you have gone through all the prepared questions, ask the interviewee if there are any items that you have failed to ask about. You may find that you have inadvertently overlooked some important matters.

End interview on time. Respect the amount of time that was granted when you set up your appointment; if you were allotted 20 minutes, stay no more than 20 minutes—unless of course the interviewee invites you to stay longer. If you still have questions when the time is up, you can ask for a second interview (perhaps a few extra questions can even be handled over the telephone).

Following up

After you leave the interview, you have two important tasks.

Promptly expand your notes. Immediately after the interview, go through your notes and expand upon them (by turning words and phrases into complete sentences) while the conversation is fresh in your mind. If you wait 2 weeks to go over the notes, they will be stale and you might puzzle over your scribbling or you might forget what a particular phrase means.

Evaluate your information. After you have expanded the notes, evaluate them to see if you got exactly what you were looking for. If you are confused on any points or if you find that you need more information on a particular item, telephone the interviewee and ask for help. This should not be a source of embarrassment for you—it shows that you care enough about the subject and the interviewee to get the information exactly right.

Other Resources

You can often get literature and visual aids from companies and agencies in your community. One student, Rhonda Murchison, visited an office of the American Red Cross and told them she wanted to give a talk on CPR (cardiopulmonary resuscitation); they lent her a portable dummy to use in her demonstration speech. Sometimes you can even get "freebies" from local sources. Student speaker Jerry Lipe was preparing a speech on stress; he went to a local mental health agency and got brochures and thirty stress detectors—small color-coded dots that can be placed on the skin to determine how much stress a person is under at that moment. Jerry had enough tabs to give one to each listener at the end of his speech.

A vast amount of literature on a wide variety of subjects can be ordered at no charge (or for a very small fee) from thousands of corporations and associations. To get addresses of national groups, go to the library and consult reference books such as *The Encyclopedia of Associations* and *The Directory of Corporations*. Another good source is the United States government, which each year puts out 25,000 new publications on subjects ranging from rabid animals to gardening to solar heating. Your librarian can help you locate or order government documents.

An important note of caution: do not rely too heavily on requested material because it may not arrive in time for your speech. I remember one student telling me that she wrote for some interesting material, but it arrived three months after she gave her speech. Also, do not overestimate the value of material that you have not yet seen. One student felt certain that some pamphlets he ordered would give him all the information he needed for his speech; they arrived the day before his speech but turned out to be worthless. He had to race to the library to do some frantic research.

Finding the Right Materials Efficiently

Many students fail to come up with good material because they spend most of their time in unproductive research. They either fail to find the right kinds of information or they get more material than they have time to process. Here are steps leading to productive research.

Start Your Research Far in Advance

Running out of time is the most common reason students give for not doing adequate research. If you start your research well ahead of the speech date and budget your time sensibly, you should be able to do a thorough job. Keep in mind that most research takes longer than you anticipate. Leave yourself more time than you think necessary.

The worst thing about waiting until the last minute to do research is that most people do not think well under pressure. The anxiety engendered by the approaching deadline can lock up the gears of your brain, causing you to think less efficiently than you normally would.

Turn Your Specific-Purpose Statement into a Research Question

Your specific purpose should be decided before you start your research. Imagine that you had written the following specific-purpose statement: "To tell my audience how people can determine if they have a serious drinking problem." For research purposes, you can turn this into a question, "How can people determine if they have a serious drinking problem?" Why use a question? Because a question brings your research efforts into sharper focus than a statement does. If you write the research question at the top of the first page of your notebook or on your first index card—and keep it in front of you at each step of your research—it will be a constant reminder of precisely what you are searching for. It will prevent you from wandering off into areas that are not related. Let's say you pick up an interesting book on alcoholism. It contains fascinating charts on the physiological effects of alcohol and fact-filled chapters on such things as cirrhosis of the liver and delirium tremens. But you notice that nothing in the book answers your specific question. So you put it back. No sense wasting your time on a book that will not contribute to your speech. (After you prepare and deliver your speech, you can always go back and read the book at your leisure.)

Establish a Research Strategy

Some people enter the library, not knowing exactly what they are looking for, and then drift from place to place inside the library, hoping to stumble upon a helpful book or magazine. Rather than drifting about, you should spend a few minutes devising a research strategy; here are two ways to achieve this.

1. *Talk to your librarians.* Explain your research question and get their advice. In your speech on alcohol, suppose that the librarian suggests that you start off by looking in the card catalog for some of the most current books on alcohol abuse with annotated bibliographies. These bibliographies might lead you immediately to the best materials. If this does not give you all that you need, the librarian might advise you to look in *The Magazine Index* because popular magazines often run checklists such as "How to Tell if You Have a Drinking Problem."

2. *Talk to an informed person on campus or in the community.* Suppose that you look in the Yellow Pages of the local telephone directory and call the number of an alcohol abuse treatment center. The woman you talk to suggests that you come by and pick up some pamphlets on the subject. She also gives you the phone number of a member of Alcoholics Anonymous who has given talks in the community on warning signals of alcoholism.

By this point you should be able to devise a firm research strategy involving a series of tasks. Assign dates for completion of each task, leaving yourself plenty of time in case you run into a delay or get sick or have some unforeseen crisis.

☐ Nov. 3—Call A.A. member to set up interview.
☐ Nov. 4—Go to alcohol abuse treatment center and get pamphlets.
☐ Nov. 5—Card catalog—alcohol abuse—look for books with annotated bibliographies.

☐ Nov. 6—Look up the books and articles obtained from the above.
☐ Nov. 7—If still need information, see *The Magazine Index*.
☐ Nov. 9—Interview A.A. member.

Post the schedule in a visible place in your room, or carry it around with you. Try to abide by it. With such a research strategy, you should be able to save time and avoid "drifting."

Evaluate All Sources

Suppose that you find twelve books and nineteen magazine articles for your speech on alcohol abuse. Should you read through all the books and articles? No, of course not. That would take too long. What you need to do now is sift through your potential sources, choosing those which will help you and discarding those which are irrelevant or unimportant. To assist you in your task, here are some questions to ask yourself.

Is the source current? In some fields, especially in the physical and social sciences, you need the most up-to-date material on a subject. If you were doing research on robotics, for example, a book published last year would be far more valuable than one published 10 years ago because there have been hundreds of new developments in this field since the older book was published. Even in history and biography, more recent sources would generally be preferred because they might include previously undiscovered information; for example, a history of Native Americans published this year might report new evidence concerning how humans first migrated to the Western Hemisphere.

Is the source credible? You should decide whether your particular audience will consider a source believable. Suppose you are doing research on UFOs and you come across an article in one of the sensational tabloids (the kind sold at grocery store checkout counters) with this headline: FLYING SAUCER ABDUCTS FARMER AND COW. You would be wise to ignore the article because most audiences would consider such a source to be laughably unreliable. If, on the other hand, you read an article in a prestigious journal such as *Aviation Week and Space Technology* on the possibility of flying saucers, your audience would most likely respect the source and therefore give serious consideration to the source's ideas.

Is the source comprehensive? If a magazine index shows that a particular article is only one page long, you may want to skip it and look for a longer article. Longer articles usually contain more information, and you can save yourself time by concentrating on them.

Is the source understandable? If you are researching volcanoes and you come across an article on the subject in *Journal of Earth Sciences*, you might find (unless you are a geology major) that parts of the article are too complicated for you to understand. You would be wasting your time if you tried to struggle with it. If, on the other hand, you find an article on volcanoes in *National Geographic*, you can be sure that it is written in language that is understandable to the nonspecialist.

Can the source lead to other sources? When you use the card catalog and you find a card for a promising book, look on the card to see if the book includes a bibliography (see Figure 6.1). A bibliography can save you an enormous amount of time if it cites the most important articles and books on your topic. Suppose you are interested in how people can interpret dreams. You find a book on the subject, and in the back is a long bibliography giving you the names of dozens of magazine articles. You choose five of the most promising articles, look them up in the library, and subsequently find all the information you need for your speech. A bibliography can be especially helpful if it is annotated, that is, if the author gives a brief description of what is contained in each book or article cited. By the way, do not overlook your textbooks; they often have extensive bibliographies in the back.

Taking Notes

As you hunt for materials in the library, you need to systematically record the key points that you find. Here are the steps you should follow.

Prepare Bibliography Cards

As you go through catalogs and indexes, jot down the names of books and articles that sound promising. Use 3 × 5 index cards (because they are easy to shuffle and place in alphabetical order). These cards help you locate materials, and they come in handy later when you put together the bibliography for your speech. In addition, if you need to consult a book or article again for clarification or amplification of facts, the data on your card should help you find it quickly. Figure 6.4 shows two sample bibliography cards.

Fill out a bibliography card for every book or article which you think might be helpful. You may end up with more sources than you have time to consult, but it is better to have too many sources than not enough. Leave space on each card for personal comments (see Figure 6.4), which can help you evaluate which sources are most likely to yield good information.

Make Note Cards

As you read through books and articles, make notes of key ideas on large cards (4 × 6 or 5 × 7). Using large cards will help you distinguish them from the smaller (3 × 5) bibliography cards and also give you ample room for note taking.

Put a subject heading on the top of each card, as shown in Figures 6.5 and 6.6 These headings will be valuable when you finish making your notes because you can group the cards into related clumps. Identify each card with the author's name. There is no need to write down full bibliographical information because those details are already on your bibliography cards.

Library call
number

Author

Title

Place of
publication,
publisher,
date of
publication

Personal comment

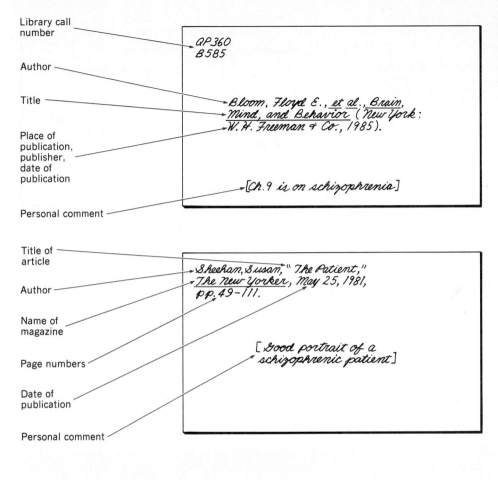

Figure 6.4
Sample bibliogra-
phy cards for a
book and a maga-
zine article.

Title of
article

Author

Name of
magazine

Page numbers

Date of
publication

Personal comment

In making notes, follow these steps:

☐ Quickly read through the material to see if there is anything worth noting.
☐ If there is, reread the material—this time very carefully.
☐ Try to summarize the key points in a few simple sentences. Avoid the temptation
   to copy down huge chunks of undigested information. Your task is to interpret,
   evaluate, and boil down ideas, not to convey a text verbatim.
☐ While striving for brevity, you must make sure that summarized information is
   in a coherent form. If you jot down a phrase like "schizophrenic—Jesus Christ
   or Napoleon," and then wait 5 days before organizing your notes, you may
   forget the meaning of that note. Write out a coherent sentence such as: "Schizophrenics who have delusions often think they are Jesus Christ or Napoleon."
☐ Occasionally, you will find an arresting phrase or a short, vivid sentence which
   you will want to convey to your listeners in the form of a direct quotation. Be
   sure to put quotation marks around such passages in your note cards. Do not
   use too many direct quotations in your notes, however, because you may fall

Figure 6.5
Sample index card
for a direct quota-
tion from a book.

Subject heading

Author and page number
(Full details are available
on bibliography card)

Direct quotation

Personal comment (in brackets)

Incidence of Schizophrenia

Bloom, p 261

"If you survive to age 55, you have a 1 in 100 chance of being diagnosed as a schizophrenic."

[use in introduction?]

into the trap discussed above—of copying down large blocks of text without proper evaluation and condensation.

☐ Take more notes than you probably will need. It is better to have too much raw material than not enough.

☐ Personal comments can be added to the bottom of note cards to provide ideas on how to use the note or how to connect it to other notes (see Figure 6.5). You can also express a personal reaction, such as "This sounds implausible—check other sources." Use square brackets or some other device to distinguish between your own comments and the text that you are summarizing.

☐ Use a separate card for each idea. This will make it easy to sort your cards by subject headings.

Giving Credit

If you have gathered information from sources, you should use oral footnotes in your speech; for example, "According to the *CBS Evening News* of March 15th of

Figure 6.6
Sample index card
for a summary
from a magazine.

Subject heading

Author and page number

Summary of author's ideas

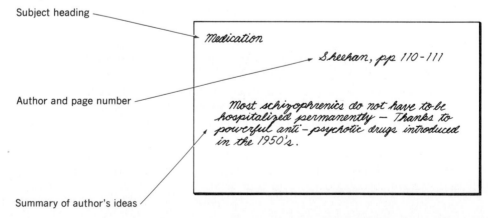

Medication

Sheehan, pp 110-111

Most schizophrenics do not have to be hospitalized permanently — Thanks to powerful anti-psychotic drugs introduced in the 1950's.

this year . . ." or "In the words of Thomas Jefferson. . . ." An oral footnote is the equivalent of a footnote in a written document and its purpose is the same: to give credit for information or ideas that did not originate with you. Oral footnotes also give credibility to your remarks. You are saying, in effect, "I didn't pull this out of thin air; I got this information from someone who is an authority on the subject."

If you got information from an interview, you could say something like this: "According to Elizabeth Smith, director of advertising for our city's biggest department store, . . ."

For material from books or magazines, you could say, "In an article in the latest issue of *Scientific American,* Dr. Paul Rhodes says that . . ." or "The graph on this slide is based on data I found in the current edition of the *World Almanac."*

When you are quoting verbatim, use "oral" quotation marks such as the following: "To quote Abraham Lincoln . . ." or "In the words of Plato. . . ." Expressions like these are a little smoother than an abrupt "Quote" at the beginning of a statement and "Unquote" at the end. A slight pause at the end of the quotation should be an adequate signal that you have finished quoting.

Summary

Your quest for speech material should begin with yourself. What personal experiences or observations can you draw upon? After you have looked inward, you can look outward—at the books, magazines, and audiovisual holdings of college and local libraries. Some of these libraries may have computer databases that can be tapped for quick retrieval of a vast amount of information.

Interviewing knowledgeable people on your campus or in your community can yield valuable, up-to-date information in many fields. To prepare for an interview, do extensive research on the topic and then draw up a list of question to be asked. Conduct the interview in a relaxed, conversational manner.

Whatever sources you draw from, start your research far in advance, devise a research strategy, and then carry out that strategy in a systematic way. Make all your notes on cards, with a subject heading at the top, and with only one idea per card. These cards can later be shuffled and arranged systematically as an aid to the writing of your outline.

Review Questions

1. What is interlibrary loan and how can it help you?
2. What are three main advantages of using computer databases?
3. Why should you not feel hesitant about asking a local expert for an interview?
4. Why should most of your research be done *before* you call someone for an interview?
5. What are the advantages and disadvantages of using a tape recorder in an interview?
6. What steps should you take after an interview is completed?

7. In your research, why should you take more notes than you probably will need?

Tip 6: Develop a Lifetime Filing System for Important Ideas

Marie Judson, a computer programmer for a large manufacturing company, takes notes at every speech, training session, and seminar she attends and then files the notes under appropriate headings in her filing cabinet. She also clips and files articles from professional journals and newsletters.

When Judson is required to write a memorandum or prepare a talk, her files provide a gold mine of good resource material. When her superiors want information about the latest developments in computers, they consult Judson first because of her extensive files. These superiors have come to regard Judson as an indispensable, "got-it together" person who tries to keep up with developments in her field.

Like Judson, you should develop personal files on topics that are relevant to your career. Such files will obviously come in handy for preparing speeches and for writing memos and reports. Also, as in Judson's case, they can be useful in establishing yourself as a valuable, up-to-date employee.

Even if your are not yet employed in your chosen field, you should still keep files so that when you do enter the field, you will have a wealth of professional information at your fingertips.

What should you file? In addition to clipping or photocopying articles, I suggest that you keep a pack of index cards or a legal pad handy so that you can jot down notes of important ideas that you encounter. These ideas may come from your own thoughts, or they may come from books, TV programs, speeches, lectures, workshops, and interviews. Since many of your instructors are experts in their fields, you may want to file lecture notes from some of your college classes. Do not worry that you might accumulate too many notes. You can always go through your files later and discard deadwood.

How should you file information? Devise whatever method works best for you. A popular arrangement is to place items in manila file folders that are labeled by topic. You might want to start with some broad categories and then later create subcategories when a folder starts overflowing. For articles that you clip or photocopy, be sure to write down the name of the publication and the date. For notes of interviews or speeches, write down the speaker, date, place, and occasion. You can start off by putting your file folders in a cardboard box; later, when your files become bulky, you can store them in a filing cabinet.

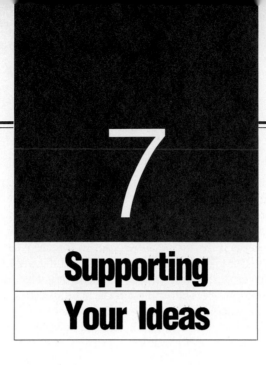

7

Supporting Your Ideas

Reasons for Using Support Materials

Types of Support Materials

In a classroom speech, a student, whom I'll call Sam, made an interesting point. "Violence on television," he contended. "causes some viewers to commit violent acts."

The reaction of the audience was undoubtedly skeptical. Some of the listeners were probably saying to themselves, "I don't believe it—prove it" or "Says who?" or "How do you know that?"

After making his assertion, Sam made these comments: "When people see violence night after night, they are going to become violent themselves. It's just common sense: seeing violence encourages people to act violently. How can you let impressionable children and teenagers watch murder, robbery, and brutality every night and then expect them not to imitate what they see?"

Do you think Sam's remarks convinced the audience that TV violence causes some viewers to become violent? Probably not. His remarks did nothing to bolster his contention. He offered no proof, no illustration, no support. All he did was repeat his original point.

Now imagine how the audience might have reacted if Sam had substantiated his assertion with these items:

☐ Following the telecast of the film *The Deer Hunter,* which showed a character playing a game of Russian roulette with a revolver, 29 Americans killed themselves while "playing" Russian roulette, according to Dr. Jon M. Shepard, professor of sociology at the University of Kentucky.[1]

☐ A TV show depicted an alcoholic "bum" being doused with gasoline and set on fire; the next day three "winos" in three different American cities were murdered in similar fashion by youths who had seen the show, according to The Associated Press.[2]

☐ The National Institute of Mental Health evaluated 2500 studies on TV violence conducted over a 10-year period and concluded that "violence on television does lead to aggressive behavior."[3]

These items, which are samples of *support materials,* help back up the contention that TV violence causes some viewers to commit violent acts. The first two provide vivid examples, while the last item brings in testimony from a prestigious source. If Sam had used these support materials, his audience would have seen that his argument had merit.

Examples and testimony are just two of the kinds of support materials that we will discuss in this chapter. The others are definitions, descriptions, narratives, comparisons, contrasts, and statistics.

Reasons for Using Support Materials

Support materials enable you to move from general and abstract concepts, which are often hard for audiences to understand and remember, to specific and concrete details, which are easily grasped. Support materials add spice and flavor to a speech, but they are more than just seasonings; they are basic nourishment that is absolutely essential to the success of a speech. Below are five reasons why support materials are so important.

1. *Support materials develop and illustrate ideas.* In a classroom speech on sharks, Austin Fitzgerald pointed out that unlike most creatures of the sea, sharks behave unpredictably. To develop and illustrate his point, he said:

> In his book on sharks, Jacques-Yves Cousteau, the famous oceanographer, says that he has seen sharks flee from an almost naked, completely unarmed diver, but soon afterward hurl themselves against a steel diving cage and bite furiously at the bars. Sometimes a diver can scare off a shark by waving flippers at it, while at other times sharks are so determined to attack that they are not deterred by the sight of five divers with spears. The terrifying thing, Cousteau says, is that sharks never give clues as to what kind of behavior they will exhibit.

Without these examples, Austin's contention that sharks behave unpredictably would have been weak. With the examples, the listeners got a clear picture of sharks' volatile nature. Notice, too, that Austin enhanced the credibility of his remarks by attributing his information to a well-known authority.

2. *Support materials can clarify ideas.* Helping the listener make sense out of your ideas is one of the main reasons for using support material. Years ago I was taught a valuable fact about statistics by a professor who used a good example to make his point. He was trying to show the class why professional pollsters interviewed only 1000 registered voters in all of America in order to predict a presidential election. Why not interview 10,000? Or 100,000? Would not a larger sample produce a more accurate prediction? No, said the professor, a small sample is just as accurate as a large one. To make his idea clear and understandable, he gave us a hypothetical example: Imagine that you place 100,000 coins in a rotating drum. Of that number, 70,000 are gold coins and the remaining 30,000 are silver coins. In another rotating drum you place 1000 coins, using the same proportion: 700 gold coins and 300 silver coins. You spin both drums, thoroughly mixing up the coins, and then you get a blindfolded man to reach in and randomly select 100 coins from each drum. The man will pull out 70 gold coins and 30 silver coins, or come very close to these numbers every time he tries, even though one drum has 100 times more coins than the other. This hypothetical example makes clear why a small sample in a public opinion poll can be as accurate as a large one.

3. *Support materials can make a speech more interesting.* In a classroom speech on how explorers from Earth would experience life on Mars, Diane Weber said,

> Most of the time Mars is much colder than the coldest regions of Earth, with summer temperatures dipping down as low as 126 degrees below zero and winter temperatures twice that cold. Sometimes, however, at the equator of

Mars, the temperature does warm up to an earthly level of comfort. For a few minutes, the temperature can climb to a high of 68 degrees—like a pleasant October afternoon in New England.

Instead of merely reciting statistics, which would have been boring, Diane made her subject interesting by comparing and contrasting the climate of the two planets, using images (such as the October afternoon in New England) that her listeners could appreciate.

4. Support materials help listeners remember key ideas. Jeffrey Scott, a high school English teacher, says that his students are more apt to remember the meaning of a word in a vocabulary lesson if they are told the story of the word's origin. For example, he tells his students that we get the word *tantalize* from the god Tantalus in Greek mythology: "As punishment for betraying Zeus, Tantalus was sentenced to hang from the branch of a fruit tree that spread out over a pool of water. Whenever he got hungry and reached for fruit, the wind would blow it out of his reach. Whenever he got thirsty and leaned over to drink from the pool, the water would recede." This story, Scott says, helps his students to remember that when we tantalize people, we torment them by showing something that is desirable but unattainable.

5. Support materials help prove an assertion. When you want to prove a point, you must have evidence. If, for example, you wanted to prove that more counterfeiters are being caught today than ever before, you could quote a Secret Service official who states that the number of counterfeiting convictions this year is ten times the number of convictions in any previous year. Such a statistic from a reliable source is solid proof of your statement.

But a note of caution: not all support materials constitute proof. Suppose that a speaker argues that flying saucers from alien planets visit the earth regularly, and to prove his claim, he cites fifteen eyewitness accounts from different parts of the country. Is this proof? No. While it may be true that flying saucers do indeed visit the earth, the fifteen eyewitness accounts do not constitute proof. Some of the people could have seen explainable phenomena, such as weather balloons or swamp-gas apparitions. Some of the individuals could have experienced hallucinations caused by drugs or psychosis.

Types of Support Materials

In this chapter we will look at *verbal* support materials, reserving *visual* supports for the next chapter. The cardinal rule in using verbal supports is that they must be relevant; they must develop, explain, illustrate, or reinforce your message. They cannot be thrown in simply to enliven a speech.

Let's now examine seven categories of verbal supports.

Definitions

One of the biggest obstacles to successful communication is the assumption that your listeners define words and phrases the same way you do. If you are speaking on gun control, it is not enough to say, "I'm in favor of gun control." Exactly what does "gun control" mean? To some members of your audience, it may mean that citizens must surrender all their firearms. To some, it may mean that citizens must give up only their handguns. To others, it may mean that citizens can keep their guns if they register them with the authorities. If you say that you are in favor of gun control without giving your definition of the term, some listeners might misunderstand your position and angrily reject everything that you say on the subject. That's why you should define your terms at the outset; for example: "When I talk about gun control, I'm not talking about confiscation of all guns; I'm talking about citizens registering the serial numbers of their guns with the authorities." Now you and your audience have a common basis for an evaluation of your views.

You should also define any jargon or specialized words that some listeners might not know. Do not assume, for example, that everyone knows military lingo such as KP and AWOL. Even though there have been dozens of movies and TV shows about military life, some people might not know that KP means "kitchen police" and AWOL means "absent without leave." If you are a computer buff, you must be careful to define concepts like RAM (random-access memory) and ROM (read-only memory) that are well known to you but not to the general public.

Avoid dictionary definitions, if possible. They tend to be tedious and hard to grasp. Instead, use informal definitions that can be easily understood by the audience. For example, *chutzpah*, a slang word that the English language has borrowed from Yiddish, is defined by the *Random House College Dictionary* as "unmitigated effrontery or impudence." I once heard a speaker give a humorous, informal definition of the word: "Chutzpah is the kind of audacity and gall that a youngster would show if he killed both of his parents and then demanded that the court be lenient to him because he was an orphan." This informal definition drives home the point that chutzpah is more than ordinary gall; it is the *ultimate* form of gall. Such a definition is very effective because it not only helps the listeners understand the meaning of the word; it also helps them remember it.

Description

One good way to support your speech is to use descriptions—verbal pictures that are created by using lots of details about specific, concrete objects or people. One of my students, Jacqueline Wilson, lived with her husband and child on a homestead in a remote rural area. To show the joys of using a wood-burning stove as a means of heating a home, she painted the following word portrait:

> The wood burner in my kitchen crackles constantly from October until March, warming our home, our hands, and our hearts. The heat that radiates from it is constant, efficient, and—best of all—free. If you wanted to, you could make

it spit out the heat so intensely you'd have to open the front door in February to keep from roasting. But heat isn't all the stove's good for. It cooks great pinto beans and chili on the top, and inside it bakes the best potatoes you'll ever eat. It can get the wettest laundry dry in nothing flat, too. And the smell— oh, the smell is what I love, like the leaves my daddy used to burn on a crisp fall day when I was a child. Every time I open the door to load the box, I get a blast from the past. The stove has also become a family gathering place. Especially in the mornings, when I've just kicked her up, there will be my little boy and my husband dressing for school and work, and warming themselves way up close to it. It warms more than just my body; it warms my soul. There is no better way to heat a home than with a good wood-burning stove.

Notice that Jacqueline used specific details to paint her word picture. Details are the brush strokes that provide richness, color, and vividness.

Examples

Examples are instances or facts that illustrate a statement or back up a generalization. In a classroom speech on counterfeiting, Bob Lanelli made the following point:

Sophisticated counterfeiters are careful not to pass bills that are crisp and new-looking.

If Bob had said no more on the subject, he would have forced his listeners to guess for themselves just how counterfeiters go about aging their bogus money. Fortunately for the audience, Bob gave examples:

To get their phony money to look old, counterfeiters might put the bills in a washing machine with a combination of water and coffee. Or they might run them through a homemade device that crinkles them up and rubs in dirt at the same time. Or they might crumple each bill by hand and tear off a corner.

Examples can be longer and more detailed than the preceding ones. In a classroom speech, Judy Korytowski made an unusual assertion which at first seemed absurd: on many occasions if you offer an item to people at no cost whatsoever, they will look down on it and consider it worthless, but if you put a price tag on the very same item, people will respect it and consider it valuable. If Judy had stopped at this point, her audience probably would have been skeptical. After all, her assertion sounded farfetched. People are not so naïve as to scorn something just because it is free, are they? But Judy did not stop there; she quickly gave a detailed example which demonstrated that her observation had merit:

Did you know that veterinarians in this city no longer give puppies away? Instead they *sell* them. They charge five dollars per puppy. Why? Not because they're money-hungry but because when they used to give puppies away, people wouldn't take proper care of them. Now, with the five-dollar charge, people take good care of the dogs, making sure they get rabies shots and a collar, making sure they're clean and well nourished. If a puppy is free, it must be a worthless mutt; if it costs five dollars, it's obviously a deserving pet.

In case this example was not enough to convince the audience, Judy gave another example:

A caretaker at [a nearby] zoo told me that a few years ago, when admission was free, they had a lot of trouble—vandalism, littering, and mistreatment of animals. Then they heard about zoos in other cities solving their problems by charging a small fee. So they tried it here; they started charging fifty cents to get in. Now, the caretaker tells me, they have very little trouble. It's not that the fee keeps the riffraff away. The same number of people come—and they look the same as patrons in previous years. It's just that paying a fee makes people think that the zoo is a place that deserves respect and good treatment.

Judy proceeded in this way, piling example on top of example. By the end of her speech she had convinced even the most skeptical of her listeners that in many circumstances people do indeed value an item more highly if it has a price tag on it than if it is free.

Judy used more than one example to make her point. How many should you use in your speech? In some cases, one illuminating, well-developed example is sufficient to develop an idea. In other cases, you may need a series of examples. Judy needed several examples because her assertion ran contrary to what the audience probably believed. She needed lots of reinforcement to make her case. To decide how many examples to use in your speech, you should analyze your listeners. Put yourself in their shoes by asking, "If I were those people sitting out there, would I be convinced on the basis of just one example?"

Narratives

Narratives, which are stories that explain or illustrate your message, are audience favorites, lingering in the mind long after a speech has ended. People *love* stories, and even a sleepy or distracted member of the audience finds it hard to resist listening. As with all support materials, narratives must be relevant to your message. Never tell a story, even though it is a spellbinding tale, if it fails to develop, explain, illustrate, or reinforce your key ideas.

Sharon Eklund, a student nurse, gave a speech in which she tried to persuade her listeners to stop driving a car whenever they became sleepy. She used a narrative to underscore her message:

Have you ever been so sleepy, you could hardly keep your eyes open? That's the way I felt one morning two years ago as I was driving home from work. I had worked the graveyard shift at the hospital and that's always tiring, but this time was worse than usual because I had slept only 3 hours out of the last 48. I was really dragging. Even though it was a nice spring morning, there was a nip in the air so when my eyelids became thick, I rolled the window down to get some cool air on my face. This helped for a few minutes but my lids started getting heavy again, so I turned the radio on. Then I got to thinking: Why don't you try singing? If you have ever heard me sing, you'll know why I thought my singing would wake me up. Well, by the time the road had wound its way around beside the river, I had resorted to threats and was even slapping myself in the face. I told myself, "Now listen, dummy. You know you can't swim. If you fall asleep, you'll drown when this car hits the river."

I made it past the river, however. I turned onto a back road and was almost home. My driveway was just beyond the next curve. Curve? What curve? I don't remember the curve for two good reasons: number one, I fell asleep, which meant that number two, I didn't make the curve. I woke up as my car smashed through several mailboxes, went over an embankment, jumped a ditch, and landed in an open field. I was shaken but unharmed.

Thank God it was Saturday. If it had been a weekday, there would have been children waiting for a school bus at that very spot. . . . They would have been *my* children.

After telling this fascinating story, Sharon pleaded with her audience to act decisively (stop for coffee or pull over for a nap) if they ever became sleepy at the wheel. I doubt if anyone in the audience remained unmoved or unpersuaded by her argument.

Notice that Sharon's narrative was filled with details, giving you a sense of what it was like to fight desperately to stay awake. Details give richness and color to narratives. They paint a picture that the listeners can see.

While Sharon's story was factual, there are occasions when you may want to use a narrative that is *hypothetical*, that is, about an imaginary situation. Here is an example from a classroom speech by Coretta Johnson:

You are riding along the highway when you see a two-car collision fifty yards in front of you. You pull over and park, and then run to offer help. You realize that you're the first to arrive at the scene of the accident, and you hear a person inside one of the cars screaming for help. What should you do?

By means of this hypothetical story, Coretta made her point—that all citizens need to know what to do if they arrive first at the scene of an accident. By putting her listeners squarely in the middle of her narrative, Coretta increased the audience's curiosity and involvement. Then, of course, she gave the steps that should be taken: Do not move the victims unless there is an imminent danger of the car exploding, keep them calm and comfortable, administer first aid if they are bleeding or choking, and call an ambulance.

Comparison and Contrast

Sometimes the best way to explain anything new or strange is to make a *comparison*, that is, show how it resembles something else. Here is a beautiful comparison of two species—ants and human beings—by Dr. Lewis Thomas:

Ants are so much like human beings as to be an embarrassment. They farm fungi, raise aphids as livestock, launch armies into wars, use chemical sprays to alarm and confuse enemies, capture slaves. The families of weaver ants engage in child labor, holding their larvae like shuttles to spin out the thread that sews the leaves together for their fungus gardens. They exchange information ceaselessly. They do everything but watch television.[4]

By comparing ant behavior to human behavior with which we are all familiar, Thomas achieves his goal of demonstrating the amazing intelligence of ants.

While a comparison shows how things are similar, a *contrast* shows how they are different. Tony Rivas, a criminal justice major, made an interesting contrast between how people view rich lawbreakers and how they view poor ones:

One Saturday, while I was at work as a security guard for a department store, we managed to catch several people who were trying to steal merchandise from the store. One of the shoplifters was caught stealing some cologne. He was about 20 years old, not very well dressed, and definitely could have used a good bath. Employees who saw us take him to the security office later asked what that "crook" had stolen. They used words like "scum" and "low-life thief" in talking about him.

Later that day, we had the opportunity to catch someone from the other side of the tracks. This woman was well-dressed, had plenty of money, and had no excuse to be stealing from anyone. Once again the same employees saw us take her to the security office. What was their attitude toward her? "Did she really steal anything?" they asked. "She looks like too nice a lady to steal—she must be a kleptomaniac."

By means of this contrast, Tony was able to clearly demonstrate society's starkly different ways of viewing lawbreakers: poor thieves are "scum"; rich thieves merely suffer from a psychological illness.

Sometimes it is helpful to use both comparison and contrast. For example, comparing and contrasting Japanese and American cars could help the listener understand more fully the features of each.

Testimony

Suppose for a moment that one of your fellow students gives a speech on America's jury system, and she tells you that the method of selecting and using jurors in most communities is inefficient, overly expensive, and demoralizing to the jurors. Would you believe her? Probably not, if all she gave was her personal opinion—after all, she is not a lawyer or a judge. But what if she quoted the Chief Justice of the United States Supreme Court saying the exact same thing? Now would you believe her? You probably would, because the Chief Justice is one of the nation's experts on what happens in our courts.

When you use what knowledgeable people have to say on your subject, you are using *testimony* to back up your assertions. The main advantage of using testimony is that it gives you instant credibility; quoting an expert is a way of saying, "I'm not the only one who has this idea; it has the backing of a leading authority on the subject."

There are three ways of using testimony:

1. *Quote verbatim.* Sometimes it is effective to quote a source word-for-word. For example, student speaker George Hassoun made the following point in a speech on the value of aerobic exercise:

> Aerobic exercise is the best preventive medicine you can find, according to Bob Anderson, sports physiologist and author of a national best-seller on exercise. He says: "If you don't find time for exercise, you'd better find time to be sick."

Quoting the expert verbatim was very effective because Anderson's statement was phrased in a colorful, yet authoritative tone that would have been weakened if it had been paraphrased.

2. *Summarize.* When a statement is lengthy, quoting it verbatim can bore the audience, so summarize any quotation that is more than one or two sentences. In another part of George Hassoun's speech, he took a long quotation and boiled it down into one brief sentence:

> Anderson says that aerobic exercise decreases the risk of heart attack, helps control weight, relieves stress-induced tension, and alleviates anxiety and depression.

3. *Paraphrase.* If a quotation has archaic or technical language or is laced with jargon, you should paraphrase it. If, for example, you are speaking on computers and you want to quote an expert who says, "Don't buy a software package that doesn't have help menus," you can paraphrase this jargon into plain English by saying, "Don't buy a program for your computer unless it has lists of options on the screen to keep you from getting lost or confused."

Here are some guidelines for using testimony:

☐ *Make sure quotations are accurate.* If you are not careful with a quotation, you can unwittingly change its meaning. For example, Ralph Waldo Emerson is often quoted as saying, "Consistency is the hobgoblin of little minds." That is an unfortunate misquotation. What he really said is quite different in meaning: "A foolish consistency is the hobgoblin of little minds." With the misquotation, consistency itself is damned, but with the correct quotation, only a *foolish* consistency is deemed stupid.

☐ *Use testimony from unbiased sources.* Ethical speakers avoid using sources that are biased. Suppose you are researching the question of whether polygraphs (lie detectors) are accurate, and you come across glowing pro-polygraph statements by two "experts" who are on the payroll of a firm that manufactures polygraph machines. Could you expect such sources to be unbiased? Of course not. They would probably lose their jobs if they said anything negative about the machines. You should reject such "evidence" and look instead for statements by people who have no vested interest in the issue.

☐ *Use testimony that your audience will respect.* As part of your prespeech audience analysis, ask yourself, "What kind of experts would this particular audience believe?" If you are speaking on foreign policy, for example, and you have a good quotation from a movie star, would your audience consider the star's views irrelevant? If so, quoting the star might weaken, rather than strengthen, your case.

☐ *State the credentials of your source.* If you quote a famous person like Abraham Lincoln, you obviously do not need to give any background information about the person. But for authorities who are not well known, be sure to give some biographical data to establish their credibility. For example, "Jack Smithson, who spent 25 yearts as a research scientist for NASA, says that. . . ."

Statistics

For a speech explaining the immense distances of space, Paula Schiller, a student speaker, began with some mind-boggling facts:

> Proxima Centauri, the star that is closest to our solar system, is only 4.28 light-years away. That doesn't sound like a very great distance, does it? Is there any chance that we can reach that star—or one of its planets—in our lifetime? Before you start fantasizing about being the first human to travel to our nearest star, consider this fact: if you traveled to Proxima Centauri in the fastest spacecraft now in existence, it would take you *40,000 years* to make the trip.

Statistics that show a startling difference can be a particularly effective means of supporting your ideas.
(John Maher/EKM-Nepenthe)

Paula was using *statistics,* which are numerical ways of expressing information. As illustrated in this example, statistics do not have to be dry and boring. They can be made interesting and even exciting.

Statistics can be especially effective in persuading an audience to accept a particular point. In our society, people put a lot of trust in statistics. If a television commercial says that 78 percent of physicians prefer Cure-All pain reliever over all competing brands, many consumers will rush out to buy Cure-All.

In a speech in which she tried to persuade her audience to drive their cars less and walk more, Carol Morris wanted to prove that the fitness of Americans has been weakened by the automobile. She could have made a vague statement such as: "Because of the automobile, we Americans are getting soft and flabby." Instead, she gave a fascinating statistic to prove her point: "Since the advent of the auto, the average waistline of American adults has increased one inch every generation." That single statistic, short and surprising, was one of the most persuasive parts of her speech.

Understanding Statistics

While statistics can provide powerful support for ideas, they also can be easily misused, either willfully or through carelessness or ignorance. Unfortunately, there is much truth in the old statement: "You can prove anything with statistics." To understand how statistics are used (and abused), let's look at several of the more popular varieties.

Averages. The most popular kind of statistic is the average. It can provide interesting views of a subject, as when one student speaker pointed out, "On an average day, twenty-four mail carriers in the United States receive animal bites." Giving the average in a case like this is much more interesting than simply stating the annual total.

Though averages seem like straightforward pieces of statistical data, there are pitfalls: most people are unaware that there are actually three different kinds of averages—the mean, the median, and the mode. Suppose a company is made up of a president with an annual salary of $290,000, a vice president with a salary of $170,000, three managers with salaries of $50,000 each, and twenty workers with wages of $20,000 each. What is the average income of the people who work at this company? The *mean,* which is what most people use when they are asked to compute an average, is derived by totaling the salaries and dividing by 25. In this case, $40,400. The *median* is derived by listing the salaries in a column, ranging from highest to lowest, and then locating the salary that falls in the middle. In this case, the median is $20,000. The *mode* is simply the figure that occurs most frequently: $20,000.

Now suppose that the company had a labor-management dispute. In an interview with the press, the president could say, "I don't see what the workers are complaining about. The average income in this company is $40,400." And she would be correct, since she chose to use the *mean* as her version of average. A representative of the workers, on the other hand, could say, "We are paid an average of only $20,000," and this would be correct, since the _median_ is also a kind of average.

Percentages. Giving percentages can be a useful way to make a point. For example, suppose that you find that 2 percent of the 1000 employees in a company are physically handicapped, and yet only 1 percent of the parking spaces has been designated for the handicapped. With these figures, you can make a good argument for increasing the number of spaces for the handicapped.

Unfortunately percentages can be misleading. A television commercial might say, "Eighty percent of the doctors interviewed said they recommend Feel Good medicated tablets for their patients." How many doctors were involved? If only 10 doctors were interviewed, and 8 of them gave the endorsement, the commercial is accurate (8 out of 10 amounts to 80 percent) but misleading.

The following statment is true: in one recent year Switzerland experienced a 50 percent jump in unemployment, causing that nation to rank number one in the world in the percentage increase of unemployed over the previous year. Sounds terrible, doesn't it? Sounds as if the prosperous little country is sliding toward economic catastrophe. But here is another way of reporting the facts: in the year cited, there were 51 jobless persons in Switzerland as compared to 34 in the previous year. This represents a 50 percent increase, but when you look at the actual number of people involved, there is obviously no reason for the Swiss to be alarmed.

Correlations. The term _correlation_ is used to show the relationship between two sets of data. For example, when IQ scores are compared with academic performance, it is clear that there is a high correlation between the two; for most people in our society, the higher the IQ, the greater the level of academic achievement. By contrast, when shoe size is compared with academic achievement, there is no correlation at all.

Correlation is a handy statistical device because it can help us predict outcomes for individuals. Because we know that a high correlation exists between high IQ and academic success, we can predict that a person with a high IQ should be able to succeed in college.

Correlation, however, is often misunderstood and misused because some people think that it proves a cause-and-effect relationship. Just because two sets of data are correlated does not necessarily mean that one causes the other. For example, some medical researchers once thought that drinking milk might cause cancer because they found a high correlation between milk consumption and the incidence of cancer in some European countries, while finding a rarity of that disease in Asian nations where milk consumption is low. When the researchers analyzed their data, however, they found that a third factor was involved: cancer most often strikes people who are over 40; most of the people studied in the backward Asian nations did not live long enough to get the disease. So a correlation between milk consumption and cancer does exist, but there is no cause-and-effect relationship.

Guidelines for Using Statistics

Here are some guidelines to consider when you are evaluating statistics for possible use in a speech.

Use statistics fairly and honestly. Sometimes a statistic is true but it is cited in such a way as to leave a false impression. A favorite ploy of unethical politicians is to make an accusation like this: "While my opponent has occupied the office of governor, state tax revenues have shot up 30 percent." To many voters hearing that statistic on TV (and seeing the accompanying graph), it sounds as if the governor has hiked their taxes. The truth is that tax revenues have gone up because they are tied to rising income—not because the tax *rate* went up. In reality, the governor should be cheered for the dramatic rise in personal income, but instead his opponent has used a clever 20-second TV commercial to discredit him. Notice that the statistic is true; the opponent cannot be charged with falsifying information.

When you prepare a speech, you should be sure to analyze a statistic for its true significance. For example, if you look at employment figures and notice a big drop in employment from December to January, does that mean the country is headed for depression and ruin? No, it does not. If you look at previous years, you will see that because of the Christmas shopping season, employment always goes up in December and then dips down in January. It would be unethical, then, for you to cite the 1-month drop as an indication of economic decline.

Make sure that your sources for statistics are unbiased. If a pharmaceutical company comes out with a new drug which it claims is 100 percent effective in eliminating migraine headaches, you would be wise to treat the claim with skepticism. Look for an evaluation by a source that has no vested interest in the product—a university medical school, for example.

Use statistics sparingly. If you use a large number of statistics, it is hard for the audience to absorb them. Be very selective, and choose only a few to make a point.

Poor: China has a population of 1 billion 45 million, India has 783 million, the Soviet Union has 279 million, the United States has 241 million, and Indonesia 176 million. So these five countries have a combined population of 2 billion 524 million. Contrast that with the entire world population, which is 5 billion 48 million. That means these five countries have half the world's population.

Better: There are 5 billion 48 million people living on earth, and one-half of them live in just five countries: China, India, the Soviet Union, the United States, and Indonesia.

The statistics in the first version would be fine in a written essay, but in a speech all those figures would be hard for the audience to grasp. The second version, streamlined and simple, would be easier for the audience to absorb.

Round off long numbers. In print, a long number is no problem, but in a speech it is hard for the listener to absorb the information. A rounded-off number is easy to say and easy for the audience to grasp.

> *Poor:* Attendance at major league baseball games last year was 44,587,874.

> *Better:* Attendance at major league baseball games last year was about 45 million.

Translate your statistics into vivid, meaningful language. If you have a statistic that would be meaningless to most listeners, translate it into language they can understand. If you are explaining disk drives to a group of students who know very little about computers, do not just say, for example, that a particular fixed-disk drive has a storage capacity of 10 megabytes. Convert that into information the students can easily grasp: "On a 10-megabyte fixed disk, you can store the equivalent of over 5000 double-spaced typewritten pages." The students can visualize 5000 sheets of paper; now they understand that you are talking about a huge amount of storage space.

In a classroom speech on energy, Jack DuVall reported that a government experimental project, a giant windmill on a mountaintop near Boone, North Carolina, was supposed to produce 2000 kilowatts of electricity. That statistic by itself would have meant nothing to most students, unless they happened to be well-versed in electricity. Fortunately, Jack translated the statistic into understandable terms: he said that 2000 kilowatts was enough electricity to satisfy the electrical needs of about 500 homes.

One student, Diane McDaniel, found a fascinating way to illustrate how cutting down on a few calories each day can result in substantial weight losses:

> If you want to lose weight, you don't have to go on a crash diet; you can shed a lot of pounds by altering your eating habits in very small ways. For example, if you eat just one pat less of butter every day, you will lose three and a half pounds in one year. If you cut out one piece of cake a week, you will lose five pounds in a year. If you omit two slices of bacon from breakfast each week, you will lose one and a half pounds in a year.

This interpretation of statistics was much more interesting to the audience than a recital of calories per food would have been.

Adapt statistics to your particular audience.. Whenever possible, you should adapt your statistics to the needs and interests of your particular audience. Imagine that you are planning a speech on Alaska, and you want to give your audience an idea of that state's immense size. All you need to do is take a pocket calculator with you to a library, look up the areas of states in a reference work like the *World Almanac,* and make a few simple calculations. If you live in California, for example, you could give your audience a sense of Alaska's size by saying, "You can put three Californias inside Alaska's borders and still have room left over for Oregon."

Relate statistics to familiar objects. One way to make statistics dramatic is to relate them to something familiar. In a speech on bats, Sally Ingle wanted to give the audience an idea of the incredible smallness of one variety of bat. Instead of giving its weight in grams, which would have meant little to most of the audience, she said, "One variety of bat is so tiny that when it is full-grown, it weighs less than a penny." Knowing the lightness of a penny, the audience could easily get a notion of the smallness of the bat.

Since everyone in America has a clear visual image of the width and length of a football field, it is convenient to use the field as a point of reference for size and distance. To show that a baseball diamond uses more space than one would suspect from its appearance, you could say, "The distance that a home run hitter travels around the bases is 60 feet more than the length of a football field." To show the smallness of a basketball court you could say, "A regulation court, if placed on a football field, will extend from the goal line to the 31-yard line; its width will cover less than a third of the field."

Summary

Verbal support materials are vital to the success of a speech. They develop, illustrate, and clarify ideas; they make a speech more interesting and meaningful, and they can help prove an assertion. Some of the more popular types of verbal supports are definitions, description, examples, narratives, comparisons, contrasts, testimony, and statistics.

Of all these types, the narrative (or story) is the favorite of most audiences. People love to hear stories and are more apt to remember them than most other parts of your speech. As with all support materials, you must make sure that a narrative explains, illustrates, or reinforces the message of your speech. Telling a story that is irrelevant to the subject is not appropriate in informative and persuasive speaking.

Statistics such as averages, percentages, and correlations can be useful in a speech, but you must be careful to use them accurately and fairly. Adapt statistics to your particular audience, making them as interesting and meaningful as possible.

Review Questions

1. List five reasons why support materials are important in a speech.
2. Why are informal definitions usually superior to dictionary definitions in a speech?
3. "The human brain is like an incredibly sophisticated computer." Is this sentence an example of a comparison or a contrast?
4. What is the main advantage of using testimony in a speech?
5. The boss of a small firm has an annual salary of $100,000. Each of his 13

employees makes $12,000 a year. Give the average salary of the firm in terms of *mean, median,* and *mode.*

6. Whenever tar on asphalt roads gets hot enough to bubble on a summer day, the incidence of heat exhaustion among citizens goes up. In other words, there is a strong correlation between bubbling tar and heat exhaustion. Does the correlation prove that tar fumes cause people to pass out? Explain your answer.

Tips
FOR YOUR CAREER

Tip 7: Let Your Subconscious Mind Help You Prepare Speeches

Many speechmakers rely upon their subconscious mind to help them prepare speeches. The subconscious is the part of the mind that simmers beneath the surface of awareness. It is especially active at night, when it creates dreams, but it is also active during the day, when it occasionally floats an idea up to the surface of our minds. You probably have had the experience of wrestling with a problem, then later, while you are taking a walk or driving your car and not consciously thinking of the matter, a good solution suddenly appears in your mind like a flash of light—your subconscious mind had continued to work until it found a solution.

The subconscious mind can provide you with topics, support materials, and organizational patterns, but unfortunately it cannot be ordered to perform like a trained dog. It is unpredictable, often mysterious, and usually requires a lot of time. Nevertheless, there are four things you can do to take advantage of this creative process.

1. Supply raw materials The subconscious cannot spin cloth out of thin air. You must fill your mind with information. Read, do research, conduct interviews.

2. Allow time to elapse Sometimes you must allow a few days—or even a few weeks or months—to give the subconscious ample time to incubate your ideas. This is where the subconscious is most unpredictable: it's hard to forecast how long the process will take. (Note: in order for the subconscious to work for classroom speeches, you must choose your topic and carry out your research far in advance of your speech date.)

3. Get away from deliberate mental activity For some reason the subconscious transmits its idea when your mind is disengaged from rational, conscious work. In other words, don't sit at your desk and flog your brain for ideas. Go for a walk or take a ride in your car. Forget about whatever you've been working on. Once you "let go," you will often be happily surprised to have an idea suddenly well up from your subconscious. Relaxation seems to unlock the subconscious. Thornton Wilder, a Pulitzer Prize–winning playwright, reported that his best ideas came to him on hikes or in the shower but never at his desk.[5] Joe W. Boyd, a professional speaker from Bellingham, Washington, says, "I get my best topics when I'm exercising (running) or driving long distances. The topics just seem to flow into my mind.";[6]

4. Be prepared to record ideas Because ideas from the subconscious often come when you are climbing out of bed, driving to work, or walking across campus between classes, you should keep paper and pen with you at all times to get these ideas down. If you do not seize an idea at once, it might slip away and be gone forever.

Margaret McFadden, a business executive, uses her subconscious in a process she calls "living with" a speech. "As soon as I receive an invitation to speak," she says, "I choose my topic and do whatever research I need to do. Then I 'live' with my speech for a few weeks. Wherever I go—to work, to the store, to the beach—I find myself thinking about the speech. Not fretting or brooding, just playing with ideas. I carry a pad with me and jot down the ideas as they come to me. At the end of each day, I drop the notes into a manila folder. After a few weeks, I sit down at my desk, pull out the folder of notes, and organize my material into an outline. Usually everything just falls into place."

Everything falls into place because her subconscious mind had been busy for weeks, sorting and editing the materials.

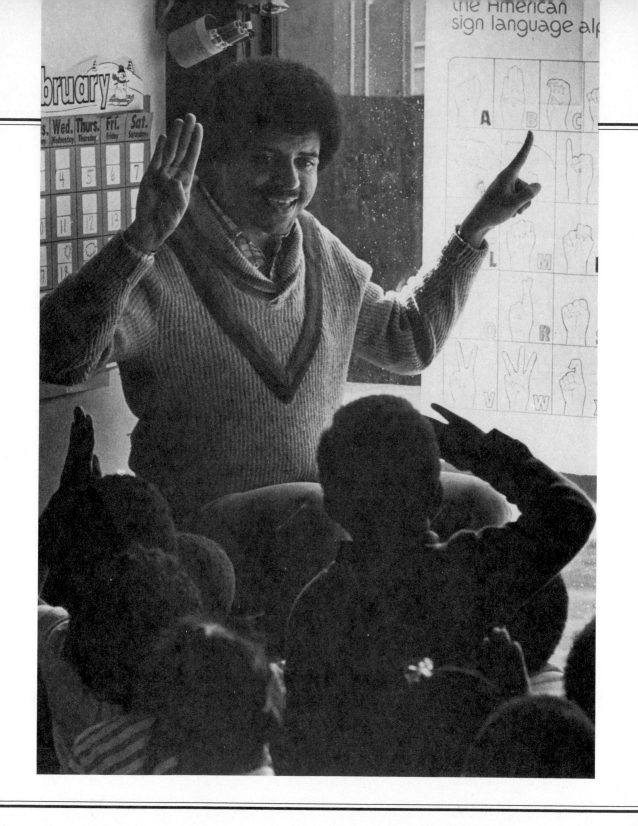

8

Visual Aids

Reasons for Using Visual Aids

Types of Visual Aids

Media for Visual Aids

Guidelines for Using Visual Aids

For several months, Megan Kennerly, a dental hygienist, tried telling her patients how to floss their teeth correctly, but "most of them didn't really catch on." Then she began coupling her instructions with a demonstration, using a string (to represent dental floss) and a large model of a row of teeth. As a result, her patients were able to understand, remember, and apply her instructions.

What Kennerly discovered is that oral instructions alone are not as effective as oral instructions combined with a visual aid. This insight has been confirmed by the research of Robert Craig, chief of the U.S. Public Health Service's audiovisual facility. He found that people who were taught orally could remember only 10 percent of the information 3 days later, but people who were taught orally and visually could recall 65 percent of the information 3 days later.[1]

Because most people have grown up with television and therefore are conditioned to learn things by means of visual images, visual aids are considered a vital part of most business and professional presentations today. The attitude throughout society is: "Don't tell me, show me."

Reasons for Using Visual Aids

While Chapter 7 dealt with *verbal* supports, this chapter will examine *visual* supports for a speech. Let us examine some good reasons for using visual supports.

Visual aids can make your ideas clear and understandable. Mary Callahan gave a classroom speech on how the United States government, when printing paper currency, uses complicated techniques that prevent counterfeiters from producing perfect imitations. Using a slide of a greatly enlarged dollar bill, she pointed out intricate designs and clever nuances that most people never would have dreamed existed. Without the blown-up dollar, her explanations would have been hard to follow. With the slide, her remarks were lucid and easy to grasp.

Visual aids can make your speech more interesting. Li Yang, a foreign student from Mauritius, showed slides to supplement his talk on his native country, which is an island in the Indian Ocean. To illustrate the geographical diversity of Mauritius, Li showed beautiful views of sparkling beaches and majestic mountains. To illustrate the racial and ethnic diversity of the island, he showed slides of citizens in a marketplace. There were also pictures of wind surfing and dancing. All in all, the slides took the audience on a vicarious trip to an exotic land and enhanced the speech.

Visual aids can help the audience remember facts and details. Research shows that visual aids help a listener retain ideas.[2] During his speech on Mauritius, Li showed a map of the world, on which he pinpointed his tiny country's location in the Indian Ocean. As we all do with visual aids, I took a mental snapshot of the map, which will help me remember where Mauritius is located.

Visual aids can make long, complicated explanations unnecessary. If you watch professional basketball on TV, you see a coach call a time out to set up one last play, with only seconds remaining in the game. He does not have time to explain to each player the complex pattern of the play, but he uses a miniature basketball court with little magnetic buttons representing the players. He moves the buttons about to show the players where they should run and what they should do. The players nod their assent, walk out onto the court, and execute the play as they saw it on the miniature board. The coach's visual aid saves time and makes a long, complicated explanation unnecessary.

Visual aids can help prove a point. A representative of Leica, the German camera manufacturer, once gave a talk to a group of photographers. He maintained that the body of the Leica (not the lens) could be dropped on a concrete floor without suffering any damage; in fact, he said, it could be dropped out the window (the group was on the third floor) to the sidewalk below, and it would still function as well as ever. To prove his point, he sent the entire audience down to the sidewalk. The group formed a semicircle and watched as he dropped the camera from the third floor to the sidewalk. Sure enough, the camera was undamaged. He challenged the photographers to take pictures with the camera if they doubted his claim. Most speakers do not have such dramatic visual aids, but even simple aids like graphs and drawings can help prove a point. As the old saying goes, "Seeing is believing."

Visual aids can add to your personal credibility. Your listeners will be impressed if it is obvious that you have expended time and energy on visual aids to make your speech interesting and understandable. Researchers have discovered that if you add visual aids to your speech, audiences are apt to rate you as being more trustworthy and more intelligent than they would if no visual aids were used.[3] But certain other research also needs to be mentioned as a warning: If listeners think that your visual aids are poor, their confidence in you falls off.[4] In other words, you are better off using no visual aids at all than poor ones.

Types of Visual Aids

Graphs

Graphs help audiences understand and retain statistical data. The *line graph* should be a familiar form to all college students because it is widely used in textbooks. It uses a horizontal and a vertical scale to show the relationship between two variables, as in Figure 8.1.

The bell-shaped curve for normal distribution is a feature known to many people through such statistical graphs as IQ scores in the general population. This

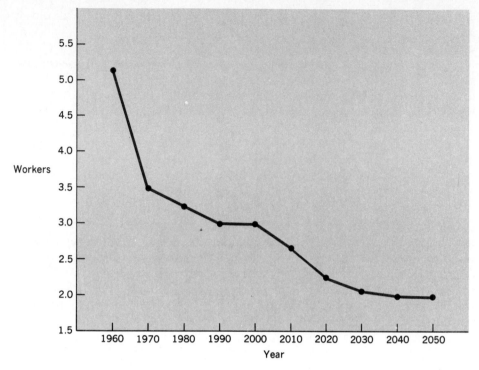

Figure 8.1

In America, workers pay Social Security taxes to finance Social Security benefits for people over 65. This graph shows the ratio of workers per Social Security dependent. In 1960, there were five people working for every person over 65 receiving Social Security benefits. By the year 2030, there will be only two workers for every Social Security retiree. Thus the tax burden on those two workers is expected to be very heavy. *(Source: U.S. Commission on Population Growth)*

curve can be used in symbolic ways (instead of in strictly mathematical terms), as Figure 8.2 demonstrates.

A *bar graph* is an easy way to show a great deal of data in a clear, easily comprehended manner. This kind of graph enables you to show comparisons within groups, as in Figure 8.3.

A *pie graph* is a circle representing 100 percent. It is easy for the audience to understand as long as there are not too many different "pieces" of pie. A textbook could have a pie graph with twenty different pieces because the reader would have ample time to analyze them, but a pie graph in a speech should have no more than six or seven pieces. Figure 8.4 shows a pie graph with four pieces.

Of all graphs, a *pictorial graph* is perhaps the easiest to read, because it visually translates information into a picture that can be grasped instantaneously. Figure 8.5 is an example of a pictorial graph.

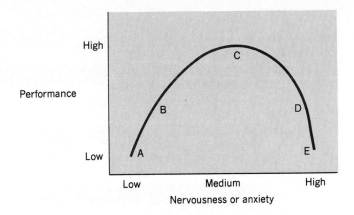

Figure 8.2
This is a graphic representation of the Yerkes-Dodson law in psychology. One speaker used this graph to discuss the anxiety that students experience in taking tests. At point A, people are asleep—no nervousness or anxiety, no mental performance. At point B, people are alert because they have a small amount of tension; their performance on tests is moderately good. At point C, people have a medium amount of nervousness so their performance is at its peak. At point D, the nervousness is getting acute and the test-taking performance is beginning to falter. At point E, panic and mental disorganization have set in and performance is zero. The purpose of the graph is to show that a moderate amount of nervousness or anxiety while taking a test is desirable. (This graph could also be used to demonstrate the point made in Chapter 3: a moderate amount of nervous energy during a speech is ideal for effective speechmaking.)

You need not be an artist to create a pictorial graph. Anyone can draw a representation of human figures, even if they are as primitive as those shown in Figure 8.6.

Charts

Charts provide information in a compact, easily digested form. An *information chart* can show the main points of your speech or list the steps in a process. In Figure 8.7, the speaker put five steps in a process on a poster.

An *organization chart* can be used to show a hierarchy in a business or agency. We are familiar with charts that show the president of the company at the top and lines of authority going downward. This kind of chart can also be used to organize information, as in Figure 8.8, which shows how the body's nervous system is organized.

A *flowchart* shows the flow, or sequence, of related events. (See Chapter 3, Figure 3.1, for a flowchart showing two possible sequences of events that can happen to a nervous speaker.) Figure 8.9 shows a flowchart involving personal computers.

Figure 8.3
This bar graph shows how long the average person can expect to live in five different countries. Notice that this graph makes it easy to show comparative figures for males and females.

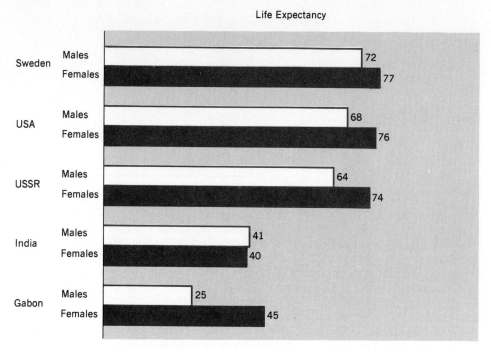

Life Expectancy

Drawings

Drawings make good visual aids because they can illustrate points that would be hard to explain in words. For example, telling an audience how to cut down a tree would be very difficult without a drawing, such as that in Figure 8.10.

Figure 8.4
This pie chart shows the results of a survey of 1267 corporate executives, who were asked what format was most often used by their companies in presenting business graphics. *(Source: PC Magazine)*

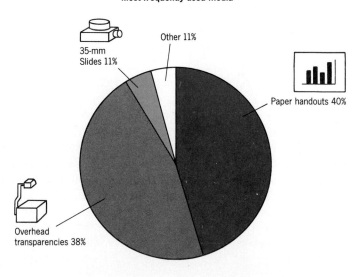

Most frequently used media

Napoleon's Invasion of Russia, 1812

Figure 8.5
Napoleon invaded Russia in 1812 with 422,000 soldiers, but only 10,000 survived the military battles and the bitter Russian winter. When the speaker points out that each figure in this pictorial graph represents 10,000 soldiers, the audience can easily see the immensity of Napoleon's disaster.

422,000 Soldiers invaded Russia

Only 10,000
returned

Some students shy away from using drawings because they consider themselves unartistic. You need not be an artist to make a simple drawing such as the one shown in Figure 8.10.

One kind of drawing that is highly effective is a map. By sketching a map yourself, you can include only those features that are pertinent to your speech. If you were speaking on the major rivers of America, for example, you could outline

Figure 8.6
These simple pictorial representations of human beings illustrate that artistic ability is not required to create a pictorial graph. Figures such as these could have been used in Figure 8.5 if the speaker had lacked access to more sophisticated graphics.

the boundaries of the United States and then draw heavy blue lines for the rivers, leaving out extraneous details, such as cities. Figure 8.11 shows a drawing with one map superimposed upon another—an effective way to show comparative size.

Photographs

Photographs have a high degree of realism; they are very good for proving points. Lawyers, for example, often use photographs of the scene of an accident to win a case. You should use photographs in a speech only if they are enlarged to poster size. If you have a small photograph that you think would make an important visual aid, have your school's audiovisual department make a 35-mm slide from it, if possible, and then project it so that everyone in the audience is able to see it.

Computer Graphics

Computers can create all kinds of graphs, charts, maps, and drawing, which can then be printed (sometimes in color) either on paper or on transparencies for overhead projection. Slides can also be made from computer graphics. Your

Figure 8.7
An information chart listing the steps in a process can make it easy for the audience to absorb the information.

Running Without Pain

1. Do stretches

2. Walk briskly

3. Run

4. Walk slowly

5. Do stretches

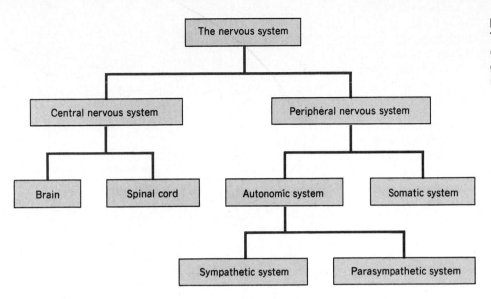

Figure 8.8
This organization chart shows sub-groupings of the nervous system.

college may have a computer that generates graphics. More and more businesses are producing visual aids by this means because computers can create graphics much more quickly than an artist can. Such graphics are highly accurate and easily updated.[5]

Objects

Three-dimensional objects make good visual aids, provided that they are large enough for everyone in the audience to see. You could bring such things as a blood-pressure gauge, a hibachi, handmade pottery, mountain-climbing equipment, and musical instruments. Living objects could also be used, but be sure to get your instructor's approval in advance. You could use a friend, for example, to illustrate self-defense methods against an attacker.

Figure 8.9
This flowchart shows how to send data from one personal computer to another, using telecommunications. There is no need to label the parts; the audience instantly recognizes all of the images except the rectangular box—the modem—which can be explained when the speaker discusses the chart.

Figure 8.10
This drawing shows how to make the cuts necessary for felling a tree. This kind of illustration helps to explain to the audience the subtleties of depth and angle.

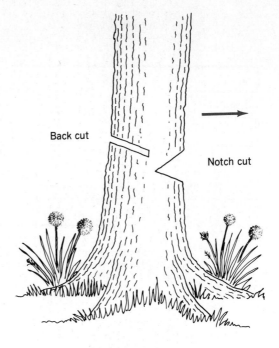

Back cut

Notch cut

Models

A model is a representation of an object. One student used a model of the pyramids to discuss how the ancient Egyptians probably built their famous pyramids. If you were discussing space travel, you could use a model of a space shuttle. One advantage of a model is that you can move it around. If you had a model airplane, for example, you could show the principles of aerodynamics more easily than if you had only a drawing of a plane. One student brought in a homemade "lung," the interior of which consisted of clean cotton. When cigarette smoke was sucked through a tube, the lung turned from white to a sickening yellow-brown.

Figure 8.11
This drawing shows Alaska superimposed on the continental United States, vividly illustrating the huge size of the state and its long span from east to west.

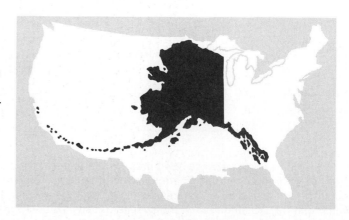

Yourself

You can use yourself as a visual aid. You can demonstrate yoga positions, judo holds, karate chops, stretching exercises, relaxation techniques, ballet steps, and tennis strokes. You can don native attire, historical costumes, or scuba-diving equipment. One student came to class dressed and made up as a clown to give a speech on her part-time job as a clown for children's birthday parties.

Media for Visual Aids

Some of the types of visual aids we looked at above—charts, graphs, drawings, etc.—can be conveyed to the audience by means of a variety of different media. Here are some of the more popular media.

Chalkboards

A chalkboard is an ideal tool for visual aids if you have a few technical words that you need to write for your audience. If you use a big word like *transmogrification* (which means "changing into a different, sometimes bizarre, form"), you can step over to the chalkboard and write it down in big letters. A chalkboard is also effective if you have complex drawings that require constant insertions and erasures—for example, diagramming plays for a soccer team.

Otherwise, a chalkboard is usually not very desirable because if you put your visual—a graph, say—on the board during your speech, you have to turn your back on the audience; while you're drawing, their attention drifts away from you, and you may find it hard to regain it. Nor is it a good idea to put your graph on the board before the speech begins because the audience will be distracted by it; they will be scrutinizing it before you are ready to talk about it. (It would do no good to say, "Don't pay any attention to this until I get to it." Such an admonition would make the graph all the more interesting—and therefore distracting.) There is one possible solution: cover the part of the chalkboard on which you have written, but this can be awkward. You would have to find something large enough to do the job but not be distracting. Another problem is that speakers preceding you may also be planning to use the board, and they might erase your visual aid.

Since people are so accustomed to seeing chalkboards after spending years in school, there is not much novelty involved, so get chalk in different colors to add sparkle to your visuals.

Posters

You can put many kinds of visual aids—graphs, drawings, charts, etc.—on posters. They do the same work as chalkboards, but they are usually a lot neater and more visually appealing.

The size of the poster will depend, of course, upon the size of the audience. Ask yourself: can the person in the back row see the words or artwork clearly? For huge audiences, posters obviously would be unsuitable; you would have to use slides.

Make sure there is a reliable place to put your posters. Propping them against a chalkboard may cause them to fall to the floor during the middle of the speech. Taping them up on a wall may cause them to fall with a thud during the speech. Using thumbtacks might work if there is a suitable place for tacking. One technique is to put the posters on a desk near the lectern and take one at a time from the pile to hold it up. If you follow this technique, be sure to hold your posters steady. The best, most reliable method is to put your poster on an easel (your school's audiovisual department may be able to provide one). Even with an easel, however, some posters tend to curl and resist standing up straight. To make a poster firm, tape a second (blank) poster to the back of it.

Flip Charts

A flip chart is a giant writing pad glued or wired together at the top. It can be mounted on an easel. It is much like a chalkboard except that when you are through with a visual, you can tear off the page or flip it over the back of the easel.

You can prepare the visuals on each page in advance, or you can "halfway" prepare them—that is, lightly pencil in your sheets at home; then during the speech, with a heavy marker, trace over the lines. (Since the audience is unaware that you are tracing, not drawing, you come across as crisp and professional.) With some flip charts, the paper might be so thin that ink will seep to the next page, so you might need a blank page between each sheet that you draw on.

Handouts

In a survey, 1267 corporate executives were asked what format was most often used by their companies in presenting business graphics. The winner was paper handouts, with 40 percent (overhead transparencies placed second with 38 percent, and 35-mm slides came in third with 11 percent).[6] At a time when businesses can use dazzling electronic media, it is surprising to see handouts used so frequently.

Or maybe it is not surprising, when you consider that handouts are easy to prepare, can be updated quickly at the last moment, and provide a permanent document that listeners can take with them when they leave a presentation.

As will be explained later in this chapter, some handouts should not be passed out until the end of a speech. Figure 8.12 gives an example of a handout.

Overhead Transparencies

Overhead projectors are light boxes that project images from transparencies onto a screen. There are five advantages in using overhead transparencies: (1) The transparencies are not hard to produce. (2) It is easy to make last-minute changes in artwork or statistics. (3) You do not need another person to operate the machine for you. (4) Since the room usually does not have to be darkened, you and the audience can see each other at all times. (5) When you want to point to an item on your visual, you do not have to turn your back to the audience by going to the screen; you can simply point to the proper place on the transparency with a pencil or pen.

Prepare transparencies well ahead of time. You can reproduce photos or

Figure 8.12
An example of a handout that can be given at the end of a speech on cancer, so that the audience will have key information for later use.

C A U T I O N

Early Cancer Symptoms:

Change in bowel or bladder habits
A sore that does not heal
Unusual bleeding or discharge
Thickening or lump in the breast or elsewhere
Indigestion or difficulty in swallowing
Obvious change in wart or mole
Nagging cough or persistent hoarseness

illustrations from magazines and books, or you can create original graphics. Using a variety of color pens, you can write directly on the film, or you can make a master copy on plain white paper, then use certain kinds of office copiers to make your transparency. (Your college's audiovisual department may be able to help you produce transparencies for a small fee, or a print shop in your community can make transparencies from your master copy.)

Make your artwork and letters larger than you think necessary. Do not try to use a typewriter to make the master copy because the letters are too small. Even large typefaces, such as IBM's Orator, are too small to be seen by people in the back of a room.

It is possible to write or draw on a transparency while you are projecting it on the screen, but I do not recommend doing so because you can lose your audience's attention while you write or draw. An exception to this would be using your pen to circle key words, draw arrows, or insert updated statistics.

When you create transparencies in advance, you must make sure that you use a marking pen especially designed for overheads. If you use an ordinary marker to prepare a transparency the night before your speech, the graphics might look fine at the time, but by the next day the ink may evaporate, leaving you with only thin traces. Avoid storing transparencies directly against one another. The ink may transfer from one to another. Put them in file folders or store them with a piece of paper between each one.

You can use a card or heavy paper to reveal one part of a transparency at a time. If, for example, you have three major points, you can cover up all but point 1 and discuss it; when you're through with point 1, pull the card down and show point 2, and so on.

Slides

Slides are popular in business, government, and military presentations. They allow a great deal of flexibility: you can insert and delete slides quickly and easily, thus adapting a slide show to meet the needs of different kinds of audiences. As an example, if during a recent trip to Mexico you took 245 slides, including 35 at an ancient Mayan excavation site, you might want to show all 35 of the Mayan slides in a talk to an archaeological society. But if you are giving a talk to a civic club, you might want to show only three or four of those slides because a general audience would not be interested in detailed information on archaeology.

Slide projectors are easy to operate. You can set your own pace, lingering over a slide that requires long explanation, while hurrying through slides that need little or no commentary. If you have a remote-control device on a long cord, you can stand next to the screen and point out items without having to walk back and forth between projector and screen.

If you have a photograph, chart, drawing, magazine ad, or cartoon that is too small for the audience to see, consider making a slide of it. If you are making a slide of a graph or chart, limit yourself to only two or three bold, contrasting colors (too many colors would be garish) and do not use many words. Keep the slide simple and vivid.

To be seen clearly, slides must be shown in a completely darkened room. This situation is both good and bad. It is good in that the attention of your audience is concentrated on one spot—the screen. This means there are no visual distractions that might cause the listeners' eyes to wander. The bad aspect is that you and your listeners lose eye communication with each other; you have to rely solely on your voice to make contact. To solve this problem, some speakers show slides in a semidark room, but this makes the slides appear washed out and therefore hard to see.

Once you have finished discussing a slide, do not leave it on the screen. If you are not yet ready to go to the next slide, project a light-colored blank slide on the screen while you talk, or turn off the projector and turn on the lights until you are ready for the next slide.

Films and Videotapes

Films are awkward to use. Time is spent starting and stopping the projector (unless you have an experienced operator to run the machine for you). Furthermore, the projector makes noise and can block the view of some listeners. If you are thinking of showing a film as part of a classroom speech, you should get permission in advance from your instructor. Even if you get approval, you will want to guard against letting the film dominate the speech or take up most of your time. Outside the classroom, a film might be very effective if you are allotted, say, 45 minutes and the film could serve as an appetizer—something to whet appetites for the main course, your speech. If you have detailed, technical material to cover, you might use a film in the middle of your speech to break the monotony. Or you can use a film at the end if it will motivate the audience to take action on your proposals.

Videotapes are replacing 16-mm films as the favorite type of motion picture. Not only are many commercially produced videotapes available, but many people can make their own tapes, using their own videocassette camcorders or one borrowed from their schools or employers. Because of the ease in rewinding and advancing, videotapes are superior to films if you want to show only a small portion of a show. Furthermore, the playback machines for videotapes do not make a loud noise, as do 16-mm projectors.

If you use videotape for your interviews, you may even be able to use some excerpts in your speech. In a community speech on the unsanitary conditions in which some children are forced to live, Linda Morales, a social worker, included videotaped interviews of children who pointed at the cockroaches and other insects in their apartment. The videotape was much more powerful than any verbal description would have been.

Guidelines for Using Visual Aids

Here are some guidelines for using visual aids effectively in your speeches.

Choose Visual Aids That Truly Support Your Speech

Before you use any visual aid, ask yourself this question: Will it help support an important idea in my speech? If the answer is "no," forget about using it. Your job is not to dazzle people with pretty colors on a screen or to impress them with your creative artwork. A beautiful drawing of an airplane, for example, would not really contribute to a speech on vacationing in Europe.

Beware of using a visual aid that is of poor quality. As we discussed earlier, a poor visual aid is worse than none at all because it can weaken your credibility with the audience. Take a candid, realistic look at your visuals. Are they really worth displaying?

Make Visual Aids Simple and Clear

Each visual aid should have just one major idea which the listeners can quickly grasp. Too much information can confuse or overwhelm them. They might spend so much time and energy trying to make sense out of your visual that they stop listening to you.

If you take graphs or charts from books, be aware that some visual aids in books are jam-packed with fascinating details which may not be suitable for a speech.

While visual aids should be appealing to the eye, they should also be clear, neat, and uncrowded. In aids such as graphs, make all labels horizontal (in a textbook, many labels are vertical because readers of a book can turn the visual sideways, but listeners should not be forced to twist their necks to read vertical lettering). You need not label every part of your visual, as you are there to explain the aid.

A common mistake made by speakers is to use visual aids that cannot be seen by everyone in the audience—for example, lettering that is too small to be read by people in the last four rows. A good rule of thumb is to make your letters and sketches much larger than you think necessary. Before the date of your speech, go to the room where you will be speaking, display your visual aid in the front of the room, and then sit in the back row and determine whether you can see it clearly.

It makes you appear amateurish when you show an aid that cannot be seen by everyone. If you have a multidimensional object, be sure to turn it during your talk so that everyone can see all sides of it. Before a speech, move any objects such as desks or tables that might block the view of some listeners.

Do Not Let Visuals Become a Substitute for a Speech

Your visual aids cannot give your speech for you. This is especially important to remember for classroom speeches. Do not show a 4-minute film on Denmark and then spend only 1 minute talking about your trip to that country. The aid is a supplement, a help, a clarifier—it is not a substitute for a speech.

Do Not Use an Excessive Number of Visual Aids

How many visual aids should you use? Only the number necessary to make your points. No more, no less. It is not true that the more aids you have, the better off you are. If there are too many, the audience might feel overwhelmed or jaded.

Practice with Your Visual Aids

When you practice your speech, do not forget to include your visual aids. It is especially important that you practice using unfamiliar equipment, such as overhead projectors or videotape machines, so that you can avoid fumbling or faltering during your speech. In order to have plenty of practice time, you obviously need to prepare your visual aids far in advance.

Make Sure Visual Aids Do Not Distract from Your Message

Never let a visual aid draw the attention of your listeners away from your message. One speaker brought in a ferret to demonstrate what great pets they make. The only trouble was that the ferret did cute impromptu stunts all during the speech, causing the audience to laugh at the antics of the animal rather than listen to the speech. (A note of caution: some instructors disapprove of using animals in speeches; be sure to get permission before using an animal in a classroom speech.)

Inanimate aids can also be distracting. Drawings or graphs that are shown prematurely might cause the audience to scrutinize them rather than listen to you. For this reason, you should display only one visual aid at a time. Show it during the time you are talking about it—do not pull it out early or leave it on display after you have discussed it. If you have, say, five posters for your speech, displaying all of them at the same time would distract your listeners from following your remarks. Display poster 1 when it is time; then cover it up or turn it over; display poster 2 and talk about it, and so forth. If you have an object to show, keep it covered or in a box. (An object in a box, by the way, can be a great suspense builder, You can refer to the mysterious item in the box early in your speech, but not reveal what it is until the climax of your speech.) When you do bring the aid out, do not just show it briefly and leave the audience wishing for more time to see it. Let the audience have a good look before you put it away.

If a visual aid is too small for listeners to see it from their seats, do not circulate it among the audience because people will look at it instead of listening to you. And there's likely to be distraction, perhaps even whispered comments, as it is being passed from one person to another. Avoid doing anything that will take the eyes and minds of the listeners away from your speech. The best way to display a small aid is to leave it in the front and invite the audience to see if after the speech. Some speakers try to handle this problem by walking from listener to listener, giving each person a close-up view. But this is a poor technique; the listeners who are not seeing the visual aid may get bored or distracted, or they may start whispering comments to their friends. Also, the listeners who are looking at the aid may ask questions that mean nothing to the rest of the audience. In a case like this, you can easily lose your audience's attention and interest.

Since handouts are so popular in the business world (see Figure 8.4), you need to know some basic rules: (1) *Never* distribute a handout until you are ready to talk about it. This is a simple rule, but one that is often violated: I have seen dozens of presenters pass out stacks of handouts at the beginning of a talk. While they go over each handout, the room is filled with the sound of rustling papers, as the listeners race ahead, reading handouts that the presenter has not yet come to and ignoring or only half-listening to what the speaker is saying. (2) Do not distribute a handout *during* a speech unless it is short and simple. If you have a simple graphic or a small amount of text on a handout, you can distribute a copy to each listener, and then discuss the content. (3) Be careful to avoid talking about a handout while you are passing copies out; wait until every listener has a copy, then start your explanation. (4) Lengthy or complex handouts that you want listeners to take home with them should be distributed at the end of the question-and-answer period. The reason for this is obvious: if a handout with many different graphics or with a lot of text is passed out during the speech, the listeners would be tempted to read or study the entire handout, rather than pay attention to you. (For classroom speeches, check with your instructor; he or she may prefer that you wait until the end of the class period; if you give out material at the end of your speech, students might read it instead of listening to the next speaker.)

Do Not Talk to Your Visual Aid

Many speakers are so intent on explaining a visual aid that they spend most of their time talking to it instead of to the audience. You should stand next to your aid and face the audience during most of your discussion. Look at the aid only in two situations: (1) When you introduce it, look at it for several seconds— this is long enough to draw the listeners' attention toward it. (2) When you want to redirect the audience's attention to a new feature, look at the aid for one or two seconds.

Explain Visual Aids

No matter how simple your visual aid is, your should explain it to your audience. Some speakers slap transparencies of graphs onto an overhead projector, talk about them for a moment, and then whisk them off. To such speakers, the graph is simple and obvious; they do not stop to think that the listeners have never seen the aid before and need time to analyze and absorb the visual information.

As you discuss a part of your visual aid, do not wave your hand in the general direction of the aid and assume that the audience can figure out what feature you are pointing out. Be precise. Point to the specific part that you are discussing. If you have a small visual aid, you can use a finger to point; if your aid is large, you may want to use a ruler, pen, or extendable pointer. To avoid twisting your body, use the hand nearer the aid.

Plan for Emergencies

With visual aids, there is always a chance of a foul-up, especially if you are using electronic media, so you need to plan how to handle any problems that might arise. Sometimes the problem is simple but nevertheless frustrating. If you plan to sketch on the board, make sure there is chalk. It is disruptive to have to send someone to another room to find chalk.

Before you use any electronic media, you should talk with your instructor or the program chairperson to get permission and to make arrangements (for darkening the room, getting an extension cord, etc.)

Be prepared for the unexpected—slides appearing upside down, the bulb in the slide projector burning out, videotape breaking in the middle of the program. Some of these disasters can be mitigated by advance planning. For example, carry a spare bulb for the slide projector; if the videotape breaks, be ready to fill in the missing information. If equipment breaks down and cannot be fixed quickly, continue with your speech as best you can. Try to keep your poise and sense of humor.

Summary

Visual aids can enrich and enliven your speech in many ways: they can make your ideas clear and understandable, they can make your speech more interesting and memorable, they can help prove a point, and they can add to your personal credibility.

Whatever type of aids you choose, you should take into consideration the following guidelines: (1) Choose visual aids that truly support your speech. (2) Make your aids as simple and as clear as possible. (3) Do not let your visuals become a substitute for the speech. (4) Do not use an excessive number of aids. (5) Practice with your aids ahead of time. (6) Make sure the aids do not distract from your message. (7) Do not talk to your aids. (8) Explain each aid, regardless of how simple it is. (9) Plan for emergencies.

Review Questions

1. List at least six types of visual aids.
2. List at least five media for visual aids.
3. Why is it a mistake to circulate small visual aids during your speech?
4. Why should a graphic in a speech be less complex than a graphic in a book?
5. What are the disadvantages of using a chalkboard for visual aids?

Tips

FOR YOUR CAREER

Tip 8: Use a Friend to Assist You

For speeches that you give on the job or in the community, you may want to consider using a friend to assist you. Here are some of the ways in which an assistant can be useful:

1. An assistant can help you set up and operate audiovisual equipment, turn lights off and on, or search for a missing extension cord. Such assistance will free you to concentrate on getting your message across to the audience.

2. If you are speaking to strangers, the presence of your friend can give you a nice psychological boost—you have an ''ally'' in the room.

3. An assistant might be able to handle any distractions or emergencies that arise. If, for example, a group of people start a loud conversation right outside the door of the room where you are speaking, the assistant can open the door and whisper a request for silence.

4. Your assistant can stand or sit in the back of the room while you are speaking and give you signals that the two of you have rehearsed. For example:

☐ ''Slow down—you're talking too fast.''

☐ ''Speak louder—I can barely hear you.''

☐ ''You're speaking too loud.''

☐ ''You're looking at your notes too much.''

5. An assistant can give you a critique of your speech afterward, so that you can learn from any mistakes you have made. Sometimes the assistant can mingle with the audience in the hall after your speech and find out how listeners responded to the presentation, so that you can learn about your strengths and weaknesses.

PART THREE

Organizing

the

Speech

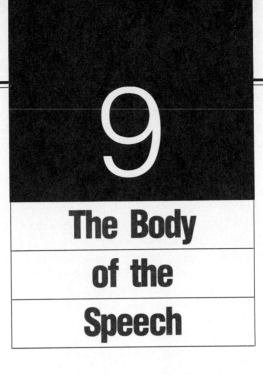

9

The Body
of the
Speech

Creating the Body

Organizing Main Points

Selecting Support Materials

Supplying Transitions

I once heard a naturalist give a talk on why the leaves of hardwood trees change colors in autumn. As he talked (without notes), it was obvious that he had no coherent plan for his speech: he rambled from one item to another, without tying things together. He would talk for a while about the chemical makeup of leaves, then throw in a few comments about rainfall and temperature, then go back to chemistry. He gave his information in random order, not following a logical sequence. He backtracked a great deal ("Oh yeah, when I was talking about rainfall, I forgot to mention..."). For me, the speech was confusing rather than enlightening. I failed to get what I came for: an understanding of the chemical process by which leaves change colors. I think I would have understood the process, however, if he had organized his material in a logical, easy-to-follow pattern, such as: "Here's how leaves change colors: First..., second..., third...," and so on.

Organizing material logically and intelligently is important in all types of communication, but it is especially important in oral communication. If readers of an essay find themselves confused, they can easily go back a few paragraphs and study the material until they make sense out of it, but people who listen to a speech do not have this option. If they fail to understand what a speaker is saying, they are out of luck. There is no instant replay. What this means to you, the speaker, is that you must organize your ideas clearly and logically, so that your listeners will understand you. If your speech is rambling, illogical, and poorly constructed, the listeners may go away confused rather than enlightened. A well-organized speech has the following advantages over a poorly organized one:

1. *A well-organized speech is easier to understand.* Just like the naturalist, many speakers have interesting, important ideas, but their speeches are so poorly organized that the audience fails to grasp the ideas. Studies have shown that a well-organized speech is much easier for a listener to understand than a poorly organized one.[1]

2. *A well-organized speech is easier for the audience to remember.* Imagine that you need to remember to buy the following items at the store:

☐ bagels	☐ butter
☐ frozen spinach	☐ tomatoes
☐ milk	☐ hamburger buns
☐ lettuce	☐ carrots
☐ rolls	☐ frozen peas
☐ frozen squash	☐ yogurt

In a number of experiments, psychologists[2] have shown that your chances of recalling all the items increase if you revise your list to look something like this:

Breads
☐ bagels
☐ rolls
☐ hamburger buns

Dairy products
☐ butter
☐ yogurt
☐ milk

Frozen foods
- ☐ spinach
- ☐ squash
- ☐ peas

Fresh produce
- ☐ lettuce
- ☐ tomatoes
- ☐ carrots

The reason the second list is easier to remember is that items are grouped in meaningful clusters. You can, for example, get a mental picture of the bread section of your grocery store, and then tell yourself that you need to pick up only three things in that section—bagels, rolls, and hamburger buns. In a good speech, you should apply the same principle: group your ideas in meaningful clusters that are easy to comprehend and recall.

3. A well-organized speech is more likely to be believed. Studies show that if you present a poorly organized speech, your listeners will find you less believable at the end than they did at the beginning of the speech.[3] But if your speech is well-organized, you will come across as someone who is in full command of the facts, and therefore believable.

All good speeches are made up of three parts: introduction, body, and conclusion. You might think it logical to formulate your introduction first, but most speakers find it is easier to begin with the body of the speech and then prepare the introduction. If you stop and think about it, this makes a lot of sense: How can you introduce the body until you know its full nature?

In this chapter we will discuss how to organize the body of the speech. In the next chapter we will look at introductions and conclusions. Then, in the chapter following, we will examine how to put all these parts together in an outline.

Creating the Body

To create the body of a speech, start with your *specific purpose,* which is the goal of your speech, and your *central idea,* which is the key concept that you want to get across to your audience. (If you are unsure about these terms, please review Chapter 5 before proceeding in this chapter.)

Suppose you want to argue against the sport of boxing, and you come up with the following purpose statement:

Specific Purpose: **To persuade my listeners that the sport of boxing should be outlawed.**

Next, you should ask yourself, "What is my essential message? What big idea do I want to leave in the minds of my listeners?" Your answer, of course, is your central idea. Here is one possibility:

Central Idea: **Boxing should be banned because it is an uncivilized form of brutality.**

This central idea is your speech boiled down to one sentence. It is what you want your listeners to remember if they forget everything else. The next step is to ask yourself this question: "How can I get my audience to believe my central idea?" The best way to get the central idea across to your audience is to firmly implant in their minds a few *main points* that are based on the central idea. In our boxing example, here are three main points that could be made:

I. Boxing can cause permanent brain injury.
II. Boxing sometimes leads to death.
III. Boxing is the only sport in which inflicting injury is the primary goal.

Next, ask yourself, "How can I make these main points stick in the minds of my listeners?" The answer is to back up each main point with supporting materials such as narratives, examples, and statistics. For example, here is how you could develop main point II:

II. Boxing sometimes leads to death.
  A. According to the American Medical Association, 439 boxers have died from boxing injuries since 1918.
  B. Willie Classen was knocked unconscious in the tenth round of a middleweight bout at Madison Square Garden and died 5 days later of massive brain damage.
  C. Duk Koo Kim, a young Korean, was killed in a televised match with lightweight champion Ray "Boom Boom" Mancini in 1982.

If you arrange a speech in this way, you will have an easy time getting your message across. Your listeners will know your central idea—that boxing should be outlawed because it is brutal—and they will know *why* boxing is brutal, thanks to your well-developed main points.

In chart form, here is what the body of a typical well-developed speech would look like:

Central idea

  Main point
    Support material
    Support material
    Support material
    Support material

  Main point
    Support material
    Support material

  Main point
    Support material
    Support material
    Support material

In this chart, note the three levels of importance: your central idea is supreme; it is developed by main points, which in turn are buttressed by support material. All three levels are necessary: your listeners will not believe your central idea unless you have some strong main points, and they will not believe your main points unless your support material is convincing.

Developing Material

I've heard people say something like this, "When I'm putting together a speech, I get lost in my notes. How do I know which are main points and which are subpoints? How do I know what to put in and what to leave out?" To develop your material, here are the steps to follow:

Cluster Your Research Notes

Your first step is to group your research notes into piles or clusters, according to subject matter. Suppose you are preparing a speech on the claims that vitamin C is a "miracle" substance for colds and cancer. You conduct extensive research and come up with a thick stack of notes. For brevity's sake, let's examine only eleven of your notes:

1. All researchers agree that vitamin C helps maintain and repair connective tissue and bones and promotes healing of wounds.
2. Since the eighteenth century, it has been known that humans must consume modest amounts of vitamin C (60 milligrams a day) to avoid the deficiency disease called scurvy.
3. Vitamin C is contained in citrus fruits and in potatoes, tomatoes, and other vegetables.

4. Dr. Linus Pauling, a Nobel Prize winner, believes that taking large amounts of vitamin C supplements can reduce the number of colds a person gets.
5. Dr. Pauling has won the Nobel Prize for his work in chemistry.
6. Dr. Pauling won a Nobel Peace Prize for working to reduce the risks of nuclear war.
7. Dr. Pauling says large doses of vitamin C can improve a cancer patient's chances of survival.

8. On the basis of several tests conducted over a 10-year period, the prestigious *New England Journal of Medicine* concluded that vitamin C does not cause a person to contract fewer colds.
9. Dr. Terence W. Anderson, a Canadian investigator who conducted three studies on more than 5000 adults, found no reduction in the frequency of colds during winters when vitamin C was taken, as compared with winters when the vitamin was not taken.
10. According to the *Harvard Medical School Health Letter,* two investigations at the famous Mayo Clinic found that cancer patients receiving vitamin C did not show any more improvement than patients not taking the vitamin.
11. Researchers have concluded that although smokers have lower blood levels of vitamin C than nonsmokers, they do not need to take extra vitamin C.

Notice that the notes have been placed into clusters—the first three items contain background information that all scientists agree on. The next four items (4 through 7) are concerned with Dr. Linus Pauling. The last four items deal with recent research on vitamin C. Grouping your research notes into clusters is an important way to gain control of your material.

Create Main Points and Support Them

Your next step is to create main points and then back them up with support materials. You can do this by systematically answering the following questions:

1. What is the specific purpose of my speech?
2. What is my central idea, the key concept that I want my listeners to understand, believe, and remember?
3. What main points can I create to drive home the central idea?
4. What support material (narratives, statistics, quotations, etc.) will I need under each main point to explain or prove it?

Let's apply these four questions to your speech on vitamin C.

1. *What is the specific purpose of my speech?* Here is one possibility:

Specific Purpose: To inform my audience of the latest research findings about vitamin C's influence on health.

Note that you have narrowed your topic to something that can be managed in a short speech. If you had tried to cover all the different kinds of vitamins, you would have created too broad a topic.

2. *What is my central idea, the key concept that I want my listeners to understand, believe, and remember?* From studying the above notes, you can see that Dr. Pauling, despite his prestige as a scientist, has formulated hypotheses about vitamin C that have been disproved by researchers. How do you know that Dr. Pauling is wrong? Because you have evidence from highly esteemed sources: The *New England Journal of Medicine* is one of the most respected medical journals in the world; the Mayo Clinic and Harvard Medical School are famous for their careful, reliable research in medicine. Armed with testimony from such highly credible sources, you can formulate the following as the gist of your speech:

Central Idea: Contrary to claims by Dr. Linus Pauling, vitamin C is not a miracle substance for colds and cancer.

3. *What main points can I create to drive home the central idea?* Put yourself in the place of the listeners. What would they say in response to your central idea? They would probably say, "How do you know that?" Based on your notes, you can create two main points—two key reasons why Dr. Pauling is wrong:

    I. Research shows that vitamin C cannot decrease a person's chances of catching colds.
   II. Research shows that vitamin C cannot increase the chances of recovery of a cancer patient.

Why these particular points? If you examine the central idea again, you will see that these are the points that are needed to explain and develop it. These are the points that summarize the findings of researchers. Our notes are important, but they are not main points. How about item 9—Dr. Anderson's research? That looks important. It *is* important, but it is not what you want your audience to remember. It would be nice if they could remember Dr. Anderson's name and the number of persons studied—5000—but is it realistic to expect an audience to remember such details a month after your speech? No, but you do hope they will remember the gist of Dr. Anderson's research, as expressed in main point I.

What about items 1 to 3? Aren't they worthy of being main points? No, because they merely give background information; they are not items that drive home the central idea. They can be included in the speech (in the introduction, as we will see in the next chapter), but not as main points.

    4. *What support material (narratives, statistics, quotations, etc.) will I need under each main point to explain or prove it?* By themselves, your main points would be unconvincing to the audience. Take a look at main point I above. If you made this statement by itself, the listeners would say to themselves, "Says who?" You would need to substantiate it by using items 8 and 9 from your notes. Here is how it would look in outline form:

    I. Research shows that vitamin C cannot decrease a person's chances of catching colds.
      A. On the basis of several tests conducted over a 10-year period, the prestigious *New England Journal of Medicine* concluded that vitamin C does not cause a person to contract fewer colds.
      B. Dr. Terence W. Anderson, a Canadian investigator who conducted three studies on more than 5000 adults, found no reduction in the frequency of colds during winters when vitamin C was taken, as compared with winters when the vitamin was not taken.

You could substantiate your other main point in the same fashion. (If this were a "real" speech, you obviously would have more notes than the samples above.)

Discard Irrelevant Material

In any speech, you need to be selective, choosing only those items that directly relate to the central idea. If you include irrelevant information, you risk confusing your listeners or overloading them with too much information.

In our vitamin C example, should all of the research notes above be used? Let's examine items 5 and 6 from our list. Item 5—the Nobel Prize in chemistry—is important in this speech because it establishes that Dr. Pauling has credentials that should be taken seriously in the field of medicine. But item 6—the Nobel

Peace Prize for working to reduce the risks of nuclear war—is irrelevant to this speech. Discard it.

How about item 11—the findings about smokers? Let's say you jotted down this research note because you thought that it might be pertinent to your speech. By now, however, you realize that although it is an interesting piece of research, it has no bearing on the narrow scope of your speech. Discard it.

Refining Main Points

"Do I need more than one main point?" some students ask. Yes. If you have only one main point to develop your central idea, you have a weak structure, like a bridge that has only one pillar to hold it up. If you provide only one main point, your listeners have only *one* reason to believe your central idea. If you give them two or three main points, you multiply your chances of convincing them.

"How many main points should I have?" you may be asking. To answer this and other questions, let's examine some guidelines for refining main points.

Limit the Number of Main Points

A common mistake of public speakers is to cram too many points into a speech. They do this because they are approaching the speech from their own personal viewpoint and not from the viewpoint of the listeners. If you ask yourself "How much information can I squeeze into the 5 minutes allotted?" you are approaching from your own viewpoint. To approach from the audience's viewpoint, you should ask, "How much information can the audience comfortably pay attention to, understand, and remember?" Remember that audiences simply cannot absorb too much new information. You should know this from your own experience; if you think for a moment, you probably can recall many speakers (including some teachers) who overwhelmed you with a barrage of ideas, facts, and figures. So do not be afraid to cut and trim your material.

Exactly how many main points should you have? In a short speech (5 to 10 minutes), you should limit yourself to two or three (or occasionally four) main points. That is as much as an audience can absorb. In a longer speech, you could have as many as five main points, but most experienced speakers cover only two or three, regardless of the length of their speech. It is a rare—and usually ineffective—veteran speaker who attempts six or more.

Make Sure All Main Points Develop the Central Idea

You should make sure that all of your main points are truly based on the central idea. In the following example, one of the main points does not belong. Can you spot it?

Specific Purpose: To inform my listeners of the valuable lessons that humans have learned from the study of dolphins.
Central Idea: Humans have learned valuable lessons by studying dolphins.

Main Points: I. People have learned how to construct faster boats by studying dolphins' skin.
II. People have learned to improve submariners' ability to "hear" underwater by studying dolphins' ears.
III. People have come to admire the intelligence and friendliness of dolphins.

The third main point fails to develop the central idea. It has nothing to do with lessons learned from dolphins, so it should be dropped as a main point (although it might be useful as part of the introduction).

Restrict Each Main Point to a Single Idea

Each main point in a speech should focus on just one idea. The following example violates this rule.

Specific Purpose: To convince my listeners that country life is superior to city life.
Central Idea: Living in the country is preferable to living in the city.
Main Points: I. Country life provides more privacy than city life.
II. Country life involves less stress than city life.
III. Country life involves less pollution, and there is little crime.

The third main point covers two different ideas. The discussion of crime should be made into a separate point or perhaps used as supporting material for the second main point.

Use Parallel Language Whenever Possible

Parallel language means that you use the same grammatical forms throughout a sentence or paragraph. Read the following sentence aloud: "Joe enjoys hunting, fishing, and to camp." There is nothing wrong with the sentence grammatically, but it doesn't sound as pleasant to the ear as this version: "Joe enjoys hunting, fishing, and camping." Rather than the discord of -ing, -ing, plus "to," our ears prefer the rhythm of -ing, -ing, -ing, as in the second sentence.

Suppose that you started an outline with the following:

Specific Purpose: To persuade my audience to swim for exercise.
Central Idea: Swimming is an ideal exercise because it dissipates nervous tension, avoids injuries, and builds endurance.

Now decide which set of main points would be most effective.
First set:

I. You can work off a lot of nervous tension while swimming.
II. Muscle and bone injuries, common with other sports, are not a problem with swimming.
III. Swimming builds endurance.

Second set:

    I. Swimming dissipates nervous tension.
   II. Swimming avoids the muscle and bone injuries that are common with other sports.
  III. Swimming builds endurance.

The second set is preferable because it follows a parallel grammatical form throughout (the noun *swimming* followed by a verb). Parallel language is not only pleasant to hear; it also helps listeners absorb your points. This consistent arrangement may not be practical in every speech, but you should strive for parallelism whenever possible.

Organizing Main Points

Information is easier to understand if it is presented in a sensible pattern rather than in an illogical manner. If, for example, someone tells you how to bake bread, you would expect to be told what to do first, then second, then third. It would be hard to follow if the person started off with oven temperature, then backtracked to kneading the dough, then went back to sifting flour. Likewise in a speech, your main points should be organized in a logical, easy-to-follow pattern. Let us look at five of the most popular patterns speakers use.

Chronological Pattern

In the chronological pattern you arrange your main points in a *time* sequence—what occurs first, what occurs second, and so on. If, for example, you are describing a process, you can use this pattern to show how something is done step by step. Here is an illustration:

Specific Purpose: To tell my listeners how to revive a person who is in danger of drowning.
Central Idea: To revive a person who is in danger of drowning, you should follow three simple procedures.
Main Points: I. With the victim on his or her back, tilt the head backward so that the chin juts upward.
II. Give mouth-to-mouth resuscitation until the victim breathes regularly again.
III. Place the victim on his or her stomach with the head facing sideways.

The chronological pattern is a logical choice for a speech dealing with periods of time in history. If, for example, you were speaking on the history of immigration in the United States, you could divide your subject into time periods—seventeenth century, eighteenth century, nineteenth century, twentieth century.

If you were speaking on the life of a person, you might want to divide the person's life into time periods, as in the following example:

Specific Purpose: To inform my listeners of the heroic life and example of Helen Keller.

Central Idea: Helen Keller demonstrated the capacity of humans to live happily and creatively despite physical handicaps.

Main Points: I. At an early age Keller was plunged into blindness and deafness.
   II. A gifted teacher helped Keller develop her native intelligence and creativity.
   III. As an adult, Keller became known internationally as a writer, lecturer, and champion of social justice.

Spatial Pattern

In the spatial pattern, you organize items according to the way in which they relate to each other in *physical space*—top to bottom, left to right, north to south, inside to outside, and so on. If you were speaking on the solar system, for example, you could discuss the sun first, then move outward in space to Mercury, Venus, Earth, Mars, and so on. Here is an example in which the speaker divides a car into space-related sections:

Specific Purpose: To tell my audience how to inspect a used car before deciding whether to buy it.

Central Idea: If a person examines a used car carefully and critically, he or she can avoid buying a "lemon,"

Main Points: I. Inspect the condition of the body of the car.
   II. Inspect the condition of the motor.
   III. Inspect the condition of the interior.

Another example of this pattern goes from bottom to top:

Specific Purpose: To describe to my audience the construction of the Leaning Tower of Pisa.

Central Idea: The Leaning Tower of Pisa was crooked from the beginning, but it still stands after 800 years.

Main Points: I. The foundation and first story of the tower went crooked when the land settled soon after construction began in 1174.
   II. The upper stories were designed with short pillars on the north side to compensate for the tilt.
   III. The bell tower on top was built at an angle to further compensate.

Causal Pattern

In some speeches, you are concerned with why something happens or has happened—a cause-and-effect relationship. For example, some people refuse to ride in elevators because they have an inordinate fear of enclosed spaces. Their claustrophobia is the *cause,* and their refusal to ride in elevators is the *effect.* Here is a sample of a cause-and-effect pattern for a speech:

A college professor discusses a point in economics. One important pattern for organizing material is the causal pattern, showing how causes lead to effects. *(Susan Lapides/Design Conceptions)*

Specific Purpose: To inform my audience of how Americans are responding to the bombardment of telephone calls by businesses, charities, and politicians.

Central Idea: Unwanted telephone solicitations by businesses, charities, and politicians are forcing many Americans to have unlisted telephone numbers.

Main Points:

(cause) I. More and more businesses, charities, and politicians are using the telephone to solicit the public.

(effect) II. A growing number of Americans are having the phone company change their telephone numbers from listed to unlisted.

Sometimes it is more effective to start with the effects and then analyze the causes, as in this case:

Specific Purpose: To explain to my listeners why people get headaches.

Central Idea: Most headaches are caused by tension, psychological frustrations and conflicts, excessive alcohol consumption, or too much caffeine.

Main Points:
   (effects) I. Severe headaches create physical and psychological problems.
             A. They can make you short-tempered and irritable.
             B. They can keep you from sleeping.
             C. They can prevent you from thinking clearly.
   (causes) II. Headaches are caused by a variety of things.
             A. A buildup of tension is a primary cause of headaches.
             B. Psychological frustrations and conflicts can lead to headaches.
             C. Excessive alcohol consumption can create headaches.
             D. Too much caffeine from coffee, tea, and soft drinks can cause headaches.

In the above pattern, putting the effects first is good strategy because the listeners can nod in agreement and say to themselves, "Yes, that's exactly what headaches do." This puts them in the proper frame of mind to hear the causes. Their unspoken response will probably be something like, "Now tell me what causes headaches so I'll know how to avoid them."

Problem-Solution Pattern

A popular pattern in persuasive speeches divides the speech into two main parts: a statement of a problem and the solution. Here is an example:

Specific Purpose: To persuade my listeners to support mandatory safety devices in all new automobiles.
Central Idea: Thousands of lives could be saved each year if all new cars sold in the United States were required to meet basic safety standards.
Main Points:
   (problem) I. Thousands of people are killed on American highways each year because of inadequate safety standards in cars.
   (solution) II. Legislation should be passed requiring all cars sold in this country to meet basic safety standards.

This pattern has the advantage of simplicity. You convince the listeners that a particular problem exists, and then you tell them how it can be solved. Here is another example:

Specific Purpose: To convince my listeners that prison overcrowding can be solved by not incarcerating nonviolent offenders such as embezzlers.
Central Idea: Overcrowded conditions in prison can be eliminated if we require nonviolent offenders, such as embezzlers, to perform community service in their hometowns rather than spend time in prison.

Main Points:
(problem) I. Most American prisons are dangerously overcrowded.
(solution) II. Nonviolent offenders such as embezzlers can be required to perform community service in their hometowns rather than spend time in prison.

Topical Pattern

In the topical pattern, you divide your central idea into components or categories, using logic and common sense as your guides. Thus, the federal government could be divided into three branches: executive, legislative, and judicial. You can divide according to whatever emphasis you wish to give; for example, politics could be divided into international, national, state, and local; or it could be divided according to the people who practice it: liberals, moderates, and conservatives. Here is an example of the topical pattern:

Specific Purpose: To inform my audience of the two kinds of sleep that all persons experience.
Central Idea: The two kinds of sleep that all persons experience at alternating times during the night are NREM (non-rapid-eye-movement) sleep and REM (rapid-eye-movement) sleep.
Main Points: I. NREM (non-rapid-eye-movement) sleep is the period in which a person does very little dreaming.
II. REM (rapid-eye-movement) sleep is the period in which a person usually dreams.

Another way of subdividing an idea is to show reasons for it, as in the following example:

Specific Purpose: To persuade my listeners to support the 55-mile-per-hour speed limit on interstate highways.
Central Idea: The 55-miles-per-hour speed limit should be maintained and enforced on America's interstate highways.
Main Points: I. The 55-miles-per-hour speed limit saves thousands of lives each year.
II. The 55-miles-per-hour speed limit conserves fuel.

When you use the topical pattern, you can arrange your main points in whatever order suits the purpose of your speech. In the persuasive speech above, the speaker chose to use the stronger of the two points—that the 55-miles-per-hour limit saves lives—at the beginning of the speech. In some speeches, on the other hand, you may want to put your least important points first and build up to your most important points. Here is such a case:

Specific Purpose: To persuade my listeners to buy a personal computer.
Central Idea: The personal computer offers the college student opportunities to have fun, keep financial records, and prepare school assignments.

Main Points: I. With a personal computer, a student can play mind-expanding games.
II. With a personal computer, a student can keep track of financial records quickly and efficiently.
III. With a personal computer, a student can prepare school assignments and papers with a huge savings of time and energy.

A note of caution: Some students make the mistake of thinking that the topical pattern is a formless bag into which anything can be dumped. Though you have a great deal of liberty to organize the points in whatever order you choose, you still must apply logic—for example, arranging points from least important to most important, or placing material under three major subdivisions.

Selecting Support Materials

In the preceding sections, we have concentrated on main points, but main points by themselves are not enough for the body of a speech. We also need support materials to develop and amplify our main points. These supports can be either verbal (as discussed in Chapter 7) or visual (as discussed in Chapter 8).

To see how support materials can be developed for main points, let us take a look at an outline by student Yolanda DeLeon:

General Purpose: To persuade.
Specific Purpose: To persuade my listeners to volunteer their time to tutor illiterate adults.
Central Idea: Illiteracy in America is widespread and harmful, but it can be eliminated if enough volunteers step forward to help.
Main Points: I. Illiteracy is a major social problem in America.
II. Illiterates can learn to read and write if given proper instruction by volunteer tutors.

Using the problem-solution pattern, Yolanda needs explanation and elaboration for both her first main point (*problem*) and her second main point (*solution*):

Commentary

The speaker uses *statistics* from prestigious sources to prove that illiteracy is a serious problem.

I. Illiteracy is a major social problem in America.
   A. Illiteracy is widespread.
      1. A U.S. Senate subcommittee estimates that 25 million American adults cannot read well enough to write a check, read a sign in a store window, or fill out a job application.
      2. The United States ranks forty-ninth in literacy out of the 158 member nations of the United Nations.
      3. The U.S. Navy found that 30 percent of its recruits were "a danger to themselves and to costly naval equipment" because they

Commentary

The speaker uses vivid *examples* to demonstrate the human cost of illiteracy.

Statistics are used to show the price society pays for this problem.

Testimony from a leading authority lends credibility to the speaker's contention.
These *statistics* are impressive evidence that adults can be taught.
The speaker uses more *testimony* from an authority on the subject.
A *narrative* provides a bright picture of the prospects for eliminating illiteracy.

couldn't read or understand written instructions.
B. Illiteracy hurts individuals and society in general.
   1. A child was hospitalized in Syracuse, New York, after her illiterate mother mistook a pink dishwashing liquid for medicine.
   2. A worker in Chicago killed a herd of cattle because he couldn't read the word "poison" on a bag that he thought was feed.
   3. A Senate subcommittee estimated the social cost of illiteracy to be $225 billion a year in welfare checks, lost taxes, and crime costs.
   4. One-half of all prison inmates are illiterate.
II. Illiterates can learn to read and write if given proper instruction by volunteer tutors.
A. Yale University Professor Jonathan Kozol, author of *Illiterate America* and a leading expert on the problem, says that illiterate adults are capable of learning to read and write, if they are given proper instruction.
B. The leading literacy organization, Laubach Literacy, teaches 60,000 adults to read and write each year.
C. Peter Waite, Laubach's national director, says that thousands of volunteer tutors are needed in each of the fifty states.
D. Lewis Meade was 43 years old when he learned how to read and write.
   1. He had masked his illiteracy in the Army by pretending to be unable to read "without my glasses."
   2. He had masked his illiteracy while employed as a salesman in a paint store by asking customers to point to the color they wanted on a paint chart, then using the corresponding number to fetch the correct can of paint.
   3. He heard a commercial for Laubach Literacy on the radio and went to an adult basic education course for training.
   4. Within 6 months he was able to read his favorite book—the Bible.

If possible, you should distribute your supporting materials evenly. In other words, don't put all your support under point I and leave nothing to bolster point II. This does not mean, however, that you should mechanically place the same number of supporting points under every main point. In some speeches, it may turn out that you need five supports for one point and only two for another. You have to consider *quality* as well as *quantity.* One powerful anecdote may be all that is required to illustrate one point, whereas five minor supports might be needed for another point.

When you are trying to decide how many supporting points to place underneath a main point, use this rule of thumb: have enough supporting points to adequately explain or bolster the main point, but not so many that you become tedious and repetitious.

Supplying Transitions

Transitions are words, phrases, or sentences that show logical connections between ideas or thoughts. They help the listeners stay with you as you move from one part of your speech to the next. To get an idea of how transitions work, take a look at the following paragraphs and decide which is superior:

1. Mayor Smythe has been involved in graft for years. He is a capable administrator. I intend to vote for him.
2. Mayor Smythe has been involved in graft for years. Nevertheless, he is a capable administrator, so I intend to vote for him.

The second paragraph is obviously superior. The reason is that it contains two transitional words: *nevertheless* and *so.*

In a speech, transitions clarify the relationship between your ideas, thereby making them easy to comprehend. They serve as signals to help the listeners follow your train of thought. Here are just some of the many transitional words or phrases in the English language:

☐ To signal addition: *and, also, besides, furthermore, moreover, in addition*
☐ To signal time: *soon, then, later, afterward, meanwhile*
☐ To signal contrast: *however, but, yet, nevertheless, instead, meanwhile, although*
☐ To signal examples: *for example, to illustrate, for instance*
☐ To signal conclusions: *in summary, therefore, consequently, as a result*
☐ To signal concession: *although it is true that, of course, granted*

In public speaking, there are some special types of transitions that can be employed to help your listener follow your remarks. Let us look at four of them:

Bridges

In crossing a bridge, a person goes from one piece of land to another. In giving a speech, the speaker can build "bridges" to tell the listeners of the terrain they are leaving behind and the terrain they are about to enter. It is a way of saying, "I've finished thought A; now I'm going to thought B."

Imagine that you had the following main points in an outline on professional wrestling:

    I. The *bad guys* are the villains of professional wrestling.
    II. The *good guys* are heroes who triumph over hatred, trickery, and diabolical enemies.

How can you go from point I to point II? You could simply finish with point I and begin Point II, but that would be too abrupt. It would fail to give the listeners time to change mental gears. One way to bridge the two points is with a sentence like this: "Well, that's all I have to say about the bad guys; let me tell you about the good guys." Such a sentence is better than no transition at all, but it is clumsy and artificial. A smoother way to make a bridge is to refer back to the bad guys at the same time you are pointing forward to the good guys. Here is an example:

> If you think that the bad guys are absurd exaggerations, you are right, of course, but what about their opponents, the good guys? Are they exaggerated to the same degree of absurdity?

This is a successful bridge because it smoothly and gracefully takes your listeners from point I to point II. It also has the virtue of stimulating their curiosity about the good guys.

Let us examine one more case: Assume that you are preparing a speech on child abuse. The first part of the speech deals with a description of the problem, and the second part deals with solutions. Here is one way to bridge the two parts:

> These examples [just given by the speaker] show that child abuse occurs in all social and economic levels of our society, but is the situation hopeless? Are there any possible solutions?

Now the audience is ready to hear the solutions.

Internal Summaries

At the end of a baseball game, announcers always give a summary of the game. But during the game itself, they occasionally give a summary of what has taken place up to the present moment ("We're in the middle of the fifth inning; Detroit is leading Milwaukee 4 to 3 on a grand-slam homer by . . . ."). Though this is primarily designed for the viewers who have tuned in late, it is also appreciated by the fans who have been watching the entire game because it gives them a feeling of security and confidence—a sense of knowing the "main facts." You can achieve the same effect in a speech. When you finish an important point or group of points, you may want to spend a few moments summarizing your ideas so that they are clear and understandable. This device, called an *internal summary,* is especially helpful if you have been discussing ideas that are complicated or abstract. An internal summary can be combined with a bridge to make an excellent transition, as follows:

> (*Internal summary*): So far we've seen that cocaine can kill a person if it is injected intravenously or if it is smoked as freebase. (*bridge*): But are these the only ways in which cocaine can be deadly? How about the person who sniffs, or "snorts," cocaine?

Here is another example:

(Internal summary): By now I hope I've convinced you that all animal bites should be reported to a doctor or health official immediately because of the possibility of rabies. *(bridge)*: While you're waiting for an ambulance or for an examination by a doctor, there is one other important thing you should do.

Signposts

Just as signposts on a road tell motorists their location, signposts in a speech tell listeners where they are or where they are headed. If you gave a speech on how to treat a cold, you could say, "Here are three things you should do the next time you catch a cold." Then the audience would find it easy to follow your points if you said, "First, you should . . . . Second, you should . . . . Third, you should . . . ." Using these signposts is much more effective than linking your points by saying, "Also . . ." or "Another point is . . . ."

Another way to enumerate points is to use repetition of phrases, as in this case:

America is great for three reasons:
America is great because . . .
America is great because . . .
America is great because . . .

Spotlights

Spotlights are transitional devices that alert the listeners that something important will soon appear. Here are some examples:

Now we come to the most important thing I have to tell you. What I'm going to explain now will help you understand the rest of the speech.

Spotlights can build up anticipation and excitement: "And now I come to an idea that can mean extra money in your pocket: . . . ." or "If you want to feel healthier and happier, listen to the advice of Dr. Jonas Knudsen: . . . ."

When you choose transitional devices, remember that your listeners are totally unfamiliar with your speech, so try to put yourself in their place at each juncture. Ask yourself, "How can I lead the listener from one point to another in a way that is logical and smooth?"

Summary

When you organize your speech, deal with the body first, leaving the introduction and conclusion for later. The best way to organize the body is to devise two or three (or sometimes four) main points based on your central idea. Arrange the main points in a logical pattern, such as chronological, spatial, causal, problem-solution, or topical.

Next, select support materials (as discussed in Chapter 7) to back up the main points, and then supply transitions to help the listeners stay with you as you move from one part of your speech to the next. Common types of transitions are bridges, internal summaries, signposts, and spotlights.

Review Questions

1. How many main points should you have in a speech?
2. How many ideas should be represented in each main point?
3. Which pattern of organization would be best-suited for a speech on the solar system?
4. Why are transitions important in a speech?

Tips FOR YOUR CAREER

Tip 9: Anticipate Audience Reactions

Will your audience understand and believe your main points? You can test your material in advance by using one or both of these techniques:

1. During your preparation, as you create each main point, think of the typical people who will be in your audience and ask yourself, "How will they react to this?" Then shape your material accordingly. If your imaginary listeners say, "How do you know this is true?" give the name and credentials of the expert from whom you derived your material. If they ask, "What do you mean by that?" give them an explanation. If they say, "Who cares?" show them the importance of your subject.[4]

2. Try out your material on friends or relatives. Victoria Vance, a hospital nutritionist who gives talks in her community on diet and nutrition, tests her ideas on her husband and teenage children at the dinner table. "I tell them, 'I'm going to give a speech at a high school next week. Here's what I plan to say.' Then I casually tell them the main points of my speech. Occasionally one of the kids will break in with something like, 'But, Mom, are you saying that *all* fast food is bad for you?' That tells me the places in the speech where I need to add some more explanations or examples."

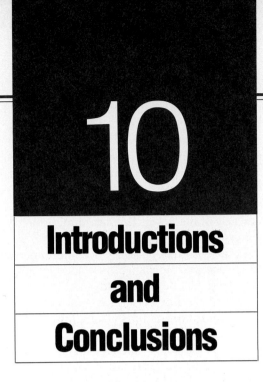

10
Introductions
and
Conclusions

Introductions

Conclusions

Sample Introduction and Conclusion

In a speech to a church group, Navy Commander William H. Withrow, a former combat pilot, began with a BB and a metal washtub. He held up the BB and told his audience to listen as he dropped it into the tub.

That little clink, he told his audience, represented "the TNT [explosive] equivalent of every shot fired in World War II, every artillery round, every conventional bomb, even the two atom bombs that were dropped on Japan."[1]

Then the commander pulled out a mason jar that was filled with BBs—6000 of them, he told the audience. Reminding the audience that each BB represented the total of all explosions in World War II, he poured the 6000 BBs noisily into the wash tub, creating a metallic roar. That sound represented "the combined nuclear arsenals of the Soviet Union and the United States [at the present time]—a terrifying overkill."[2]

Having captured the audience's attention and interest, Withrow gave an impassioned speech on the dangers of an uncontrolled arms race between the superpowers, and then he closed with an eloquent plea for the listeners to support arms reductions. Whether or not the audience agreed with Withrow, his speech demonstrated the power of a fascinating introduction and a forceful conclusion.

Some speakers give little thought to what they are going to say at the beginning of a speech and at the end. Some wait until the actual hour of delivery, preferring to let the mood of the moment determine what they will say. But these speakers are making a big mistake. A faltering or dull introduction can cause the audience to lose interest in both speaker and speech. A conclusion that is weak or clumsy can leave the audience with a bad opinion of what otherwise might have been a good speech.

Since both introduction and conclusion are crucial to the success of any speech, you should spend as much care and thought in devising them as you would in planning the body of the speech.

Introductions

The introduction to your speech has two parts: *attention material,* to get your audience's attention and interest, and *orienting material,* which prepares your audience intellectually and psychologically for the body of the speech. Here is a sample, from the beginning of a speech by Jennifer Sheldon:

Attention Material
Sheldon grabs the attention and interest of her listeners with two intriguing narratives.

I. Distraught over losing thousands of dollars on the stock market, a New York stockbroker went out one day with his American Express card and bought a gold Rolex watch costing $5,000, a new video and sound system costing $20,000, and a set of golf clubs costing $7,000. The problem was: he lacked enough money to pay for the credit card charges. In Arizona, a secretary spent $36,000 in one afternoon, using her credit card to buy shoes, dresses, and furniture. She had the same problem as the stockbroker: not enough money to cover her purchases. In both cases, the merchandise had to be returned.

Orienting Material
The speaker prepares her audience for the body of her speech by giving background information, by revealing the central idea of the speech, and by telling the listeners what she will cover.

II. You have heard of alcoholism and compulsive gambling. Now psychologists are taking note of a new addiction—people who are unable to control their desire to go on wild shopping sprees. They are called shopaholics because their compulsive shopping disrupts their personal, business, and family lives, as well as plunging them into a deep hole of debt. The credit card is to them what the bottle is to an alcoholic, according to Janet Damon, a New York City psychotherapist who has written a book called *Shopaholics*. From reading her book and several magazine articles, I believe that people go on shopping binges as a way of escaping from an emotional problem— whether it be depression, loneliness, or low self-esteem—so the best way for them to "recover" is to eliminate the problem or learn to cope with it constructively. To show you why I have come to this conclusion, I'd like to give you some details on who shopaholics are, why they go on binges, and what can be done to help them.

In the rest of her speech, Sheldon developed her central idea, giving examples and psychologists' insights.

Let's look at some techniques for gaining attention and interest (attention material), and then how to orient your audience (orienting material).

Gain Attention and Interest

If you were sitting in an audience, would you want to listen to a speech that began with this statement: "I'd like to talk to you today about one of our state's most important crops"?

Crops? Who besides farmers and agricultural students would want to hear about corn or wheat or barley? If you are like most people, you would say to yourself, "I don't want to hear about crops," and your mind would drift to something more interesting, such as the party you are planning to attend next weekend.

Now imagine that you were sitting in the audience when Rex Kent, a student speaker, gave his speech on a crop. Rex began by raising a clenched fist and saying, "I'm holding in my hand something which no human being has ever seen before. And in a few moments, it will be transformed so that no human being will ever see it again." After pausing dramatically, he opened his hand and revealed a peanut in a shell. He cracked open the shell, ate the peanut, and said, "The lowly peanut may seem like an insignificant munchie to you, but it has hundreds of uses that most of you have never heard about. Did you know that peanuts are used to make explosives? And to make shampoos and shaving creams? Today I'd like to tell you about some of these amazing products."

The listeners were hooked. How could they possibly turn their attention away after such an interesting, dynamic beginning? Rex's technique was to use attention material as a lure, just as a fisher dangles bait in front of a fish.

A lure needs to be dangled in front of listeners because of an unfortunate fact: Audiences do not automatically give every speaker their full, undivided, respectful attention. As you begin a speech, you may find that some listeners are engaged in whispered conversations with their neighbors (and they do not necessarily stop in midsentence when you start speaking); some are looking at you, but their minds are far away, floating in a daydream or enmeshed in a personal problem; some are shifting in their seats to get comfortable; others are thinking about what the preceding speaker said, or looking about the room to see who they know, or trying to figure out when they should slip out if you talk too long. So your task is clear: grab their attention when you start talking.

But grabbing their attention is not enough: your introduction must also *keep* their attention, so that they will want to hear your entire speech. Your introduction must deprive them of any possible excuse to sink back into their private thoughts and daydreams. If you simply say, "I'm going to talk about peanuts," you leave it up to the listeners to decide whether they want to listen to the rest of the speech. Do not give them a choice! Devise attention material that is so interesting that it is impossible for anyone *not* to listen to the entire speech.

Let us examine some common attention getters. Keep in mind that sometimes these can be combined.

Relating a Story

Telling a story is one of the most effective ways to begin a speech because people love to listen to narrative accounts. If you start a speech by saying—"While fishing early one summer morning, I heard a rustle in the brush behind me and then an awful buzzing sound; I knew instantly that it must be a rattlesnake"—who could resist listening to you?

Whatever story you tell must be relevant to your central idea and it must provide an easy and natural entry into the rest of your speech. Such an entry was provided by law enforcement student Kerrie Lee's attention material:

> One August morning in 1953, a stranger accosted Eric Gronwell, manager of a branch of Franklin National Bank. Holding a gun, the stranger ordered Gronwell to drive to the bank and open it as he always did. The gunman was very nervous; he adjusted the rear-view mirror so that he could hide in the back seat and still see whether Gronwell's car was being followed. When they arrived at the bank, Gronwell was forced to hand over two hundred thousand dollars from the bank's vault. Then the gunman made a quick, successful getaway. He disappeared from sight.
>
> One year later, however, police arrested George Patrick McKinney and

charged him with bank robbery. The robbery had been well planned and executed, but McKinney left behind one small piece of evidence. What was this evidence?

In her orienting material, the speaker revealed that McKinney left a single thumbprint on the rear-view mirror as he adjusted it. Then she told the audience that her speech would explain how fingerprinting is used to locate criminals and missing persons.

One kind of story you can use is the hypothetical illustration, as demonstrated by Jerome David Smith, an attorney, who said in a speech:

> One day you become angry over the nasty pollution of a river near your home, so you sit down and write a letter to the editor of your local newspaper. The letter is a scathing attack on a corporation that you believe is responsible for ruining the river. Two weeks later, you get a letter from the corporation's attorney informing you that you are being sued for $100,000 for "harming the reputation, prestige, and credibility of the corporation." Does this sound incredible? Can this happen in a country that celebrates freedom of speech? Yes, it can happen. . . .

In the rest of his speech, he explained how lawsuits have become a popular way for companies and public officials to retaliate against criticism.

Asking a Question

Asking a question can be an effective way to intrigue your listeners and encourage them to think about your subject matter as you discuss it. There are two kinds of questions that you can use as attention material: rhetorical and overt-response.

With a *rhetorical* question, you do not want or expect the listeners to answer overtly by raising their hands or answering out loud. Instead, you want to trigger an inner curiosity. For example:

> With powerful radio signals being beamed into outer space at this very moment, is there any realistic chance that during our lifetime we human beings will establish radio contact with other civilizations in the universe?

Such a question not only catches the attention of the listeners, but it also makes them want to hear more. It entices them into listening to your speech for the answer to the question.

With an *overt-response* question, you want the audience to reply by raising their hands or answering out loud. Here is an example:

> Dave Rodriguez, a student speaker, began his speech by asking, "Other than swimming, what is the most dangerous sport or recreational activity in America, considering the number of people who lose their lives? Would anyone like to take a guess?
> The listeners were intrigued. "Football?" asked one student.
> "No, its not football."

"Mountain climbing?" asked another person.

"No, it's not mountain climbing."

"Hang gliding?" asked a third student.

"No, it's not hang gliding. Other than swimming, the most dangerous outdoor recreational activity in America is . . . bicycling. Last year, 1200 Americans were killed while riding their bicycles."

Thus, Dave effectively launched his speech on the importance of bicycle safety. Note that he did not drag out the suspense too long. If listeners are forced to guess and guess and guess until the right answer is found, they might become exasperated, wishing that the speaker would get to the point.

Never ask embarrassing or personal questions such as, "How many of you have ever tried cocaine?" or "How many of you use an underarm deodorant every day?" An audience would rightfully resent such questions as intrusions into their private lives.

Never divide your audience into opposing camps by asking "loaded" questions like this: "How many of you are smart enough to realize that capital punishment is an absolute necessity in a society based on law and order?" By phrasing your question in this way, you insult those who disagree with you.

With some overt-response questions, you can try to get every member of the audience to participate, but this can be very risky, especially if you poll the audience in this way: "How many of you favor the death penalty? Raise your hands. Okay . . . now, how many of you are opposed to the death penalty? Okay, thanks . . . how many of you are undecided or unsure?" What if three people raised their hands for the first question, five for the second question, ten for the third, while the remaining sixty-seven people in the audience refused to cooperate? This can happen, and often does, much to the embarrassment of the speaker. Sometimes audiences are in a passive or even grumpy mood; this is especially true with "captive" audiences—that is, audiences that are required (at work or at school) to listen to a speech. In such a case, refrain from asking questions that require the participation of the entire audience.

Make sure the audience is clear on whether you are asking a rhetorical question or an overt-response question. If you ask, "How long will Americans continue to tolerate shoddy products?" the audience knows you are not expecting someone to answer, "Five years." It is clearly a rhetorical question. But suppose you ask a question like this: "How many of you have ever gone swimming in the ocean?" The listeners might be confused about whether you want them to raise their hands. Make it clear. If you want a show of hands, say so at the beginning: "I'd like to see a show of hands, please: How many of you have ever gone swimming in the ocean?" Alerting them in advance not only helps them know what you want, but also makes them pay special attention to the question, since they know you are expecting them to respond.

Making a Startling Statement

An opening remark that shocks or surprises the listeners can certainly get their attention. Rhonda Ercolano, an attorney for a corporation, began a speech in the following way:

> Today each of you will be robbed of ten dollars. Tomorrow you will be robbed again of ten dollars. The next day, another ten dollars. In fact you will be robbed of ten dollars every day this year.

Then Ercolano explained:

> The robber will not be holding a gun, wearing a mask, and emerging from some dark alley. No, this robber will be well-dressed and well-to-do and possibly very polite. I am talking about so-called white-collar criminals, who steal billions from corporations and consumers alike, and plunder our national treasury through their tax frauds and evasions. The director of the FBI estimates that white-collar crime costs the average American about ten dollars per day in higher prices and taxes.

Ercolano used the technique of transforming statistics into a provocative statement. Here is another example of the technique: you could take the fact that 25 percent of all Americans will be afflicted by cancer, and restate it in terms that can shock an audience.

> There are forty of you sitting out there in the audience. According to medical statistics, ten of you will someday be afflicted by one of the most dreaded of all diseases—cancer.

Such an opener is certain to draw your listeners in.

Citing a Quotation

Quotations can provide a lively beginning for a speech. In a speech urging the audience to read good literature, librarian Mary Channing Russell began by saying:

> The semanticist and former U.S. Senator S.I. Hayakawa once said: "In a very real sense, people who have read good literature have lived more than people who cannot or will not read. . . . It is not true that we have only one life to live; if we can read, we can live as many more lives and as many kinds of lives as we wish." Let us look at what good literature is, and how we can use literature to add those extra lives to our time here on earth.

Quotations usually work best when they are short. Do not have a quotation that is so long that listeners lose track of where the quotation ends and your remarks begin. The best way to indicate that you have finished quoting is to pause at the end of the quotation. The pause acts as an oral "punctuation" device, signaling the end of one thought and the beginning of another.

I do not recommend beginning with the actual quotation itself. Consider the following:

> *Poor:* "Science has promised us truth. It has never promised us either peace or happiness." These words, by French psychologist Gustave Le Bon, offer a valuable insight into the nature of science.

> *Better:* A French psychologist named Gustave Le Bon once made an inter-
> esting observation about science. He said, "Science has promised us
> truth. It has never promised us either peace or happiness."

While the first version is better for a written composition, the second is better for a speech because the listeners need time to tune out distracting thoughts and to tune in to you. If they fail to pick up the name of the French psychologist, no harm has been done; what you want them to absorb is the quotation.

If a quotation is too concise, it may go by so fast that the audience does not have a chance to absorb it. In such cases, it is a good idea to repeat it, as in this example:

> Bertrand Russell once said, "The opposite of love is not hate, but indiffer-
> ence." Think about that for a moment: "The opposite of love is not hate, but
> indifference."

In print, the repetition looks silly, but in a speech the audience is grateful for the instant replay. It allows time for the idea to sink in.

Arousing Curiosity

An effective attention getter is one that piques the curiosity of the audience. In a speech on common misconceptions about snakes and snakebites, student speaker Lynn Baker began by saying:

> When a person gets bit by a poisonous snake, some people think that the
> best thing to use is a tourniquet to tie around the injured limb, but they're
> wrong. Some people think the best thing to use is a knife to make an incision,
> but they're wrong. Some people think the best thing to use is a suction device
> to suck out the venom, but they're wrong. All of these devices have serious
> medical drawbacks, as I shall explain in a moment. So, what is the best thing
> to use?

Having aroused the curiosity of her listeners, Lynn picked up her purse; as she reached inside, she said:

> The best thing to have for a snakebite is a little item that all of you carry in
> your pocket or your purse. Here it is.

With a flourish, she displayed her car keys. Then she went on to explain that driving a snakebite victim to a hospital is more likely to save the person's life than giving first aid. At the hospital, the victim can be given an injection of antivenin, which she said is the best life-saving method of all.

Providing a Visual Aid or Demonstration

Any of the visual aids we discussed in Chapter 8 could be used to introduce a speech, but you must be sure that while the aids get the audience's attention, they also are relevant to the main points of your speech. One student showed slides of sunbathers on a beach to begin a talk on sharks. Though there was a logical link (sometimes sunbathers who go into the water must worry about sharks), the connection was too weak to justify using these particular slides. In a case like this, it would be better to show a slide of a ferocious shark while describing a shark attack.

A demonstration can make an effective opener. Working with a friend, one student gave a demonstration of how to fight off an attacker, and then talked on martial arts. If you want to give a demonstration, you should get permission from your instructor beforehand. One note of caution: never do anything that might upset the listeners. Holding a revolver and firing a blank to start off a speech on gun control or suicide would upset some people and put them out of a receptive mood.

Giving an Incentive to Listen

At the beginning of a speech, many listeners have an attitude that can be summed up in these two questions: "What's in it for me? Why should I pay attention to this speech?" Such people need to be given an incentive to listen to the entire speech. So, whenever possible, you should state explicitly why the listeners will benefit by hearing you out. It is not enough to simply say, "My speech is very important." You must *show* them how your topic relates to their personal lives and their own best interests. If, for example, you were giving a talk on cardiopulmonary resuscitation (CPR), you could say, "Everyone in this room may someday have a friend or loved one collapse from a heart attack right in front of your eyes.

An introduction should get your listeners' attention and interest, and make them want to hear the rest of your speech. *(John Maher/EKM-Nepenthe)*

If you know CPR, you might be able to save that person's life." Now each person in the audience sees clearly that your speech is important to his or her personal life.

Be careful about promising too much. Do not say, "How would you like to live in perfect happiness for the rest of your life?" and then discuss the joys of the macrobiotic diet. Though you may be enthusiastic about such a diet, your listeners will distrust what you have to say because you have overstated your case.

If you know some listeners have probably heard most of your speech material before, you can try to use incentives especially designed for them. Professional speaker Joel Weldon gave a talk to over 700 business and industrial trainers at a national convention of the American Society for Training and Development. His speech consisted of tips on how to train people. In his introduction, he said:

> I know some of you are pros who have been involved in training for twenty years. When you hear some of these ideas, you're going to say, "I've heard all this before." I'm sure you have. But as you say that to yourself, ask yourself these two questions: Am I using this idea? And how can I improve it?[3]

Weldon's technique was effective because he acknowledged the presence and the experiences of the "pros," and then he challenged them to give the "old" ideas a fresh look. The incentive he dangled in front of them was the possibility of doing an even better job of training than they had done in the past.

Orient the Audience

Once you have snared the interest of your listeners by means of the attention material, you should go into the second part of your introduction, the *orienting material,* which gives an orientation—a clear sense of what your speech is about, and any other information that the audience might need in order to understand and absorb your ideas. The orienting material is a road map that makes it easy for the listeners to stay with you on the journey of your speech and not get lost and confused.

The orienting material does more than prepare the listeners intellectually for your speech; it also prepares them psychologically. It reassures them that you are well-prepared, purposeful, and considerate of their needs and interests. It shows them you are someone they can trust.

The three most common ways of orienting the audience are: (1) preview the body of the speech, (2) give background information, and (3) establish credibility.

Previewing the Body of the Speech

Have you ever listened to a speech or a lecture and realized afterward that you had listened with the "wrong set of ears"—that is, your mental apparatus had been attuned to evaluating one thing when it should have been attuned to evaluating something else? I once heard a man speak on wood stoves. He plunged right into his speech, giving details about various wood stoves. Sitting out in the audience, I guessed that he was trying to show the advantages of wood as a heating source. I geared my mind to pick out those advantages. Halfway through the speech, however, I realized that I had guessed wrong. His real subject was safety features of wood stoves. Unfortunately I had not paid close enough attention to the safety features—I had listened with the wrong set of ears—so I failed to absorb some of his points. It was too late to retrieve the information, of course; in a speech, there is no instant replay.

To help your listeners use the "right set of ears," give them a preview of the body of the speech. In the example just cited, the speaker should have said something like this as orienting material: "Today I want to show you that wood stoves can be used in a safe way, so that your house doesn't catch fire. I plan to give you three tips to follow. . . ." With such a preview, all the listeners would have known what to listen for.

Your instructor may have specific requirements for what you must put in your preview. Unless he or she advises you otherwise, I recommend that you include your central idea and/or main points.

1. *State the central idea*. Your audience can listen intelligently to your speech if you stress your central idea in the orienting material. For example, "Acid rain is killing all the trees on our highest peaks in the East. Today I'd like to give you evidence to back up my claim."

2. *State the main points.* In most speeches listeners appreciate being given a brief preview of your main points. For example, student speaker Barbara LeBlanc said, "I believe that passive solar heating should be used in every home. Today I'd like to show you two reasons why you should consider using passive solar: First, it's easy to adapt your house to passive solar. Second, the energy from passive solar is absolutely free. Let me explain what I'm talking about." By stating the main points, Barbara not only helped the audience listen intelligently but she also gave them an incentive to listen: she mentioned the possibility of saving money.

Giving a preview by stating the central idea and/or main points reassures the listeners that you are not going to ramble. In other words, you give the audience a message that says, loud and clear, "I'm well-prepared; I know exactly what I'm going to say; I'm not going to waste your time." This last "message" is important, because audiences like speakers who don't waste their time, and they resent speakers who do.

Giving Background Information

Part of your orienting material can be devoted to giving background information—definitions, explanations, and so on—to help your listeners understand your speech. For example in a classroom speech on hypochondriacs, Lucinda Howard used her orienting material to define the term:

Hypochondriacs are people who have a morbid preoccupation with disease. They usually think that they are ill in some way or another. I want to make clear that they are *not* malingering. *Malingerers* are people who fake illness; they know they're not really sick. Hypochondriacs, on the other hand, truly believe that they're ill.

Notice that Lucinda not only defined her term but she clarified her definition by contrasting hypochondriacs with malingerers to make sure that her audience did not confuse the two.

Sometimes it helps the audience if you explain the limitations of your speech. For example, assume that you are giving a speech on the notion that criminals should make restitution to their victims. If you are not careful, many people in your audience will reject your argument immediately by saying to themselves, "Restitution, baloney! How can a murderer make restitution to his victim?" So in your orienting material, you head off such objections by saying, "In this speech I will talk about criminals making restitution to their victims, but I'm only talking about nonviolent criminals such as swindlers, embezzlers, and bad-check writers. I'm not talking about rapists and murderers." By showing the boundaries of your subject, you increase the chances that the audience will listen with open minds.

Establishing Credibility

No one expects you to be the world's authority on your subject, but you can increase your audience's chances of accepting your ideas if you can give some credentials or reasons why you are qualified to speak on the subject. Here is how three student speakers established their credibility: In the orienting material of her speech on schizophrenia, Rachel Weintraub told of her experiences as a psychiatric assistant in a mental hospital. In the introduction of a speech arguing for better treatment of Native Americans, William Lone Wolf briefly described his childhood on a reservation. Before demonstrating the correct way to resuscitate a person who is in danger of drowning, Cynthia Cunningham related her experiences as a lifeguard. In all three of these cases, the students strengthened their speeches by establishing their credibility as part of the orienting material.

Do not be shy about giving your credentials or background; listeners appreciate information about your degree of interest and expertise. It helps them evaluate what you have to say. Be sure, however, to give this information in a way that is modest and tactful, rather than boastful and arrogant. Here are two ways of saying the same thing:

> *Poor:* "I lived on the Mexican border for ten years, so I know more about the illegal alien situation than anybody in this room."
> *Better:* "Before I moved here, I lived in a town on the Mexican border for ten years. I talked to a lot of illegal aliens and their employers during those years. I'd like to share some of the insights I gained from those conversations."

In the first example, the speaker would irritate the audience by the claims of superiority. The second example is preferable because the speaker is giving background experience in a way that is straightforward and inoffensive.

Sometimes you can enhance your credibility by explaining how you arrived at your central idea. Student speaker Jimmy Williams said:

> Do you think electroshock treatment for mental patients is really just a form of torture? I certainly did when I chose this topic. I intended to argue for the

abolition of shock treatments. I had seen the movie *One Flew over the Cuckoo's Nest,* and I thought electroshock was a sadistic form of punishment used by cruel people like Nurse Ratched in the movie. But after reading books and magazine articles on the subject and interviewing staff members at [a local psychiatric] hospital, I changed my mind. I now believe that electroshock treatment is humane, responsible, and very effective in relieving the agony of severely depressed patients.

By relating his change of mind, the speaker enhanced his credibility. He showed himself to be honest and open-minded, a person who could be trusted.

Guidelines for Introductions

Here are some points to keep in mind for introductions:

   1. *Do not prepare your introduction first.* When you prepare a speech, it usually works best to complete the body of the speech and *then* work on your introduction. Once you have developed your main points, you are in a stronger position to decide how to introduce them.

   2. *Make your introduction simple and easy to follow, but avoid making it too brief.* Your audience needs time to get into the groove of your speech. If the introduction is too short, it may go by too fast for the listeners to absorb. That is why effective joke tellers stretch out their introduction to give the listeners time to get "into" the joke. If the idea of stretching out an introduction sounds wrong to you, it is probably because you have been taught in English classes to write concisely. While it is a sin in English composition to stretch out an essay, it is a virtue to do so with a speech's introduction that might otherwise be too abrupt for an audience. A note of caution: do not let this tip cause you to go to the opposite extreme—being tedious and long-winded. Be brief, but not too brief. If you are unsure about whether you have achieved a happy medium, deliver your speech to relatives or friends and then ask them if they thought your introduction was too long or too short.

   3. *Make sure that your introduction has a direct and obvious tie-in with the body of the speech.* A common mistake is for speakers to give an introduction that has a weak or dubious link with the rest of the speech. This kind of introduction can be annoying and confusing to the listeners.

Conclusions

When movies are made, the producers spend a lot of time and energy on getting a "perfect" ending because they know that if the ending is unsatisfying, the viewers will tend to downplay the film as a whole. As with the movies, the ending of a speech can either add to or subtract from the audience's opinion of the entire speech. So it is worthwhile to spend a lot of time working on your conclusion.

In your conclusion, you should do three important things: (1) signal the end of a speech to satisfy the audience's psychological need for a sense of completion, (2) summarize the key ideas of the speech, and (3) reinforce the central idea with a clincher. Let us discuss these points in greater detail.

Signal the End

You should always give the audience some sort of advance signal that you are nearing the end of your speech. Do not come to an abrupt halt and then sit down. An abrupt ending jars the audience.

Imagine that you are listening to your favorite song on the radio and letting your mind float freely with the music. Then suddenly, before the song is finished, the disc jockey cuts in with a commercial or a news bulletin. You missed only the last 10 seconds of the song, but you feel annoyed. Why? Because most people need to experience a sense of completion. In listening to a speech, we have the same need for a sense of finality. We like to hear a conclusion that is psychologically satisfying, one that ties up all loose ends and wraps the speech into a nice, neat package. When a speaker ends a speech abruptly, we feel a vague dissatisfaction.

Just as a musical composition provides flourishes and other "signals" that indicate that the end is approaching,[4] a speech can give signals—both verbal and nonverbal.

Verbal signals. You can openly announce that you are coming to your conclusion by using such expressions as, "So, in conclusion, I'd like to say,..." "Let me end by saying,..." or "Let me remind you of the three major points I've been trying to explain today."

Nonverbal signals. Whether or not you use verbal signals, you can always give two nonverbal cues: (1) say your conclusion with a tone of dramatic finality, and (2) subtly intensify your facial expression and gestures. These cues should come naturally to you, since you have observed numerous speakers use them in your lifetime. If you feel unsure of yourself, practice your conclusion in front of a mirror or, better yet, in front of a friend (who can give you feedback). You can also say it into a tape recorder and listen to see if you have the appropriate tone of finality in your voice.

Summarize Key Ideas

Because listening is often a difficult mental task, some people in the audience might get drowsy or inattentive toward the end of your speech. When you signal to the listeners that you are about to finish, you do more than provide them with the pleasant anticipation of an ending; you also increase their alertness. If they know they can rest soon, they may summon the mental energy required to stay alert for a few more minutes. Like runners near the finish line, they can bring forth an extra burst of energy.

This mental alertness of your listeners gives you a good opportunity to drive home your message one more time. One of the best ways to do this is to summarize your key ideas. There is a formula for giving a speech that has been around for over 100 years. Sometimes it is attributed to a spellbinding country preacher, sometimes to a savvy Irish politician. The true originator will probably never be known, but the formula is worth heeding:

> Tell 'em what you're going to tell 'em.
> Tell 'em.
> Then tell 'em what you told 'em.

The first sentence refers to the introduction, the second to the body, and the third to a summary in the conclusion. The summary gives you a chance to restate the central idea and/or the main points.

If you are like a lot of people, you may say, "Why do I need to repeat my message? After all, in the body of my speech, I give the audience 5 minutes' worth of beautifully organized, forcefully delivered information. If I hit this stuff again in the conclusion, won't I be guilty of overkill?" No, research shows that a restatement of your main points will increase the likelihood that the listeners will remember them.[5]

A summary should be brief. Do not get bogged down in explaining each point a second time; do all your explaining in the body of the speech. The following summary, for example, succinctly boils down the body of a speech into a few brief sentences, reiterating how a person can prevent car theft:

> So remember, you can prevent your car from being stolen if you follow these guidelines: Always park in a well-lighted area. Always remove your key from the ignition. Always close all windows and lock all doors.

Listeners do not mind hearing this kind of information again; it helps them retain it. I recommend that you try to combine a summary with at least one other technique, as discussed in the following section. For example, the summary of guidelines on avoiding car theft could be followed by a brief story about a person whose car was stolen because he or she did not follow one of the guidelines.

Reinforce the Central Idea with a Clincher

In addition to providing a summary, you should try to end your speech with a clinching statement that reinforces the central idea—a statement that drives home the main theme of your entire speech. Edward L. Friedman explains the process:

> It has been said that the speaker drives home his talk in the same way that the carpenter drives a nail into a floor. He begins with the introduction, which generally consists of a few preliminary taps to get the speech started right. Then he gets into the body of the speech, which is like delivering one hammer blow after another to drive the nail into its proper place with carefully executed strokes. In conclusion the carpenter executes a powerful, clinching blow. The experienced speaker also endeavors in his conclusion to deal a powerful, clinching blow.[6]

Use a clincher that is memorable, that leaves a lasting impression with the listener. You can find clinchers by using some of the techniques mentioned earlier in this chapter for the introduction (such as a rhetorical question or a visual aid), or by using some of the following techniques.

Citing a Quotation

A good quotation can dramatize and reinforce a speaker's central idea. One of the best examples of this technique can be found in the closing words of Martin Luther King's famous "I Have a Dream" speech:

> When we let freedom ring, when we let it ring from every village and every hamlet, from every state and every city, we will be able to speed up that day when all of God's children, black men and white men, Jews and Gentiles, Protestants and Catholics, will be able to join hands and sing in the words of the old Negro spiritual, "Free at last! Free at last! Thank God almighty, we are free at last!"[7]

Eye contact is important at the end of your speech, so if you use a quotation, practice it so that you can say it while looking at the audience, with only occasional glances at your notes.

Issuing an Appeal or Challenge

In a persuasive speech, you can end by making an appeal or issuing a challenge to the audience. If you are trying to persuade the listeners to donate blood, you can end by saying:

> Next week the bloodmobile will be on campus. I call upon each of you to spend a few minutes donating your blood so that others may live.

If you are trying to convince the listeners that they should develop physical fitness, you can issue a challenge:

> Don't start exercising tomorrow or next week or next month. Start exercising *today.*

Giving an Illustration

An illustration is a popular way to reinforce the central idea of a speech. For example, Angela Di Napoli gave a classroom speech in which she urged her listeners to seek an evaluation of any old coins they possessed, and she concluded with a true story that illustrated her point:

> Several years ago a woman in New England was rummaging through a trunk in her attic when she came across a box full of old coins. She took them to a coin dealer and got an evaluation. All of the coins were worthless except one. It was a five-dollar gold piece issued in 1849. The coin dealer informed the woman of its present-day value—*five thousand dollars.* So if you have some old coins lying around your house, take them to a reputable coin dealer for an evaluation. You, too, may be the owner of a very valuable coin.

Referring to the Introduction

Using the conclusion to hearken back to something said in the introduction is an effective way to wrap up your speech. One way to do this is to answer a question asked at the beginning of a speech. Student speaker Daniel Hirata asked in his introduction, "Should we permit job discrimination on the basis of a person's weight?" In the conclusion, Daniel repeated the question and answered it: "Should we allow job discrimination against overweight people? From what I've said today, I hope you'll agree that the answer is 'no.' To deny a person a job simply because he or she is overweight is as wrong as to deny a person a job because of skin color or ethnic background."

Guidelines for Conclusions

1. *Do not drag out the ending.* Some speakers fail to prepare a conclusion in advance. When they reach what should be the end of their remarks, they cannot think of a graceful way to wrap things up, so they keep on talking. Other speakers signal the end of their speech (by saying something like, "So, in closing, let me say . . . ."), but then they drone on and on. This gives false hope to the listeners. When they see that the speaker is not keeping the promise, they feel deceived and become restless.

2. *Do not end weakly.* If you close with a statement such as, "I guess that's about all I've got to say," and your voice is nonchalant and unenthusiastic, you encourage your listeners to downgrade your entire speech. End with confidence.

3. *Do not end apologetically.* Earlier, we discussed the reasons why you should not apologize at the start of a speech. The same principles apply to the conclusion. There is no need to say: "That just about does it. I'm sorry I didn't have more time to prepare . . . ." or "That's it, folks. I guess I should have looked up more facts on . . . ." Apologies make you look incompetent. Besides, some people may not have noticed anything wrong with your speech or your delivery; you may have done better than you realized. So why apologize?

4. *Never bring in new main points.* It is okay to bring in fresh material for your conclusion; in fact, it is a good idea to do so, as long as the material does not constitute a new main point. For an illustration, look at the following conclusions, which are based on a speech about the advantages of swimming.

> *Poor:* So if you're looking for a good sport to take up for fun and health, remember that swimming dissipates your accumulated tension; it builds up your endurance, and it gives you a good workout without putting a strain on your muscles and joints. And, oh yes, another good reason for swimming: it can prevent you from developing back problems in old age.
> *Better:* So if you're looking for a good sport to take up for fun and health, remember that swimming dissipates your accumulated tension; it builds up your endurance, and it gives you a good workout without putting a strain on your muscles and joints. I go over to the Y for a 20-minute swim

3 days a week, and I always come out feeling healthy and invigorated. I wouldn't trade swimming for any other sport in the world.

The first conclusion is faulty because it lets a whole new point (the issue of back problems) slip in. Since this is the first the listeners have heard of the matter, it could confuse them. "Huh?" they may say to themselves. "Did I miss something that was said earlier?" Some listeners would expect you to elaborate on this new main point, but if you did, you would drag out your conclusion and spoil the sense of finality. The second conclusion has fresh material, but this material is not a new main point. It is merely a testimonial that underlines the message of the speech.

Sample Introduction and Conclusion

To see how the principles discussed in this chapter can be applied to a speech, let us examine how one speaker, student Thomas Vandenberg, developed an introduction and a conclusion for a speech on consumer fraud.[8]

Consumer Scams

Specific Purpose: To persuade my audience to investigate gimmicks and prizes before getting involved with a company.

Central Idea: To avoid being cheated, consumers should skeptically investigate companies that offer "free prizes."

Attention Material

The speaker begins with an interesting narrative that gains the listeners' attention and interest.

INTRODUCTION

I. A few months ago, I received a letter that informed me that I had won a free cruise to the Bahamas. Sounds wonderful, doesn't it? I fantasized something like *Love Boat* on TV, a beautiful ocean voyage with dancing and dining and, of course, shipboard romances in the moonlight. I was skeptical, however, because I had done nothing to win a prize. But I was also curious, so I called the phone number listed in the letter. I was told that yes, I definitely had won a cruise. The catch was that in order to receive my ticket, I would have to buy $450 worth of vitamins. But this would still be a wonderful deal, they told me, because the cruise itself was worth far more than $450. I said I would think about it. Next, I called the Better Business Bureau, and they gave me the facts about this so-called cruise. Yes, the company would indeed give me a boat ticket from Miami to the Bahamas, but it would not be on a luxury liner—it would be on a commercial ferry. In other words, I would travel on a deck filled with cars and crates—a depressing scene when contrasted with my *Love Boat* fantasies. The Better

Orienting Material
The speaker gives some background information on the subject.

The speaker tells the audience precisely what will be covered in the speech, giving a preview of the central idea and the two main points.

Business Bureau said my ticket would be worth only $30, and in the meantime I would be stuck with vitamins that cost me $450 but would retail in drugstores for about $50.

II. This "cruise" is just one of hundreds of scams that are cheating thousands of consumers every day. A subcommittee of the U.S. Senate estimates that consumer scams, especially health schemes, cost Americans 25 billion dollars per year. I would like to tell you how these scams operate, and I'd like to convince you that you can avoid being a victim of a scam if you follow two guidelines: Number one, always remember the maxim that in life, you rarely get something for nothing. Number two, never get involved in a scheme unless the Better Business Bureau assures you that the company is honest.

[Using the problem-solution pattern, the speaker devotes the first half of his speech to describing the nature and extent of the problem. In the second half, he outlines the steps that a consumer should take to avoid being victimized.]

CONCLUSION

In the first part of the conclusion, the speaker summarizes the main points. Repetition in a speech is a good idea, so that the speaker is sure that the listeners have retained the key information.

I. If you get a letter in the mail today offering you a fabulous free prize, I hope you will remember the two guidelines I have discussed: First, remind yourself that in life, you rarely get something for nothing. So don't be surprised if the "prize" turns out to be worthless junk, like the grandfather clock I told you about that was made of cardboard or the fishing boat that turned out to be a tiny plastic toy. Secondly, before getting involved with a company, investigate it by calling your local Better Business Bureau. If they have never heard of the company, you would be wise to avoid doing business with it; many scams operate for a few months and then quickly fold, to elude the authorities.

The speaker ends gracefully with a wry reference to the story told in the introduction.

II. If you follow these two guidelines, you can avoid being ripped off. Just imagine how you would feel if your *Love Boat* fantasy turned into the grim reality of a ferry boat ride with cars and crates as your unromantic companions.

Summary

Much of the success of a speech depends upon how well the speaker handles the introduction and conclusion. The introduction consists of two parts: attention material (to gain the audience's attention and interest) and orienting material (to prepare the audience intellectually and psychologically for the rest of the speech).

For attention material, you can use one or more of the following techniques: tell a story, ask a question, make a provocative statement, cite a quotation, arouse curiosity, provide a visual aid or demonstration, and provide the audience with an incentive to listen. For orienting material, you can preview the body of the speech, give background information, and establish your credibility.

The conclusion of your speech should signal the end, summarize your key ideas, and reinforce the central idea with a clincher. Examples of clinchers are any of the above techniques (mentioned for attention material), a quotation, an appeal or challenge, an illustration, and a reference to the introduction.

Review Questions

1. Why is it necessary to have attention material at the beginning of a speech?
2. What is the purpose of the orienting material?
3. What is a rhetorical question?
4. Why is it a mistake to use a quotation as the first sentence of your speech?
5. Why is it a mistake to end a speech abruptly?

Tips
FOR YOUR CAREER

Tip 10: Use an "Icebreaker" to Start Off a Community Speech

You have probably noticed that many speakers at business and professional meetings start off by saying something like this: "I'm glad to have a chance to speak to you today." They are giving what I call an *icebreaker*—a polite little prologue to "break the ice" before getting into their speech.

In outline form, here is how an introduction with an icebreaker would look:

I. Icebreaker

II. Attention material

III. Orienting material

An icebreaker is helpful because it eases your nervous tension and it lets the audience get accustomed to your voice. You do not need an icebreaker for classroom speeches because your audience has already settled down and is ready to listen (besides, most instructors would disapprove of using one), but when you give speeches out in the community, you may want to use it.

I do not like "Hello, how are you?" as an icebreaker. It sounds too breezy and flip. It leaves a question as to whether the speaker wants the audience to roar a response like "Fine, thank you!" It is much better to say, "I appreciate the opportunity to speak to you tonight." But, you might object, phrases like this have been used so often, they are meaningless. Yes, they are. They are clichés. Nevertheless, they are valuable aids to smooth social relationships. When you engage in small talk with your friends, you use sentences like, "Hi, how are you?"

Such expressions are trite, but they are necessary because they lubricate the wheels of human discourse.

In addition to expressing appreciation for the invitation to speak, you can include a thank-you to the person who introduced you or a reference to the occasion ("I'm delighted to take part in the celebration of Martin Luther King's birthday"). Some speakers also use the icebreaker to formally greet the audience. This custom, however, has fallen out of fashion. In the old days, orators would begin speeches like this: "Madame President, Distinguished Members of the Paradox Society, Honored Guests, Ladies and Gentlemen, Greetings!" Such introductions are used today only in formal, traditional settings, such as a college commencement. In most of the speeches you will give in your life, a flowery greeting would sound pompous.

A note of caution: An icebreaker should be very brief—just a sentence or two. If you are too slow getting into your attention material, you may cause your listeners to tune you out.

11

Outlining
the
Speech

Guidelines for Outlining

Parts of the Outline

Sample Outline

Speaking Notes

Controlling Your Material

Speech as Presented

I n 1912, a new hotel was built in Baltimore—the New Howard Hotel. When the furnaces in the basement were fired up, a startling discovery was made. The builders of the hotel had failed to include chimneys![1]

This spectacular blunder illustrates the importance of using an architect's blueprint, or detailed plan, when constructing a building. The New Howard builders had failed to follow a well-defined master plan.

Just as a blueprint helps a builder construct a building, an outline helps you construct a speech. An outline permits you to organize your thoughts into a logical sequence, and to see which points are irrelevant or improperly placed or poorly developed.

Some students dislike writing an outline because they consider it unnecessary, a total waste of time. As one student put it, "I know what I'm going to say—I've got the outline in my head." However, most people who shun written outlines discover sooner or later that their method hurts them. They may fail to present information in the clearest, most logical manner possible; they may annoy the audience with confusing or irrelevant material, or they may sit down after a speech and suddenly realize that they left out a very important point.

I strongly recommend that you use an outline not only for your classroom speeches, but for any speech that you give in life. An outline will remind you to include chimneys, and it will help you construct solid, livable hotels that your audience will enjoy staying in.

So far, we have talked about gathering materials (Chapters 6, 7, and 8) and then organizing them in the body (Chapter 9) and in the introduction and conclusion (Chapter 10). Now we will discuss how to put all these things together in an outline.

There are three steps in the outline-to-speech process: first, create an outline; second, use the outline to prepare speaking notes, and third, use the speaking notes to deliver the speech. (For your classroom speeches, your instructor may have guidelines that differ in some degree from this sequence; you should, of course, follow his or her rules.)

If you are confused at this point over the difference between an outline and speaking notes, don't worry. This will be explained shortly. For the time being, take a look at Figure 11.1, an overview of the three-step process. Study this chart, and refer to it as you read the pages that follow. (Step 3, delivering the speech, will be discussed in Chapter 13.)

Guidelines for Outlining

Why use an outline? Why not just write out the entire speech?

A word-for-word script would create a sea of material that might overwhelm you. Even worse, you might be tempted to read the script, a method (as we will see in Chapter 13) that could put the audience to sleep.

An outline is better than a script because it shows the basic structure of your ideas in a streamlined form. It helps you see the relationship between ideas.

FROM OUTLINE TO SPEECH

Figure 11.1
These are the three steps in the outline-to-speech process. (For classroom speeches, find out if your instructor wants you to use this system or some other plan.)

Step 1: Create an Outline

This sample is taken from a student's outline for a speech on poisonous snakes. An outline provides the basic structure of the speaker's ideas in streamlined form; it is not a word-for-word script. A detailed outline (like this one) is used only for preparation—it is *not* taken to the lectern for the actual speech.

Outline

I. Out of a population of 245,000,000, very few Americans die from snakebite.

   A. Only 7000 are bitten by poisonous snakes each year.
   B. Of that number, only 30 die.

Step 2: Prepare Speaking Notes

The speaker prepares brief notes—derived from her outline—to be used in practicing and delivering the speech. These notes contain only a few key phrases—just enough to jog her memory. By using brief notes instead of her outline, she avoids the mistake of reading a speech.

Speaking notes

I. 245,000,000
   7,000 bitten
   30 die

Step 3: Deliver the Speech

These are the speaker's actual words. Using her speaking notes to jog her memory, she presents the information in a natural, conversational manner.

Speech as delivered

There are 245 million people living in the United States. How many of them do you think are bitten each year by poisonous snakes? Only 7,000 are bitten. What happens to them? Do most of these people die from the snakebite? No, only 30. When you think of 245 million and then think of 30, you realize that the odds are in your favor—very few people die from snakebite.

In essence, outlining is a commonsense way of arranging information in a logical pattern. The Federal Bureau of Investigation's Crime Index, for example, can be organized in the following way:

FBI Crime Index

I. Half of the eight crimes in the FBI Crime Index are considered *violent* crimes.
II. The other half of the eight crimes are considered *property* crimes.

Each of these major headings could be subdivided; for example, let's take the first one:

I. Half of the eight crimes in the FBI Crime Index are considered *violent* crimes.
   A. *Murder* means killing a person yourself, or hiring or manipulating someone else to do the killing for you.
   B. *Rape* means sexual assault or an attempt to commit sexual assault.

C. *Robbery* differs from other forms of theft in that its victims are threatened with harm if they do not surrender their property.

D. *Aggravated assault* means an attack on a person with intent to kill or cause injury.

If we wanted to, we could divide items A, B, C, and D into subcategories. For example, we could break murder down into categories of weapons used, with one category for guns, one for knives, and so on.

Here are some important points to keep in mind as you prepare your outlines.

Choose an Outline Format

The two most popular formats for outlines are the *topic outline* and the *complete-sentence outline*. Find out if your instructor prefers or requires one or the other. Some instructors and professional speakers recommend using both methods—the topic format in the early stages of preparation (when you are struggling to impose order on your material) and the complete-sentence format in the later stages (when you are refining and polishing your ideas).

Topic Outline

In a topic outline, you express your ideas in key words or phrases. The advantage of this format is that it is quicker and easier to prepare than a complete-sentence outline.

At the beginning of this chapter, we saw a complete-sentence outline on the FBI Crime Index. If we put that information into a topic outline, it would look like this:

FBI Crime Index

I. Violent crimes
   A. Murder
   B. Rape
   C. Robbery
   D. Aggravated assault
II. Property crimes
   A. Burglary
   B. Larceny/theft
   C. Motor vehicle theft
   D. Arson

Complete-Sentence Outline

In the complete-sentence format, all your main points and subpoints are expressed in complete sentences. Unless your instructor tells you otherwise, I would recommend that you use complete sentences for your final outline. Here is why: (1) Writing complete sentences forces you to clarify and sharpen your thinking. You are able to go beyond fuzzy, generalized notions and create whole, fully developed ideas. (2) If another person (such as an instructor) helps you with your outline, complete sentences will be easier to understand than mere phrases, thus permitting that person to give you the best possible critique.

All the sample outlines in the rest of this book, including the one featured in this chapter, use the complete-sentence format.

A note of caution: the complete-sentence outline is not your speech written out exactly as you will present it. Rather, it is a representation of your key ideas; the actual speech should elaborate on these ideas. This means that your actual speech will contain many more words than the outline. See Figure 11.1 for an example.

Use Standard Subdivisions

In the standard system of subdividing, you mark your main points with roman numerals (I, II, III, etc.), then place the next level of supporting materials underneath in capital letters (A, B, C, etc.), then go to arabic numerals, then to small letters, and so on. Here is the standard form:

I. Major division
II. Major division
   A. First-level subdivision
   B. First-level subdivision
      1. Second-level subdivision
      2. Second-level subdivision
         a. Third-level subdivision
         b. Third-level subdivision
            (1) Fourth-level subdivision
            (2) Fourth-level subdivision
   C. First-level subdivision

Notice that each time you subdivide a point, you indent. For most speeches you will not need to break your material down into as many subdivisions as illustrated here.

Avoid Single Subdivisions

Each heading should have at least two subdivisions—or none at all. In other words, for every heading marked "A," there should be at least a "B." For every "1" there should be a "2." The reason is obvious: how can you divide something and end up with only one part? If you divide an orange, you must end up with at least two pieces. If you end up with only one, you have not really divided the orange. One problem that arises is how to show a single example for a particular point. Below is the *wrong* way to handle the problem:

A. Many counterfeiters are turning to items other than paper money.
   1. Counterfeit credit cards now outnumber counterfeit bills.
B. . . .

This is wrong because item A cannot logically be subdivided into just one piece. There are two ways to correct the problem. One way is to simply eliminate the single item and combine it with the heading above:

> A. Many counterfeiters are turning to items other than paper money: counterfeit credit cards now outnumber counterfeit bills.
> B. . . .

Another way to handle the problem is to not number the item but simply list it as "example":

> A. Many counterfeiters are turning to items other than paper money. *Example:* Counterfeit credit cards now outnumber counterfeit bills.
> B. . . .

Test Your Material

One of the reasons for creating an outline is to *test* your material to see if it is well-organized, logical, and sufficient. Here are some questions that you should ask yourself as you construct your outline:

- ☐ Does the introduction provoke interest and give sufficient orienting material?
- ☐ Do I preview the central idea and/or main points?
- ☐ Do the main points explain or prove my central idea?
- ☐ Are the main points organized logically?
- ☐ Is there enough support material for each main point? Is there too much?
- ☐ Do I have smooth transitions between introduction and body, between main points, and between body and conclusion?
- ☐ Have I eliminated extraneous material that doesn't truly relate to my central idea?
- ☐ Does my conclusion summarize the main points and reinforce the central idea?
- ☐ Is my conclusion strong and effective?

Use Cards for Preliminary Outlines

One reason some students hate writing an outline is that they think they must sit down and write it all at once, then laboriously rewrite it whenever a change is made.

Here is a technique that can save you a lot of time and labor: For your preliminary work (before you write your final outline), use extra-large (4 × 6 or larger) cards, putting one point on each card. Sit at a desk or table and display the cards containing your main points (which we discussed in Chapter 9). Then underneath each main point, place those cards that support it. (If you want to get fancy, you can use a color code—yellow cards, say, for main points and white cards for supporting points.) Figure 11.2 shows examples of cards for a preliminary outline on how to change a flat tire.

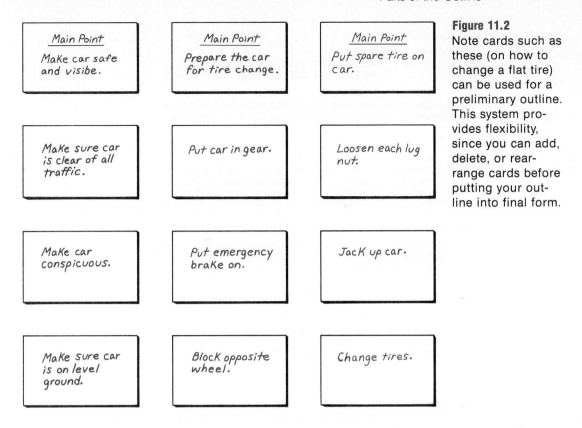

Figure 11.2
Note cards such as these (on how to change a flat tire) can be used for a preliminary outline. This system provides flexibility, since you can add, delete, or rearrange cards before putting your outline into final form.

With this system, you can move cards about to try different sequences. As you develop your ideas, you can add or eliminate cards. After you have arranged the cards in logical sequences, you can number them according to the standard outline form, as discussed earlier in the chapter. Then you are ready to write out your final outline on a full sheet of paper. The cards in Figure 11.2 represent the early stages of the outline that can be found later in this chapter.

Note to computer users: If you use word-processing software to create your outline, you will not need to use this card system because you can easily add, delete, and rearrange text on-screen.

Parts of the Outline

The parts of the outline discussed below are keyed to the sample outline that follows this section. Your instructor may have requirements for your outline that deviate somewhat from the description in these pages. (See Figure 11.3 for a schematic overview of a typical outline.)

1. *Title.* Your outline should have a title, but you *do not actually say it in your speech.* In other words, do not begin your speech by saying, "How to Lose

Figure 11.3
This is a schematic overview of a typical outline. Although this outline shows three main points, some speeches may have two or, occasionally, four.

TITLE

General Purpose: �
Specific Purpose:
Central Idea:

INTRODUCTION
I.
II.

(Transition)

BODY
I.
    A.
    B.
    C.

(Transition)

II.
    A.
    B.
    C.

(Transition)

III.
    A.
    B.
    C.

(Transition)

CONCLUSION
I.
II.

BIBLIOGRAPHY

VISUAL AIDS

Weight Permanently" or "The title of my speech is 'How to Lose Weight Permanently.'"

If you should not say the title, why have one? For classroom speeches, your instructor may want you to write one simply to give you experience in devising titles. For some out-of-class speeches, a title might be requested so that your speech can be publicized in advance.

Your title should be brief and descriptive; that is, it should give a clear idea of what your speech is about. For example, "Why State Lotteries Should Be Abolished" is a short and helpful guide. If you want an attractive, catchy title, you can use a colorful phrase coupled with a descriptive subtitle. For example:

☐ A Lousy Bet: Why State Lotteries Should Be Abolished
☐ Ouch! What to Do When a Bee Stings You
☐ Are You Living Beyond Your Means? A Brief Look at Credit Cards

2. *Purposes and central idea.* Having your general purpose, specific purpose, and central idea listed on your outline will help you bring into sharp focus the main points and supporting materials.

3. *Introduction and conclusion.* As we pointed out in the previous chapter, the introduction and conclusion are so vitally important in a speech that they deserve special attention and care. Some speakers recommend that you write out both of these items in full so you can make sure that they are well developed. Both sections should have their own numbering system, independent of the body of the speech.

4. *Body.* The body of the outline was discussed in Chapter 9. Each main point should be identified by roman numerals. The body has its own numbering system, independent of the introduction and conclusion. In other words, the first main point of the body is roman number I.

5. *Transitions.* The transitional devices we discussed in Chapter 9 should be inserted in the outline at appropriate places. They are labeled and placed in parentheses, but they are not included in the numbering system of the outline.

While transitional devices should be placed wherever they are needed to help the listener, make sure you have them in three crucial places: (1) between the introduction and the body of the speech, (2) between each of the main points, and (3) between the body of the speech and the conclusion.

6. *Bibliography.* At the end of the outline, place a list of your sources—books, magazines, interviews, etc.—which you used in preparing the speech. Give standard bibliographical data; for a book, for example, give the author, title, publisher, place of publication, date of publication, and the specific pages that you used. (Check with your instructor to see if he or she wants you to use a special format, such as that of the Modern Language Association.) If you used your own personal experiences, you should cite yourself as a source. The bibliography is useful not only to give your instructor a list of your sources but also to provide you with a record if you ever give the speech again and need to return to your sources to refresh your memory or to find additional information.

7. *Visual aids.* If you plan to use visual aids, give a brief description of them. This will help the instructor to give you guidance on whether the visual aids are effective.

Sample Outline

Your outline should *not* include every word in your speech. It is merely the skeleton. Your actual speech will be longer.

Below is an outline by student speaker Joan Cohen.[2] Read it and then study the commentary in the left-hand column.

COMMENTARY

OUTLINE

How to Change a Tire without Getting Hurt or Killed

Purposes and central idea should always appear at the top of outline to help bring content into sharp focus.

General Purpose: To inform
Specific Purpose: To explain to my listeners how to change tires on a car safely and easily.
   Central Idea: To change a tire without getting hurt or killed, a person should follow three important steps: Make the car safe and visible, prepare the car for tire change, and correctly put the spare tire on the car.

The introduction is set off from the rest of the outline by its own heading and numbering system. Part I is designed to grab the listeners' attention and interest. Part II previews the central idea and main points and gives background information.

INTRODUCTION

I. A flat tire is more than an irritation. It can endanger your life. Last year, the National Safety Council said, more than 1400 Americans were killed or hurt while working on their cars on the roadways.

II. You can follow three simple steps to avoid being hurt or killed while changing a flat. First, make the car safe and visible. Second, prepare the car for a safe change. Third, change tires correctly. I am assuming that you always carry a spare, a tire-changing kit, and an owner's manual.

By planning transitions, the speaker insures smooth passage from one part of the speech to another. Transitions are placed in parentheses and are not part of the outline's number system.

(*Transition:* Let me give you the details of these steps.)

BODY

I. Make car safe and visible.
 A. Make sure car is clear of all traffic.
  1. Drive as far off the road as possible.
  2. Leave enough room for you to work.
 B. Make car conspicuous.
  1. Put on emergency flashers.
  2. Raise the hood.
  3. Put a white cloth on the door handle.
 C. Make sure car is on level ground.

(*Transition:* Once the car is safe and visible, you are ready for the second step.)

The body contains the main points, marked by roman numerals. Under each main point,

II. Prepare the car for tire change.
 A. Put car in gear.
  1. For automatic transmission, put in "park."
  2. For standard transmission, put in lowest gear.
 B. Put emergency brake on.

---

subpoints are marked with capital letters (A, B, C) and subsubpoints with arabic numerals (1, 2, 3).

Each level of subordination is shown by indentation.

The final transition prepares the audience for the conclusion.

The conclusion has its own label and numbering system.

The speaker reviews the main points. In an essay, such a restatement would be repetitious, but in a speech, it is needed to help the listeners retain the information.

  C. Block opposite wheel.
    1. This will prevent car from rolling.
    2. Use piece of wood or stone.

(*Transition:* If you follow all the procedures so far, you can feel confident that you are safe for the actual operation you are about to perform.)

III. Put spare tire on car.
  A. Loosen each lug nut.
    1. Use lug wrench.
    2. Loosen each lug nut one turn.
  B. Jack up car.
    1. Follow owners' manual for your car.
    2. Remove lug nuts.
  C. Change tires.
    1. Put spare tire on.
    2. Be careful not to jar car off jack.
    3. Tighten lug nuts snugly but not as hard as possible.
      a. Don't tighten in a circle.
      b. Tighten one, then the one opposite, and so on.
    4. Lower car to ground.
    5. Tighten nuts as hard as you can.

(*Transition:* As you can see, these steps are easy to follow; let's review the highlights.)

CONCLUSION

I. The first thing to do is make sure your car is in a safe place—on level ground, clear of all traffic, and with plenty of room for you to work. Make the car conspicuous by turning on your emergency flashers, raising the hood, and tying a white cloth to the door handle. Put your car in gear, put the emergency brake on, and block the opposite wheel. Then loosen the lug nuts, jack up the car, and change tires, using your owners' manual as your guide.

II. If you follow the steps I have given you today, a flat tire is just a nuisance. If you don't follow them, it could mean injury or death.

The speaker lists all sources of information used in the preparation of the speech.

BIBLIOGRAPHY

Sandra Bundy, *The Breakdown Book* (New York: Shell Oil Co., undated), pp. 3–6.

Ted Mathis, owner, Mathis Gulf Station, Merrimon Ave., personal interview, August 11, 1988.

The speaker describes the visual aids.

VISUAL AIDS

Three posters showing the three main points.

Speaking Notes

After you have devised an outline, what do you do with it? Do you use it to practice your speech? No. Do you take it with you to the lectern to assist you in the delivery of your speech? No. The outline should be used only for *organizing* your ideas. When it comes to *practicing* and then *delivering* the speech, you should use brief speaking notes that are based upon the outline.

What is so bad about using your outline to give the speech? If you are using a complete-sentence outline, you might be tempted to read the outline, and nothing is duller than a read-aloud speech. As we will discuss in Chapter 13, you should deliver your speech extemporaneously; that is, in a conversational manner, looking at the audience most of the time, only occasionally glancing down at your notes. When you glance at your notes, you pick up ideas and then convey those ideas in whatever words come to mind at the moment. Thus you end up sounding natural and spontaneous.

While a complete-sentence outline is undesirable for delivery, the other extreme—using no notes at all—is equally bad. Without notes, you might forget important points, and you might fail to present your ideas in a logical, easy-to-follow sequence.

Notes bolster your sense of security. Even if you are in full command of the content of your speech, you feel more confident and self-assured knowing that you have notes to fall back on in case your mind goes blank and you fail to recall your next point.

By the way, some people (I used to be one of them) have the idea that using notes is a sign of mental weakness or a lack of self-confidence, but this is unfounded. Most good speakers use them without losing the respect of an audience. After all, your notes represent a kind of compliment to your listeners. They show that you cared enough about the occasion to spend time getting your best thoughts together in a coherent form. The kind of speaker that audiences *do* look down on is the windbag who stands up without notes and rambles on without making much sense.

Here are some guidelines for preparing notes. As you read them, you may want to refer to the sample speaking notes that appear in the next section.

☐ Make indentations in your speaking notes that correspond to those in your outline. This will help reinforce the structure of the speech in your mind. You may also want to repeat the numbering system; some speakers use only the roman numerals from their outline, some use all the numbers and letters.

☐ Use only one side of a sheet of paper or note card because you might forget to turn the paper or card over.

☐ Write down only the minimum number of words or phrases necessary to trigger your memory. If you have too many words written down, you might overlook some key ideas, or you might spend too much time looking at the notes instead of at the audience. An exception to this rule would be long quotations or statistics that you would need to write out in full for the sake of accuracy.

☐ Write words in large letters that are neat and legible so that you have no trouble seeing them when you glance down during a speech.

☐ Include cues for effective delivery, such as when to pause and when to use visual aids (see the sample notes that follow). Some speakers use black ink for their actual notes and red ink for delivery cues.

☐ For speaking, use the same set of notes you used while rehearsing, so that you will be thoroughly familiar with the location of items on your prompts. I once practiced with a set of notes on which I penciled in so many editing marks that I made a fresh set of notes right before I delivered the speech. This turned out to be a mistake because the notes were so "new" that some of the key words failed to trigger my memory quickly, causing me to falter at several points. I should have stayed with the original notes. Even though they were filled with arrows and insertions and deletions, I knew them intimately; I had a strong mental picture of where each point was located. The new notes, on the other hand, had not "burned" an image in my brain.

Sample Speaking Notes

The following speaking notes are based on the outline shown earlier in this chapter.

COMMENTARY
These cues remind the speaker to look at audience and speak slowly during introduction. The speaker writes "Fingers" as a cue to hold up three fingers.

INTRODUCTION
[E Y E C O N T A C T]
[G O S L O W L Y]
  I. More than irritation
     1400—Ntl. S. C.

 II. Three steps . . . [F I N G E R S]
     1. Safe and visible
     2. Prepare for change
     3. Put spare on
     Assume spare, kit, manual
(Let's look at details)
[P A U S E]

BODY
This cue reminds the speaker to show her first pos-

  I. Safe and visible [S H O W P O S T E R]
     Clear of all traffic
     Conspicuous

ter, on which is printed her first main point in large block letters.

The speaker reminds herself to pause at this point. Pauses are effective transition devices because they signal that you are through with one idea and ready to begin another.

The speaker uses only a few key words to jog her memory.

Transitions are included in the speaking notes, just as they were in the outline, but of course they are shortened.

      Emergency flashers
      Raise hood
      White cloth
    Level ground
(Once safe and visible, ready for II)
[P A U S E]
II. Prepare for safe change [S H O W P O S T E R]
    Car in gear
    Emergency brake on
    Block opposite wheel

(If follow, can feel confident)
[P A U S E]
III. Put spare on [S H O W P O S T E R]
    Loosen each lug nut
    Jack up car
    Change tires
      Don't jar
      Snug, but not hard
      Not a circle
    Lower, then hard
    (steps easy—let's review)

CONCLUSION
  I. Review [U S E P O S T E R S]
 II. If follow, just nuisance
    If don't, injury or death

Using Speaking Notes

Your instructor may require you to use one particular kind of note system, but if you have a choice, I recommend that you use either of two popular types: note cards or a full sheet of paper.

Option 1: Note Cards

Your speaking notes can be put on note cards, as shown in Figure 11.4.

Note cards (especially the 3 × 5 size) are compact and rather inconspicuous, and they are easy to hold (especially if there is no lectern to place notes on). Because of the small size of the card, you are forced to write just a few key words rather than long sentences that you might be tempted to read. If you use cards, be sure to number each one in case you drop them and need to quickly reassemble them.

Introduction
<u>EYE CONTACT</u>
<u>GO SLOWLY</u>

I. More than irritation
1400 – Ntl. S.C.

II Three steps [FINGERS]
1. Safe & visible
2. Prepare for
change
3. Put spare on.

Figure 11.4
Here is how the speaker used note cards for the speech about changing a flat tire. Each card is numbered so that if the speaker accidentally drops the cards, they can be put back into proper order very easily. (Only the first card is shown.)

Option 2: Full Sheet of Paper

If you use a full sheet of paper, your notes will look like the sample speaking notes on pages 223–224. The advantage of this option is that you have your entire speech spread out in front of you. A short speech can usually fit on one side of a single sheet, so you do not have to do any shuffling, as with cards.

There are, however, several disadvantages: (1) Because a whole sheet of paper is a large writing surface, many speakers succumb to the temptation to put down copious notes. This hurts them in speechmaking because they end up spending too much time looking at their notes at the expense of eye contact with the audience. (2) I have found that a full sheet of paper can cause a speaker's eyes to glide over key points because the "map" is too large to be scrutinized at a glance. (3) If sheets of paper are brought to the room curled up, they can curl up on the lectern, much to the speaker's dismay. (4) if no lectern is available, a hand-held sheet of paper tends to shake and rustle, causing a distraction to the listeners. (5) It is harder to make corrections on paper than on note cards. With paper, you may have to rewrite all your notes, whereas with note cards, you simply delete the card containing the undesired section and write your corrected version on a fresh card.

Controlling Your Material

While preparing an outline and speaking notes, it is important that you control your material, rather than letting your material control you. Here are two things you can do to make sure that you stay in control:

1. *Revise your outline and speaking notes whenever they need alterations.* Some students mistakenly view an outline as a device that plants their feet in concrete; once they have written an outline, they think that they are stuck with it—even if they yearn to make changes. An outline should be treated as a flexible aid that can be altered as you see fit. That is why I recommended earlier that you write your preliminary outline on large note cards—so that you can freely add, delete, or move points around. Whatever technique you use, feel free to make revisions at any stage of preparation.

Often an outline looks good on paper, but when you make your speaking notes and start practicing, you find that some parts are disharmonious, clumsy, or illogical. A speech needs a nice even flow, carrying the audience smoothly from one point to another. If your speech lacks this smooth flow, go back and alter the outline until you achieve a continuity that you are comfortable with. (If you practice in front of friends, ask them to point out parts that are clumsy or confusing.)

2. *Make deletions if you are in danger of exceeding your time limit.* After you make your speaking notes, you should practice delivering your speech while you clock yourself to see how much time it takes. If the speech exceeds the time limit (set by your instructor or by the people who invited you to speak), you must go back to your outline and speaking notes and trim them down.

Deleting material can be painful, especially if you have worked hard to get a

Asking a friend, relative, or instructor to critique an outline is a good way to get feedback on weaknesses in a speech. *(Kathy Sloane)*

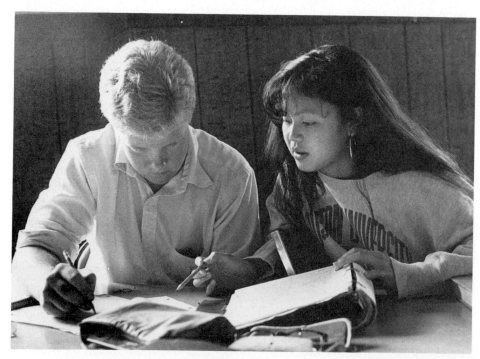

particular example or statistic. But it is a job that *must* be done. Be ruthless. Be brave. Even if you exceed the limit by only 5 minutes, you must cut. A speech that exceeds its allotted time can spoil a program that features other speakers or events in a tight schedule.

Speech as Presented

The following is a transcript of the speech about changing a flat tire as it was delivered by Joan Cohen. Note that the wording is not identical to that used in the outline. The reason, of course, is that Cohen was delivering the speech extemporaneously, using the speaking notes on page 223. If she had read from her outline or from a complete text, she might have sounded stilted and artificial. By choosing her words as she went along, she made her speech vigorous, forthright, and easy to follow. If she gave this speech ten different times, the wording would be different each time, although the ideas would remain basically the same.

How to Change a Tire without Getting Hurt or Killed

It's time for your annual vacation, and you pack your car, and head for the beach. But trouble comes along: somewhere out on the highway, your car starts to ride rough and you realize that you have a flat tire. This is really irritating—isn't it—to have your first day of vacation delayed by a flat tire. But a flat tire can be more than irritating. It can endanger your life. Last year, according to the National Safety Council, more than 1400 Americans were killed or injured while working on their cars on our roadways.

There are some simple steps that you can follow to make sure that you change a tire without getting hurt or killed; first, you must make sure that your car is safe and visible; second, you must prepare your car for a safe change; and third, you must change tires correctly. Everything I say in this speech rests on the assumption that your car always carries a spare tire, a tire-changing kit, and an owner's manual in the glove compartment.

Now let's look at the details of the steps. First, you should make your car safe and visible. Is it clear of all traffic? Have you driven it as far off the road as possible? Have you left enough room so that you can work on the car without getting hit by a passing vehicle? You should make your car as conspicuous as possible, so that you don't get sideswiped by someone who doesn't notice you. Put on emergency flashers and raise the hood. If possible put a white cloth such as a towel or handkerchief on the door handle. Then make sure the car is on level ground. If you are on a slope, even a slight one, the car could slide off the jack and crush you.

Now you've made your car safe and visible, so you are ready for the second step. Prepare the car for a safe tire change. Put it in gear. If you have an automatic transmission, put it in ''park.'' If you have a standard transmission, put it in the lowest gear. Put your emergency brake on. And then block the wheel that is opposite to the one you're working on. You can use a piece of wood or a big stone. This will prevent the car from rolling.

If you follow all of the procedures so far, you are as safe as a person can be and you can feel confident that you can carry out the remaining procedures.

Our third step is obviously to put the spare on. You should loosen all the lug nuts, using the lug wrench in your tire-changing kit. Loosen each lug nut just one turn. Put your jack in the proper place and jack up your car. To do this, you should follow your owner's manual. The reason I say this is that each car is different, and I can't give you directions that will apply to all cars. After you have jacked up the wheel, remove the lug nuts and put on your spare. While you're doing this, be careful not to jar the car because it could get jarred right off your jack. Tighten the lug nuts snugly but not as hard as you can. As you tighten, don't go in a circular pattern. Tighten one nut, then go to the one opposite, and so on. Now you're ready to lower the car to the ground. Then, tighten the nuts as hard as you can.

As you can see, these steps are easy to follow. Let's review the key information I've given you. The first thing to do is make sure your car is in a safe place. Is it on level ground? Is it clear of all traffic? Do you have plenty of room to work and move around without getting hit by a passing car? Make the car conspicuous by turning on your emergency flashers, raising the hood, and tying a white cloth to the door handle. Prepare the car for a safe change by putting it in gear, putting the emergency brake on, and blocking the opposite wheel. Then loosen the lug nuts, jack up the car, and change tires, using your owners' manual as your guide. If you follow these steps, a flat tire will be nothing more than a nuisance to you. If you *don't* follow them, a flat tire could mean injury or death.

Summary

An outline is as important to the speechmaker as a blueprint is to a builder. The outline provides a detailed plan to help the speaker organize thoughts into a logical sequence and to make sure nothing important is left out.

After you complete your outline, prepare speaking notes based upon it. You have two options—note cards or a full sheet of paper. Whichever you choose, avoid writing too many words because when you use notes in a speech, you want to be able to glance down quickly and retrieve just enough words to jog your memory.

Review Questions

1. Why is an outline recommended for all speeches?
2. What is the advantage of using complete sentences in an outline?
3. What are the parts of an outline?
4. Why should each subdivision of an outline have at least two parts?

Tip 11: When No Time Limit Is Set, Speak Briefly

We have already discussed the need to abide by the time limits placed on a speech, but what should you do when no time limit is set—that is, you are invited to speak for as long as you like? The best advice I can give you is this: Be brief. Keep it short. In the words of Owen Feltham, a seventeenth-century English author, every person "should study conciseness in speaking; it is a sign of ignorance not to know that long speeches, though they may please the speaker, are the torture of the hearer."

How brief is brief? For a short speech, a good rule of thumb is to aim for about 5 minutes. Many clubs ask for 5-minute talks; many executives ask for 5-minute presentations, and all Toastmasters' clubs stipulate five minutes for their members' speeches. For longer speeches, such as after-dinner addresses, you would need to assess the audience and the occasion. I would recommend no more than 20 minutes, although some after-dinner speakers go 45 to 60. In any situation, if you go over 60 minutes, you will usually see the audience become fatigued and fidgety.

In general, audiences prefer—and are getting—shorter and shorter speeches, possibly because television has conditioned people to assimilate only short bursts of material. The demand for brevity is even being voiced in America's churches, which once featured sermons lasting well over an hour. Most ministers today preach for no more than 30 minutes. Donald Macleod, who teaches sermon preparation at Princeton Theological Seminary, tells his seminarians that 18 minutes is the maximum time for an effective sermon.[3]

Whenever you are in doubt about length, remember that if one must err, it is always best to err on the side of brevity. If, when you finish a speech, the listeners are still hungering for more wisdom from your mouth, no harm is done. They will probably invite you to come back and speak again. But if you speak so long that they become bored, weary, and sleepy, they will resent you for wasting their time.

PART FOUR

Presenting

the

Speech

12

Wording the Speech

he power of a single word is incredible. Take, for instance, the world of advertising. A book on automobile repair was once advertised under the headline "How to Repair Cars." When the advertsing agency changed the headline to read, "How to Fix Cars," sales jumped by 20 percent.[1] Why is *fix* more likely to garner sales than its synonym *repair?* No one is sure exactly why— perhaps it sounds easier to fix a car than to repair it. Whatever the reason, ad agencies know that while the right word can help an ad, the wrong word can hurt it. David Ogilvy, an advertising copywriter once wondered why one of his ads failed to lure buyers. He conducted a survey which showed that he made the mistake of using the word *obsolete* in the ad's headline. The survey revealed that 43 percent of consumers in the group targeted had no idea what "obsolete" meant.[2]

The producers of television commercials know that the right word can be worth millions of dollars in increased sales. They have learned, for example, that the words *new* and *improved* in a commercial will boost sales significantly. That is why TV viewers so often hear a product touted as "the new, improved . . . ."

While finding the right word is obviously vital in advertising, it is also important in public speaking. The difference between the right word and the *almost* right word, Mark Twain once observed, is the difference between lightning . . . and the lightning bug.

The truth of Twain's remark can be seen in the following historical vignette: one of President Franklin Roosevelt's most famous speeches was his address to Congress asking for a declaration of war against Japan in the aftermath of the Japanese attack on the American fleet at Pearl Harbor. As written by an assistant, the speech began this way:

December 7, 1941: A date which will live in world history.

Before speaking, Roosevelt crossed out the words *world history* and substituted the word *infamy.* Here is what he ended up saying:

December 7, 1941: A date which will live in infamy.

This has become one of the most famous sentences in American history, along with such memorable statements as "Give me liberty or give me death!" And yet, if Roosevelt had used the original sentence, it never would have become celebrated. Why? Because *infamy*—a pungent word tinged with evil and anger—was the right description for the occasion; *world history*—dull and unemotional—was merely "almost right." Lightning . . . and the lightning bug.

In this chapter, we will look at how you can choose the right words for your speeches.

Using Appropriate Words

In choosing words for your speeches, your goal should not be to select the most beautiful or the most sophisticated, but to use the "right" words for the "right" audience. As you analyze your audience before a speech, you should ask yourself, "How can I best express my ideas so that the audience will understand and accept them?" A word that might be ideal for one audience might be inappropriate for another.

Dr. Martin Luther King, the brilliant leader of the civil rights movement of the 1960s, was a master at using the right words with the right group. To a highly educated audience, for example, he would employ sophisticated language and abstract concepts, such as this sentence from his Nobel Peace Prize acceptance speech:

Civilization and violence are antithetical concepts.

Such a sentence, appropriate for an erudite audience, would have been incomprehensible if used in one of his speeches to poor, uneducated sharecroppers in Mississippi. For them, he used simple words and down-to-earth illustrations. For example, in defending himself against accusations of being allied with communists, Dr. King used a simple, but vivid, comparison that could be grasped by the least educated of his listeners:

There are as many communists in the freedom movement as there are Eskimos in Florida.

With either kind of audience, Dr. King was highly persuasive, but what did he do when he spoke to a group made up of both educated and uneducated people? He used inspirational messages designed to appeal to every listener. In his famous "I Have a Dream" speech, delivered to 200,000 people who had marched on Washington to demand equal rights for blacks, Dr. King used stirring words that appealed to everyone:

I have a dream that my four little children will one day live in a nation where they will not be judged by the color of their skin but by the content of their character.

There was nothing phony about Dr. King's adaptation to his audiences. All good speakers pitch their language to the appropriate level for their audience.

In addition to choosing words that are appropriate to your audience, you should also use words that are appropriate to the occasion. If you speak at a fundraiser, your words should be uplifting and encouraging; at a funeral, solemn and respectful; at a pep rally, rousing and emotional.

Always use words that are in good taste. Avoid political, religious, racial, ethnic, or sexual references that might alienate anyone in your audience. Ask yourself, "Is there any chance at all that what I'm planning to say might offend someone in the audience?" If you cannot decide whether a word is appropriate, do not use it.

Stay away from sex-related stereotypical expressions such as *little old lady, broad, chick,* and *typical male brutality.* Try to eliminate sexism from sex-linked occupational terms. Here are some examples:

Original	Preferred form
workman	worker
stewardess	flight attendant
fireman	firefighter
policeman	police officer
mailman	mail carrier
man-made	artificial
cleaning lady	housekeeper
foreman	supervisor

Janet Elliott of Los Angeles writes, "I recently attended a meeting in which nearly 80 percent of the audience was composed of young college women. The speaker was addressing the subject of career options for communications majors in business. Throughout his speech he used the term 'businessman' when referring to a business executive in general. Many members of his audience were offended by the exclusion."[3]

Using Words Accurately

To use words accurately, you need to be sensitive to two types of meanings—denotations and connotations—and also to the use of correct grammar.

Use Precise Denotations

The *denotation* of a word is the thing or idea that it refers to—its dictionary definition. The denotation of *chair* is "a piece of furniture for one person to sit on." Complications arise when a word has more than one denotation. The word *verbal,* for example, means "in words, either spoken or written." If I asked you to give a verbal report, you would not know whether I wanted your words spoken or written. I would have to come up with a more precise word; *oral,* for example, would be clear and unambiguous.

Another complication is that words sometimes change their denotations. Several years ago a middle-aged student was giving a classroom speech, in which he said, "When some people get intoxicated with alcohol, they became carefree and gay." The younger members of the audience reacted with laughter and looks of surprise. The speaker got flustered. What was wrong? Later he realized that when he was growing up, the word *gay* had no other meaning than "merry" and "exuberant"; to his youthful audience, *gay* had a different denotation—the word had become a synonym for "homosexual."

Sometimes a word has different meanings in different parts of the nation. If, for example, you say, "In considering your nutritional needs, pay special attention to dinner," what time of day are you referring to? You would need to give an explanation because not all Americans use the word *dinner* in the same way. While most people think of dinner as the third and final meal of the day, some Americans, especially those from rural areas and from certain geographical regions, picture dinner as the meal served in the middle of the day.

You should never use a word, advises Dr. Kenneth McFarland, a professional speaker, "unless you know . . . that it means what you think it means." Dr. McFarland tells of hearing a county agricultural agent make a speech on the problems of the farm surplus. "A dozen times in his discourse he spoke of the 'dearth of wheat' and the 'dearth of corn.' At first his audience was bewildered but eventually it became obvious to most of the hearers that the speaker thought dearth meant abundance or surplus. [Actually, *dearth* is the opposite of surplus—it means "scarcity."] The misuse of this one word killed the effect of what could have been a good speech."[14]

Do you see why the county agent wounded his credibility? From the audience's point of view, how could they accept the ideas of a man who was so sloppy with language that he used a word in a sense that was opposite its true meaning?

Control Connotations

The *connotation* of a word is the emotional meaning that is associated with it. The words *slender, thin,* and *skinny* are synonyms; they have the same denotation, but the connotations are different: *slender* has a positive connotation, *thin* is neutral, and *skinny* has negative overtones. The words *fat, obese,* and *overweight* have similar denotations, but different connotations. Most fat people would prefer to be termed overweight, and if given a choice, they would rather be called fat than obese. Why? *Fat* sounds "fatter" than *overweight,* and *obese* suggests a "gross fatness that is health endangering." Other synonyms like *chubby* or *plump* have special connotations—*chubby* is often used to refer to children and suggests a "healthy condition"; *plump* suggests a "pleasing roundness."

As a listener and as a speaker, you should be aware of how connotations express a person's attitude. Let's say that some filmmakers produce a documentary on Senator Sally Jones. If they want to remain objective about the senator, they can describe her with a word that has a neutral connotation—*legislator.* If they want to convey approval, they can choose a word that has positive connotations—*national leader.* If they want to express disapproval, they can use a word that has negative connotations—*politician.* If they describe one of her campaign events, they could call it a *gathering* (neutral), a *rally* (positive), or a *mob* (negative). When she travels to Central America, the *trip* (neutral) could be called a *fact-finding mission* (positive) or a *junket* (negative).

With some synonyms, the connotations are so subtly different that you have to be especially thoughtful in selecting the right one. If, for example, you wanted to speak on the need for individuals to get away from other people occasionally and be by themselves, which word would have the more positive connotations—*loneliness* or *solitude?* When people hear the word *loneliness,* they often think of feeling sad, being friendless, craving companionship. *Solitude,* on the other hand, conjures images of peaceful serenity—walking alone on the beach, curling up with a book in front of the fireplace on a wintry night, or relaxing in a bathtub. *Solitude,* then, is the word you would want for describing the joys of being alone.

In exploring connotations, you do not have to rely solely on your own judgment. Many dictionaries have synonym notes, which are usually located after a word's definitions. While I have found that the best synonym notes are in the giant *Webster's Third New International Dictionary* (which most libraries have), you can also find helpful notes in many abridged dictionaries.

Use Correct Grammar

Although I would never devalue a person for using incorrect grammar, many people downgrade individuals if they make serious grammatical mistakes. To these people, bad grammar is as offensive as body odor or food stains on the front of a shirt. Recently, I was talking to a corporation executive who told me, "I just can't stand to be around people who use bad English. I would never hire a person who said things like 'I done it.'" And I know of a man who was passed over for a promotion (even though he was better qualified than the person who got the position) simply because he had the habit of saying "he don't" instead of "he doesn't."

Poor grammar hurts you because it makes you sound (to some people) as if you are not very intelligent. To make matters worse, people will usually refrain from telling you when your grammar offends them. A boss, for example, often is too ashamed to tell an employee that he or she uses unacceptable grammar; it is as embarrassing as telling friends that they have bad breath. So the employee is never told the real reason why he or she is being denied a promotion.

Poor grammar can damage a speaker's credibility, according to Roy Fenstermaker, winner of the 1983 Toastmasters' International Speech Contest. "Careless syntax, ungrammatical expressions, or gross mispronunciation of common words," he said, are apt to be interpreted by listeners "as evidence of lack of education or disrespect for the standards of the audience."[5]

From my observations, the following mistakes seem to be the ones that are most likely to cause some people to downgrade you:

Incorrect	*Correct*
He (or she) don't	He (or she) doesn't
You was	You were
I done it	I did it
Between you and I	Between you and me
I had went	I had gone
She's (he's) already went	She's (he's) already gone
I been thinking	I've been thinking
I've already took algebra	I've already taken algebra
hisself	himself
theirself	themselves
We seen it	We saw it
Her and me went	She and I went
Him and me went	He and I went
I come to see you yesterday	I came to see you yesterday
She ain't here	She isn't here
She don't love me no more	She doesn't love me anymore
He be late	He is late
I had wrote it	I had written it
Give me them apples	Give me those apples

If you make these or similar errors, I strongly urge you to learn how to correct your grammar and usage. Your school may have a tutoring service that can help you identify your grammatical mistakes and then correct them. Or perhaps you can find a book in a library or bookstore on improving one's English.

Achieving Clarity

To be clear in the words you use, you must first be clear in your thinking. Think about a word before you use it. Ask yourself, will it be clear to someone who is new to my subject? In this section we will examine how you can achieve clarity by using words that are simple, concrete, and precise.

Use Simple Words

A speechwriter for President Franklin D. Roosevelt once wrote, "We are endeavoring to construct a more inclusive society." President Roosevelt changed the wording to, "We're going to make a country in which no one is left out."[6]

Roosevelt obviously believed in the value of the old public speaker's maxim: "Never use a long word when a short one will do just as well." Some people think the best way to convey complex ideas is to use complex language—big words and weighty phrases. This is nonsense. If you examine great works of literature, you will see that profound thoughts can be expressed easily and beautifully by simple words. Some of the greatest pieces of literature in the English language—the King James Bible and Shakespeare's works—use simple words to convey big ideas. For example, in Hamlet's famous soliloquy ("To be or not to be") 205 of the 261 words are of one syllable. Of an American literary classic, Abraham Lincoln's Second Inaugural Address, writer William Zinsser says: "Of the 701 words in [the address], 505 are words of one syllable and 122 are words of two syllables."[7]

Some speakers are pretentious, trying to show off instead of making sure that their ideas are clear to the audience. In contrast, audience-centered speakers will choose the simple word whenever possible because they want their listeners to understand what they are saying. A pretentious speaker or an audience-centered speaker—which would you prefer to listen to? Which would you prefer to be? Here are some examples of the contrasting styles:

> *Pretentious speaker:* It is incumbent upon the citizens of this country to find alternatives to the widespread distribution of discarded objects on the nation's roads and highways.
> *Audience-centered speaker:* People ought to throw their trash some place other than on the streets.

> *Pretentious speaker:* People who are experiencing intense negative emotions directed at the significant other would be well advised to disclose their condition to that individual.
> *Audience-centered speaker:* If you're extremely angry at a loved one, don't keep it bottled up—tell the person how you feel.

As these examples show, communicating with your listeners is more important than showing off with big words.

Use Concrete Words

Concrete words name or describe things that listeners can see, smell, hear, taste, and touch—for example, *balloon, rose, gun blast, pizza,* and *chair.* They differ from abstract words, which refer to intangible ideas, qualities, or classes of things—for example, *democracy, mercy,* and *science.* While a certain amount of abstract language is necessary in a speech, you should try to keep it to a minimum. Instead, use concrete language because it is more specific and vivid, and therefore more likely to be remembered by your audience. Concrete words help you create the mental images that you want to convey to your listeners. Here are some examples:

Abstract	Concrete
She is wealthy	She makes $400,000 a year, has a winter home in San Diego and a summer home in Switzerland, and owns four different sports cars.
It was a stormy day.	The sky was gray and gloomy, and the cold, moist wind stung my face.
Rattlesnakes are scary.	A rattlesnake is ominous-looking, with its beady eyes staring at you without ever blinking, and with its agile ability to slither through the brush without making a sound—until it suddenly coils and makes its terrible buzzing rattle.

Use Precise Words

The most commonly quoted authority in America is "they," as in the following sentences:

They say that too much salt is bad for you.
They say that the murder rate goes up during a full moon.

Who are "they"? Whoever they are, avoid using them as a source for information. Be specific. Be precise. For the first sentence above, find reliable sources: "Researchers at Johns Hopkins University have found that too much salt in one's diet can cause . . . ." For the second sentence, if you try to find who "they" are, you may discover, as did one student speaker, that reliable experts have concluded that the murder rate does *not* increase during a full moon, contrary to popular opinion. The mysterious "they" can be wrong.

Two kinds of word usage—jargon and euphemisms—rob a speech of precision. Let us examine each.

Avoid Jargon

Can you understand everything being said in the following sentence?

During an attitude-adjustment period, a government official explained to reporters that his department would effect a transformation in the preexisting regulations concerning domiciles for the lower socioeconomic bracket.

Translated into plain English:

During a coffee break, a government official told reporters that his department would change the regulations concerning housing for the poor.

The government official was speaking in jargon, the specialized language of a group or profession. Some persons get so accustomed to using certain words at work that they fail to realize that people outside their field may be unaware of the words' meanings.

You may use jargon when you are talking to an audience made up entirely of people who share your specialty, but you should avoid jargon as much as possible in speeches to people of varying backgrounds. If you are forced to use a technical word because of the nature of your talk, you should always define it. One student speaker worked part-time in a hospital and gave a speech on a medical situation that she had agonized over—dealing with "no code" patients. Much to the frustration of the audience, she failed to define "no code"—until she was asked about it during the question-and-answer period. It turns out that *no code* is the term written on a patient's chart to indicate that no artifical life-support measures should be used if the patient's condition is determined to be hopeless. In other words,

Explaining a topic in your specialty to people of varying backgrounds requires you to use clear language and to avoid jargon.
(Harvey Stein)

doctors and nurses should not make heroic efforts to keep such patients alive if they are comatose and irreversibly brain-damaged. The speaker had failed to define "no code" because she assumed that everyone knew what it meant.

Be careful about using sports terms that the general public may not know. For example, if you argued for "a full-court press against communist expansion," only people familiar with basketball would know that the term means "trying to keep opponents from advancing."

Always explain abbreviations the first time you use them—even fairly well-known ones such as NATO and UNICEF. Some members of the audience may be unaware of what they stand for, and sometimes an abbreviation has several meanings. For example, *CO* is a popular military term that stands for "commanding officer," but it also means "conscientious objector," someone who refuses to participate in war. At one training seminar, a participant referred to a "PC" in a rather broad context, and it turned out that the other participants interpreted his abbreviation in four different ways: personal computer, program console, personal copier, and penal code.[8]

A friend who is a real estate agent tells a story which may be fictional, but it illustrates why we need to explain abbreviations: A college student was hired to work as an intern at a real estate agency for the summer. On the first morning of his new job, his boss sent him a message, "Mr. John Smith is in my office. Please get BLT for him." The young intern dutifully left the office, went down the street to a restaurant, and purchased a bacon, lettuce, and tomato sandwich. When he returned, he carried the sandwich into the boss's office, where the boss and Mr. Smith were conferring. "Here's Mr. Smith's BLT," said the young man. "Thanks," said the boss, laughing. "Now would you please go to the files and get Mr. Smith's Block, Lot, and Tract file?"

Avoid Euphemisms

Refrain from using *euphemisms*—pleasant, mild, or inoffensive words that are used in place of blunt, direct words. Here are some examples of euphemisms:

- ☐ Instead of saying that Bill died, we say that he *departed* or *passed away.*
- ☐ Undertakers, who prefer to be called *funeral directors,* don't handle corpses; they deal with *cases* or *patients.*
- ☐ In many cities, public toilets are now called *comfort stations.*
- ☐ Nations that are poor and backward are termed *developing* and *emerging.*
- ☐ A used car is often advertised as a *preowned* automobile.

Sometimes euphemisms are harmless. If garbage collectors prefer to be called *sanitation engineers,* I may wince at the misuse of language but I cannot object too strenuously. If it makes them feel better about their valuable, but unglamorous, work, if it increases their dignity and self-esteem, why should I criticize their euphemism?

But euphemisms become harmful when they mask a problem that should be dealt with. When a *slum* is called not a slum, but *substandard housing,* does this help the public turn its eyes away from a problem that needs attention?

Using Vivid Language

Vivid words have the magical ability to paint pictures in your listeners' minds—clear, memorable pictures. Let us examine two techniques—imagery and rhythm—which can help you create these pictures.

Create Imagery

You can bring an abstract idea to life by using precise, descriptive words to create images. For example, David Fields, a criminal justice major who had visited several prisons, painted a chilling picture of prison life:

> Prison is a jungle. When you're inside, you're as vulnerable as a lion tamer who steps inside a cage with snarling lions. At any moment the prisoners might erupt in violence. You can find yourself with a dozen knife wounds as a result of an argument over something insignificant. For example, you get a box of chocolate chip cookies from home, and another prisoner wants those cookies and will stab you with a crude, homemade shank if you don't hand them over. There is always noise in prison—even in the dead middle of night; you never have peace and quiet. Glaring lights are on all the time; you're never allowed the luxury of sleeping in the dark. And the place stinks with the odor of fear.

David's picture conveys the reality of prison life better than a long recital of dry statistics could ever convey.

Two devices that are especially effective for creating mental pictures are the simile and the metaphor. With a *simile,* you make a direct comparison of things that are dissimilar, using the words *like* or *as.* For example, "The stars are like diamonds in the sky." Like a simile, a *metaphor* compares dissimilar things, but it leaves off the words *like* and *as.* Thus, the simile just described can be changed into the following metaphor: "The stars are diamonds in the sky."

If fresh images are involved, similes and metaphors can be quite vivid. Here are some examples of the effective use of these devices:

> Marriage is a cozy, calm harbor where you are protected from the storms of the outside world. (*Pamela Smith, student speaker*)

> The snow covered up all the brown humps and furrows of the field, like white frosting on a chocolate cake. (*Joshua Burns, student speaker*)

> Manic-depressives are like passengers on an emotional roller-coaster that goes up, up, up to a high of exhilaration and then down, down, down to a low of despair—without ever stopping to let them off. (*Sarah Gentry, student speaker*)

Beware of *mixed metaphors.* These occur when the speaker combines two images that do not logically go together. Such an arrangement either confuses the

Vivid language can help bring ideas to life. *(Jeffrey Dunn/ The Picture Cube)*

listeners or leaves them smiling in amusement. President Dwight Eisenhower once said that "the Japanese have a tough row to hoe to keep their economic heads above water." This incongruous mixture of images paints the absurd picture of farmers scratching at the soil while struggling to keep from drowning. To correct the problem, one would have to say something like this: "The Japanese will have to swim vigorously to keep their economic heads above water."

Ernest Bevin, former foreign minister of Great Britain, once used this mixed metaphor: "If you let that sort of thing go on, your bread and butter will be cut out from under your feet." This ridiculous picture of people standing on their own food could be altered in the following way: "Your bread and butter will be snatched from your table."

Avoid Clichés

Try to use lively words and phrases. Avoid *clichés,* which are trite, wornout words or phrases that have lost their freshness and vividness. Here are some examples:

- ☐ bored to death
- ☐ ripe old age
- ☐ last but not least
- ☐ far and wide
- ☐ at the crack of dawn
- ☐ a needle in a haystack
- ☐ beat the bushes
- ☐ slow but sure

To eliminate clichés from our speech, we should try to find simple alternatives. For example, instead of saying, "His tie stuck out like a sore thumb," we could say, "His tie was gaudy." Or, if we want a fresh, lively alternative, we could say, "His tie was as garish as a clown at a funeral."

Use Rhythm

You can make your language vivid by taking advantage of rhythmic patterns. One such pattern is *parallel structure,* wherein words, phrases, or clauses are arranged in the same form. Here are some examples, placed in poetic form to emphasize the parallels:

Duty,
Honor,
Country.
These are the watchwords of the American soldier.

We want a government . . . of the people,
by the people,
for the people.

We need parents who will . . . praise honest efforts,
punish bad behavior, and
ignore inconsequential acts.

Parallel structure can intensify the speaker's emotions, as in this example by student speaker Georgia Adams:

When I see fish dying in our streams because of acid rain, I am enraged. When I see trees dying on our highest peaks because of acid rain, I am enraged. When I see animal habitats destroyed because of acid rain, I am enraged.

In addition to using parallel structure, Georgia also used another effective rhythmic technique—*repetition.* Notice that by repeating "I am enraged," she conveyed the full measure of her anger.

In the next section of this chapter we will discuss repetition of key ideas to help the audience remember; here we are talking about repetition for its emotional, rhythmic effect. In the conclusion to a classroom speech on preventing nuclear war, Michael Browning repeated the words "we must work hard" over and over to dramatically challenge his listeners:

Preventing a nuclear war will not be easy. We must all work hard. We must work hard to stop the arms race. We must work hard to create trust and understanding betwen ourselves and other nations. We must work hard to make sure that nuclear weapons are never used accidentally. We must work hard to keep new nations from joining the nuclear "club." It will not be easy. We must work hard.

If you go back and read Michael's conclusion out loud, you will *feel* the power of repetition.

Oral versus Written Language

One of the biggest mistakes some speakers make is to treat oral language in a speech as being no different from written language. While the two forms of communication are similar, oral language has two significant requirements which you should be aware of:

1. *Oral language requires more elaboration than written language.* If you are watching a football game on TV and you fail to see a key block that makes a touchdown possible, you have the luxury of watching an instant replay in slow motion. If you are reading a complicated passage in your chemistry text and you find yourself hopelessly confused, you can go back a few paragraphs and study the material again. Unfortunately, these opportunities are not available when you listen to a speech. If you fail to understand what a speaker is saying, you are out of luck. There is no instant replay. There is no way to back up a few paragraphs.

Because of this handicap, oral language requires more elaboration than is necessary in written language. If a statement is too terse, the audience has trouble absorbing it. Consider the following example, which is the opening sentence of an article about immigrants:

> The first generation tries to retain as much as possible; the second to forget, the third to remember.[9]

That terse sentence is excellent in an essay. The reader can study it at leisure if the meaning does not pop up immediately. But can you imagine sitting in an audience and immediately understanding it? It is too compact for easy comprehension. It would have to be spoken in an expanded form, such as this:

> When immigrants come to America, how do they treat their cultural heritage from the old country? The first generation of immigrants tries to retain as much as possible of the customs, cuisine, and language of the old country. But the second generation wants to forget all of that; these children of immigrants want to become "100 percent American," with no reminders of their foreign roots. But then along comes the third generation; these grandchildren want to celebrate the past, to find out all they can about their old-country heritage.

With this expanded version, the audience would be able to absorb the information.

A note of caution: Just because it is a good idea to amplify your spoken message does not mean that you should pad your oral language with meaningless or windy phrases. In spoken as well as in written communication, you should omit needless words. For example, don't say, "In terms of the future, the military expects to meet its recruiting goals." Leave off the unnecessary five words at the beginning and say, "The military expects to meet its recruiting goals." Don't say, "in the area of statistics." Say simply, "statistics."

2. Oral language requires more repetition of key ideas than written language. "If you have an important point to make," British Prime Minister Winston Churchill advised the young Prince of Wales, "don't try to be subtle or clever. Use a pile driver. Hit the point once. Then come back and hit it again. Then hit it a third time—a tremendous whack."[10]

One of the reasons Churchill is considered one of the greatest orators of the twentieth century is that he followed his own advice. For example, on the subject of resolution, he said:

> Never give in! Never, never, never, never, never, never. In nothing great or small, large or petty—never give in except to convictions of honor and good sense.[11]

Too much repetition? For an essay, yes. For a speech, no.

One trainer of salespersons recommends that a sales message be repeated six times to prospective customers. Why? Because a week after you give a sales spiel without repeating your key ideas, the customers will remember only 10 percent of your message, but if you repeat the key idea six times, they will remember 60 percent of the message.[12] In a public speech, it is hard to predict how much information listeners will retain because there are many variables, such as how much they already know about the subject and how interesting the speech is. But the trainer's estimates do not sound farfetched. In general, listeners do not remember ideas unless they are repeated by the speaker.

Your task is to repeat key ideas, but do it without boring the audience. As an example, suppose that a speaker wanted to make the following point:

> When you're driving in late afternoon and it starts to get dark, turn on your lights so that other motorists can see your car.

While this sentence would be acceptable in an essay, it needs some elaboration and repetition if used in a speech. Here is the way student speaker Stanley Morgan made the point:

> When should you turn on your headlights in the evening? When it gets too dark for you to see other cars? No! That's too late. You should turn on your headlights at the first hint of darkness—not to help *you* see, but to make sure that the *other drivers* see you. I'm constantly amazed at the people who ignore this simple rule of survival. Next time you're driving at dusk, look at the other cars and you'll see what I'm saying is true. Some drivers wait until it's pitch black to turn on their lights. I think it's a matter of personal pride. They have the attitude, "Well, I can still see." The real question is: Can they be seen by other drivers? Remember what I'm telling you; it could prevent you from being in an accident—turn on your lights at dusk so that other drivers can see *you.*

In print, this passage looks too wordy—and it is. But in Stanley's speech, repeating his key idea (but using different words each time) was an effective way of driving home his point. If Stanley had limited himself to only one sentence, his point might have failed to stick in the minds of the audience.

Summary

The words that you use in a speech should be chosen with care and sensitivity. Always use language that is appropriate for your particular audience and occasion, avoiding words that might be over the heads of the listeners or that might offend any member of the audience. To use words accurately, you must be sensitive to both denotations and connotations, and you must use correct grammar.

You can achieve clarity in your language by choosing words that are simple, concrete, and precise. You can achieve vividness by creating word images and by using rhythm.

Oral language and written language are similar in many ways, but there are two significant differences: (1) Oral language requires more elaboration than written language, and (2) oral language requires more repetition of key ideas than written language.

Review Questions

1. Why did Dr. Martin Luther King use different words with different audiences?
2. What is the difference between the denotation and connotation of a word?
3. Where can one find explanations of the synonyms of words?
4. Why is incorrect grammar a handicap for a speaker?
5. What are euphemisms? Give two examples.
6. What are the two major differences between oral and written language?

Tips
FOR YOUR CAREER

Tip 12: Be Sensitive to the Issue of Sexist Pronoun Usage

For centuries the masculine pronouns *he, his,* and *him* were used in the English language to designate an individual when gender was immaterial. In a sentence such as "Every driver should buckle *his* seat belt before *he* starts the engine," the pronouns *his* and *he* were understood to refer to drivers in general, both male and female. Today, however, according to Frederick Crews, a professor of English at the University of California, Berkeley, "many [people] find those words an offensive reminder of second-class citizenship for women."[13]

To avoid offending anyone in your audience, you can handle this pronoun issue in one of three ways:

1. Use masculine and feminine pronouns in tandem. In other words, use *he* or *she* (or *she* or *he*) when referring to an indefinite person. For example, "Every driver should buckle *his* or *her* seat belt before *he* or *she* starts the engine." A problem arises, however, in sentences like this: "Each participant should ask *himself* or *herself* whether *he* or *she* really needs *his* or *her* umbrella." If you continued in this way, the pronouns could become cumbersome, perhaps even distracting the listeners from your ideas. This problem has caused many people to prefer either of the two remaining alternatives.

2. Use plural pronouns. Say simply, "All drivers should buckle *their* seat belts before *they* start the engine." This alternative has the advantage of being simple, while offending no one.

3. Use the pronoun "you." For example, "Whenever *you* get behind the wheel, *you* should buckle *your* seat belt before starting *your* engine." For speeches, this is often the best of the alternatives because it is not only simple and inoffensive, but it also has the virtue of being direct and personal.

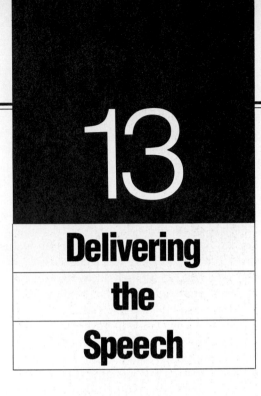

13

Delivering
the
Speech

Methods of Speaking

Voice

Nonverbal Communication

Question-and-Answer Period

Practice

Roger Howard was one of the bravest speakers I have ever seen. A young man from New York City who had been addicted to heroin as a teenager, he founded a chapter of Narcotics Anonymous, which was devoted to salvaging the lives of drug addicts. He appeared at a government-sponsored symposium that dealt with the use and abuse of heroin. Though he was a high school dropout with limited public speaking experience, he had the courage to stand before 300 highly educated people (government officials, professors, and journalists) and try to convince them that the government should provide funds to help victims of what he called the "heroin epidemic."

When Howard started speaking, his delivery was terrible: his eyes were cast downward at a spot on the floor in front of the first row; instead of standing up straight, he was hunched over the microphone; he used no gestures because his hands were too busy clutching the lectern as if it were a life raft; his voice was raspy and tremulous. He seemed shaky and unsure of himself—I'm certain that he was scared to death and wished to be a hundred miles from that room. Yet, at the same time, I sensed that he felt a strong compulsion to tell his story. And what a story it was—a harrowing tale of slavery to a narcotic habit that was so expensive that he had to commit crimes to get enough money for his daily fix. As he got into his story, I observed a remarkable transformation. He came out of his hunched-over position and stood up straight. His eyes looked directly at the listeners, imploring their understanding and support. His hands started moving with power and emphasis. His voice gained strength and confidence. The audience responded by listening with rapt attention. There was absolute stillness in the room. At the end of the speech, the listeners gave him a round of hearty, appreciative applause. His speech was a success.

As you read this chapter, I hope you will keep Roger Howard in mind because he exemplifies an important point: _The key to good delivery is a strong desire to communicate with the audience_. Though Howard started out with ragged, unpolished delivery, he had a burning desire to communicate with the audience, and before long he was unconsciously using good delivery techniques. I have observed this phenomenon time and time again: speakers who lack professional polish and training but who care deeply about conveying their ideas to the audience almost always do an adequate job with their delivery. A General Motors executive, R. T. Kingman, expressed it this way: "If a speaker knows what he wants to say, really wants to say it, and wants everybody in the room to understand what it is he wants to say, all the other things like looking people in the eye and using good gestures will just come naturally."[1]

The speaker's desire to communicate is emphasized so that you can put the ideas of this chapter into proper perspective. The dozens of tips about delivery in the pages that follow are important; you should study them carefully. But bear in mind that a strong desire to communicate with your audience is the dynamo of power that makes it possible for you to deliver a speech with strength and effectiveness.

For extra information on delivery, be sure to read the Tips for Your Career at the end of this chapter and on pages 295 and 352.

Methods of Speaking

There are four basic speaking methods used by public speakers today. You need to ask yourself which method is best suited for your particular audience.

Impromptu

Speaking impromptu means speaking on the spur of the moment—with no chance to prepare. For example, without warning you are asked give a talk to your fellow employees about your recent convention trip to New Orleans. In such a situation, you simply have to do the best that you can. If you get a few minutes' advance warning, jot down your central idea and as many supporting ideas as possible. Formulate your introduction and conclusion. If you have no advance warning at all, try to formulate your main idea as you stand to speak. As best you can, try to present your speech along the lines suggested in this book. The most important advice is this: be brief. When asked to speak impromptu, some speakers spend an hour saying the same thing over and over again because they are afraid of leaving out something important or of being unable to finish the speech smoothly. The sins of leaving something out or having a clumsy conclusion are minor compared to the wickedness of boring an audience for an hour. Brevity is almost always a virtue.

Try to foresee situations where you are likely to be called upon to speak impromptu, and prepare yourself accordingly. In other words, when you return from New Orleans and you are driving to work, rehearse in your mind what you will say if the boss asks you to make a little speech about the convention.

Manuscript

Delivering an entire speech from a manuscript is another method of delivery. There are two ways to deliver such a speech. The first is to simply read the manuscript. Elayne Snyder, a speech consultant, says this approach is used primarily "if you are to testify at a congressional committee hearing or other official hearing where every word will appear in permanent form in an official record, or if you have been asked to deliver a paper at a scientific or educational conference and every word will appear in a conference journal." The problem with this approach, says Snyder, is that it "destroys spontaneity and enthusiasm." The speaker fails to look at the audience, fails to speak with adequate expression, and often reads too quickly.[2]

The second way to deliver a manuscript speech is to use the written text but not actually read it. Here is how this method works: You practice the speech over and over until you are thoroughly familiar with it. When you give the speech, you glance at the text to refresh your memory but most of the time you look at the listeners and speak to them as if the words were coming from the heart—fresh and newly minted. This technique is very effective, but I must warn you: it is much more difficult than it looks. Some actors, experienced politicians, and professional speechmakers use this method with great success, but most speakers—even those with a lot of experience—fail to pull it off. They sound dull and lifeless, rather than natural and spontaneous.

Unless you are a veteran orator, do not use a manuscript. You might fail to maintain good eye contact with your audience, and your words—if they are read instead of spoken naturally—might be hard for the audience to absorb.

Memorized

Memorizing a speech is a bad idea for the following reasons.

☐ You would be forced to spend an enormous amount of time in committing the speech to memory.

☐ At some point in your speech, you might suddenly forget what comes next. This could cause you to become acutely embarrassed or even panic-stricken. Once derailed from your speech, you might be unable to get back on track.

☐ Even if you remembered your entire speech, you would be speaking from your memory, not from your heart. This could cause you to sound remote, lifeless, unenergetic—more like a robot than a human being.

Memorizing does have one virtue: it lets you figure out your *exact* wording ahead of time. But this gain in precision fails to outweigh the disadvantages. Though a few popular speechmakers say that they memorize their speeches, I would not recommend this method for anyone. Certainly not for the inexperienced speaker.

Extemporaneous

The extemporaneous method is the most popular style of speaking in America today. The idea is to sound as if you are speaking spontaneously, but instead of giving the clumsy, faltering speech that many off-the-cuff speakers give, you present a beautifully organized, well-developed speech that you have spent many hours preparing and practicing.

You speak from notes, but these notes do not contain your speech written out word-for-word. Instead they contain only your basic ideas, expressed in a few key words. When you speak, therefore, you make up the exact words as you go along. You glance at your notes occasionally to remind yourself of your next point, but most of the time you look at the listeners, speaking to them in a natural, conversational tone of voice.

This conversational tone is valued in a speech because it is the easiest kind for an audience to listen to, understand, and remember. When you speak conversationally, you are speaking directly, warmly, sincerely. You are speaking as closely as possible to the way you talk to your best friends: your voice is full of life and color; your words are fresh and vital rather than stale and warmed-over.

Though the extemporaneous method is popular and effective, it provides no guarantee of success. In fact, if you are not careful, it can lure you to failure. For this method to work, *you must spend a lot of time preparing and rehearsing your speech*. Mark Twain said, "It takes three weeks to prepare a good ad-lib speech." In other words, if you want to *sound* as if you are ad-libbing beautifully, you have to spend a lot of time in preparation and practice. Speakers who use the extemporaneous method correctly are like the Olympic divers you see on television. These athletes make their high dives look natural and easy, but in reality they have achieved their graceful, "effortless" coordination through hours of hard practice. In public speaking, if you do not put forth time and effort in preparing and practicing, you are really no better off than if you give an impromptu speech. For example, if you fail to prepare a well-organized outline, you might find that your ideas do not hang together and your words are fuzzy and imprecise. If you fail to practice, you might find that your delivery is ragged, with awkward silences and many "uhs" and "ers."

Speaking extemporaneously permits more flexibility than reading from a written speech because you can adjust the speech to meet the needs of a particular audience. If, for example, you see that some of your listeners do not understand a point, you can restate your message in different words or you can insert additional explanations. If you are the last speaker of the evening at a banquet and you sense that your audience is about to go to sleep because of the long-winded speakers who preceded you, you can shorten your speech by cutting out some of your minor points.

Voice

Some people think that to be an excellent speaker, you must have a golden voice, so rich and resonant that it enthralls anyone who listens to it. This is not true. Some of the greatest orators in history had imperfect voices. Abraham Lincoln's voice was described by his contemporaries as "thin, high-pitched, shrill, not musical, and . . . disagreeable"[3] and Winston Churchill "stammered and even had a slight lisp."[4] In our own day, I have observed a popular evangelist whose voice is thin and weak, a successful TV commentator who talks in an irritatingly abrasive manner, and a leading politician who speaks with an unpleasant nasal whine. Yet all three are in demand as public speakers. It is nice to have a rich, resonant voice, but there are other characteristics of the human voice which are of greater importance for effective speechmaking: your voice should have proper volume; it should be clear and understandable, and it should be expressive.

Volume

The larger the room, the louder you have to speak. You can tell if your volume is loud enough by observing the people in the back row. Are they leaning forward with quizzical expressions as they strain to hear your words? Then obviously you need to speak louder. In some cases you may want to ask directly, "Can the people in the back row hear me all right?" There are some circumstances in which you

In a larger room, a speaker must be sure to speak more loudly. *(Ulrike Welsch)*

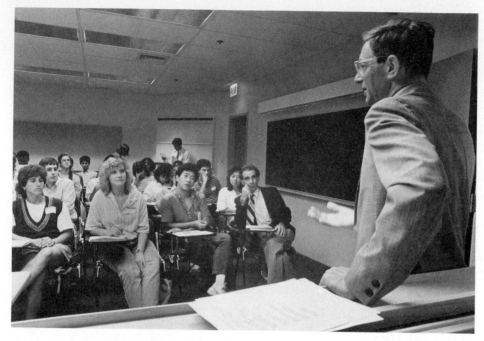

may have to raise your voice to overcome unavoidable noises, such as the hum of air conditioners, the chatter of people in a hallway, the clatter of dishes and silverware during a banquet, or even the sound of a band blaring in the next room.

Speaking loud enough for all to hear does not mean shouting. It means *projecting* your voice a bit beyond its normal range. If you have never spoken to a large group or if your instructor tells you that you have problems in projecting your voice, practice with a friend. Find an empty classroom, have your friend sit in the back row, and practice speaking with extra force—not shouting—so that your friend can hear you easily.

If a speech requires the use of a microphone, go to the meeting site early and spend a few minutes testing your voice before the listeners arrive. Adjust it to your height; if someone readjusts it during the ceremonies, spend a few moments getting it just right for yourself. Your audience will not mind the slight delay. When you speak into a mike, it is not necessary to have your lips almost touching it; in fact, your voice will sound better if your mouth is 6 to 12 inches away from the mike. Position the mike so that you can forget that it is there. This frees you to speak naturally, without having to bend over or lean forward. At large meetings, I have heard speakers raise their voices while talking into a microphone; this makes their voice sound strident. A microphone means that you *don't* have to raise your voice. In fact, says professional speaker Arnold "Nick" Carter, "the invention of the microphone made it possible for me to speak to 18,000 people with a whisper."[5]

Clarity

The words that you speak should be uttered clearly and understandably, with good
articulation and correct pronunciation.

Here is the kind of dialogue you might hear on any college campus in America:

"Watcha doin?"
"Stud'n a liddle histry."
"Howbout that lass test? Wajagit?"
"Dunno, probly flunked."
"Jeatyet?"
"Nah."
"Lessgo getta pizza."

Most of us are lazy in our daily conversations; we slur sounds, drop syllables,
and mumble words. While poor articulation may not hurt us in conversation as
long as our friends understand what we are saying, it can hinder communication
in a speech. We need to enunciate our words crisply and precisely to make sure
that everything we say is intelligible to our listeners.

If you tend to slur words, you can improve your speech by reading poems or
essays aloud 15 minutes a day for three weeks. Say the words with exaggerated
emphasis, and move your mouth and tongue vigorously. Enunciate consonants
firmly and make vowel sounds last longer than normal. In real situations you
should not exaggerate in this way, but the practice will help you avoid the pitfalls
of slurring and mumbling.

While poor articulation stems from sloppy habits, mispronunciation is a matter
of not knowing the correct way to say a word. Here are some common pronunciation mistakes:

	Incorrect	*Correct*
recognize	reck-uh-nize	rec-og-nize
library	li-berry	li-brar-y
nuclear	nu-cu-lar	nu-cle-ar
picture	pitch-er	pic-ture
hundred	hun-derd	hun-dred
realtor	reel-a-tor	re-al-tor
perspiration	press-pi-ra-tion	per-spi-ra-tion
drowned	drown-did	drownd
athlete	ath-uh-lete	ath-lete

If you are like most people, you use words which you have picked up from
books but have never heard pronounced. If you rely on your own guess, it can
sometimes cause embarrassment, as in the case of one student who had read all
about the Sioux Indians, but apparently had never heard the tribal name pronounced. He called them the *sigh-ox* Indians. On other occasions you may confuse
words that sound a lot alike. For example, one of my students said that a man and
woman contemplating marriage should make sure they are compatible before

they say their *vowels*. (One of the listeners couldn't resist the temptation to ask, at the end of the speech, whether consonants were also important for marriage.)

These kinds of mistakes can be avoided by looking up a word's meaning and pronunciation in a dictionary.

Expressiveness

The most boring voices in the world are probably those of elementary school chidren when they stand on a stage for a holiday skit and mouth sentences they have been required to memorize, often using words whose meanings they are blithely unaware of. Their lines are uttered in a flat monotone, without any flair or meaning.

In sharp contrast, a dynamic speaker has a voice that is warm and expressive, producing a rich variety of sounds. Audiences find such a voice more interesting to listen to than a monotonous one, and therefore they are more likely to respond favorably to what the speaker says. To achieve expressiveness, one must make good use of the following elements.

Pitch

The highness or lowness of your voice is called *pitch*. The ups and downs of pitch—called *intonation patterns*—give our language its distinctive melody. Consider the following sentence: "I was angry." Say it in a variety of ways—with anger, with sarcasm, with humor, with disbelief. Each time you say it, you are using a different intonation pattern.

In conversation, almost everyone uses a variety of intonation patterns and emphasizes particular words, but in public speaking, some speakers fail to use any variety at all. They speak in a monotone—a dull, flat drone that will put many listeners to sleep. Even worse, they run the risk of appearing insincere. They may say, for example, something dramatic like "This is a terrible tragedy for America," but say it in such a casual, offhand way that the audience thinks they do not really mean it.

One of the problems with a monotone is that some words fail to receive the emphasis they deserve. For example, take a sentence like this: "Mr. Smith made $600,000 last year, while Mr. Jones made $6000." Speakers who talk in a monotone will say the two figures as if there were no difference between $600,000 and $6000. But listeners need help in *hearing* the disparity. A speaker should let his or her voice place heavy emphasis on the $600,000.

Loudness and Softness

Besides having the proper volume, so that everyone in the audience can hear you, you can raise or lower your voice for dramatic effect or to emphasize a point. Try saying the following out loud:

(*Soft:*) "Should we give in to the kidnappers' demands? (*Switch to loud:*) NEVER!"

Did you notice that raising your voice for the last word conveys that you truly mean what you say? Now try another selection out loud:

> (*Start softly and make your voice grow louder as you near the end of this sentence:*) Edwin Arlington Robinson's character Richard Cory had everything that a man could want—good looks, lots of money, popularity. (*Now make your voice switch to soft:*) But he went home one night and put a bullet through his head.

Changing from loud to soft helps the listeners *feel* the tragic discrepancy between Richard Cory's outer appearance and his inner reality.

Rate

How quickly or slowly should you speak? The ideal speed for giving a speech is like the ideal speed for driving a car—it all depends on conditions. Driving a car at 55 miles per hour is fine for a highway but too fast for a school zone. In similar fashion, a rapid rate of speaking is appropriate in certain conditions—if, for example, you are describing a thrilling high-speed police chase. A slow pace, on the other hand, is preferred if you are introducing a technical, hard-to-understand concept.

One of the biggest mistakes inexperienced speakers make is to speak too rapidly. It is especially important that you speak at a slow, deliberate rate during your introduction (except in special situations, as when you lead off with an adventure story). Have you ever noticed that TV dramas start out very slowly? They do not divulge important details of the story until you are 3 or 4 minutes into the show. One obvious reason for this is to have mercy on the viewers who have gone to the kitchen to get a snack and are slow in returning to the television. But the main reason is to give the viewers a chance to "tune in" to the story, to get adjusted to what is happening on the screen, to get accustomed to the characters. If too much action or dialogue takes place in the first minute, viewers are unable to absorb the story. In like fashion, you need to give your audience a chance to "tune in" to you, to get accustomed to your voice and subject matter. If you race through your introduction, they might become lost and confused, and they might decide to spend the time daydreaming rather than struggling to follow your racehorse delivery.

Speaking slowly—and using pauses, especially at the beginning—will make you come across to the audience as someone who is confident and in control, as someone who cares about whether the listeners understand.

You can avoid speaking too rapidly by practicing your speech at home. Use a tape recorder and listen to yourself. Have friends or relatives listen to your speech; ask them to tell you frankly if you are speaking too fast for easy comprehension.

Some people speak too rapidly because they write out all or most of their speech on their note cards or a sheet of paper and then when they rise to speak, they succumb to the temptation of reading rapidly from their script. The solution is to have brief notes, not a written script, when you stand up to speak.

Pauses

When you read printed material, you have punctuation marks to help you make sense out of your reading—commas tell you when to pause, periods when to stop, etc. In a speech, there are no punctuation marks; listeners must rely on oral cues to guide them. One of these cues is the pause, which lets your listeners know when you have finished one thought and are ready to go to the next. Audiences appreciate a pause. It gives them time to digest what you have said. And it gives you a moment to think of what you are going to say next.

A pause before an important idea or the climax of a story can create suspense. For example, student speaker Stephanie Johnson told of an adventure that happened while she was camping:

> It was late at night when I finally crawled into my sleeping bag. The fire had died down, but the moon cast a faint, spooky light on our campsite. I must have been asleep a couple of hours when I suddenly woke up. Something was brushing up against my sleeping bag. My heart started pounding like crazy. I peeked out of the slit I had left for air. Do you know what I saw? [*pause*]

By pausing at this point, Stephanie had the audience on the edge of their chairs. What was it? A bear? A human intruder? After a few moments of dramatic tension, she ended the suspense: "By the light of the moon, I could see a dark little animal with a distinctive white stripe. [*pause*] It was a skunk."

A pause can also be used to emphasize an important statement. It is a way of saying, "Let this sink in." Notice how student speaker Erik Swenson used pauses in his speech:

> Albert Einstein was once asked whether he thought that World War III would be fought with nuclear weapons. [*pause to give the listeners a chance to think about the momentous nature of the question*] Einstein, the man who made possible the construction of the atomic bomb, gave this answer: "I don't know what weapons will be used for World War III, but I do know what weapons will be used for World War IV: [*pause to create dramatic tension and suspense*] sticks and stones." [*pause to let the audience reflect on the irony*]

Erik's dramatic pauses captivated his audience. Notice that his final pause gave the listeners time to reflect on Einstein's insight.

In some speeches you might find yourself pausing not because you want to, but because you have forgotten what you were planning to say next and you need to look at your notes. Or you might pause while searching your mind for the right word. Such a pause seems like an eternity, so you are tempted to fill in the horrible silence with verbal fillers like "uh" or "er" or "um." Try hard not to make these sounds. There is nothing wrong with silence; there is no need to be embarrassed by it. The audience does not mind. In fact, a few such pauses can enhance your credibility, making you seem more conversational and natural, and less artificial and contrived. You look as if you are concerned about giving the audience the most precise words possible.

Conversational Quality

Many inexperienced speakers give their speeches in a dull, plodding, colorless voice. Yet 5 minutes afterward, chatting with their friends in the hall, they speak with animation and warmth.

What they need to do, obviously, is bring that same conversational quality into their speeches. How can this be done? How can a person sound as lively and as "real" in talking to thirty people as in chatting with a friend? If this problem applies to you, here are two suggestions:

1. *Treat your audience not as an impersonal mass, not as a blur of faces, but as a collection of individuals.* Some students sound wooden and artificial when giving a speech, but during the question-and-answer period, they respond to questions in a natural, conversational manner. Why does this happen? One reason is that they are engaged in a conversation with the person who asked the question. They are now talking one-on-one. To capture this style of talking during the speech itself, here is a mental ploy you can use from the very beginning: look at one or two or three individuals in different parts of the room and act as if you are talking to them one-on-one. You should avoid staring, of course, but if you look at them briefly, it will help you develop a conversational attitude. As the speech goes on, you can add other faces to your "conversation."

2. *Be yourself—but somewhat intensified.* To speak to an audience with the same natural, conversational tone you use with your friends, you must speak with greater energy and forcefulness. We are not talking now about projecting your voice so that the people in the back of the room can hear you, but rather about *intensifying* the psychological dimensions of your voice—the emotional tones and the vibrancy. How can you do this? Here are two ways.

First, let your natural enthusiasm come forth. If you have chosen a topic wisely, you are speaking on something you care a great deal about and want very much to communicate to the audience. When you stand in front of your audience, don't keep a lid on your feelings. Don't hold yourself back; let your voice convey all the enthusiasm that you feel inside. Many speakers are afraid they will look or sound ridiculous if they get involved with their subject. 'I'll come on too strong," they say. But the truth is that your audience will not react this way; they will be impressed by your energy and zest. Think back to the speakers you have heard: Didn't you respond favorably to those who were alive and enthusiastic?

Second, practice loosening up. Some novice speakers sound and look stiff because they simply have had no practice in loosening up. Here is something you can try: find a private location (such as a room at home or a clearing in the woods or an empty classroom late in the afternoon when no one else is around). For subject matter, you can practice a speech that you are working on, recite poetry, read from the morning newspaper, or simply ad-lib. Whatever words you use, say them dramatically. "Ham it up." Be theatrical. Act as if you are running for President and you are trying to persuade 10,000 people to vote for you. Or act as if you are giving a poetry reading to 500 of your most enthusiastic fans. You will not speak so dramatically to a real audience, of course, but the practice of "letting go" will help you break out of your normal reserve. It will help you learn to be yourself, to convey your natural enthusiasm.

Nonverbal Communication

Nonverbal communication consists of the messages that you send without words—what you convey with your eyes, facial expression, posture, body movement, and tone of voice.

The words of a speech, says Roger Ailes, a communications consultant who has advised various presidential candidates, "are meaningless unless the rest of you is in synchronization."[6] Corporate executives, he says, "often get up and send all sorts of weird signals to their audience. My favorite is, 'Ladies and gentlemen, I'm very happy to be here.' But they're looking at their shoes as they say it. They have no enthusiasm whatsoever. They look either angry, frightened, or depressed about being there."[7]

When there is a discrepancy between words and nonverbal behavior, the audience "will always go with the visual signals over the verbal ones," says Ailes. "They'll say to themselves unconsciously, 'He's telling me he's happy to be here, but he's really not. Therefore, he's either uncomfortable or a liar, or both.'"[8]

To get your nonverbal signals synchronized with your words, you need to show enthusiasm (with your eyes, facial expression, posture, and tone of voice) as you speak to your audience. Let your body confirm that you believe in what you are saying and that you want your audience to accept your ideas.

If you are truly enthusiastic about your speech and eager to share it with your audience, much of your body language will take care of itself, as we discussed at the beginning of this chapter. But you may be asking, "What if I don't really feel happy and confident? I can't lie with my body, can I?" This is a good question, because there are times in your life when you will resent having to give a speech, as when the boss orders you to give a presentation to the board of directors or an instructor assigns you to give an oral report to the class. Also there are times when you simply do not feel like standing up in front of a group. Maybe you did not get much sleep the night before, and you have no zip, no spark. At times like these, what should you do?

Pretend. Yes, pretend to be confident in yourself and in your ideas. Pretend to be glad to appear before your audience. Pretend to be enthusiastic. But isn't this phony? Isn't this forcing the body to tell a lie? Yes, but we often must be "deceitful" in order to carry out life's tasks. We force ourselves to be cheerful and animated for a crucial job interview, for conferences with the boss, for an important date with someone we love, and for myriad other situations in life. By *acting* as if you are confident, poised, and enthusiastic, you will often find that after a few minutes, the pretense gives way to reality. You truly become confident, poised, and enthusiastic. Consider the comedians and talk-show hosts who appear night after night on television. Do you think they are always "up"? No, they are like you and me. They have their bad days, their sluggish days, their down-in-the-dumps days, their head-cold and stomach-ache days, but they force themselves to perform;

they pretend to be enthusiastic. After about 60 seconds (most of them report), the pretense gives way to reality, and they truly *are* enthusiastic. (A word of advice: If this transformation fails to happen to you—if you do not feel enthusiastic after a few minutes—you should still pretend.)

How do you carry out this pretense? How can you make the body "lie" for you? The answer is to be sensitive to the "signals" that the body sends out to show confidence and energy, and then to force yourself to use these signals. To familiarize yourself with these signals, take a look at the major nonverbal aspects of public speaking.

Personal Appearance

Your audience will size up your personal appearance and start forming opinions about you even before you open your mouth to begin your speech. You should be clean, well-groomed, and attractively dressed.

Janet Stone and Jane Bachner, who conduct workshops for women executives, have some good advice for both men and women:

> As a general rule of thumb, find out what the audience will be wearing and then wear something yourself that is just a trifle dressier than their clothes. The idea is to establish yourself as "The Speaker," to set yourself slightly apart from the crowd, to show them that you are taking their invitation seriously enough to dress up a little for them, and yet to look enough like them to establish yourself as a person they can identify with.[9]

Your attire should always be appropriate. In other words, do not wear anything that would distract or offend the audience. A T-shirt with a ribald or controversial slogan printed on the front, for example, might direct attention away from the speech itself, and it might offend some members of the audience.

Eye Contact

You should look at your audience 95 percent of the time while you are talking. The other 5 percent is for occasional glances at your notes. Having good eye contact with your listeners is important for three reasons: (1) It creates an important bond of communication and rapport between you and them. It is, in the words of professional speaker Jack Valenti, a "figurative handshake."[10] (2) It shows your sincerity. There's an old saying, "Don't buy a used car from a dealer who won't look you in the eye." We distrust people who won't look at us openly and candidly. If you want your listeners to have confidence in what you are saying, look at *them,* not at a spot on the back wall. (3) It enables you to get audience feedback. Looking directly at your listeners makes you instantly aware of any lapses in communication. For example, did a number of listeners look puzzled when you made your last statement? Then you obviously confused them; you need to explain your point in a different way.

The biggest spoiler of good eye contact is looking at your notes too much.

This is usually caused by one of the following: (1) Not being prepared. This can be corrected, of course, by rehearsing your speech so many times that you need only glance at your notes to remind yourself of what comes next. (2) Nervousness. Some speakers are well prepared and do not really need to look at their notes very often, but they are so nervous that they scrutinize their notes to gain security and avoid the audience. One way to correct this is to put reminders, in giant red letters, on your notes—LOOK AT AUDIENCE—to shake you out of this habit.

Eye contact is more than darting furtive glances at the audience from time to time. It is more than mechanically moving your head from side to side like an oscillating fan. You must have meaningful contact similar to the eye-to-eye communication you engage in with your friends. For a large audience, the best technique is to have a "conversation" with three or four people in different parts of the room (so that you seem to be giving your attention to the entire audience). Professional speaker James "Doc" Blakely expains how to do this:

> Many speakers, especially inexperienced ones, don't see an audience at all. To them, it is just a blur of faces. I have found that the real key in natural, conversational speaking is to pick out the friendliest faces in the audience and speak to them as if you were speaking only to that person. It's like everyone else is eavesdropping on the conversation. By shifting eye contact from one point to another scattered throughout the room, but still speaking to those friendly faces, you give the listeners the feeling that you are speaking to them as individuals.[11]

While picking out faces in different parts of the room is a good technique for large audiences, you should actually look at *every* listener when the audience is small. Professional speaker Danny Cox uses a technique called "locking" whenever he speaks to a small gathering:

> I learned something once from a piano player. I couldn't believe how she held an audience in a cocktail bar. It was so quiet in there you couldn't believe it. I realized one night what she was doing. She was looking at each person and as soon as she made eye contact with them, she smiled at them. And then moved on to the next one, and smiled. She was "locking" everybody in. This is a good technique in public speaking—very simple, too.[12]

Facial Expressions

You should let your face express whatever emotion is appropriate at any given moment in a speech. A student told me he was planning to speak on how to perform under pressure; his primary example was the thrilling moment in high school when he kicked the winning field goal in the final seconds of a championship football game. When he described that triumphant feat, his face was suffused with excitement, but when he got up in front of the class and told the same story in his speech, his face was blank. Gone was the joy, gone was the exhilaration. By having a facial expression that was incongruous with the event he was describing, he weakened the impact of the story.

If you are speaking about sad topics, your face should not be grinning; if you are speaking about happy times, your face should not be grimacing. And whatever you are talking about, your face should not be devoid of emotion—it should be animated. "Animation," says speech consultant Dorothy Sarnoff, "is the greatest cosmetic you can use, and it doesn't cost a cent. Animation is energy in the face. . . . It's action that comes not only through the eyes, but around the mouth and the whole face. It tells the listener you're glad to be right where you are—at the lectern, around a conference table or across a desk."[13] How can you make your face become animated? By choosing a subject that you care a great deal about, by having a strong desire to communicate your message to your listeners, and by delivering your speech with energy and enthusiasm.

Posture

Stand in front of your audience poised, with your weight equally distributed on your feet. Your body language should convey the message, "I am confident; I am in command of this situation." This does not mean that you should be cocky and arrogant, but simply that you should convey an appearance of relaxed alertness.

If you are speaking at a lectern, here are some things *not* to do: Do not lean on it. Do not slouch to one side of it. Do not prop your feet on its base. Do not rock back and forth with it.

Some speakers like to sit on the edge of a desk to deliver a speech. This posture is fine for one-hour classroom lectures because the speaker gets a chance to relax, and his or her body language bespeaks openness and informality. But for short speeches, especially the kind you are expected to deliver in a public speaking class, stand up straight, primarily because it is easier to be alert and enthusiastic if you are standing up than if your body is in a relaxed sitting position.

Movement

You do not have to stand in one place throughout your speech as if you were glued to the spot. Feel free to move about. You can walk to the chalkboard and write a key word, or walk to your visual aid. Occasionally you can move left or right from the lectern to a new position in front of the audience.

Movement gives your body a chance to dissipate nervous energy. It can also be used to recapture your listeners' attention if they are getting bored or tired; an animated speaker is easier to follow than an unanimated speaker who stays frozen in one spot.

You can use movement to emphasize a transition from one point to the next. For example, walking three steps to the left of the lectern while giving the audience a verbal "bridge" to your next point is a good way to emphasize that you are moving from one idea to another.

Movement can also be used to drive home an important point. At a crucial juncture in your speech, when you want strong audience involvement, you can take a few steps toward the listeners as you state a key idea. Moving toward them signals nonverbally that you are keenly interested in having them understand and accept what you are saying.

All your movements should be purposeful and confident—not random and nervous. If you roam back and forth across the front of the room like a tiger in a cage, your audience will be distracted and even annoyed. Don't sway back and forth; don't rock on your heels. In short, make your movements add to your speech, rather than subtract from it.

Using Notes

For classroom speeches, your instructor will tell you whether you may use notes and whether you may use a lectern.

For speeches in your career, the note system that was explained in Chapter 11 is highly recommended. It is a system that most professional speakers use. (Even speakers who talk without looking at notes often have notes with them as insurance—in case they lose their train of thought.)

If you do take cards or sheets of paper to the lectern, display them in whatever way works best for you. Some speakers place them in a stack on the lectern and consult one at a time. Other speakers spread them out, so that several are visible at a time.

Here is a technique that has become popular in business and professional speeches (but you should check with your instructor before trying it in a classroom speech): Using the lectern as "home base," walk a few paces to the left or right of it each time you make a point. In other words, glance at your notes on the lectern to remind yourself of the point you want to make, move away from the lectern a few paces, make the point, then walk back to the lectern to pick up your next point. The rationale for this technique is that you remove the physical barrier (the lectern) that separates you from your listeners so that you strengthen your bond of communication with them.

In some situations, you may find that the location for your speech has no lectern. How should you handle your notes? Simply hold them in one hand and glance at them occasionally. You should of course leave your other hand free for gesturing.

Whatever note system is used, remember our earlier warning: *Use notes sparingly.* Look at your audience 95 percent of the time; look at your notes only 5 percent.

Gestures

What should you do with your hands during a speech? The best advice is to let your hands be free to make gestures whenever you feel like making them. This, after all, is how you make gestures in conversation—naturally and without thinking. To make sure that your hands are free for gesturing, you can let them hang by your side, or allow them to rest on the lectern. Beware of doing things that prevent your hands from being free to gesture: (1) *Don't* grip the lectern with your hands.

Gestures should be
natural and com-
fortable to the
speaker. *(McGraw-
Hill photo by Lisa
Willinger, courtesy of
Pace University)*

(2) *Don't* clutch your notes with both hands. (3) *Don't* stuff both hands into your
pockets.

Gestures are good if they reinforce your message or help the audience
understand what you are saying; gestures are bad if they draw attention to themselves. If, to show anger, you slam your fist down on the lectern, knocking over a
glass of water and scaring the audience, you have called attention to the gesture
and distracted the audience from your message.

If you use a lectern, do not let it hide your gestures. Some speakers rest their
hands on the lectern and make tiny, flickering gestures that cannot be seen by the
audience. This is distracting to many listeners. Better no gestures at all than half-
hidden ones.

Some speeches call for lots of gestures, some call for little or none. If you
were describing your battle to catch a huge fish in the ocean, you would find your
hands and arms constantly in motion. If you were giving a funeral eulogy, on the
other hand, you might not make any gestures at all.

Most gestures should not be mechanically planned in advance because if you
are not using gestures naturally, your timing might be off. One student gave a
speech in which he planned ahead of time to slam his fist on the lectern at the
climax of his remarks. He said to the audience, "We must close down all nuclear
plants!" But then he waited a few seconds before he slammed his fist down on
the lectern, as if he had forgotten to do it until he had seen the cue on his note
cards. The effect was comical rather than serious.

Though most of the time you should not plan gestures in advance, there are a few occasions when this is appropriate. If you have three major points to make, you can practice in advance holding up the correct number of fingers to assist the audience in following your points. If you are discussing two contrasting ideas, you can hold up your left hand when you say "On the one hand, . . ." and then hold up your right hand when you say "On the other hand, . . ."

The larger the audience, the more sweeping your gestures. The evangelists who use windmill-like arm movements in addressing their multitudes in arenas are doing so for a good reason: they are able to establish a bond with people who are hundreds of yards away; small gestures would be lost in the vastness of the arena.

One last comment about gestures: if you are the kind of person who simply does not gesture much, don't worry about it. You have enough on your mind without having to add this item to your list of worries. Just be sure to keep your hands free (not clutching notes or the lectern), so that if a gesture wells up inside you and cries out for expression, you will be able to make it naturally and forcefully.

Beginning and Ending

First impressions are important in many human events. The first impression we make on a person at a party, for example, often determines whether the person will want to spend much time chatting with us. In a speech, as one IBM executive told me, "You have only one chance to make a first impression." You make this first impression as you walk to the front and as you say your first few sentences.

When they are introduced, many inexperienced speakers rush forward and start speaking even before they get to the front. The problem is that the listeners are not ready. They need time to get settled, so that they can clear their minds of other things and tune in to you.

When you are called upon, you should walk confidently to the front, face your audience, and then pause a few seconds before speaking. Do not say a word—just stand in silence. Some inexperienced speakers are terrified by this silence; they view it as a horrible event that makes the audience think they are too frozen with fear to speak. If you have had this concern, relax. A brief period of silence is a very effective technique which all good speakers use. It is a punctuation device, separating what went before from what is to come—your speech. It creates drama, giving the audience a sense of expectancy. It is a dignified quietness that establishes your confidence and authority. In some cases, you may need to wait longer than a few seconds. If you are speaking to a civic club, for example, and a large number of people are arriving late, it is best to wait until the noise created by the latecomers has settled down. Or if many members of the audience are still whispering comments related to the previous speaker, you should simply stand and wait until you have their attention.

During these opening moments of silence, you have a chance to make sure your notes are in order and to review once again what you will say in your introduction. The next step is very important. Before you say a word, give your audience a friendly, confident look (if possible, smile) and then, continuing to look at your listeners instead of at your notes, say your first few sentences. You should have practiced your introduction thoroughly, so that you can say it without looking down at your notes. It is important to establish eye contact at this point. By looking at the listeners directly, your body language is saying, "I'm talking to you—I'm not up here just going through the motions of making a speech. I want to communicate. I want to reach out to you."

While first impressions are vital, final impressions are also important. Like your introduction, your conclusion should be well rehearsed (though not memorized), so that you can say it without looking at your notes. At the end of your speech, pause a few moments, look at your audience, and say, "Are there any questions?" or "I'll be happy to answer your questions now."

Question-and-Answer Period

In classroom speeches, the question-and-answer period usually represents a small percentage of the total time spent in front of the audience, but in some presentations in business, professional, and technical fields, the question-and-answer period is *the* most important part. Your speech is just a prelude—a little warm-up to get the audience ready for the questions. In some sales presentations, for example, the speaker will talk for, say, 10 minutes and then the question-and-answer period will go on for over an hour, with the listeners getting down to the nitty-gritty ("Okay, you say this machine will never wear out, but what happens if...").

Many listeners are so accustomed to listener-speaker interaction that they will interrupt during a speech to ask questions. In some technical presentations or classroom lectures, such interruptions might be appropriate and acceptable, but in other speeches, they are a nuisance. The continuity of the speaker's remarks is broken because listeners are prematurely asking questions that will be answered later in the speech. If you feel that your speech would be marred by interruptions, you should announce early in the orienting material of your introduction, "I know many of you will have questions. I'd like to ask you to hold them until I finish my presentation and then I'll be happy to try to answer them."

Here are some guidelines:

☐ Find out ahead of time if the person planning the program will want or permit a question-and-answer period and, if so, how much time will be allotted.

☐ Decide in advance if you want to invite comments as well as questions. If you do, you can say, "Are there questions or comments?" (In some situations, you may not want comments because they could mushroom into long-winded rebuttals that detract from your message and leave no time for short, clarifying questions.)

☐ Plan for the question-and-answer period as carefully as you plan for the speech itself. Jot down all the possible questions that you think might come from the audience, and then decide exactly how you will answer them if they are asked.

☐ Try to regard the question-and-answer period as a blessing, not a curse. It gives you valuable feedback—it helps insure that the message you intended the listeners to receive is indeed the one they end up with. If a misunderstanding has occurred, you have an excellent opportunity to clear it up.

☐ Ask for questions as if you really wanted them. If you lean toward your seat and let your facial expression and tone of voice say, "Please don't ask me any questions," you won't get any, and the audience will be deprived of an opportunity to get clarification and elaboration.

☐ Do not feel defeated if you are not asked any questions. It could mean that you have covered everything so well that the listeners truly have nothing to ask.

☐ Give the audience time to think of questions. Some speakers wind up their conclusion, hastily ask if there are any questions, impatiently wait 3 seconds, and then dash back to their seats. They do not really give the audience a fair chance. When you ask for questions, pause for as long as 10 seconds. If you get the feeling that no questions at all will be asked, you can say "Thank you" and sit down. But if you sense that the audience is simply shy (some listeners want to ask questions but are afraid that their question will be considered "dumb"), you may want to give them some encouragement. One way is to say, "While you're thinking of questions, let me answer one that a lot of people ask me...." In some community and career contexts, you may even want to involve the listeners by asking *them* a question; for example, "What do *you* think of my proposal?"

☐ When a person asks a question, look directly at him or her, but when you give your answer, look at the entire audience, so that no one feels left out.

☐ In a large room, when a question is asked, repeat it for the benefit of listeners who may not have heard it. Repeating it also gives you time to think of your answer. If a question is unclear to you, ask the listener to clarify it.

☐ Don't reward some questions with "That's a good question" or "I'm glad you asked that," because the questioners who receive no praise from you will feel that their questions have been judged inferior.

☐ If you do not know the answer to a question, say so. Your listeners will not think less of you for an honest admission of ignorance on a particular point; they *will* think less of you if you try to fake expertise. In some situations, you may want to ask the audience for help: "I don't know the answer. Is there anyone here who can help us out?"

☐ If a listener points out a flaw in the logic of your argument or casts doubt on some of your facts and figures, try to avoid being defensive. If the listener seems to have merit to his or her point, say so. You can say something like "You've got a good point. I'm going to have to think about this some more," or "You may be right: that statistic could be outdated. I'll have to check it. Thanks for mentioning it." Such a conciliatory approach is not only honest, it is also a good way to gain respect from the listeners. No one expects you to be perfect; if a listener finds an error in your speech, it does not mean that your whole effort has been discredited.

☐ Do not let one listener "hog" the question-and-answer period, especially if a number of other people have questions. If a person persists in asking one question after another or launches into a long monologue, you should interrupt and say, "Let's give others a chance to ask questions; if we have time later, I'll get back to you."

☐ Decline to answer questions that are not appropriate for a discussion in front of the entire audience—for example, questions that are too personal or that would require a long, technical explanation that most of the listeners would find boring and tedious. You can deflect such questions by politely explaining your reasons; for example, "That's a little too personal—I'd rather not go into that," or "I'm afraid it would take up too much time to go into the details right now." In some cases, you might tell the questioner to see you afterward for a one-on-one discussion.

☐ Don't let the question-and-answer period drag on interminably. If you have been allotted an hour, say, for both your speech and the question-and-answer period, end the session promptly at the end of an hour—even if some listeners still have questions. (As we have already discussed, it is important that you avoid going over your time limit.) If your speech is the last item on the program and you sense that some listeners would like to continue the question-and-answer period, you could say, "I'm going to end the formal part of my presentation now because I promised I would take up only 1 hour of your time and I know that some of you have other business to take care of. However, if any of you would like to stay, you can move to the seats here at the front and we'll continue with an informal question-and-answer period."

Practice

After you have written your outline and made notes based on it (as discussed in Chapter 11), you should spend a great deal of time rehearsing your speech. Practice, practice, practice—it's a crucial step that some inexperienced speakers leave out. Practice makes you look and sound fluent, smooth, and spontaneous. Practice bolsters your confidence, giving you a sense of mastery and competence.

Here are some tips:

☐ Start early. If you wait until the eve of your speech, you will not have enough time to develop and polish your delivery. Allow yourself at least 4 days of practice before your speech date.

☐ Practice going through your entire speech at least 4 times, more if necessary. Space your practice sessions; in other words, avoid doing most of your practicing on a single day. You will find that you make greater progress if you have time intervals between practice sessions.

☐ "Practice ideas, not words" is a maxim worth heeding; in other words, learn your speech point by point, not word by word.[14] Remember that your goal in extemporaneous speaking is not to memorize or read a speech. Every time you say your speech (whether in practice or in delivery to an audience), the wording should be different. The ideas will be the same, but not the words.

☐ Time yourself during practice sessions. If your speech exceeds the time limit set by your instructor or by the group that invited you, go back to your outline and notes and trim them down.

☐ During most of your practice sessions, go all the way through the speech. Do not stop if you hit a problem (you can work it out later). Going all the way through helps you see whether your ideas fit together snugly, and whether your transitions from point to point are smooth.

☐ Some speakers find it helpful to practice in front of a mirror or to use a video or audio tape recorder. Whether or not you use one of these techniques, you should practice at least once in front of a *live* audience—friends or relatives who can give you a candid appraisal. Don't make an imprecise request like "Tell me how I do on this," because your evaluators will probably say at the end of your speech, "You did fine—good speech," to avoid hurting your feelings. Instead give them a specific assignment: "Please make a note of at least two things I do well and at least two things that I need to improve on." Now your listeners have an assignment that they know will not hurt your feelings, and you are likely to get some helpful feedback.

☐ Some speakers find it helpful to make a trial run in the very room in which they will give the speech. This would be an especially good idea if you have visual aids and equipment; you can practice the mechanics, for example, of showing overhead transparencies.

☐ In addition to practicing the entire speech, devote special practice time to your beginning and ending—two parts that should be smooth and effective.

☐ Be sure that you don't put too many words down on your notes. Have just the bare minimum necessary to jog your memory. Practice from the actual notes that you will use in the speech. Don't make a clean set right before the speech; the old marked-up notes are more reliable because you're very familiar with them from your practice sessions.

Summary

The key to good delivery is a strong desire to communicate with the audience. Speakers who concentrate on getting their ideas across to their listeners usually find themselves using good delivery techniques.

There are four methods of delivering a speech: impromptu, manuscript, memorized, and extemporaneous. Of the four, extemporaneous is the most popular and usually the most effective because the speaker delivers a well-prepared, well-rehearsed speech in a lively, conversational manner.

In delivering a speech, your voice should be loud enough for everyone to hear; your words should be spoken clearly so that they are easily understood, and your voice should be expressive so that you sound interesting and lively.

Nonverbal communication is the message you give with your body by means of personal appearance, eye contact, facial expressions, posture, movement, and gestures. All these elements should convey confidence and a positive regard for the audience. Of special importance is eye contact. You should look at your listeners during 95 percent of your speech to maintain a bond of communication and rapport with them and to monitor their feedback.

Practice is a vital part in the success of your speech. You should practice the entire speech over and over again—until you can deliver it with power and confidence.

Review Questions

1. What are the disadvantages of impromptu, manuscript, and memorized speeches?
2. What ingredient is essential for the success of an extemporaneous speech?
3. Why is it a serious mistake to speak too rapidly at the beginning of a speech?
4. What are the characteristics of good eye contact?
5. What can speakers do with their hands to make sure that they are free for gesturing?
6. Why should a speech be learned and practiced point by point, instead of word for word?

Tips

FOR YOUR CAREER

Tip 13: Deal with Distractions in a Direct, but Good-Humored, Manner

In classroom speeches you will have an attentive, courteous audience, but at some point in your career, you may encounter an audience that contains a few rude listeners who chat among themselves while you are trying to speak, thus causing a distraction for other listeners.

Professional speakers stress that you should *not* ignore the disturbance that the rude listeners are creating. You should confront these listeners, but do so in a calm, friendly, good-humored manner.

One technique is to simply stop your speech and look directly at the rude listeners (try to look friendly and not irritated). This nonverbal nudge is often all it takes to cause the persons to stop talking. Sometimes people sitting near the offenders will pick up on your cue and help you out by turning and saying "shh."

Professional speaker Rosita Perez of Brandon, Florida, says that you may lose the respect of your entire audience if you ignore the talkative few. "Confront them *kindly*," she advises. "Say, 'It seems to me you must have a lot of catching up to do with your friends. I wonder if you would visit outside so I can continue?' " In most such cases, the listeners will stay in the room and give the speaker respectful silence for the rest of the speech.[15]

Speech consultant Sandy Linver says that in a large audience, "I take the trouble to gently zero in on . . . the chatterers and pull them back in. I say something like, 'Are you with me?' . . . If it's a small group, side conversations often are important to the subject at hand, so it is important not to ignore them. If I were speaking at a business meeting of fifteen people or so, I might say to the three people talking among themselves, 'That looks as if it might be important. Would you like to share it with the group?' Often they are discussing something I have said that needs clarification or elaboration, and the whole group benefits when they are encouraged to speak up."[16]

Some speeches are marred by the incessant crying of a baby. Even though members of the audience turn and give annoyed, disapproving looks, the parents of the baby sometimes refuse to take the infant out of the room. Actor and orator Steve Allen once handled this situation by saying, "As the father of four sons I've more than once been in the position of the parents of that child. Personally I could go on even if there were several children crying at the same time, but I know that most people are too distracted by that sort of thing to concentrate on what is being said. So if you wouldn't mind taking the child out—at least until he stops crying— I'm sure the rest of our audience would appreciate it." This remark, says Allen, prompted applause from the audience and "gracious cooperation from the parents."[17]

PART FIVE

Types
of
Public
Speaking

14

Speaking
to
Inform

Types of Informative Speeches

Guidelines for Informative Speaking

Sample Informative Speech

At a shopping mall not long ago, I ran into Pete Gentry, a former student of mine. "Listen," he asked, "do you remember that speech Julie Parris gave about whatever-it's-called—the way you help a person who's choking on food?"

"Yes," I said, "the Heimlich Maneuver."

"Well," continued Pete, "it was a lucky thing I learned about it because a couple of months ago I used it on my kid brother. He got some food caught in his throat and was turning white as a sheet. I grabbed him and did what Julie taught us—made a fist on his stomach and forced the air up from his lungs. It worked—it cleared his windpipe. He could have died if I hadn't known exactly what to do."

Thus was a life saved because a speaker had presented information so clearly that a listener was able to remember it months later. Pete had forgotten the name of the technique, but so what? He had remembered the essence of Julie's speech— how to rescue a choking person.

Julie's talk on the Heimlich Maneuver is an example of an informative speech, one of the most popular kinds of speeches given in the classroom and in the community. In the informative speech your task is primarily to educate—to give new information to your listeners and help them understand it.

What you hope to achieve is what Julie achieved: having your audience remember the essence of your speech months later. To reach this goal, your speech must be interesting (so that the audience *wants* to listen) and it must be clear (so that the audience can understand what you are saying). In this chapter, we will look at four types of informative speeches and then discuss guidelines to help you create speeches that are clear, interesting, and memorable.

Types of Informative Speeches

Informative speeches can be categorized in many different ways, with many different labels, but in this chapter we will concentrate on four of the most popular types: definition, description, process, and expository.

Definition Speech

Suppose that one of your friends confides that she has dyslexia, but you do not know the meaning of this word. Obviously, then, you are going to say "What do you mean by dyslexia?"

Your friend could give you a dictionary definition—"the impairment of the ability to read"—but that would not do much to satisfy your curiosity. You would want her to give examples such as this: "When I was in elementary school, I scrambled letters when I tried to read; the word *was* looked to me like *saw*." You would want her to relate how the affliction has affected her life: "I flunked first grade and I thought I was dumb. I had a terrible inferiority complex." And so on.

What your friend would give you is an *extended* definition, one that goes beyond the dictionary explanation. That is what a definition speech is all about—

giving an extended definition of a concept so that the listeners get a full, richly detailed picture of its meaning. While a dictionary definition would settle lightly on the listeners' brains and probably vanish overnight, an extended definition is likely to stick firmly. Here are some sample specific-purpose statements for definition speeches:

☐ To explain to my listeners the meaning of feminism in modern America.
☐ To explain to the audience my definition of an ideal marriage.
☐ To define astrology for my listeners.
☐ To explain to my audience what constitutes true intelligence.

Any of the support materials that we discussed in Chapter 7 (narratives, examples, description, statistics, etc.) can be applied to defining a topic. If you were speaking on phobias, for example, you could give *examples* of the types of phobias, such as claustrophobia and agoraphobia, and *narratives* from the lives of phobic individuals.

Sometimes the best way to define a topic is to compare or contrast it with a similar item. If you were trying to define what constitutes child abuse, for example, it would be helpful to contrast abuse with firm, but loving, discipline, as in the following outline:

Specific Purpose: To explain to my audience what constitutes child abuse.
Central Idea: Child abuse, unlike firm discipline, damages a child's emotional growth.
Main Points: I. Firm, but loving discipline is healthy for the child's emotional growth.
    A. It involves punishment that is fair and not excessive.
    B. It does not harm the child's self-esteem.
    C. It causes the child to feel protected and cherished.
II. Abuse is damaging to the child's emotional growth.
    A. It is harsh and extreme.
    B. It hurts the child's self-esteem.
    C. It causes the child to feel insecure, angry, and unloved.

Contrasting abuse and discipline in this way helps the listeners see the line that separates the two.

One method of defining a topic is to break it down into logical subtopics. For example, here is one way of defining mental retardation:

Specific Purpose: To explain to my listeners the wide range of diversity among mentally retarded people.
Central Idea: The mentally retarded are a diverse group, ranging from the mildly retarded, who are capable of holding jobs, to the severely retarded, who require constant care.
Main Points: I. The highest functioning group of retardates is the mildly retarded, with IQs of 55 to 70.

> II. The second group of retardates is the moderately re-
>   tarded, with IQs of 40 to 55.
> III. The lowest functioning group of retardates is the se-
>   verely retarded, with IQs below 40.

By the time the speaker has finished analyzing the three categories of retardation, the listener has a good extended definition of retardation.

Description Speech

Describing a person, place, object, or event is a technique that can be used in any kind of speech. In a definition speech on alcoholism, for example, you might include a description of an alcoholic. In some cases, however, you may want to devote your entire speech to description. Here are some specific-purpose statements for description speeches:

☐ To tell my listeners how a tornado looks, sounds, and feels.
☐ To describe to my listeners the glories of the Grand Canyon.
☐ To inform my audience about living conditions in an institution for autistic children.
☐ To describe to my audience the highlights of the life of Margaret Sanger.

If you were describing an object or place, you might want to use the *spatial* pattern of organization. Here is an example as used in an outline on the Blue Ridge Parkway:

Specific Purpose: To describe to my listeners the Blue Ridge Parkway.
Central Idea: The Blue Ridge Parkway is a motor route through spectacular mountain and valley scenery.
Main Points: I. The northern leg of the Parkway covers the highlands overlooking the Shenandoah Valley.
II. The southern leg of the Parkway takes the motorist to the highest peaks east of the Mississippi.

The Parkway could also be described by means of another scheme of organization: the *topical* pattern. Here is one possible arrangement:

Main Points: I. The roadway itself is a marvel of engineering.
II. Spectacular scenery is visible from strategic overlooks.
III. There are many campgrounds and off-road recreational sites.

Describing a person, living or dead, can make a fascinating speech. If you were describing a historical figure, you might want to use the *chronological* pattern; in a speech on Susan B. Anthony, for example, you could· discuss the major events of her life, in the order in which they occurred, from birth to death.

For some descriptions of persons, you might prefer to use the *topical* pattern, as in the following outline:

Specific Purpose: To describe to my audience the exploits that made Harry Houdini a famous and controversial figure in American history.

Central Idea: Harry Houdini, the most famous magician of the early part of the twentieth century, was best known for his amazing ability to escape from any bond imaginable and for his campaign to expose fraudulent "mediums."

Main Points: I. Houdini was a magician who could extricate himself from any containment device then in existence—handcuffs, straitjackets, jail cells, and sealed coffins.

II. Houdini tried to expose the trickery of "mediums" who claimed to have direct communication with the dead.

Process Speech

In a *process speech*, you are concerned with explaining the steps or stages by which something is done or made. There are two kinds of process speeches. In the first kind, you show the listeners how to *perform* a process so that they can actually use the skills later (this is sometimes called a *demonstration* speech). (For a sample demonstration speech, see the one featured in Chapter 11.) Here are some examples of specific-purpose statements for this kind of speech:

☐ To teach my listeners how to apply first aid for snakebites.
☐ To explain to my audience how to perform yoga exercises.
☐ To show my audience how to identify and pick nonpoisonous mushrooms.
☐ To demonstrate to my listeners how to build kites.

In the second kind of process speech, you provide information on "how something is done" or "how something works." Your goal is to explain a process so that the listeners *understand* the process, not necessarily so that they can perform it themselves. For example, let's say that you outline the steps by which counterfeiters print bogus money. You are showing these steps to satisfy the listeners' intellectual curiosity and also to teach them how to spot a counterfeit bill, not so that they can perform the job themselves. Here are some samples of specific-purpose statements for this kind of speech:

☐ To explain to my audience how magicians saw a person in half.
☐ To tell my listeners how porpoises are trained to do out-of-water stunts.
☐ To explain to my listeners how a hurricane is tracked.
☐ To inform my listeners about how a guitar makes music.

If your instructor consents, you may want to use humor to make serious points in a process spech. For example, if your speech purported to be on "how to flunk

One common type
of informative
speech is a dem-
onstration of a pro-
cess. *(Joseph
Schuyler/Stock,
Boston)*

a test," you could discuss such items as "Be sure to party all night on the eve of
the test." Though you do not state it explicitly, your true point, of course, is that
a person should get plenty of sleep before taking a big test. One student gave a
process speech on how to burglarize a house or apartment; by speaking tongue-
in-cheek from the burglar's point of view, he effectively conveyed his real message—how to make sure your home is protected from burglars.

Here are five guidelines on preparing a process speech:

1. *Be sure to include all steps, even obvious ones.* A lawyer bought a
huge aquarium for his new office and then went out and spent hundreds of dollars
at a pet shop on an assortment of exotic tropical fish. He returned to his office,
filled the aquarium with water, and dumped the fish in. When all the fish died,
he called the pet shop and found out why: the directions for the aquarium had
neglected to mention that tap water must sit 24 hours before fish are inserted so
that all the chlorine can evaporate. Otherwise, the fish will die of chlorine poi-
soning. Whoever wrote the directions for the aquarium probably assumed that
any fish lover would be familiar with this piece of information, but such an
assumption was a mistake.

In a process speech, you should give all the steps involved, including the ones that are simple and self-evident. What seems obvious to you may not be obvious to some of your listeners.

2. *Use visual aids whenever possible.* Because processes are often complicated, you should use visual aids, if at all possible, to help the listeners understand and retain your points. One of the most effective visual aids is the demonstration, wherein you actually perform the process while talking. For example, if you wanted to teach cardiopulmonary resuscitation (CPR), you could demonstrate the steps on a dummy while you go through your explanations.

3. *Involve the audience in physical activity whenever possible.* If you involve the audience in a physical activity, you capitalize on more than just the listeners' sense of hearing and seeing; you also bring in touch and movement. There is an ancient Chinese proverb that says:

- ☐ I hear—and I forget.
- ☐ I see—and I remember.
- ☐ I do—and I understand.

The wisdom of this saying has been confirmed by psychologists, who have found that of the three main channels for learning new information, the auditory is weakest, the visual is stronger, and physical action is strongest of all. The best approach is to bring all three together. For example, if you were explaining how to do stretching exercises, you could explain the techniques (auditory) as you give a demonstration (visual); then you could have each listener stand and perform the exercises (physical action). Some audience involvement can be accomplished while the listeners remain in their chairs; for example, if you are speaking on sign language, you could have the listeners practice the hand signals as you teach them.

Note of caution: Get your instructor's approval before you use any physical activity in a classroom speech. When you give a talk in the community beyond the college campus, use your best judgment. Make sure that you do not ask your audience to do something that would be embarrassing or awkward for some of the listeners. If, for example, there are physically handicapped people in the audience, would they be able to perform the task? One student, who was ecstatic about the hug-everybody philosophy of Leo Buscaglia, tried to get the entire audience to hug each other. Some of the students were embarrassed.

4. *Proceed slowly.* Always bear in mind that much of what you say might be brand-new to the listeners. If you are giving instruction about how to make leather belts, for example, you might be describing activities that are so easy for you that you could perform them blindfolded, but they might be completely foreign to some members of the audience. That's why you should talk slowly and repeat key ideas if necessary. Give the listeners ample time to absorb the points and form mental images.

5. *Give advance warning of difficult steps.* When you are ready to discuss especially difficult steps, you can use transitions to give the listeners a warning. For example, you can say, "The next step is a little tricky," or "This next step is the hardest one of all." This alerts the listeners that they need to pay extra-special attention.

Expository Speech

An *expository speech* (also called an *oral report*, or *lecture*) involves explaining a concept or situation to the audience. For this speech, your instructor may want you to choose a topic that you are not thoroughly familiar with and then conduct research (in the library and/or by means of interviews) to gain command of the subject.

The expository speech may contain many features of the definition, descriptive, or process speeches. For example, if you chose to speak on "how the bail system works," you would be explaining a process. What makes the expository speech different from the other types is that you must conduct in-depth research, using books and articles and interviews, rather than rely upon your own personal experiences.

Here are examples of specific-purpose statements for expository speeches:

- ☐ To explain to my listeners the major causes of kleptomania.
- ☐ To inform my audience of the courting customs of colonial Americans.
- ☐ To explain to my listeners the effects of captivity (in zoos) upon wild animals.
- ☐ To report to the audience on the condition of America's passenger trains.
- ☐ To inform my audience of the opposing arguments concerning sex education.

Expository speeches are often organized in the *topical* pattern. As we saw in Chapter 9, you use the topical pattern to subdivide a central idea into main points, using logic and common sense as your guides. Here is an outline for an expository speech that uses the topical pattern:

Specific Purpose: To inform my audience about the dangers of quicksand.
Central Idea: Found in almost every state of the United States, quicksand is a terrifying natural trap from which people can extricate themselves if they follow the correct steps.
Main Points: I. Quicksand is as treacherous as the movies depict it.
  A. It has swallowed people.
  B. It has swallowed cars and trucks.
II. Quicksand is deceptive.
  A. The surface can appear as solid as the surrounding terrain.
  B. Underneath the surface is a sandy brew that is formed by water flowing upward from hidden springs.

III. If you step into quicksand, you can follow four easy steps that will save your life.
   A. Get rid of extra weight such as a backpack or coat.
   B. Throw yourself flat on your back and "float."
   C. Press your arms out onto the surface of the quicksand.
   D. Moving with snail-like slowness, roll your way to firm ground.

Notice that there are elements of description (point I), definition (point II), and process (point III) in this outline.

Another pattern is the *fallacy-fact* pattern (or it could be called *myth-reality*). In this pattern, the speaker cites a popular fallacy and then presents facts that refute it. Here is a sample outline from a speech given by student speaker Sarah Stepanovich, in which she refutes three popular misconceptions about sharks:

Specific Purpose: To refute, for my audience, common fallacies about sharks.
Central Idea: Sharks are not as dangerous to humans as most people think they are.

Main Points:
(fallacy) I. It is widely believed fallacy that there are hundreds of shark attacks each year, most of which are fatal.
(facts) A. Worldwide, there is an average of twenty-eight attacks each year.
B. Only three or four are fatal.
(fallacy) II. It is a widely believed fallacy that when a shark attacks one person, it will attack anyone else who is nearby.
(facts) A. Sharks select a single person and ignore others.
B. Rescuers are usually unharmed.
(fallacy) III. It is widely believed fallacy that sharks attack people when they get hungry.
(facts) A. Very few attacks are made by sharks that are hungry.
B. In most attacks, the shark takes one bite and then leaves.

Guidelines for Informative Speaking

In informative speaking, you should strive to make your message clear, interesting, and memorable. You can achieve this goal by applying the principles that we have covered so far in this book, being especially careful to select good support materials (Chapters 7 and 8). In addition to techniques already covered, here are some guidelines that should be useful for informative speeches.

Relate the Speech to the Listeners' Self-Interest

Many listeners seem to approach a speech with an attitude of: "Why should I care? Why should I pay attention? What's in it for me?" The best motivator in a speech, therefore, is something that relates directly to their self-interest, and has an impact on their lives in one way or another.

"When I was in the Navy," a friend recalls, "I was assigned to duty as a parachute packer. On our first day, we were given a talk on what people do to prepare themselves for jumping out of planes with a parachute. I didn't pay much attention because I figured my only contact with parachutes would be packing them. Then the next day they announced that in a few weeks *we* would have to parachute out of a plane! They wanted to make us appreciate—the hard way—just how important it is to pack a parachute correctly and carefully. When I heard this, I was scared, and I kicked myself for not paying attention to all that stuff they had said about getting ready for a jump."

Whoever gave that lecture failed to provide the audience with motivation to listen closely. The lecturer should have said something like this: "You may think your only contact with parachutes is packing them, but you're wrong. In a few weeks you will all jump out of an airplane with a parachute. Now here's how you do it. . . ." Hearing such a comment, my friend undoubtedly would have listened to the lecture with rapt attention.

Hoang Pham, a computer programmer, gave a talk to a business group on "bugs," or tiny glitches, in computer software. He knew that some listeners might be tempted to tune him out, figuring that his speech was about an esoteric subject of no real consequence to them. So, to make sure that everyone in his audience realized the bugs could someday affect their lives, he said, "According to the *Wall Street Journal*, Verdon Kidd, an East Texas bus driver, was using a computerized radiation-therapy machine to fight his skin cancer last spring; the therapy was going along okay until a defect in the machine's software caused Kidd to receive a massive dose of radiation that killed him. This is not just an isolated case: the *Journal* says that during the past five years, 'software defects have killed sailors, maimed patients, wounded corporations, and threatened to cause the government-securities market to collapse.' "[1]

Realizing that computer bugs could have a life-or-death and dollars-and-cents impact on their lives, the business executives in the audience probably listened intently to the rest of the speech.

Relate every speech you give to the listeners' self-interest, if at all possible. Show them that what you have to say is important to their individual lives.

Make Information Interesting

Listeners usually don't absorb information that is presented in generalized or dull packages, so you should try to make your ideas as interesting as possible by using verbal support materials such as narratives, examples, quotations, and statistics (see Chapter 7) and visual aids (see Chapter 8). Here is an example of a generalized statement:

> **Some dogs are trained by their owners to be aggressive and dangerous. The dogs are chosen and bred for their hostile tendencies. These dogs sometimes attack without warning.**

By itself, this statement is colorless and not likely to make much of an impression on the listeners' minds. As a contrast, let's look at a portion of a speech by Gina Hawkins, a professional dog breeder:

> Some dogs are trained to be vicious. For example, some pit bulls (the popular name for American Staffordshire Terriers) have been bred and trained to be savage attack dogs. Last April, a two-year-old girl in Michigan was killed instantly when the family's pit bull suddenly turned on her and bit her in the throat. That same day, Dr. William Eckman was attacked by two pit bulls; nine people spent 25 minutes trying to pry off the dogs with poles and brooms. Dr. Eckman died soon thereafter, from the wounds. Last year, a 71-year-old woman in Stone Mountain, Georgia, was dragged across her driveway by a pit bull and bitten so severely that she needed 100 stitches. Of the 34 fatal canine attacks in the U.S. in the last five years, pit bulls have inflicted 27 of them.[2]

This excerpt shows the use of interesting support materials—examples and statistics. In the same speech, Hawkins also used visual aids—pictures of two breeds that are often confused. The first photograph showed a snarling pit bull; Hawkins pointed out the blunt face and unfriendly "look" of this breed. For contrast, she displayed a poster of Spuds McKenzie, the famous bull terrier of TV commercials, so that the audience could see that bull terriers have elongated oval heads and a gentle, friendly look—characteristics that distinguish them from their cousins, the pit bulls.

Assess the Knowledge of Listeners

You should analyze your listeners thoroughly before a speech (as discussed in Chapter 4) to find out what they know and what they don't know. This will keep you from committing two common mistakes.

1. Don't give information the audience already knows. A famous psychiatrist who had developed innovative programs for training mentally retarded individuals gave the keynote speech at a state convention of the Association for Retarded Citizens. For one hour, he explained the revolution that had taken place in recent years in educating retarded students.

At the conclusion of his speech, he was given polite applause, but throughout the hall, at the individual tables, there were mutterings of discontent. The famous man had spent an hour imparting information that all the delegates already knew. "What a waste of time!" exclaimed one disappointed listener, who had been hungry for new insights. Apparently the psychiatrist had failed to analyze his audience; he thought they were primarily parents who knew little about the scientific aspects of retardation. If he had analyzed them correctly, he would have known that half of the audience consisted of knowledgeable professionals—psychologists, social workers, and teachers—and the other half consisted of parents who had spent months or years learning the basic information of the field.

2. Don't talk over the listeners' heads, or use words, concepts, references, and allusions the audience doesn't understand. It is easy to commit this mistake if you assume that your listeners possess a common body of information.[3] Recent polls have shown that many Americans, especially high school students, lack a body of knowledge that earlier generations possessed. For example, a Gallup poll found that 40 percent of American high school students did not know that Israel is a Jewish nation—they thought it was an Arab state; some 45 percent could not locate Central America on a map, and 10 percent thought that Latin was the language spoken in Latin America.[4]

If you find out in advance what your audience doesn't know, you can define words or explain concepts whenever necessary. You can give background information and examples.

What should you do when your audience is mixed—that is, some know your information already and some don't? How can you give explanations in a way that does not insult the intelligence of the listeners who already know the material? In some cases, you can give information in a casual, unobtrusive way. For example, let's say you are planning in your speech to cite a quotation by Adolf Hitler. Most college students know who Hitler was, but there are some who do not. To inform the latter without insulting the intelligence of the former, you can say something like this: "In the 1920s, long before Adolf Hitler rose to power in Germany and long before he launched the German nation into World War II, he made the following prophetic statement." An indirect approach like this permits you to "sneak" in a lot of background information.

In other cases, you may need to be straightforward in giving definitions or explanations. For example, if you need to define *recession* for a speech on economic cycles, do so directly and clearly. As long as most of your speech supplies them with new material, the knowledgeable listeners will not be offended by a quick definition; in fact, they will probably welcome a chance to affirm the accuracy of their own understanding of the term.

Use the Familiar to Explain the Unfamiliar

A few years ago an Israeli leader toured the United States to drum up support for increased military aid to Israel. Dorothy Sarnoff, an American consultant who was hired to help him prepare his speeches, gave him the following advice.

> If you describe Israel at its narrowest point by saying, "Israel is so narrow that we can be [easily] attacked," the Americans won't get it . . . Instead say, "Israel is so narrow that if you were driving on a[n] [American-style] highway, it would take you only twenty minutes to get from one side of Israel to the other."[5]

Sarnoff's advice was sound. When you want to explain or describe something that is unfamiliar to your audience, relate it to something that is familiar. You can use some of the devices we discussed in Chapter 7, such as comparisons, contrasts, and analogies. If, for example, you point out that divers in Acapulco, Mexico, astound tourists by diving into water from rocks 118 feet high, that statistic does not have much impact unless you point out that a 118-foot plunge is equal to a dive from the roof of an 11-story building.[6]

To give listeners a mental picture of what the inside of a tornado is like, student speaker Dale Higgins said: "A tornado's funnel is like the vortex you see when you let water go down a drain." Since everyone has seen the swirling action of water going down a drain, the comparison helped the audience visualize a tornado's vortex.

Sample Informative Speech

Student Martha Penland prepared and delivered a classroom speech on how to avoid being struck by lightning. She conducted an interview with an expert to get most of her material. Her outline is presented first, followed by a transcript of the actual speech.[7]

The Outline

How to Avoid Being Struck by Lightning

General Purpose: To inform
Specific Purpose: To inform my listeners of how to avoid being struck by lightning.
Central Idea: You can decrease your chances of being struck by lightning if you rid yourself of three common misconceptions—that a vehicle with rubber tires guarantees safety, that you are safe inside a house, and that you are safe if a thunderstorm is not overhead.

INTRODUCTION

I. Lightning is one of the most terrifying things on earth, especially if you are caught outdoors in a sudden thunderstorm, with gigantic bolts of raw electricity cracking and crashing all around you. Last year, four golfers in Michigan were killed when the oak tree they were standing under was blasted by a lightning bolt. In New Mexico, a 21-year-old college student was killed by lightning as he rode his bike on a highway near Santa Fe. And in Florida, a family was struck while on a picnic—the mother and a son were killed, and the other three members of the family were seriously injured. Every year an average of 100 Americans are killed by lightning and 250 are injured, according to Bill Skinner, a meterologist with the National Climatic Data Center, whom I interviewed for this speech. Mr. Skinner said that the worst month for lightning deaths and injuries is July, followed by August, and then June. The most common victims are farmers, fishers, golfers, and cyclists.

II. Do you know how to avoid being hit by lightning? To test your knowledge, see if you can answer the following true-false questions correctly. True or False? If you are outdoors during a thunderstorm, you are guaranteed safety by climbing in or on a vehicle with rubber tires, such as a car, motorcycle, or bicycle. True or False? If you are inside a house during a thunderstorm, you are safe. True or False? If a thunderstorm is not over-head, you are safe. Now for the answers. All three of these statements are false. Today I would like to tell you why they are untrue. The information I will give you could save your life someday. My information comes from my interview with Mr. Skinner and from a booklet published by the Lightning Protection Institute.

(*Transition:* Let us take a look at the first misconception.)

BODY

I. It is a misconception to think that if you are outdoors during a thunder-storm, you are guaranteed safety by climbing in or on a vehicle with rubber tires, such as a car, motorcycle, or bicycle.
  A. Contrary to what many think, rubber tires do *not* protect humans.
    1. If a car is struck by lightning and nobody is hurt, it is not because the rubber tires offered protection but because the blast of electricity was conducted to the ground by the metal shell of the car.
    2. Thus it is risky to sit or lean on the outside of a car or golf cart.
    3. It is extremely dangerous to stay on a bicycle or motorcycle.
      a. In an open area, lightning seeks the highest point.
      b. Since the rubber tires of a bike or motorcycle provide absolutely no protection, a rider is very vulnerable.
  B. It is true that the inside of a car is a safe place to be, but only if you follow certain precautions.
    1. Keep the windows rolled up.
    2. Do not touch the radio dial or metal parts of the car.
  C. If you are caught outdoors, and there is no car to climb into, make sure you are the lowest object in the area.
    1. Get in a ditch or ravine.
    2. Do not stand under lone trees or tall trees.
      a. Pick a small tree.
      b. Stand 5 feet from the trunk.
    3. Do not swim; do not stay in a boat.
    4. If you are caught in a boat, lie down and place cushions between you and the metal parts.
    5. Avoid unprotected structures, such as golf course shelters.
    6. If you are with a group, spread out—don't bunch together.

(*Transition:* Now that you know how to protect yourself outdoors, let us move indoors.)

II. It is a misconception to think that if you are inside a house during a thunderstorm, you are safe.
  A. It is true that only 1 percent of lightning fatalities occur indoors, but you still must be careful.
  B. You can be safe inside if you follow some simple precautions.
    1. Stay away from open doors, open windows, and fireplaces.
    2. Stay away from appliances and computers.
    3. Do not use the telephone.
    4. Do not take a bath or shower during a storm.

(*Transition:* So far we have talked about what to do *during* a thunderstorm, but is there anything that you should do if a thunderstorm has not yet arrived where you are?)

III. It is a misconception to think that if a thunderstorm is not overhead, you are safe.
 A. Lightning can strike several miles away from a storm.
 B. You should take precautions as soon as you hear lightning within 5 miles.
  1. You can tell how close a storm is by counting the seconds between a lightning bolt and thunder.
  2. Divide the number of seconds by 5 to find the distance in miles.
  3. If you see lightning and then hear thunder 25 seconds later, the lightning is 5 miles away.
  4. It is time for you to seek shelter because lightning could soon be upon you.

(*Transition:* I hope that you will remember the key ideas that I have given you today.)

CONCLUSION
 I. Let me review: If you are caught outdoors, climb into a car, being careful to roll up the windows and avoid touching the radio dial or metal parts. If you cannot get into a car, make sure you are the lowest object in the area. Get into a ditch or ravine. Do not stand under lone or tall trees. If you are indoors, be sure to stay away from open windows and doors and fireplaces. Do not talk on the phone or take a bath or shower. Last of all, do not wait for a storm to come overhead. When it is within 5 miles of you, start looking for shelter.
 II. If you follow the precautions I have suggested today, you can avoid being one of the 100 Americans who will be killed by lightning in the next 12 months.

BIBLIOGRAPHY
Bill Skinner, meteorologist, National Climatic Data Center, personal interview, May 11, 1988.
Protection from Lightning, booklet published by the Lightning Protection Institute, Harvard, Illinois, 1988.

VISUAL AIDS

☐ Three posters presenting the main points as true-false questions
☐ Poster showing a car, motorcycle, and bicycle
☐ Poster showing a lone tree, a tall tree, and an "ideal" tree for safety

The Speech as Delivered

Here is a transcript of the speech as it was delivered.

Commentary	**How to Avoid Being Struck by Lightning**
The speaker begins with a description that all the listeners can identify with.	One of the most terrifying things on earth is lightning. It's especially terrifying if you get caught outside during a thunderstorm, when huge bolts of raw electricity crack and crash all around you. Last year, four men playing golf in Michigan took refuge under an oak tree during a thunder-

storm. Lightning hit the tree and killed all four men. In New Mexico, there was a 21-year-old college student who was riding his bike on a highway near Santa Fe. A bolt of lightning killed him. In Florida, a family was on a picnic when lightning struck. The mother and son were killed; the other three members of the family were seriously injured. Every year there is an average of 100 people who are killed in the U.S. by lightning and 250 are injured. I got these statistics from a meteorologist at the National Climatic Data Center, Bill Skinner. Mr. Skinner said that July is the worst month for lightning fatalities, followed by August as the second-worst, and June as the third-worst. He said the most common victims are farmers, fishers, golfers, and cyclists.

Three dramatic examples gain the listeners' attention and interest.

Citing an expert as her source gives the speaker credibility.

If you ask questions, you should make it clear (as this speaker does) whether you want the listeners to respond overtly.

Do you know how to avoid being struck by lightning? To test your knowledge, I'd like to give you a little quiz. I'm not going to embarrass you by calling on someone or by asking for a show of hands, but I wonder if you can answer the following true-false questions correctly. I'll tell you the answers in a moment. Here we go with number one: True or False? If you are outdoors during a thunderstorm, you can guarantee safety by climbing on top of or going inside of a vehicle with rubber tires, such as a car, a bicycle, or a motorcycle. [*Pause.*] Now for number two: True or False? If you are inside a house during a thunderstorm, you are safe. [*Pause.*] And now number three: True or False? If a thunderstorm is not overhead, you are safe. [*Pause.*] Now let's see how you did. The answer to all three statements is . . . false! Today I would like to explain all three of these misconceptions, so you can see why they are false. The information I will give you could save your life someday. By the way, all of this information comes from an interview with Mr. Skinner and from a booklet published by the Lightning Protection Institute.

The "quiz" stimulates the listeners' curiosity.

The speaker uses her questions to forecast the three main points of her speech. This gives the audience a preview of the body of the speech.

The speaker makes a smooth transition from her introduction to her first main point.

Notice how direct and conversational the speaker's words are—very easy for listeners to understand and absorb.

Let's take a look at the first misconception: that if you're outdoors during a thunderstorm, you're certain to be safe if you're on or in a vehicle with rubber tires. This is a very common misconception. The truth is that rubber tires do not protect humans. If you're in a car and lightning hits it and you're not hurt, it's not the rubber tires that saved you. Its the metal shell of the car. The metal shell conducts the electricity to the ground. So don't make the mistake a lot of people make and say, "Well, I'm leaning on the car—the rubber tires will save me." Or "I'm sitting on this golf cart, so I'm safe." Some of you ride bicycles or motorcycles—two of the most dangerous things to be on in a thunderstorm. In an open area, lightning seeks the highest point, and that could be you. Your rubber tires provide absolutely no protection at all. Now it is true that the inside of a car is a safe place to be, but only if you are careful. You must keep the windows rolled up, and you must not touch the radio dial or metal parts of the car.

Rhetorical questions are used to pique the audience's curiosity.

What happens if you get caught out in a storm, and you don't have a car to climb into? What should you do? Mr. Skinner says the primary rule is to make sure you are the lowest object in the area. Get in a ditch or a ravine. Don't get close to tall objects. In other words, don't stand next to the only tree on a hill. Don't stand next to the tallest tree in the vicinity. If you want to get under a tree, pick a small tree and even then, stand 5 feet from the trunk. If you're swimming, get out of the water; if you're in a boat, get out of it as quickly as possible. If you're caught in a boat, lie down and put cushions between you and the metal parts of the boat. You should also stay out of unprotected structures like golf course shelters. If you're with a group of people, split up and spread out. Don't bunch together.

By saying "you" throughout her speech, the speaker draws in every member of the audience and gives a flavor of warm, personal conversation.

The speaker uses a bridge, a transitional device to transport the listeners from one section of the speech to the next.

Now that you know how to be safe outdoors, let's move indoors and talk about the second misconception people have—that if you're inside a house during a thunderstorm, you are safe. Now it is true that of all lightning fatalities, only 1 percent occurs indoors, but you don't want to be part of that 1 percent, do you? So here's how you can be safe inside your house. Stay away from open doors; stay away from open windows; stay away from fireplaces. Stay away from appliances and computers. Don't use the telephone during a storm and don't take a bath or a shower.

The speaker makes a smooth transition from the second main point to the third.

Up to this point I have talked about what to do and not do *during* a thunderstorm, but is there anything you should do before a storm looms over your head? Yes, and that leads us to consider the third misconception—that if a thunderstorm is not overhead, you are safe. A lot of people don't know this, but lightning can strike several miles away from a storm. So you should start taking action as soon as lightning approaches your area. How soon? When lightning gets within 5 miles of you, you should take precautions. Here's an easy way to tell how close lightning is: Count the seconds between the time you see a lightning flash and the time you hear the thunder. Divide the number of seconds by 5 to find the distance in miles. For example, if you see lightning and then hear thunder 25 seconds later, 25 divided by 5 is of course 5, so the lightning is 5 miles away. It's time for you to take action. Let me repeat the technique: count the seconds between lightning and thunder and divide by 5. That's how many miles away the lightning is.

Repetition of a point, though undesirable in a written essay, is valuable in a speech because the listeners may fail to absorb the information the first time it is mentioned.

I hope that you will remember the safety rules that I have given you today. Let me review the key ones: If you're out-

The conclusion gives the speaker one last chance to drive home the key ideas of the speech.

The speaker ends gracefully by echoing the statistic used in the introduction.

doors, you can be safe by climbing into a car, provided that you roll up the windows and don't touch the radio dial or metal parts. If you can't find a car, make sure you're the lowest object in the area. Get in a ditch or a ravine. Don't stand under the only tree in an area and don't stand under the tallest tree. If you're indoors, stay away from open windows, doors, and fireplaces. Don't take a bath or shower, and don't talk on the phone. And remember not to wait for a storm to come to you. When it's within 5 miles, that's the time to seek shelter.

If you follow these precautions, you can avoid becoming one of the 100 Americans who will be killed by lightning in the next 12 months.

Summary

The informative speech is one of the most popular kinds of speeches given in the classroom and in the community. Your goal in this kind of speech is to give new information to your listeners and help them understand and remember it. Four subcategories of the informative speech are definition, description, process, and expository.

In developing an informative speech, you can draw from all the techniques and methods discussed in the book so far, plus the following guidelines: (1) Relate the speech to the listeners' self-interest, if at all possible. Show them explicitly the connection between your material and their personal lives. (2) Make the information interesting by using verbal and visual supports. (3) Assess the knowledge level of the listeners. Don't give them information they already know, and don't talk over their heads. (4) Use the known to explain the unknown. When you want to explain or describe something that is unfamiliar to your audience, relate it to something that is familiar.

Review Questions

1. What is an extended definition? Why is it preferable in a speech to a dictionary definition?
2. What are the two kinds of process speeches?
3. List the five guidelines for preparing a process speech.
4. Why is it important to relate a speech, if possible, to the listeners' self-interest?

Tips

FOR YOUR CAREER

Tip 14: For Long Presentations, Plan a Variety of Activities

Your boss asks you to conduct a 3-hour workshop Friday afternoon to explain important procedures to a group of new employees. What do you do? Do you spend 3 hours talking? No, not unless you want to put them to sleep.

For long presentations, you should provide a variety of activities to keep your audience awake and attentive. Here are some suggested activities:

1. Invite audience participation. At various intervals, or even throughout the entire presentation, you can encourage listeners to ask questions or make comments. By letting them take an active role, instead of sitting passively for 3 hours, you invigorate them and prevent them from daydreaming.

2. Use visual aids whenever possible. Visuals give variety and sparkle to the presentation.

3. Give coffee or "stretch" breaks at various intervals. A good rule of thumb for marathon sessions is to give a 15-minute break after every 45-minute period, even if the audience does not seem tired. In other words, don't wait until fatigue sets in. If you wait until the audience is nodding, you might lose their interest for the rest of the day. When you give a break, always an-

nounce the time for reassembly; when that time arrives, politely but firmly remind any stragglers that it is time to return to their seats. If you do not remind them, you will find that a 15-minute coffee break can stretch to 30 minutes.

4. Call on people at random. If your presentation is in the form of a lecture, you can use the teachers' technique of calling on people to answer questions. This causes every listener to perk up because he or she is thinking, "I'd better pay attention because my name might be called next, and I don't want to be caught daydreaming." An embellishment of this pedagogical ploy is to call the person's name *after* you ask the question. (If you call the name before the question, everyone in the audience except the designated person might breathe a sigh of relief and fail to pay close attention to the question.)

5. Encourage the listeners to take notes. Some business speakers pass out complimentary pens and pads at the beginning of their presentations in hopes that the listeners will use them to write down key points. There is, of course, a side benefit: taking notes helps the listeners to stay alert and listen intelligently.

15

Speaking

to

Persuade

Types of Persuasive Speeches

Elements of Persuasion

Sample Persuasive Speech

When Nancy Gibson, a dance instructor at a small college, asked the coach of the football team for permission to talk to the team, some people thought she was crazy, for her professed goal was to persuade the football players to sign up for her ballet class.

When the players assembled in front of her, their initial attitude was derisive glee. "Can you believe it?" one player snickered. "She wants us to learn that sissy ballet stuff." In her talk, Gibson told of certain well-known professional football players who had taken ballet lessons in college because it made them more agile and quick-footed on the playing field. Then she explained how the techniques learned in her class could help the students play football more effectively. So convincing was her speech that after she finished, there was a virtual stampede, led by the first-string players, to sign up.

This anecdote illustrates the art of persuasion—getting people to think or act a certain way. In your lifetime, you will be faced with many tasks that require persuasion, ranging from one-to-one situations (such as convincing a bank executive to give you a loan for a new car), to small groups (persuading your fellow employees to join with you in a grievance about working conditions), to large audiences (talking your club into holding its annual picnic at a particular site). In this chapter we will discuss the strategies that you can use in these many kinds of persuasion, with special emphasis on preparing persuasive speeches.

Types of Persuasive Speeches

Persuasive speeches can be categorized in a variety of ways, but one of the most popular classification schemes divides them according to two objectives: (1) to influence thinking and (2) to motivate action. While these categories sometimes overlap (for example, you often have to influence thinking before you can motivate action), they nevertheless provide a handy framework for developing the content of a persuasive speech.

Speech to Influence Thinking

The speech to influence thinking is an effort to convince people to adopt your position on a particular subject. (If some listeners agree with your ideas even before you speak, your job is to reinforce what they already think.) In some cases, you may want to implant ideas that are completely new to the listeners; for example, you argue that we should experiment to see if tobacco can be used as a source of protein. In other cases, you may want to alter the audience's preexisting ideas; for example, let's say that from your audience analysis, you know that your listeners consider white-collar criminals to be rather harmless wrongdoers who do not deserve to be put behind bars. So, in your speech you show that white-collar criminals who steal from companies and banks hurt everyone in society— by jeopardizing the continued existence of those institutions and by causing prices to be raised—and, therefore, they deserve to be imprisoned.

Here are some samples of specific-purpose statements for this kind of speech:

☐ To convince my audience that dinosaurs became extinct because a rain of comets stirred up so much debris that sunlight was blocked from the earth for months.

☐ To convince my listeners that the metric system is superior to the traditional American system of weights and measures.

☐ To convince my audience that the President of the United States should be limited to one term lasting 6 years.

☐ To convince my listeners that unchecked population growth is a threat to world peace.

In a speech to influence thinking, you may want to use the *statement-of-reasons* pattern of organization (which is a variation of the *topical* pattern discussed in Chapter 9), in which you state the reasons why your central idea has merit. Student speaker Frank Collins used the statement-of-reasons pattern in the following outline:

Specific Purpose: To persuade my audience that schools should stop using IQ tests.

Central Idea: IQ tests should not be used to evaluate or place students.

Main Points:

(reason 1) I. Because they reflect only a small part of human intelligence, IQ tests are not valid measurements.

(reason 2) II. Students who score poorly on IQ tests get unfairly labeled—and then treated—as slow or dumb.

Frank's two main points are outgrowths of his central idea, giving good reasons why IQ tests should not be used.

Sometimes, the *problem-solution* pattern is the best way to organize a persuasive speech. You show that a problem exists, and then you present the solution. This pattern is especially effective when the audience does not know that a particular problem exists, or it does not know how serious it is. For example, student speaker Rebecca Carter gave a speech on frivolous lawsuits (such as children suing their mother and father for "malparenting," and patients suing their plastic surgeons for a belly button left askew). Rebecca showed how these suits created a problem and then she presented her solution to the problem. Here is part of her outline:

Specific Purpose: To persuade my audience that frivolous lawsuits should be kept out of court.

Central Idea: Settlement of frivolous lawsuits should be made not by the courts but by citizens acting as voluntary arbitrators.

Main Points:

(problem) I. Frivolous lawsuits cost the taxpayers millions of dollars annually in court expenses.

(solution) II. Congress and state legislatures should pass laws that move settlement of frivolous disputes from the courts to nonprofit arbitration centers run by citizen volunteers.

A subcategory of the speech to influence thinking is the *speech of refutation,* in which your main goal is to knock down arguments or ideas that you feel are false. In this kind of speech, you may want to attack what another speaker has said, or you might want to refute popularly held ideas or beliefs which you think are false. One student, for example, tried to explode the myth that mentally retarded people can contribute little to the work force.

Here are some sample specific-purpose statements for speeches of refutation:

☐ To convince my listeners that Christopher Columbus was not the first European to explore the New World.
☐ To persuade my audience to reject the false picture of pigs as dirty, stupid animals.
☐ To convince my audience that the present laws forbidding mercy killing are based on outdated concepts.
☐ To persuade my listeners that dowsers (people who claim to find water by means of divining rods) are no more capable of locating underground water than a child with a stick.

Refuting an argument is easier when you are dealing with facts than when you are dealing with deeply held beliefs. Suppose, for example, that you want to demolish the commonly held idea that during the American Revolution, solid ranks of red-coated British soldiers marched to battle in open fields, while crafty American patriots hid behind nearby trees in guerrilla fashion and shot the unsuspecting British with ease. You could refute this idea by citing the works of scholars and by pointing out that the British army in North America had adapted to guerrilla-style warfare during decades of fighting the Indians—long before the American Revolution. All this is a matter of historical record, so your persuasive task is easy. But suppose that you wanted to persuade an audience to reject the belief that children should be reared by their parents; instead, you argue, children should be reared by communes like the kibbutzim in Israel. Though you may win some respect for the value of your idea, you are highly unlikely to demolish the deeply held belief that children should grow up under the wings of their parents. Core beliefs are extremely difficult to change.

Let us turn now to an example of the right way to refute arguments. Jim Lawter heard a speech by a classmate who advocated state-operated gambling. Jim disagreed so strongly that he prepared a speech to try to refute some of the points made by the earlier speaker. Here is the gist of his speech:

Specific Purpose: To convince my listeners that state and local governments should not sponsor gambling in any form.
Central Idea: Government-sponsored gambling exploits the poor and corrupts society's work ethic.
Main Points: I. The argument that "no one is hurt in legalized gambling" is erroneous.

    A. Studies show that poor people, who can least afford to gamble, are in fact the heaviest gamblers.

    B. In states that have legalized gambling, there has been a dramatic increase in the number of compulsive gamblers, who sometimes lose all their possessions in their obsessive desire to "strike it rich."

II. The argument that "gambling does not weaken society" is erroneous.

    A. Government-sponsored gambling whets the public's appetite for illegal gambling, which is usually controlled by organized crime.

    B. Heavy advertising for government-sponsored gambling creates a lust for quick riches that runs contrary to the work ethic needed for social stability.

Notice that Jim stuck to the issues; he wisely refrained from questioning the intelligence or morality of his opponent.

Speech to Motivate Action

The speech to motivate action is like the above speech in that it tries to win people over to your way of thinking, but it also attempts one of the most challenging tasks of persuasion—getting people to take action. This action can be either positive or negative: you can urge people to *start* doing something (start using dental floss, start buying U.S. savings bonds, start collecting stamps), or *stop* doing certain things (stop smoking, stop tailgating, stop wasting time). Sometimes you want immediate action from your listeners ("Please vote for my candidate in today's election"); at other times, you simply want them to respond at any appropriate point in the future ("Whenever you see a child riding a bike, please slow down and drive very cautiously").

Here are some sample specific-purpose statements for speeches to motivate action:

☐ To persuade my audience to walk 3 miles a day.
☐ To persuade my listeners to sign a petition aimed at outlawing corporal punishment in elementary schools.
☐ To persuade my audience to take a course in first aid.
☐ To persuade my listeners to stop buying merchandise on credit.

A popular way to organize a speech for motivating action is the *statement-of-reasons* pattern (discussed earlier in this chapter), as shown in this outline by student speaker Brett Clayton:

Specific Purpose: To persuade my listeners to vote in all elections.
    Central Idea: Every citizen should vote in every general election.
    Main Points: I. Universal voting would prevent small, special-interest groups from gaining power.

II. Since some elections are won by razor-thin margins, every vote counts.

III. In a democracy, it's important for all citizens to express their views via the election process.

The statement-of-reasons pattern was appropriate because Brett's strategy involved backing up his central idea with three good reasons.

Another way of organizing this kind of speech is the *motivated sequence,* a commonsense approach to persuasion that was developed by the late Alan Monroe.[1] There are five steps in this method.

1. *Attention.* Grab the audience's attention at the beginning of your introduction, as discussed in Chapter 10.
2. *Need.* Show your audience that there is a serious problem that needs action.
3. *Satisfaction.* Satisfy the need by presenting a solution, and show how your solution works.
4. *Visualization.* Paint a picture of results. Help the listeners visualize what will happen when your solution has been put into effect. If possible, show how they personally will benefit.
5. *Action.* Request action from the listeners. Be specific: "Sign this petition" or "Write your legislators today—here are their addresses" or "You can volunteer in Room 211 this afternoon."

To see how the motivated sequence works, imagine that you want to persuade your audience to support expanded research on energy alternatives to oil. You could develop the following strategy:

1. *Attention.* To grab the listeners' attention, you could describe the disaster that would occur if America suddenly found itself without oil for cars, homes, and factories.
2. *Need.* To describe the problem and show the need for action, you could explain that a war in the Middle East would cut off much of our oil supply and strangle our economy, so we need to become independent of foreign oil.
3. *Satisfaction.* You can satisfy the need by presenting a solution: alternative energy sources such as solar, geothermal, and hydrogen can be developed.
4. *Visualization.* To help the audience visualize the results, you paint a picture of a future war that breaks out in the Middle East, disrupting oil supplies to the West, but you describe the United States as serenely continuing to thrive, thanks to the alternative energy sources.
5. *Action.* You request that the audience take immediate action by writing legislators and asking them to support expanded research on energy alternatives.

Jennifer Wade, a student speaker, used the motivated sequence to create the following outline:

INTRODUCTION

Attention   I. You are driving down a steep road when suddenly your brakes fail. You try to gear down, and you try to steer your car to a safe spot, but there's not enough time. Your car goes out of control and smashes into a tree. You are thrown against the windshield. When the paramedics arrive on the scene, you are alive, but you're bleeding profusely. The paramedics quickly put you into an ambulance and race you to the hospital. Time is of the essence. If you don't get a blood transfusion in the next few minutes, you will die.

Need   II. Where is the blood going to come from? Obviously it must come from the blood bank, but will there be blood of your type in the bank? Will there be enough blood? Did you know that today our local blood bank has a critical shortage of blood? The Red Cross has issued an emergency appeal for people to donate blood.

BODY

Satisfaction   I. The Bloodmobile will be on campus next week.
Visualization   II. Blood donors save the lives of many people.
    A. Accident victims need blood transfusions.
    B. Leukemia and cancer patients need blood transfusions.
    C. Some new babies need a complete change of blood supply.
    D. Hemophiliacs will die without regular transfusions.

CONCLUSION

  I. Donating blood is giving the gift of life.
Action   II. When the Bloodmobile comes to our campus next week, step forward and give the gift of life.

Elements of Persuasion

As you prepare a persuasive speech, there are six questions that you should ask yourself about the listeners:

1. Who are my listeners?
2. How can I build credibility with the audience?
3. What evidence should I provide to convince this particular audience?
4. What form of reasoning would be most compelling to the audience?
5. How can I appeal to the listeners' motivations?
6. How can I arouse the listeners' emotions?

To help you answer these questions, let us examine each point in greater detail.

Knowing Your Audience

Dr. Frank C. Laubach was an educator who launched a nationwide crusade in the 1950s to teach illiterate adults how to read. In the early days of his crusade, when he went to factories to try to recruit illiterates for his reading classes, he would make the following appeal: "Would any of you people like to learn how to read?" Much to Dr. Laubach's disappointment, only a few of the illiterates in each factory would sign up—even though the classes were free.

What was wrong? Didn't the illiterates know that their inability to read was a big handicap in an advanced industrial society such as ours? Yes, Dr. Laubach reasoned, these people were keenly aware that their illiteracy condemned them to spend their lives on the margins of society. Why, then, did they pass up a chance to take free classes to better themselves?

As Dr. Laubach analyzed his audiences, he realized that most illiterates were ashamed to admit in public that they could not read. So he altered his pitch. At a factory in Charlotte, North Carolina, he asked, "Would any of you people like to learn to improve your reading?" This time, scores of illiterates stepped forward. The new pitch was effective because it enabled the men and women to maintain their self-respect. Instead of embarrassing themselves with an open admission that they could not read, they could identify themselves as simply people wanting to improve a skill. Thenceforth, Dr. Laubach used the revised version for all his spiels, with the same good results.

This story, which I heard from a reading teacher who uses the still-popular Laubach teaching method, demonstrates that persuasion involves more than simply "giving the facts." To get people to think or act a certain way, you must know who they are. What are their backgrounds? What are their needs and desires? What are their fears? Though he had a fabulous free offer that he handed to each audience on a silver platter, Dr. Laubach was ineffective in his attempts at persuasion until he accurately analyzed and understood the listeners. (At first glance Dr. Laubach's change of words seems a bit deceitful, but it really was not; all of the illiterates certainly could have read their own names and a few other simple words, so it was not stretching the truth to talk of "improving" their reading.)

As Dr. Laubach discovered, the first step in persuasion is understanding your listeners. To truly understand them, you must find out where they are standing, then go over to that spot, stand inside their shoes, and see the world as they see it. Only after you have seen the world from their perspective will you have a ghost of a chance of leading them to where you want them to stand.

While you need to understand your listeners, it is important to realize that failure to win every listener to your way of thinking does not indicate failure as a speaker. You should try to persuade every listener, but it would be unrealistic to expect that you can succeed with all people at all times. If you were trying to get your audience to accept the theory that our solar system contains a mysterious, as-yet-undiscovered planet on its outer fringes, you would have a good chance of convincing all the listeners because that theory has some solid scientific support and, more importantly, your listeners would probably have no strong emotional commitment to a competing theory. But what if you were trying to convince your audience that private ownership of handguns should be outlawed? That is an issue that polarizes many Americans, with people on both sides strongly committed to their position. It would be unrealistic to hope that you could persuade every opponent to march over to your camp.

On controversial issues, you often have three "audiences" listening to you. First, you have the people who already agree with you. Your goal with them is to reinforce their belief and perhaps even give them new reasons for supporting your cause. On the other extreme, you have the people who oppose your views. While not compromising your integrity (by doing such things as watering down your beliefs), you should show respect for these people and their views. *Never* insult or belittle the opposition; sarcastic or belligerent remarks make people defensive and all the more committed to their side. Try to persuade these people, but if that fails, be content if you can move them a few inches toward your camp. Sometimes the best you can hope for is to plant some seeds of doubt about their position which might someday sprout into full-blown conversion to your side. Finally, your third "audience" consists of people in-between the two extremes—those who are neutral. This group is obviously your ripest field for converts. The tips in the rest of this chapter are designed to help you reach them.

Building Credibility

A few years ago I was looking for a good pair of running shoes. I was picky: I wanted a brand that would provide support for the peculiar contours of my feet. When I went to a sporting goods store and explained to a clerk what I was looking for, he grabbed a pair of shoes off the shelf and said, "Try these. They're perfect for your feet." I tried them on, and they seemed all right, but I had a vague uneasiness about the clerk's judgment. I decided to wait.

Later, I placed a long-distance call to an old Army friend who is a dedicated long-distance runner and frequently writes articles about running. When I explained my situation, my friend recommended a particular brand. The next day I went out and bought a pair of the kind that he suggested.

This story illustrates the nature of credibility. Whether you are selling shoes or selling ideas, you must have high credibility with your listeners. How do you achieve this? By showing that you are *trustworthy* and *competent*. In my search for the perfect shoe, I rejected the advice of the clerk because he had low credibility with me. I did not know him well enough to judge whether he was trustworthy (maybe he was just trying to make a sale and did not care what kind of shoe he sold me), and I had no way of knowing whether he was competent (maybe he knew nothing at all about runners and their special needs). My friend, on the other hand, had high credibility with me because I knew he was trustworthy and I knew he was competent to give advice on runners' foot problems.

Showing that you are trustworthy and competent is a process that goes on from the time you are called to speak until the time you sit down. You enhance your credibility if your delivery is enthusiastic and if your speech is clear, well-organized, and well-reasoned. In addition, you can build credibility through the following methods.

Explain Your Competence

If you have special expertise, be sure to let your audience know about it—modestly, of course. Do not boast or brag, just give the facts. Telling about your special competence enhances your credibility because it shows that you are speaking from personal experience. It says, "I've been there—I know what I'm talking about." Here is how student speaker Lauren Shriver bolstered her credibility during a speech:

> Deep-sea diving is not dangerous—if you follow all the safety rules. I've made over 50 dives myself, and I feel very safe because I'm very careful each time. I never allow myself to get slack and overconfident.

Lauren's information about her dives was necessary to give credibility to her remarks. Notice how she inserted her personal background in a modest way.

If you do not have personal knowledge of a subject and therefore must rely on the authority of others, you can enhance your own credibility by showing that your sources are competent. For example, in arguing that computers in the future will be capable of humanlike thinking, Don Stafford knew that his ideas might sound farfetched coming from a student, so he said:

> My information comes from the work of Dr. Patrick Winston, who for the past 10 years has been director of the Artificial Intelligence Laboratory at the Massachusetts Institute of Technology. Let me explain an experiment that Dr. Winston carried out. . . .

By quoting from an eminent authority, Don was able to give his speech instant credibility.

Be Honest and Careful with Speech Material

You must be careful in your research, and you must be honest and straightforward in your presentation of ideas. Otherwise, the audience will lose confidence in you.

If people are convinced that one part of your speech is erroneous, they often discount your entire speech. In arguing against the Darwinian theory of evolution, one student gave an incorrect example of Charles Darwin's ideas:

> Darwin taught that giraffes have long necks because thousands of years ago they had to stretch their necks to reach food in trees. All this exercise made their necks longer, and when they reproduced, their offspring had long necks. This went on generation after generation until you got giraffes with very long necks. This is ridiculous. I can spend years and years stretching my neck and maybe make my neck a little bit longer than it is. But I can't pass on long-neck genes to my children.

There is nothing wrong with arguing against Darwin's theories, but in this case, the student misrepresented Darwin's writings. As biology students in the audience quickly pointed out during the question-and-answer period, Darwin contended that as food became available only at high levels in trees, giraffes with short necks died off because they couldn't reach enough leaves to stay alive. Only giraffes with necks long enough to reach leaves were able to survive. That left only long-necked males and long-necked females for mating, and their offspring inherited the tendency to have long necks.

I don't think the student deliberately twisted Darwin's theory in an unethical attempt to disprove the theory of evolution. He simply had failed to do his homework. His blunder, however, probably caused his whole speech to be discredited in the eyes of many listeners.

Show Your Open-Mindedness

"If you would convince others," Lord Chesterfield once said, "seem open to conviction yourself."[2] In other words, show that you are a reasonable person who is open-minded and receptive, and quite capable of being wrong. This approach is not only an ethical one, but it is also highly effective in building credibility. Audiences distrust fanatical know-it-alls who never admit that they might be mistaken.

In a community speech, Patricia Caldwell argued for the right of parents to teach their children at home instead of sending them to school. After citing cases where home-taught children excelled in college, she showed her open-mindedness by conceding that some parents are bad teachers:

> In one well-publicized case in Chicago a few months ago, the authorities brought legal action against a husband and wife for not sending their children to school. Their idea of a home school was to make the children—ages 7, 9, and 10—work all day instead of teaching them to read and write.[3]

Was it stupid for the speaker to relate an incident that seemed to negate her central idea (that some parents can do a better job of teaching than the public schools)? No, because she went on to say that bad parent-teachers are rare, and that periodic state inspections can weed out such cases. Rather than damaging her case, her concession strengthened it, for she showed herself to the audience as a fair-minded individual who could be trusted. If you were a listener, wouldn't you trust her more than someone who said *all* parents are good teachers?

It is especially important to be reasonable and open-minded during the question-and-answer period. I have seen some speakers do a good job in their speech, but when they are asked questions by listeners, they become rigid and defensive, refusing to admit error, refusing to concede that a listener has a good point. These speakers severely damage their own credibility and undo much of the persuasiveness of the speech itself.

Show Common Ground with Your Audience

When you are introduced to someone at a party, you try to find things that you have in common. You ask each other questions ("What is your major?") until you hit upon some interest that you share. Often a person introducing you will try to help you find common ground: "Bill, I'd like you to meet Susan. She's like you: loves to ski." We try to find common ground because it not only helps us to make conversation but it also helps us to feel comfortable with another person.

Likewise in a speech, listeners like and trust a speaker who is similar to themselves. Your job is to show that to some degree you are like your listeners. This does not mean compromising your beliefs; it means highlighting those characteristics you share with the audience. This is especially important if some of the listeners are hostile to your ideas. Say, for example, that you are speaking on gun control and you know that half the listeners are already against your position. Here is what you can say: "I'm talking on gun control today. I know that a lot of you are opposed to the position I'm going to take. I ask only that you hear me out and see if my arguments have any merit whatsoever. Though we may disagree on this subject, you and I have at least one thing in common: we want to see a reduction in the number of violent, gun-related crimes in our society." With this kind of statement, you not only pinpoint common ground (opposition to crime), but you also appeal to the audience's sense of fair play.

One of the best ways to build credibility is to show the listeners that you identify with them—that you share (or have shared) their ideas or feelings. For example, actress Carol Burnett made the following revelation in a talk show on how relatives of an alcoholic should deal with the problem drinker in their lives:

> You may wonder why I'm here to talk about alcoholism. It's easy to explain: Both of my parents died when they were 46 years old because they were both drunks.[4]

Thus, Carol Burnett demonstrated that she was not an aloof, imperious star being paid to talk to the "lowly" masses about a problem that *they* had. She showed, by means of a revelation that must have been painful to make, that she shared the heartbreak of so many people in her audience—the heartbreak of being related to an alcoholic. Her revelation undoubtedly caused her audience to draw closer to her emotionally and to become especially receptive to the rest of her talk.

Providing Evidence

When you make an assertion in a speech, it is not enough to say, "Trust me on this" or "I know I'm right." The audience wants *evidence,* or proof. Evidence can be presented in the forms we discussed in Chapter 7: narratives, statistics, examples, testimony, etc. For each main point in your speech, you should ask yourself, "What evidence is most likely to prove my point with this particular audience?"

Catherine Huseman, a student speaker, gave a talk in which she urged her listeners to cut down on their consumption of salt. Her first step was to prove that excessive salt intake was harmful to one's health. Here are some statistics (from a reliable source) that she used as evidence:

> Salt is a combination of two chemical elements—sodium and chlorine. It's sodium that we need to worry about. The American Medical Association has

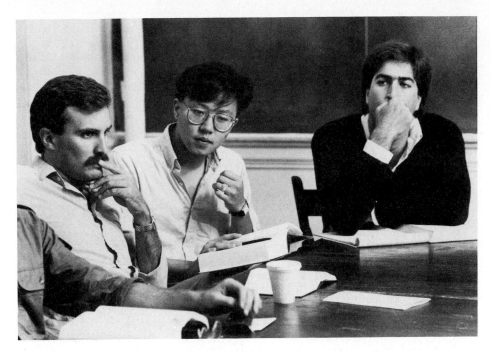

Evidence in a form your listeners will accept is vital to successful persuasion. *(David Wells/ The Image Works)*

concluded that too much sodium leads to hypertension (high blood pressure). Hypertension is known as the "silent killer" because one-fourth of all Americans suffer from the disease without knowing it—until one day they suddenly suffer heart or brain damage. The AMA says that hypertension is a factor in one-half of all the deaths in the U.S. each year.

Catherine also used testimony from an eminent authority:

Dr. Mark Hegsted, head of the Human Nutrition Center of the U.S. Department of Agriculture, says, "If salt were a new food additive, it is doubtful that it would be classified as safe and certainly not at the level most of us consume."

Having argued that sodium was harmful, Catherine next had to convince her listeners that they probably use too much salt. She employed statistics that had been fashioned into an easily grasped contrast:

The body needs a small amount of sodium every day, but most Americans consume more than 20 times the amount of sodium that the body needs. A lot of people think that if they give up potato chips, pretzels, and crackers, they can forget about overconsumption of sodium. What they don't know is that sodium is found in lots of surprising places: Two slices of white bread have twice as much sodium as a small bag of potato chips. Cottage cheese has 3 times as much sodium as a comparable amount of salted peanuts. A one-half cup of instant chocolate pudding has more sodium than three slices of bacon.

Next, Catherine used some examples to drive home her point:

> The following are just a few of the foods that are very high in sodium: bread, milk, cottage cheese, tomato soup, canned tuna, canned corn, margarine, and ham. Also, fast foods are very high in sodium: fried chicken, hamburgers, french fries. In other words, many of the foods we eat every day are loaded with sodium.

After giving all this evidence, Catherine spent the rest of her speech telling the listeners how to cut down on salt in their daily meals. The audience should have been highly receptive to her suggestions because she had done such a good job in presenting evidence of salt's dangers.

Although a speaker should use a variety of supports, is there one type that is more persuasive than others? Yes, there is, but before we discuss the answer, imagine that you are planning a speech on drunk driving. If you want to convince your audience that they stand a chance of being victimized by a drunk driver, which of the following would be the more persuasive piece of evidence?

1. You relate the sad, shocking details of an automobile accident in which a drunk driver hit your car and killed one of your passengers.
2. You cite the fact that 25,000 people are killed in America each year in alcohol-related car accidents.

Though you would need to use both of these items in your speech, the more persuasive item for most listeners would be item 1. But, you might ask, how can one, solitary case be more persuasive than a statistic encompassing 25,000 people? Psychologists have conducted scores of experiments which indicate that one vivid narrative, told from the speaker's personal experience, is much more persuasive than its statistical status would imply.[5] "All other things being equal," writes social psychologist Eliot Aronson, "most people are more deeply influenced by one clear, vivid personal example than by an abundance of statistical data."[6]

So, use a variety of evidence in your persuasive speeches, remembering that your most powerful evidence might be found in your own pool of personal experiences.

Reasoning

Reasoning is the act of reaching conclusions on the basis of logical thinking. While it is true that people are not always logical and rational, it is also true that they frequently can be persuaded by a message that appeals to their powers of reasoning.[7] Let us take a look at two major types of reasoning.

Deduction

Imagine that you are driving a car on a highway at a speed about 15 miles per hour over the speed limit. Suddenly you see a police car parked behind a billboard; as you whiz past, you notice that a radar device is protruding from the police car. You slow down but you know it is too late: you are certain to be stopped. Sure enough, you glance in your rear-view mirror and see a second police car with lights flashing; the officer motions you to pull over.

How did you know that you were going to be stopped? By using *deduction*—a chain of reasoning that carries you from a generalization to a specific conclusion. In formal logic, this chain of reasoning is expressed in the form of a syllogism:

> *Major premise (generalization):* Motorists who are speeding when they pass a radar point are usually stopped by police.
> *Minor premise (specific instance):* I was speeding when I passed a radar point.
> *Conclusion:* Therefore, I will probably be stopped.

In a speech, deductive reasoning is convincing *only if both premises are accepted by the audience as true.*[8] Would an audience be likely to accept the following chain of reasoning?

> *Major premise:* Aerobic exercise improves eyesight.
> *Minor premise:* Jogging is a form of aerobic exercise.
> *Conclusion:* Therefore, jogging improves eyesight.

The minor premise is true, but the major premise is false, so the entire syllogism is flawed. An audience would reject the conclusion.

Placing your deductive reasoning in the form of a syllogism can sometimes help you prepare a persuasive speech. For example, let's say that you wanted to argue that acupuncture should be a legal form of medical therapy. You could set up the following syllogism:

> *Major premise:* Any medical technique that relieves pain should be legal, as long as it has no adverse side effects.
> *Minor premise:* Acupuncture is a medical technique that relieves pain and has no adverse side effects.
> *Conclusion:* Therefore, acupuncture should be legal.

Remember that your deductive argument will be strong only if the listeners believe both your major and minor premises. So, to convince your audience of the truth of the major premise, you can point out that a person in pain deserves relief, regardless of whether the relief comes from orthodox western medicine or from ancient oriental practices. To convince your audience of the minor premise, you can cite studies by reputable researchers on the effectiveness and safety of acupuncture, and you can relate testimonials from patients who found relief from pain by means of the technique.

Once your listeners are convinced of your major and minor premises, they should be receptive to your conclusion (which is really the central idea of your speech)—that acupuncture should be legal.

When lawyers stand in front of the U.S. Supreme Court to argue against a particular law, they use a deductive argument. In the form of a syllogism, the argument looks like this:

Major premise: All laws that violate the Constitution must be struck down.
Minor premise: This law violates the Constitution.
Conclusion: Therefore, this law must be struck down.[9]

Since the Supreme Court justices already accept the major premise as true, the task of the lawyers is to convince them that the minor premise is true. If they succeed, the justices move to the inescapable conclusion—the law must be struck down.

Induction

While deductive reasoning moves from the general to the specific, *inductive reasoning* proceeds from the specific to the general. Assume, for example, that you are sitting in a windowless room in the library and you make the following observations:

☐ A student enters the room carrying an umbrella that is dripping.
☐ Another student walks into the room and appears to be wet on the head and shoulders.
☐ A third student enters and takes off a raincoat that glistens with water.

Based on what you have seen, you reason inductively that it has been raining outside. You use specific evidence to reach a general conclusion. In reaching this conclusion, however, you must take an *inductive leap*. You cannot prove that it has been raining simply because of what you have seen. You are probably right, but your conclusion has to remain tentative (until you walk outside and see for yourself) because there is always the chance that some other explanation can account for the three students' wetness: perhaps they have just participated in a science experiment (involving water) that took place outside the library. Perhaps there has not been a drop of rain all day. The chances are overwhelming that rain *is* the explanation, of course, but the point is that induction, unlike deduction, never leads to a certain conclusion, only a *very likely* one.

To construct an inductive argument, you should follow these steps: (1) ask a question, (2) answer the question by collecting as much specific evidence as possible, and (3) reach a conclusion based on the evidence. Here is an example:

Question: Do air bags in cars save lives?

Evidence:

Item 1: Joan Baxter of San Diego survived a head-on crash because of the air bag in her car.
Item 2: Dr. Arnold Arms, a Kansas City physician, survived a 35-mile-per-hour crash into a city bus; the bus suffered $15,000 damage, while Dr. Arms was spared any injury because of the air bag in his car.

Item 3: Mrs. Mattie Lansing of Chicago was involved in a head-on collision at 50 miles per hour, but suffered no injuries because of the air bag in her car.

Conclusion: Air bags save lives.

Is this all you need for evidence? No, although the inductive reasoning is powerful, you would need to show that your examples are not isolated flukes. You could, for example, cite statistics from national authorities, such as: "The Department of Transportation estimates that 11,000 lives would be saved each year if air bags were used in all cars."

When you use inductive reasoning, you will convince an audience only if your evidence is strong. If you have weak evidence, your conclusion will be weak. In the preceding example, if you had used such vague statements as "The manufacturers of air bags assure us that the bags will save lives," your evidence would have been too flimsy to support the conclusion.

Earlier, we discussed the value of stating your central idea in the introduction of your speech; there are occasions, however, when this is not the best strategy. One such occasion is when you have an audience that is likely to be hostile or skeptical to your central idea. With such listeners, a wise strategy is to lead them through an inductive chain, saving your central idea for the latter part of the speech. Here's an example.

Student speaker Robert Burnham had the following as his central idea: "We could cut down on street crime in America if heroin addicts could legally get their daily 'fix' from government-sponsored clinics at no cost." If he had said this in the introduction, many of the listeners might have dismissed the idea as crazy and the speaker as a crackpot. But Robert used a smart approach. In his introduction, he made no mention of his central idea; he merely said, "I want to talk to you about one of America's worst drugs, heroin." Using the inductive approach, he built his case:

☐ He gave true accounts of heroin addicts robbing citizens in order to get money to support their expensive addiction.

☐ He told of an experiment in Great Britain where addicts were treated as patients rather than as criminals and were given heroin in government-sponsored clinics so that they would not have to mug people on the street.

☐ He quoted a judge who said that if heroin were legally available to addicts, there would be a big drop in muggings and other street crimes.

Toward the end of his speech, having built a good case, Robert stated his argument: society should give addicts the heroin they crave so that they won't engage in street crimes. By then, the listeners were probably more open-minded about the idea than they would have been if they had heard it at the beginning of the speech. Even if they rejected the idea, they at least saw it as having some merit rather than being completely off-base.

Fallacies in Reasoning

A fallacy is an error in reasoning that renders an argument false or unreliable. You should become adept at recognizing fallacies so that you can avoid using them in your own speeches and so that you can prevent yourself from being influenced by them when you listen to the speeches of others. Here are some of the more common fallacies:

1. *Hasty generalization.* A hasty generalization is a conclusion that is reached on the basis of insufficient evidence. For example, "The mayor was convicted of accepting bribes and a city council member was indicted for vote fraud. So we can conclude that all the politicians in this city are corrupt." The fact that two politicians are corrupt does not prove that all are. Make sure that you have ample evidence before you reach a conclusion.

2. *Sweeping generalization.* A sweeping generalization is a statement that is so broad and so categorical that it ends up being unfair and inaccurate. It often includes words like *always, never, all,* and *none.* In a speech on America's neglect of old people, one student said, "America is the only country in the world that has no regard for its elderly family members. All other countries have great respect for the age and wisdom of the elderly."

The speaker had a good point to make—that we need to take better care of our elderly—but he damaged his credibility by indulging in such an outrageously unfair generalization. Is it true that *all* Americans have *no* regard for the elderly? Don't some Americans have high regard for old people? Even if his accusation were true, how can he say that America is the *only* country exhibiting such neglect? Has he researched the situation in such nations as Zaire, Luxembourg, and Sri Lanka?

To make his argument reasonable and accurate, the speaker would need to modify the generalization to say: "Some Americans do not give their elderly family members the honor and attention that they deserve." Now the generalization would be acceptable to most listeners.

3. *Attack on a person.* Some speakers try to win an argument by attacking a person rather than the person's ideas. For example: "Rodney has lived in upper-class luxury all his life, so how can we believe anything he says about changing the welfare system for the poor? He obviously knows nothing about poverty." This tactic, sometimes known as *argumentum ad hominem* (argument against the man), is unfair and unethical. Rodney's arguments should be judged on how sound his ideas are, not on any aspect of his personal life.

Attacks on a person are often used in the courtroom to discredit a witness ("Ladies and gentlemen of the jury, this witness admits that he's an atheist, so how can we trust him to tell us the truth?) and in politics to discredit a foe ("My opponent has gambled in Las Vegas at least 5 times. Do you want such a person to manage your tax dollars?"). Though this tactic may be effective in the hands of such speakers, it should never be used by the ethical speaker, not only because it is dishonest and unfair, but also because it can backfire and cause careful listeners to lose respect for the speaker.

4. *False cause.* Beware of the fallacy of assuming that because events occur close together in time, they are necessarily related as cause and effect. A President takes office, and 4 months later the unemployment rate goes up 1 percent. Can we say that the President's policies caused the rise in unemployment? It is possible that they did, but there may be many other factors that caused the problem—for example, the economic policies of the previous administration.

The fallacy of false cause can also occur when a speaker oversimplifies the causes of complex problems. Take, for example, a speaker who says that *the* cause of cancer is negative thinking. That explanation is simple and understandable—and wrong. While negative thinking—and the stress and tension that go with it—may be implicated someday as contributing factors in cancer, medical researchers say that no one thing has been isolated as *the* cause of cancer. The disease is probably caused by an interaction of several factors, including genetic predisposition, susceptibility of the immune system, the presence of a carcinogenic virus, and environmental irritants. Cancer is too complex to be explained by a single causative factor.

5. *Begging the question.* When speakers "beg the question," they act as if an assertion has been proved when in fact it has not. Suppose that a speaker made the following statement: "Since the Japanese never make a product that will last a long time, we should stop buying Japanese products and start buying American-made products." The speaker is acting as if the impermanence of Japanese products is an established fact, when in reality many listeners would probably disagree. An ethical speaker would first try to prove that Japanese products are less enduring than American products and then urge the audience not to buy Japanese-made goods.

When a speaker begs the question, careful listeners are resentful because they feel as if they are being tricked into giving assent to a proposition that they do not believe.

6. *False analogy.* When speakers use a false analogy, they make the mistake of assuming that just because two things are alike in minor ways, they are also alike in major ways. For example, some people say, "Feed a dog every day, and it will be your friend forever. Likewise, if we give generous aid, especially food, to foreign countries, they will always be our friends." This analogy is erroneous. Although it is true that dogs and humans are similar in some respects, they are different psychologically in many important ways. While dogs may never bite the hand that feeds them, the same cannot be said of humans. In fact, receiving food from the United States has sometimes caused peoples in other lands, embarrassed by their poverty, to resent and even hate their American benefactors.

Here is another false analogy: "We can communicate effectively via satellite with people on the other side of the planet. Why, therefore, can't parents and children do a better job of communicating within the intimate environment of their own homes?" Upon close examination, this analogy falls apart. Satellite communication between nations is a purely technical matter of transmitting radio and television signals, whereas communication among family members involves psychological complexities and subtleties that are beyond the reach of technology.

7. *Either-or reasoning.* The either-or fallacy occurs when the speaker states that there are only two alternatives, when in fact there may be many. For example: "Either we wipe out our national deficit or we watch our economy die." Is there truly no other way? Is it not possible that we can trim the deficit, without totally eliminating it, and still preserve our economic health? Stating an argument in stark, either-or terms makes a speaker appear unreasonable and dogmatic.

Here is another example: "Intelligence is determined by either heredity or environment, and I say that heredity is the key. How smart you are is determined by your genes." Most psychologists would disagree with this statement because intelligence seems to be determined by a complex interplay of both genetic and environmental factors. People like Albert Einstein or Margaret Mead would probably never have thrived intellectually if their entire lives had been stunted by extreme poverty and malnutrition.

8. *Straw man.* Some people try to win arguments by creating a straw man, a ridiculous caricature of what their opponents believe, and then beating it down with great ease. For example, one speaker, while arguing in favor of the death penalty for convicted murderers, said, "These people [who oppose the death penalty] say that a murderer is not really to blame for his crime. They say that society is to blame for not providing better educational and economic opportunities. So the murderer shouldn't be executed; he shouldn't even be sent to prison. We should simply say to him, 'Naughty boy, you did a no-no. Don't do it again.'"

Was this a fair summary of the belief of his opponents? Of course not. Most opponents of the death penalty favor long prison sentences for murderers. A speaker like this creates a straw man in order to look like a victor. Careful listeners, however, will spot the deception and lose confidence in the speaker.

Appealing to Motivations

Motivations are the needs, desires, or drives that impel a person toward a goal or away from some negative situation. People have hundreds of motivations, including love, happiness, health, social acceptance, financial security, adventure, and creativity.[10] If you show your listeners how your ideas can help them satisfy such needs and desires, you increase your chances of persuading them to adopt your point of view. Here are some examples of how student speakers appealed to the motivations of their audiences:

☐ To raise money to buy food for starving people in Africa, Lee Anne Washington appealed to the motivation that most Americans have to help those less fortunate than themselves.

It is ethical for a speaker to arouse strong emotions in listeners, but he or she should accompany emotional appeals with valid evidence and sound logic. *(Brent Jones)*

☐ To try to persuade listeners to use seat belts at all times in a car, Jason Bradley appealed to the strong drive that people have to protect themselves from harm.

☐ To try to convince listeners to invest in real estate, Glenda Jorgensen tapped the public's desire for financial security and wealth.

Let's examine some of the more common motivations that audiences have. (This is a partial list—there are dozens of other motivations.)

☐ *Love and esteem.* People want to love and be loved, to have good friends, to be esteemed at work and at home.

☐ *Health.* Your listeners want to avoid sickness, maintain their health, and live a long time.

☐ *Safety.* People want to be protected from crime, and they want to use products that will not injure or kill them.

☐ *Success.* Most men and women wish for success of some sort, depending upon their individual definition of the term; for one person, success means making a million dollars, whereas for another, it is becoming the best violinist in an orchestra.

☐ *Financial security.* Most men and women desire a degree of financial security, though they would disagree on just how much money they need to achieve it.

☐ *Self-improvement.* Most people want to improve themselves, whether by learning a new skill or learning more effective ways of coping with life.

☐ *Recreational pleasure.* People of all ages love to get away from the stress and toil of work by taking vacations, going to movies, eating at fine restaurants, and so on.

☐ *Altruism.* Many people have a sincere desire to help others, whether through donating blood in their communities or through sending food to starving children in a faraway land.

Whenever possible, you should appeal to several motivations at the same time. Listeners who are not reached by one appeal can still be influenced by another. Suppose, for example, that you are trying to persuade your listeners to take up bicycling. Here are some of the motivations that you could identify, coupled with appropriate appeals:

Motivation	*Appeal*
Feeling good	Bicycling works out tension and makes you feel energetic and happy.
Looking good	Bicycling burns lots of calories so it's ideal for weight control. It also tones up leg muscles.
Long-term health	Bicycling is excellent exercise for heart and lungs, thus helping prevent cardiovascular disease.
Friendship	Being on a bicycle is an instant passport to the world of cyclists. It's easy to strike up conversations with other riders, and you can often make new friends. Cycling also provides an enjoyable activity to share with old friends.
Adventure	With a bicycle you can explore out-of-the-way places, travel long distances in a single day, and experience the thrill of flying down a steep mountain road.
Competition	If you enjoy competing, there are bike races in almost every city or town.

By appealing to more than one motivation, you increase your chances of persuading the audience. For example, the listener who is already in superb health may not be reached by the first three items, but might be swayed by one of the last three.

As part of your audience analysis in the early stages of preparing a speech, you should ask yourself, "What are the strongest motivational appeals that I can make to this audience?" Then determine how you can work those appeals into your speech. As an example, let's take a look at how one speaker handled this matter: Vanessa Rivers is a real estate agent who frequently gives a talk in her community on the advantages of living in a condominium (a unit in a cooperative apartment building that a person owns instead of rents). Here are her main points, followed by an explanation of the motivational appeal in each.[11]

I. Owning a condo is more advantageous financially than renting an apartment. [She explains that a condo owner's monthly mortgage payment is an investment and that a condo owner can write off these mortgage payments on federal income taxes. Thus she appeals to the audience's desire for *financial security.*]

II. A condo owner does not have to worry about house and yard maintenance. [This point appeals to a person's desire for *independence* (in this case not being tied down to such tasks as mowing a lawn or repairing gutters) and for *leisure time.*]

III. A condo owner, along with all the other residents, owns and has unlimited access to the recreational facilities, which may include a swimming pool, tennis courts, and health club. [This item appeals to the audience's desire for *good health, recreational pleasure,* and *companionship.*]

In analyzing the motivations of your listeners, you need to ask yourself, "Will anything I plan to say conflict with some of their strongest desires and needs?" If so, you need to confront the problem explicitly in your speech (in other words, don't pretend that the problem doesn't exist). For example, in the case of bicycling above, you might find that all your descriptions of the wonderful benefits of cycling fail to move some listeners who are worried that sharing a highway with fast-moving trucks is too dangerous. Thus the motivation they have to be safe outweighs all of the benefits. To win over such listeners, you must either convince them that cycling is really not dangerous if precautions are taken (such as riding only on back roads in the country) or persuade them that the risks are minimal and are worth taking.

In some cases where motivations conflict, you can offer a countervailing reward. In the condominiums speech mentioned above, for instance, some listeners might feel that condos do not satisfy their desire for complete privacy (of the kind they would experience in a private home). The speaker could acknowledge that condos are, as far as privacy is concerned, the same as apartments, but that the advantages of a condo—health facilities, lack of maintenance requirements, tax advantages, and so on—far outweigh the disadvantage of lack of privacy.

Arousing Emotions

Emotions are "stirred up" feelings that can be either positive (amusement, love, joy) or negative (fear, anger, sadness). In a speech, emotional appeals can stir listeners and rouse them to action.

To give an example of how emotion can be used effectively, here is an excerpt from a speech by a student, Stacey Brooks, who was arguing for a crackdown on divorced parents who kidnap their children and thereby deprive the other parent of seeing them:

> One morning Martha Greer, a divorced woman, woke up her kids, Samantha, aged 8, and Bruce, aged 6. She rubbed their backs to help them get awake, then she helped them find their school clothes. She made them a breakfast of orange juice, toast and jelly, bacon, hashed browns, and milk. Then she walked with them to the place where they caught the bus to school.
> That was the last time Martha saw them. They were kidnapped by their father that afternoon as they left school. That was 6 months ago, and Martha has no idea where they are. The police have not been able to find them. Think how frantic Martha is, think how angry she is, as she wonders where her kids are and how they're getting along without their mother. Imagine how you would feel if your kids were suddenly snatched from your life.

This story was very effective in arousing anger and pity in the listeners. However, this kind of emotional appeal has its limits: churning up emotions can be a potent tool, but you should take care that it never becomes a substitute for well-reasoned arguments. A speaker who does nothing but tug on heart strings, completely neglecting the listeners' minds, will usually be less effective than the speaker who uses both emotional and rational appeals. In general, emotional appeals work best when they are used sparingly. Just as too much icing can cause a cake to change from sweet to sickening, too much emotion can cause a speech to change from effective to excessive. After giving this introduction, Stacey relied upon sound evidence and logic in the rest of her speech, thus making sure that her emotional appeal was an accompaniment to solid arguments, rather than a substitute for them.

Fear, one of the most powerful emotions, deserves special mention. Over the years, communicators have wondered how much fear one should evoke in trying to persuade people. For example, if you want to convince an audience to wear seat belts, would you be most successful with some low-fear visual aids, such as a chart on traffic fatalities, or with some high-fear graphics, such as a gory, full-color videotape of victims of a terrible car wreck? Research favors the latter. "The overwhelming weight of experimental data," says psychologist Eliot Aronson, "suggests that . . . the more frightened a person is by a communication, the more likely he or she is to take positive preventive action."[12] Research also indicates that high-fear messages are most effective when they are coupled with specific instructions on how to take action. For example, a high-fear message on rabies would be more persuasive if it included instructions on how to avoid the disease than if it left out such instructions.[13]

Sample Persuasive Speech

In a speech to motivate action, student Jeffrey Cordell argued for tougher laws against drunk driving. His outline is presented first, followed by the speech as delivered.[14] In the commentary alongside the outline, note the discussion of the five steps of the motivated sequence.

The Outline

What Can We Do about Drunk Drivers?

General Purpose: To persuade
Specific Purpose: To persuade my audience to support tough legislation aimed at getting drunk drivers off our highways.
Central Idea: Tough new laws should be enacted to rid our highways of drunk drivers.

Motivated Sequence: **INTRODUCTION**
Attention
Jeffrey grabs the listeners' attention with a tragic story.

I. According to *Newsweek* magazine, a 4-year-old boy in Memphis, Tennessee, David Gunderman, was run over by a car as he stood on the sidewalk waiting for an ice cream truck. His killer, a drunk driver who had eight prior convictions ranging from hit-and-run to drunk driving, was sentenced to 5 years in prison.

Need

Jeffrey shows the scope of the problem and why action must be taken.

II. David Gunderman's story is just one out of thousands. The FBI estimates that 25,000 people are killed in alcohol-related traffic accidents each year in the United States. The National Safety Council estimates that one-half of all Americans will be victimized by a drunk driver in some way during their lifetimes—either in a serious crash or a fender-bender. We, the public, do not have to put up with this slaughter. We can—and we must—get drunk drivers off our highways, permanently. We can do so if we pass tough new laws that do two things—one, let police set up roadblocks, and two, give drunk drivers harsh penalties.

(*Transition:* Let's start off by taking a look at what police can do.)

BODY

Satisfaction

Jeffrey presents his solution to the problem.

I. Police should set up roadblocks at random sites every night of the week to apprehend drunk drivers.
   A. Breathalyzers can be used to test blood alcohol level.
   B. Roadblocks in Sweden have apparently been successful.

(*Transition:* Now that we've talked about what police can do, let's turn our attention to the courts.)

II. Persons convicted of drunk driving should receive harsh penalties.
   A. They should get mandatory prison sentences.
   B. They should lose their licenses permanently.
   C. Though some experts doubt that jurors would convict under such stern penalties, it's worthwhile to try harsh measures.

(*Transition:* Would tough new laws be likely to get drunks off the roads?)

Visualization

By showing what happened in other states, he helps his audience see what he believes will happen if his proposals are adopted.

III. States that have instituted tough policies have experienced a drop in traffic fatalities.
   A. California saw a 14 percent drop in traffic deaths.
   B. Maine reported a 24 percent drop.
   C. Minnesota and Maryland had a 30 percent reduction.

(*Transition:* Let me review my two proposals.)

CONCLUSION

I. I have proposed police roadblocks and stronger punishment.

Action

Jeffrey makes a request for immediate action by the audience.

II. All states should adopt these stringent new laws to get drunks off the road—permanently.

III. At the end of class, I will have a petition for you to sign, urging our state lawmakers to enact the proposals I've outlined for you today. I hope you will sign. The life you save may be your own.

BIBLIOGRAPHY

"Drunken-driving laws vary across USA," *USA Today,* May 6, 1985, p. 4.

"One less for the road," *Time,* May 20, 1985, pp. 76–78.

Shelley Patterson, exchange student, personal interview, April 1985.

The Speech as Delivered

Here is the transcript of Jeffrey Cordell's speech. Notice that the speaker uses the ideas of his outline without using the exact wording. In an extemporaneous speech, the speaker does not read or memorize a speech, but speaks from brief notes.

Commentary

The story of the little boy is an effective device to arouse a well-justified emotion in the listeners—anger.

What Can We Do about Drunk Drivers?

David Gunderman was a 4-year-old boy who lived with his parents in Memphis, Tennessee. One summer day, as David stood on the sidewalk waiting for an ice cream truck, he was run over and killed by a driver who had lost control of his car. According to *Newsweek* magazine, the driver was drunk. And it wasn't the first time he had been drunk behind the wheel. He had *eight* previous convictions ranging from hit-and-run to drunk driving. For killing David, he was sentenced to only 5 years in prison.

The speaker previews the body of the speech by giving his central idea.

The story of David Gunderman is just one out of thousands. The FBI estimates that 25,000 Americans are killed each year in alcohol-related traffic accidents. The National Safety Council estimates that one-half of all drivers in the U.S. will become the victim of a drunk driver in some way during their lives. It might be a serious accident or it might be a fender-bender, but one-half of you will be victimized at some point in your lives. Is there anything we can do about this slaughter on our highways? I say that we can get drunk drivers off our roads and highways, and keep them off, if we pass tough new laws that do two things: one, let police set up roadblocks, and two, give drunk drivers strong punishment.

First of all, let's see what police can do. I think that the police should be permitted—and encouraged—to set up

The speaker anticipates an objection that is likely to arise in the listeners and tries to rebut it.
The testimony of an observer can provide stronger support than a recital of dry statistics.

roadblocks at random places every night of the week to catch drunk drivers. Breathalyzers could be used to test blood alcohol level. Some people say this is too drastic, this is too much like a police state, but I say that the law-abiding driver has nothing to worry about. The roadblocks would cause people to think twice before using a car on a night when they are planning to drink heavily. A friend of mine lived in Sweden for a year on a student-exchange program, and she said that Swedish police set up roadblocks at different places every night. She said that most Swedes are very reluctant to drink if they are planning to drive.

While the police can set up roadblocks, what can the courts do? My second recommendation is that we make the penalty for drunk driving much more severe than it is right now in most states. I believe that people who have been convicted of drunk driving should receive a mandatory prison sentence and should lose their driver's licenses permanently. Some legal experts say that if we have penalties that are real tough like this, some juries will be reluctant to convict. They may turn out to be right, but I believe that we at least ought to try it. If it proves to be unworkable, then we can modify the laws later. We have nothing to lose by trying tough sentencing and possibly many lives to gain.

By admitting that his plan might have flaws, the speaker shows his moderation and open-mindedness, thus enhancing his credibility with the audience.

Are tough new laws likely to get drunk drivers off the highways? Several states have already adopted stringent laws that include some or all of my proposals. What has happened in these states? Are the new laws working? Yes, most definitely they are. In the first year of their new laws, here's what happened, according to *Time* magazine: In California, the traffic death rate went down 14 percent; in Maine, it went down 24 percent; and in Minnesota and Maryland, it went down 30 percent. Those percentages translate of course into lives saved. Tough laws *do* work.

Statistics provide good support for the speaker's point.
The speaker summarizes his two key ideas.
If the speaker gets the audience to sign a petition, he increases their commitment to his cause.

Today I have made two proposals—that police should set up frequent roadblocks at random places and that a drunk driver who is convicted should lose his license permanently and be sent to jail. I believe that all states should put these proposals into law. These laws would be a giant step toward getting the drunks off the roads—permanently. At the end of class, I will have a petition at the table by the door. This petition urges our state legislators to pass the laws I've talked about. I hope you will sign the petition. The life you save may be your own.

Summary

Persuasion—getting people to think or act in a certain way—is one of the most frequent tasks of the public speaker. There are many patterns that can be used for the persuasive speech, but one of the most effective is the motivated sequence, in which you (1) gain the listeners' attention, (2) show them the need for action, (3) offer a solution that satisfies that need, (4) help them visualize what will happen if the solution is put into effect, and (5) request that they take action.

To be effective in persuasion, you should analyze your audience carefully, asking six key questions: (1) Exactly who are my listeners? (2) How can I build credibility with them? (3) What evidence should I provide to convince them? (4) What form of reasoning would be most compelling to them? (5) How can I appeal to their motivations? (6) How can I arouse their emotions?

In using logic, you must be careful to avoid these fallacies: hasty generalization, sweeping generalization, attack on a person, false cause, begging the question, false analogy, either-or reasoning, and straw man attacks.

Review Questions

1. Why is it a good idea in many cases to tell the audience why you are competent to speak on your particular subject matter?
2. How is an audience likely to react if you are careless with your facts and ideas?
3. What is the difference between deduction and induction?
4. Why should a speaker never use the logical fallacy called "attack on a person"?
5. List at least five motivations that all listeners have.

Tip 15: Provide Supplementary Material at the End of a Speech

At the end of a speech, especially a persuasive talk to a community or business audience, it is sometimes effective to offer the listeners supplementary materials that support or elaborate your message. Here are some possibilities:

1. Pass out a brief written summary of your key ideas. This reinforces your message and give the listeners, many of whom probably did not take notes, an accurate record of what you said. A summary is especially helpful for technical presentations that include complex ideas and detailed statistics.

2. Pass out a supplementary reading list. If you get your listeners interested or excited about a particular subject, they will appreciate receiving a list of books and articles that they can read to delve further into the subject.

3. Offer written documentation of your sources. You might say, for example, "I don't have time to name all the books and articles from which I got my information, but I have a bibliography which I'll place on the table at the front, and you're welcome to pick this up after I finish.'' Such a list is not only helpful to listeners who want to pursue your subject further, but it also suggests to the audience that you are a careful researcher who is concerned about getting the information correct.

16

Special
Types of
Speeches

Entertaining (or After-Dinner) Speech

Speech of Introduction

Speech of Presentation

Speech of Acceptance

Speech of Tribute

Speech of Inspiration

Though most of the speeches that you will give in your lifetime will probably be informative or persuasive, there are occasions when you may be called upon to give other kinds—an entertaining speech at a banquet, a brief speech introducing the main speaker at a convention, a eulogy at a funeral to honor a close friend, an acceptance speech to thank an organization for giving you an award, or an inspirational speech to lift the morale of your subordinates or fellow employees. In this chapter, we will take a look at these special types of speeches.

Entertaining (or After-Dinner) Speech

An entertaining speech provides amusement or diversion for the audience. It should be light and enjoyable, and easy to listen to. There should be no lecturing, no preaching, no doomsaying.

An entertaining speech can be given in a variety of circumstances, but it is most often delivered at meetings such as conventions and annual club dinners. It is frequently referred to as an "after-dinner speech" because it is usually given after luncheon or dinner. People who have just eaten a big meal want to sit back, relax, and enjoy a talk. They don't want to work hard mentally; they don't want to be told anything negative and gloomy. So if you are an after-dinner speaker, do not challenge their beliefs or pump them with statistics. Strive to entertain them.

An entertaining speech can consist of a series of jokes, but joke telling is a difficult and risky business (see Tip 16 at the end of this chapter); besides, an entertaining speech does not have to be humorous to be effective. In other words, to entertain you do not have a elicit belly laughs, shrieks of glee, or deep chuckles. You can entertain an audience with stories and word pictures; for example, a well-told story about the calamities that occurred on your first date, a dramatic account of Sir Edmund Hillary's conquest of Mt. Everest, a description of the weird behavior of the South American sloth, or an imaginative forecast of life in America 100 years from now. All these speeches could be given without thigh-slapping jokes, but they nevertheless would be highly entertaining.

Students have given entertaining speeches on such topics as:

- ☐ My first piano recital—a total disaster
- ☐ Hitchhiking from East Coast to West Coast
- ☐ My grandfather's favorite ghost stories
- ☐ The wit and wisdom of Mark Twain
- ☐ The best rock concert I ever attended

While entertaining the audience is the general purpose of this kind of speech, this does not mean that you cannot include a few elements of persuasion, information, or inspiration; it just means that you should weave them unobtrusively and gracefully into the cloth of entertainment. To see how one speaker dispensed information in a light, entertaining manner, read the speech "Blue Beans and Purple Potatoes" in Appendix B.

Speech of Introduction

☐ At a meeting of her civic club, Paula Moreno spoke briefly on why she was supporting a particular candidate for Congress and then turned the lectern over to the candidate.

☐ Theodore Lansing, a university librarian, stood up in front of 1500 delegates at a national librarians' convention and introduced the keynote speaker, a renowned writer of science fiction.

These are examples of speeches of introduction. When you introduce one friend to another, you want them to get interested in each other and to like each other. When you introduce a speaker to an audience, you want to achieve the same goal. You want speaker and audience to be interested in each other and to feel warmth and friendliness.

An introduction should mention the speaker's name several times (so that everyone can catch it), and it should give background information to enhance the speaker's credibility with the audience. Your tone of voice and facial expression should convey enthusiasm for the speech to come.

Here are some guidelines for speeches of introduction.

☐ *Ask the speaker ahead of time what kind of introduction he or she would like.* Some speakers will write out their introduction and send it to you in advance. While you should not actually read the document (because this would be boring to the audience), you should use it as the basis for your remarks. If the speaker provides you with a lengthy résumé or list of accomplishments, select those items that would be most appropriate for the audience and the occasion. Also, the speaker may want you to establish ground rules about questions; for example, "John will take questions at the end of the speech."

☐ *Be sure to pronounce the speaker's name correctly.* If you have any doubt about how to pronounce the speaker's name, verify the pronunciation beforehand. If the name is difficult to pronounce, practice saying it in advance so that you do not stumble during the introduction.

☐ *Use the name the speaker prefers.* If you are scheduled to introduce Dr. Elizabeth Wilson, find out beforehand what she wants to be called. Do not assume that she prefers to be called "Dr. Wilson." It could be that for this particular audience she prefers the informality of "Elizabeth" or even her nickname "Liz."

☐ *Set the proper tone.* When you introduce someone, you help set the tone for the speech to follow. Be careful to set the right tone—a humorous tone for a humorous speech, a serious tone for a serious speech. Consulting with the speaker in advance will ensure that you understand the tone he or she wants you to set.

☐ *Avoid long introductions.* A good rule of thumb is to keep an introduction under 3 minutes. After all, an audience wants to hear the speaker, not the introducer.

☐ *Avoid exaggeration.* If you exaggerate the speaker's abilities or credentials, you build up unrealistic expectations in the audience. Consider this kind of introduction: "Our speaker tonight is a funny person who will have you laughing so hard you'll have to clutch your sides," or "The speaker will give us insights that are wise and brilliant." Such statements raise expectations that are very difficult for the speaker to meet. If the listeners are expecting one of the world's funniest speakers or one of the wisest, they may be disappointed. Overpraising a speaker also puts enormous pressure on him or her. The introduction "Our speaker is a dynamic personality who is known far and wide for her flawless platform technique" not only will cause the audience to focus on the speaker's delivery rather than on the message, but will also place great pressure on the speaker to perform perfectly.

☐ *Find out whether the speaker wants you to discuss the topic.* Some speakers will want you to discuss the significance of their topic (to help prepare the audience for the speech); other speakers prefer to save all discussion of the topic until *they* step to the lectern.

☐ *Never steal the speaker's material.* Imagine this scenario: you are about to deliver a speech to an audience of 1000 people, and suddenly you realize that the person introducing you is telling the very anecdote that you had carefully planned as the opener of your speech. How in the world are you going to begin your talk? Such nightmares actually happen, say professional speakers. The introducer uses a joke, anecdote, key statistic, or quotation that the speaker had planned to include. Or the introducer summarizes the subject matter in a way that duplicates or contradicts the subsequent speech. When you are an introducer, stay away from the speaker's material unless you and the speaker have worked out an agreement on exactly what you may cover. Your job is to set the stage, not steal it.

The following introduction of Joseph Conte was delivered at a meeting of a genealogical society:

> Our speaker tonight, Joseph Conte, will talk to us about how to set up a computerized ancestry record. Mr. Conte brings a lot of personal experience to this subject. The great-grandson of immigrants from Italy, he has traced his own family roots back to Florence. He has put all of his genealogical records onto a computer, using a program that was created by a Mormon group in Salt Lake City. Mr. Conte has a background of expertise in scholarly detective work: for the past decade he has been a researcher for the National Archives in Washington, D.C., specializing in nineteenth and twentieth century immigration. Mr. Conte, welcome to our society and thank you for taking the time to share your knowledge with us.

Speech of Presentation

Awards or honors are often bestowed upon individuals for their service to business, institution, community, church, or club. It is customary for a brief speech to be made before the award is presented.

The speech of presentation should give (1) any background information that would help the audience understand the purpose or circumstances of the award, (2) the criteria used for selecting the recipient, and (3) the achievements of the recipient. In many cases, it is customary to withhold the name of the recipient until the very end of the speech, as a way of building suspense.

If humor is used, it should be handled very carefully. If you try to make a joke about the recipient, it may seem as if you are belittling her or him. At one company banquet, a department head gave an award for 10 years of service to a subordinate and used the occasion to tease him with a mock insult—"the only reason we keep him on the payroll is because his father worked here for 40 years." The "humor" was similar to the kind of bantering that the boss and the subordinate engaged in during a typical workday, but at the awards banquet, with his family present, the subordinate felt humiliated.

Here is a speech of presentation delivered by Meredith Brody at the annual meeting of a community theater:

> The John Cleese Award is given each year to the top actor or actress in our theater. As most of you know, the award is given in honor of the British actor John Cleese of *Monty Python* and *Fawlty Towers* fame. The winner is selected by ballots circulated to all our members. Our winner this year is a seasoned veteran of our stage, a person who always performs with intelligence, audacity, and élan. I am pleased to announce that the winner of the third annual John Cleese Award is . . . James Colton!

Speech of Acceptance

If you are ever given an award, a promotion, or some other sort of public recognition, you may be called upon to "say a few words." Giving a speech of acceptance is difficult because you want to sound appreciative without being syrupy; you want to sound deserving without being egotistical. Here are some guidelines to follow:

☐ *Thank those who played a part in your achieving the honor.* If a few individuals made your recognition possible, mention them by name; if a lot of people did, mention the most important contributors to your success and say something like this, "There are many others but they are too numerous to name. Nevertheless, I am grateful to all of them."

☐ *Thank the organization giving you the award and recognize the work they are doing.* If, for example, you are cited by the United Way as top fund-raiser of the year, spend a few moments extolling the great work that United Way does in helping the unfortunate and needy.

☐ *Do not exaggerate.* If you receive an award for perfect attendance at your club's meetings, do not say, "This is the greatest honor I've ever received or ever hope to receive," unless, of course, you mean it. Exaggeration makes you seem insincere.

☐ *Be brief.* I have seen some ceremonies marred because an award recipient viewed the acceptance speech as a chance to expound on his or her pet ideas. If you deliver a lengthy oration, the people who gave you the honor might regret that they did. Make a few sincere remarks—and then sit down.

A sample acceptance speech is the one given by Rita Goldberg, who was honored by a chapter of the Lions Club for her work with the handicapped:

> I want to thank you for choosing me to receive your Distinguished Service Award. In the past year I couldn't have accomplished half of what I did without the help of Henry and Judith Fletcher. I am grateful to them for their valuable assistance. And I am grateful to you Lions for setting up programs for the visually handicapped. Because of your compassion and your work, you have made it easy for volunteers like me to help the handicapped. Again, thank you for this honor.

Speech of Tribute

A speech of tribute praises or celebrates a person, a group, an institution, or an event. For example, the leader of a veterans' organization might pay tribute on Memorial Day to comrades who had died on the field of battle. At a retirement banquet, you might give a brief talk lauding the work of a colleague who is stepping down after 25 years with your organization.

A speech of tribute should be completely positive. It is not appropriate to point out faults or dredge up old disputes. Concentrate all remarks on the praiseworthy and noble.

In the U.S. House of Representatives, Congressman Jim Courter of New Jersey delivered the following speech of tribute. (In keeping with the tradition of the House, he addressed his remarks to the Speaker of the House, though he was actually speaking to the entire House.)

A Tribute to Tammy Hitchcock

Mr. Speaker, I rise today to honor my constituent, Ms. Tammy Hitchcock of Pittstown, New Jersey.

Tammy Hitchcock is a skydiver, which certainly takes a great deal of courage and determination. But what makes her accomplishments even more significant is that Tammy has multiple sclerosis, a disease that short-circuits the central nervous system and reduces stamina and coordination. Despite her disability, Tammy spends almost every weekend skydiving, using equipment modified to compensate for balance problems, visual distortion, and faulty depth perception.

Ever since Tammy learned she has multiple sclerosis, she has been resolved to continue leading an active and productive life. Her spirit has earned her a place in the National Multiple Sclerosis Society's new ''Profiles in Courage'' public service advertising campaign. This campaign is designed to educate the public about the personal achievements that can be accomplished by persons with disabilities. The society deserves commendation for its dedication to aiding the more than 250,000 Americans who suffer from multiple sclerosis. The society's funding enables hospitals and universities to continue important research in virology, genetics, and immunology in order to find a cure for this crippling disease.

All too often, people allow obstacles to stand in their way of achieving their goals. Through the National Multiple Sclerosis Society's "Profiles in Courage" campaign, Tammy is serving as an inspiration to us all.[1]

One kind of tribute speech that you are likely to make is a eulogy—a speech of praise for a friend or colleague who has died. A eulogy should be dignified, without exaggerated sentimentality. (Though humor is often out of place in a eulogy, it is sometimes appropriate: one student described the funeral of an uncle who had been a "colorful character," known for his story-telling abilities; during one eulogy, the speaker recited some of the humorous tales, and everyone smiled in warm remembrance of the yarn-spinning uncle.)

A eulogy should focus on the *significance* of the person's life and deeds, rather than on a mere recital of biographical facts. In other words, how did this man or woman enrich our lives? What inspiration or lessons can we draw from this person's life?

Speech of Inspiration

The goal of the inspirational speech is to stir positive emotions—to cause people to feel excited, uplifted, encouraged. You may need to give inspirational speeches at various times in your life. Let us say, for example, that you are manager of an office or department, and you give your staff an upbeat, "you-can-do-it" speech to get them fired up to do good work. Or let us say you coach a children's softball team and you give the boys and girls a "pep talk" before a game to make them feel confident that they can win.

The inspirational speech is similar to the persuasive speech, with the two purposes often overlapping. The main difference is that in the inspirational speech, you devote yourself almost solely to stirring emotions, while in the persuasive speech, you use emotional appeals as just one of many techniques.

Delivery is an important dimension of inspirational speaking. To get other people fired up, you must be "on fire" yourself. Your facial expression, your posture, your tone of voice—everything about you must convey zest and enthusiasm.

An inspirational speech should tap the emotional power of vivid language. An example of effective language can be found in a speech by Benjamin L. Hooks, executive director of the National Association for the Advancement of Colored People (NAACP), to the annual convention of the group. In the early part of his speech, Hooks lamented the limited educational and job opportunities for many blacks. Then, in a style reminiscent of the oratory of Dr. Martin Luther King, Hooks closed with an emotional plea for the delegates to "struggle on" in the fight to gain equality for blacks in America:

My brother and sisters . . . I want you to know that the struggle that we will face through the remaining period of the eighties and on through the twenty-first century will not be an easy one. It is fraught with pitfalls and plagued with setbacks, but we as a people have developed a resiliency which has made it possible for us to survive slavery and vicious discrimination. We must never tire or become frustrated by difficulties. We must transform stumbling blocks into stepping stones and march on with the determination that we will make America a better nation. . . .

Struggle on: We want more schoolhouses and less jail houses,
Struggle on: We want more books and less weapons,
Struggle on: We want more learning and less vice,
Struggle on: We want more employment and less crime in our communities,
Struggle on: We want more justice and less vengeance,
Struggle on: We want more of our children to graduate from high school able
　　　　　to read and write, not more on unemployment lines,
Struggle on: We want more statesmen and less politicians.
Struggle on: We want more workers in our ranks and less cynics,
Struggle on: We want more hope and less dope,
Struggle on: We want more faith and less despair. . . .[2]

Hooks made effective use of the techniques of *repetition* and *parallel structure* (which we discussed in Chapter 12), causing his speech to grow in power and intensity.

Summary

While informative and persuasive speeches are the most frequent types, there are speeches when other purposes must be served. When you need to entertain an audience, as in an after-dinner talk, your remarks should be light and diverting; any elements of information or persuasion should be gracefully interwoven into the fabric of entertainment. When you are asked to introduce a speaker, you should convey enthusiasm for the speaker and the topic, and you should give whatever background information is necessary to enhance the speaker's credibility. When you make a speech of presentation, you should focus your remarks on the award and the recipient. When you are called upon to "say a few words" in acceptance of an award or promotion, you should thank the people who gave you the honor and acknowledge the help of those who made your success possible. When you give a speech of tribute, you should praise the person, group, institution, or event being honored, avoiding any negativity. When you speak to inspire an audience, you should devote yourself to stirring emotions, using a dynamic delivery to convey your zest and enthusiasm.

Review Questions

1. Why would an informative speech on a difficult, highly technical subject usually be inappropriate for an after-dinner audience?

2. If you are asked to introduce a speaker, why should you coordinate your remarks with those of the speaker?
3. Name four guidelines for the speech of acceptance.
4. What is the difference between an inspirational speech and a persuasive speech?

Tips

FOR YOUR CAREER

Tip 16: Inject Humor—If It Is Appropriate

If you can use humor effectively, it is a good way to keep an audience interested in your speech. It creates a bond of friendship between you and the listeners, and it puts them into a receptive, trusting mood. You should use humor only when it is appropriate—a speech about a solemn subject such as euthanasia would not lend itself to an injection of humor.

One kind of humor is the joke, a funny story that depends upon a punch line for its success. I do not recommend that any novice speaker use jokes, for these reasons: (1) jokes usually do not tie in smoothly with the rest of the speech; (2) most speakers (both inexperienced and experienced) cannot tell jokes well; and (3) the audience may have already heard the joke.

I have seen speakers tell a joke that no one laughed at. And I mean *no one.* Maybe the audience had heard the joke before, or maybe it was too early in the morning or too late in the evening. Whatever the reason, a joke that fizzles can be devastating to the speaker's morale. "But it looks so easy on TV," some students say. It looks easy and *is* easy because TV joketellers have advantages that most speakers lack: They have studio audiences that are predisposed to laugh at virtually any joke the comedians tell (your audiences will probably not be poised for laughter in this way). They have a supporting cast of gag writers

who test the jokes out before they are used. Most important of all, they have years of joke-telling experience before they appear on national television.

You can use other kinds of humor beside jokes. A mildly amusing story, quotation, or observation can be as effective as a side-splitting joke. The best thing about low-key humor is that it's safe. While the success of a joke depends upon the audience laughing immediately after the punch line, the success of a light story or witty observation does not depend on laughter or even smiles. Sometimes the only audience response is an inner delight. In a speech urging his listeners to exercise regularly, student speaker Jerry Cohen began with a humorous quotation:

> The late Robert Maynard Hutchins, president of the University of Chicago, once said, "Whenever I feel like exercising, I lie down until the feeling passes." Is this your attitude toward exercise? Do you think of exercise as an odious chore to be avoided if possible?

Notice that Jerry's quotation was the kind of wry humor that does not depend on belly laughs; also notice that he tied the humor in with the purpose of his speech. This is an example of how you can sneak humor in, so that the audience sees it as part of your speech, not as a "joke." If they laugh or smile, fine; if they don't, no harm has been done. It's still enjoyable and relevant. If you use humor, here are some points to remember.

1. Humor must always relate to the subject matter.   In other words, never tell an amusing story about a farmer unless your speech is about farming and the story ties in with the rest of the speech.

2. Never use humor that might be offensive to any person in the audience.   You should avoid humor that is obscene or that ridicules members of any group in society (racial, ethnic, religious, political, gender, etc.). Even if the audience contains no members of the group being ridiculed, you risk alienating listeners who disapprove of such humor.

3. Never let your face show that you expect laughter or smiles.   Let us say that you cleverly insert a delicious piece of ironic humor into your introduction. After you make your humorous remark, do not stand there with an expectant grin on your face. If no one smiles back or laughs, you

will feel very foolish. By the way, if you do fail to get any smiles or laughs, this does not mean that the listeners did not appreciate your humor. As I mentioned previously, some kinds of humor elicit only an inner delight.

4. If you use jokes, use self-deprecating ones.   Although jokes are inappropriate in classroom speeches and are risky in community addresses (as discussed previously), you may decide someday that you want to tell a joke to your audience. You can minimize the risks if you make *yourself* the target of your humor. Professional speaker Hope Mihalap says, "I always try to start with a line that will get a laugh, usually something about myself (slightly derogatory, of course)."[3] And former Olympic Gold Medalist John Naber says: "I always begin with a cute joke *at my expense*."[4] Poking fun at yourself is fairly safe because you escape the possibility of telling a joke the audience has already heard and you avoid offending anyone (as long as you don't resort to vulgarity or obscenity).

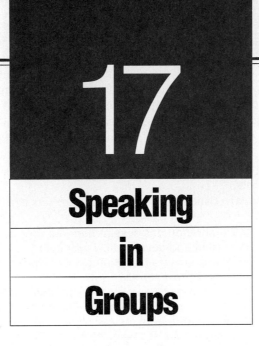

17

Speaking in Groups

Responsibilities of Leaders

Responsibilities of Participants

The Reflective-Thinking Method

Team Presentations

Small groups do much of the work of our society, at all levels of government, education, business, and industry. For example, NASA (National Aeronautics and Space Administration) uses small task forces to develop space programs. Colleges and universities use committees to set policy and develop new curricula. Businesses use small sales teams to sell their products.

The value of small groups is even recognized by giant corporations. After studying forty-three successful American companies for their best-seller *In Search of Excellence,* management consultants Thomas J. Peters and Robert H. Waterman wrote, "Small groups are, quite simply, the basic organizational building blocks of excellent companies." The most effective groups, they say, range from four to ten members.[1]

Here are some of the examples that Peters and Waterman cite:

- ☐ 3M Corporation has several hundred four- to ten-person "venture teams" that design and develop new products.[2]
- ☐ Texas Instruments has 9000 teams "zipping about looking for small productivity improvements."[3]
- ☐ To solve problems quickly and effectively, many corporations such as General Motors and IBM bypass the chain of command—the formal organizational structure—and instead, form task forces made up of "champions"— a few key employees who are known for their creativity and dedication.[4]

For creativity and problem solving, small groups have obvious advantages over individuals: they provide a pooling of resources, ideas, and labor. Errors can be caught and corrected. Small groups also have advantages over large conglomerations of people: they act with greater quickness and flexibility. In this chapter, we will focus on meetings, the means by which small groups do their collective work. If carried out properly, meetings give group members a chance to discuss ideas, solve problems, reach decisions, resolve differences, and reduce tensions. Meetings provide close eye-to-eye contact with lively interaction between participants.

To perform well in meetings, groups should (1) have a purpose, (2) secure the cooperation of all members, and (3) have effective leadership. Everyone in the meeting should possess a spirit of goodwill or, to use the term of etiquette expert Letitia Baldrige, *good manners.* "I have observed," says Baldrige, "that every well-run meeting invariably has a combination of a chairman with good manners and participants with good manners—it is like an excellent symphony conductor who needs an excellent corps of musicians in order to make truly beautiful music."[5]

Let us take a closer look at the roles of the leader and the participants.

Responsibilities of Leaders

Meg Slubiski, head of the sales force at a car dealership, called a meeting of salespersons to try to work out a problem that was causing hard feelings among the staff: whenever a potential customer walked into the automobile showroom, the salespersons would elbow each other aside in an effort to be the one to greet the person (and possibly make a sale). Patiently, Meg listened to the complaints and accusations, and then shepherded the group toward a compromise that everyone seemed happy with: the staff would use a rotating system for greeting potential customers so that each salesperson got the same number of contacts as everyone else.

Meg demonstrated the importance of firm, but friendly leadership in small groups. When you are the leader of a small group, here are some guidelines for planning and conducting a meeting.

1. *Establish an agenda.* An agenda is a list of items that need to be covered in a meeting. When there is no agenda, groups often fail to work efficiently and productively. They waste time pursuing irrelevant matters, or they spend all their time and energy on minor items and never get around to the major issues. When you are a leader of a group, decide in advance what issues should be discussed (be sure to consult the participants on what topics they want to discuss), then write out an agenda, ranking items from most important to least important. Be sure the group members receive the agenda well before the meeting so that they can prepare themselves. At the beginning of the meeting, ask the participants if they want to add items to the agenda or make alterations in the order of priorities. If circumstances prevent you from preparing an agenda in advance, take a few moments at the beginning of the meeting to establish the agenda, asking group members for their suggestions and then rank-ordering the items on a chalkboard for everyone to see. Though setting the agenda may take a few minutes, it is time well spent, for it will help the group stick to the relevant and important issues. If your group is working against a deadline, you may need to establish a timetable for the agenda—for example, allotting 10 minutes for discussion of item A, 15 minutes for item B, and so on. (A special kind of agenda, using the reflective-thinking method, will be discussed in detail later in this chapter.)

2. *Start the meeting on time.* If some group members fail to arrive at the designated time, you may be tempted to delay the start of the meeting in hopes that they will soon appear. This is a mistake for two reasons: (1) You are being discourteous to the group members who were punctual; their time is valuable and should not be wasted. (2) You are setting a bad precedent for future meetings. If the people who arrived on time see you wait for latecomers, they will perceive you as a leader who starts meetings late, so they will probably also arrive late for the next meeting. If the same thing happens again, some group members will arrive later and later for meetings.

3. *Set a friendly tone.* Start off with a friendly, upbeat welcome. If some of the participants do not know each other, introduce all the members of the group, one at a time, or let them introduce themselves.

4. *Make sure that minutes are kept.* If the group is not a formal committee with a previously designated secretary, the leader should appoint someone to take notes and later prepare minutes of the meeting. Minutes are a record of what was discussed and accomplished during a meeting. They should be circulated to group members as soon after the meeting as possible. While minutes are obviously valuable for absentees who need to get caught up on events, they are also important for people who were present—to remind them of their responsibilities for the next meeting. Minutes should consist of five elements: (1) agenda item, (2) decision reached, (3) action required, (4) person(s) responsible for taking action, and (5) target date for completion of action.[6] At each meeting, the minutes of the previous session should be briefly reviewed to make sure that tasks have been completed.

5. ***Make sure all participants know the purpose of the meeting and the scope of the group's power.*** Even if you have circulated an agenda in advance, you should still review the purpose of the meeting. Some of the participants may have failed to read the agenda carefully or correctly, while others may have forgotten what it contained. Refresh their memories; make sure everyone knows the task that the group faces. Also review the scope of the group's power, so that participants do not labor under false ideas of what the group can or cannot do. Group members need to know the following: Does the group have the power to make a decision, or is it being asked simply to recommend a decision? Will the group reach a decision and then carry it out, or will someone else actually carry out the decision? Is the group's decision subject to revision by a higher authority?

6. ***Encourage participation.*** In some groups, especially ones led by a boss, group members say nothing while the leader does all the talking. Such groups are little more than rubber stamps for whatever the leader wants—the meetings are really a waste of time. When you are a leader, do not be dictatorial or directive. Guide the discussion, but do not dominate it. Encourage the free flow of ideas from all members of the group. This is more than a matter of politeness: group-created decisions are usually better than leader-dictated decisions because people tend to support what they have helped create. If, for example, you are the manager of five employees and you call them together and dictate a policy, there may be grumbling behind your back and passive resistance in implementing the policy, but if you call your people together and spend a few hours letting *them* hammer out the same policy, they will feel a strong commitment to it—now it is *their* idea, *their* policy.

7. ***Guide the discussion.*** As leader, you should move the discussion along from point to point on the agenda. If participants go off on tangents, you should diplomatically pull them back to the task at hand. (You can say something like "That's an interesting point, but let's stick to our agenda; if we have any time left over, we can come back to your idea.") If a participant talks too much, not giving others a chance to speak, you should gently but firmly intervene. (You can say, for example, "Good point; if I may interrupt, I would like to hear how the others are reacting to what you just said.") If a participant is shy or unusually quiet, you can try to elicit comments. Do not ask a "yes or no" question, such as "Do you have anything you would like to say?" Instead, ask open-ended questions, such as "How do you think we can solve this problem?" If the person says "I don't know," do not press any further. Thus you avoid badgering or embarrassing the person. It may be that he or she truly has no particular contribution to make on the issue. If participants become hostile toward one another, try to mediate by finding common ground and by helping them stick to issues rather than resorting to personal attacks.

8. *Discourage side conversations.* Meetings can be marred if two or more people break off from the group's activities and hold a private discussion. This, of course, is rude to the other group members, and it prevents the group from staying together as a unified team. As leader, you should gently shepherd the wayward group back into the fold; for example, if two members are carrying on a private conversation, you can say, "It looks as if you've come up with something interesting. Could you share it with the group?" This technique usually has one of two results: the offenders share their comments with the group, or (if they have been chatting about unrelated matters) they grin sheepishly, decline to reveal the content of their discussion, and return to participation with the group.

9. *Summarize periodically.* Since you are playing the role of guide, you should occasionally let the participants know where they are on their journey toward the group's goal. Summarize what has been accomplished, and indicate work that still needs to be done. For example: "Let's see where we stand. We have decided that item A and item B should be recommended to the board of directors. But we still need to tackle problem C. . . ." Keep your summaries brief—just say enough to help the participants gain their bearings.

10. *Keep meetings short.* Most small-group meetings should last no longer than 1 hour. Anything longer will cause fatigue and a dropoff in the group's effectiveness. If 1 hour is not enough time to handle the group's work, a series of 1-hour meetings should be set up. If, for some reason, the group is obliged to conduct all its business in one day or during an afternoon, 1-hour sessions should be interspersed with coffee or "stretch" breaks.

11. *End the meeting.* At the end of a meeting, summarize what the group has accomplished, make sure that all participants know their assignments for the next meeting, and express appreciation for the work that the group has done.

12. *Follow up.* After the meeting, make sure that the minutes are written and distributed to each participant and that all participants carry out their assignments.

Responsibilities of Participants

In one community, a committee was formed to plan and finance the construction of a new swimming pool for a YMCA. The committee included a cross section of community talent—for example, a financier who was experienced at fund-raising, an engineer who was knowledgeable about pool construction, and a swimming instructor who knew what kind of pool the public wanted. When the committee met, it was effective in overseeing the design and construction of an excellent pool because the participants were able to share their ideas and expertise.

This story illustrates that while leadership of a small group is important, the participants themselves play a vital role. When you are a participant in a small group, here are some guidelines to keep in mind.

1. *Prepare for every meeting.* Find out in advance what is going to be discussed at the meeting, and then decide what contributions you can make. Jot down items that you think need to be discussed. Do whatever research, background reading, and interviewing that might be necessary to make you well-informed or to bolster your position on an issue. If documentation is likely to be requested for some of your data, bring notes to the meeting so that you can cite your sources.

2. *Arrive on time.* Meetings cannot work effectively if some participants straggle in late. Make sure that you arrive at the appointed time. Even better, arrive a bit early; this will give you a chance to chat informally with your fellow participants and create a mood of friendliness.

3. *Participate in group discussions.* Do not sit back and let others carry on the work of the group. Throw yourself wholeheartedly into the discussion,

Because the resources of all the members of the group are important, each member should participate fully. *(McGraw-Hill photo by Stacey Pleasant)*

contributing your ideas and opinions. This does not necessarily mean giving a brief speech or saying something brilliant. You can enter the discussion by asking questions, especially when points need to be clarified, by expressing support for ideas that you like, and by paraphrasing other members' ideas to determine if you are understanding them correctly.

4. *If possible, speak up early in the meeting.* If you have the opportunity to make a contribution to the group, do so at the earliest possible time. This serves as an "icebreaker," causing you to draw closer (psychologically) to the other members of the group and making you more attentive to the discussion. The longer you wait to speak, the harder it becomes to enter the discussion. This does not mean that you should blurt out the first thing that pops into your head; you should never speak impulsively or aimlessly. But when a chance to make a genuine contribution arises, take advantage of it.

5. *Exhibit positive nonverbal behavior.* Nonverbal cues, such as clothes, facial expression, posture, and eye contact, speak as powerfully as words. In a meeting, you should avoid slumping in your chair because that conveys boredom, negativity, or lack of confidence. Instead, sit in an alert but relaxed posture that shows you are both comfortable and confident. Whether you are playing the role of speaker or listener, look people in the eye. Your facial expression should convey openness and friendliness.

6. *Do not treat your own ideas as beyond criticism.* Some group members act as if criticism of their ideas is an attack upon themselves, so they fight ferociously to defend their position. What they are really defending is not their ideas, but their ego. Unfortunately when people are busy defending their ego, they refuse to listen to what their critics are saying, they refuse to budge an inch from their position, and they sometimes prevent a group from making progress. When you present your ideas to a group, you should recognize that no human is perfect and that a wise and mature person readily admits the possibility of being in error.

7. *Do not monopolize the meeting.* Give others a fair chance to state their views.

8. *Stick to the point.* A common problem in meetings is for participants to stray off the subject and get bogged down in irrelevant matters. Before speaking, ask yourself if what you plan to say is truly related to the purpose of the meeting.

9. *Treat all group members fairly.* All too often, some group members form coalitions with people who already agree with them and then freeze out the rest of the group (by not listening carefully to what they say, by not giving them sufficient eye contact, by not soliciting and respecting their ideas). Aside from being rude, this cold-shoulder treatment cripples the effectiveness of the group;

members who feel frozen-out tend to contribute little. You should treat each person in the group with dignity and respect, offering a friendly ear and an open mind to her or his ideas.

10. *Express dissenting views.* Some group members never raise objections or express views contrary to the majority. There are a number of reasons for this timidity: fear of being ridiculed, fear of antagonizing others, or fear of displeasing the leader (especially if he or she is the person's boss). When you disagree with an idea being discussed by the group, it is a mistake to remain silent. Group decisions that are made in a mood of pseudo-unanimity are often poor decisions.

11. *Avoid personal attacks.* Conflict—a clash of ideas or opinions—is healthy in group discussion. It helps the group see weaknesses in plans, to separate the workable from the unworkable. While conflict is desirable, it should always be centered on *issues,* not on personalities. In other words, disagree without being disagreeable.

12. *Whenever possible, express objections in the form of a question.* Even though you should certainly speak up when you think an idea is poor, there is a diplomatic way to offer criticism. If you blurt out, "Oh, no, that will never work," you might deflate the person who suggested the idea, and even provoke hostility. A better approach is to ask a question, such as "How could we make this work?" As the group members try to answer the question, there is a spirit of cooperation, and often they come to the conclusion you hoped they would reach—that the idea *is* unworkable—without hostility or bad feelings.

13. *Do not work from a hidden agenda.* A group's work can be sabotaged if some members pretend to be committed to the goals of the group, but in reality have hidden agendas—that is, unannounced private goals that conflict with the group's goals. Examples of hidden agendas are a desire to gain personal power over other participants, a striving to impress a superior, and a secret wish to see the group fail.

14. *Do not carry on private conversations.* Group unity can be undermined if two or three participants engage in a whispered conversation, which is rude and insulting to the speaker; it is also damaging to the work of the group since it cuts off teamwork and a spirit of cooperation.

The Reflective-Thinking Method

When a group must solve a problem, one of the most effective techniques is the *reflective-thinking* method derived from the writings of the American philosopher John Dewey.[7] To illustrate the steps of this method, imagine that you and I and several other people are joint owners of a restaurant, and suppose that we have a problem that must be solved: many customers have been complaining about slow service.

Define the Problem

Since a group will sputter and falter unless everyone has a clear idea of exactly what is wrong, the first step is to define the problem. Sometimes the problem is obvious (for example, what prices to set for each item on the menu at our restaurant). But sometimes a problem is vague; for example, "We need to improve our restaurant." This statement is so vague that it would probably mean different things to each of the owners. To one, it might mean that we need to improve the food; to another, it might mean that we need to improve the skills of our waiters and waitresses. One of the best ways to define a problem is to phrase it in the form of a question. In the case of our restaurant's problem, we could ask, "What steps can be taken to improve the service in our restaurant?"

Analyze the Problem

A problem-solving group should scrutinize the problem in order to learn as much as it can. Some of the questions that should be asked are: What is the nature of the problem? How severe is the problem? What are the causes?

In our restaurant, we need to focus on causes so that we can correct the situation. Is slow service caused by the waiters and waitresses? If so, is it because they are lazy or inefficient, or is it because they are forced to serve too many tables? Or can the slow service be blamed solely on the kitchen staff? Are *they* the lazy or inefficient ones? Are *they* understaffed? At this point, if we cannot get a clear picture of the cause of the problem, we need to stop the problem-solving process and get answers to these questions before continuing. Let us assume that we ascertain the cause of the problem: the kitchen staff is slow in getting items into the hands of our waiters and waitresses.

Establish Criteria for Evaluating Solutions

Suppose that you are asked by a friend to pick up "a good movie" for her while you are visiting a videotape store. What should you do? Grab the first videocassette you see? No, before going to the shop, you would need to find out your friend's tastes—her criteria for what constitutes a good movie. For example, does she enjoy comedy? If so, does she lean toward subtle British humor or slapstick Hollywood farces? Armed with the answers to such questions, you can choose a movie likely to appeal to her.

The same strategy works well for problem-solving groups. Instead of rushing to find a solution, a group should first decide the criteria—the standards or conditions—by which to judge a solution. To establish criteria, a group should ask: What must a proposed solution do? What must it avoid? What restrictions of time, money, and space must be considered? If there are more than one criteria, they should be rank-ordered in terms of importance.

In our restaurant example, the most obvious solution might be to hire more cooks, but what if we simply cannot afford to hire any new people? If at this stage we establish criteria, we can avoid pursuing solutions that are ultimately impossible. For our restaurant's problem, let us set the following standards, rank-ordered from most important to least important: (1) Orders need to be taken to tables 10 minutes quicker than at present; (2) we must take action immediately; (3) we must not lower the quality of food; and (4) whatever solution we come up with must cost no more than $1000.

Suggest Possible Solutions

The next step is for group members to suggest possible solutions. It is important for groups to show patience and avoid leaping at the first solution that comes along. Spreading out on the table a wide variety of possible solutions can enhance the chances of the group arriving at a sound decision. One of the best techniques for generating these potential solutions is *brainstorming,* wherein participants rapidly throw out ideas and the group leader writes them on a chalkboard. For brainstorming to work effectively, there should be an atmosphere of total acceptance—no one analyzes, judges, ridicules, or rejects any of the ideas. Let us say that for our restaurant, we generate a dozen potential solutions, ranging from "use frozen (instead of fresh) foods" to "hire an efficiency consultant to teach the kitchen staff to work faster."

Choose the Best Solution

After the brainstorming session, a group should analyze, weigh, and discuss the various ideas in order to come up with the best solution (or solutions). Each possibility should be measured against the criteria previously established. In our restaurant example, let us say that the idea of using frozen foods is examined. Since the chef tells us that frozen food is not as tasty as fresh, we would now reject the idea because it would violate our criterion about not compromising the quality of our food. The idea about hiring an efficiency expert would be rejected because one of our criteria stipulates immediate action. Let's say that another idea is to buy two more microwave ovens to speed up the kitchen's work. The two ovens would cost a total of $750; this would permit us to meet the under-$1000 requirement, and the chef assures us that two ovens would help get the food out to the customers quickly without lowering the quality. So we choose this option.

Decide How to Implement the Solution

A solution may sound fine at the talking stage, but can it be realistically implemented? Our next step is to decide how to put the solution into action. In our restaurant's case, we authorize our bookkeeper to write the necessary check and we verify that a certain restaurant-supply store can send us the ovens within 24 hours.

Decide How to Test the Solution

Many groups hammer out a solution to a problem, but never follow it up to determine whether their solution really solved the problem. The last task of the problem-solving group is to decide how to find out if the solution, when put into effect, really works. In our restaurant's case, we can create customer response cards to be placed at each table. The customers are asked to rate, among other things, whether the service was fast enough to suit them. We decide that if 99 percent of our customers express satisfaction with the service, then our solution has indeed worked. (We aim for 99 percent rather than 100 percent because we know from our studies of restaurant management that there is always an irritable 1 percent of customers who are never happy with the service—no matter how fast it may be.)

Team Presentations

While most group work is done in private, there are some occasions when you may act as part of a team in making a presentation to an audience. Two of the most popular forms of team presentations are the symposium and the panel discussion.

Symposium

A symposium is a series of brief speeches on a common topic, each usually discussing a different aspect of the topic. In some cases, the speakers might be members of a problem-solving group who present their ideas and conclusions to a larger group. A symposium usually features a question-and-answer period after the speeches, and sometimes includes a panel discussion.

When you prepare and deliver a speech as part of a symposium, you should use the same skills and techniques as those of solo speechmaking, but you should work in advance with other members of your team to avoid duplication of material.

Panel Discussion

A panel is usually made up of three to eight members and is led by a moderator. Though there are many different methods of conducting panel discussions, a common pattern is to have the panelists give a brief opening statement, then permit them to discuss the subject among themselves, with the moderator serving as referee. At the end of the discussion, the audience is usually invited to ask questions.

Because of the variety of viewpoints and the liveliness of informed conversation, audiences enjoy a good panel discussion.

Guidelines for the Moderator

Much of the success (or failure) of a panel discussion is determined by the moderator. He or she must keep the discussion moving along smoothly, restrain the long-winded or domineering panelist from hogging the show, draw out the reticent panelist, and field questions from the audience. Here are some guidelines to follow when you are a moderator.

☐ *Arrange the setting.* You and the panelists can be seated at a table facing the audience. Or, even better, you can be seated in a semicircle so that all members of the panel can see one another while still remaining visible to the audience. A large name card should be placed in front of each panelist so that the audience will know the participants' names.

☐ *Brief panel members in advance.* Well before the meeting, give panel members clear instructions on exactly what they are expected to cover in their opening remarks. Are they supposed to argue the "pro" or "con" position? Are they supposed to speak on only one aspect of the topic? (For information-giving discussions, you may want to assign each panel member a subtopic, according to his or her area of expertise, so that there is not much overlap among speakers.) Instruct the panelists not to bring and read written statements because this would kill the spontaneity that is desired in a panel discussion, but tell them that they are free to bring notes.

☐ *Before the meeting, prepare a list of items that you think should be discussed.* By so doing, you can make sure that no important issues are inadvertently omitted. If the discussion begins to lag or go off into irrelevancies, you will have, at your fingertips, material from which to derive questions.

☐ *Prepare and deliver an introduction.* At the beginning of the program, introduce the topic and the speakers, and explain the ground rules for the discussion; be sure to let listeners know if and when they will be permitted to ask questions.

☐ *Moderate the discussion.* Give each panelist a chance to make opening statements (within the time constraints previously announced) and then encourage the panelists to question one another or comment upon one another's remarks. Be neutral in the discussion but be prepared to ask questions if there is an awkward lull or if a panelist says something confusing or leaves out important information. Listen carefully to what each panelist says so that you do not embarrass yourself by asking questions on subjects that have already been discussed.

☐ *Maintain friendly, but firm control.* Do not let a panelist lead everyone off on a tangent that is far afield of the speech topic. During the question-and-answer session, do not let a member of the audience make a long-winded speech: interrupt kindly but firmly and say, "We need to give other people a chance to ask questions." If a panelist exceeds the time limit for opening remarks or monopolizes the discussion time, gently break in and say, "I'm sorry to interrupt, but let's hear from other members of the panel on their ideas concerning. . . ." If a panelist is reticent and says very little, draw him or her out with specific, pertinent questions.

☐ *Be respectful of all panelists, including those with whom you disagree.* Think of yourself not as a district attorney who must interrogate and skewer criminal defendants, but as a gracious host or hostess who stimulates guests to engage in lively conversation.

☐ *Ask open-ended questions, ones that require elaboration, rather than questions that elicit a simple "yes" or "no."* For example, "How can we make sure our homes are safe from burglars?" rather than "Is burglary on the increase in our community?"

☐ *End the program at the agreed-upon time.* Wrap up the proceedings on time and in a prearranged way, perhaps by letting each panelist summarize briefly his or her position. Another option is for you to summarize the key points made during the discussion (to do this, you would need to take notes throughout the program). Thank the panelists and the audience for their participation. If some members of the audience are still interested in continuing the discussion, you may want to invite them to talk to the panelists individually after the program is over.

Guidelines for Panelists

If you are a member of a panel, here are some guidelines to keep in mind.

☐ *Prepare for the discussion in the same way you prepare for a speech.* Find out all that you can about the audience and the occasion: What particular aspect of the topic are you expected to speak on? Who are the other panelists and what will they cover? Will there be questions from the audience? What are the time constraints?

☐ *Prepare notes for the panel, but not a written statement.* If you write out your remarks, you may be tempted to read them and thereby spoil the spontaneity that is desired in a panel discussion. In addition to notes, you may want to bring supporting data (such as bibliographical sources or statistics) to draw from in case you are asked for substantiation of a point.

☐ *Respect the time limits set by the moderator.* If, for example, you are asked to keep your opening remarks under 2 minutes, be careful to do so.

☐ *In the give-and-take of the discussion, be brief.* If the other panelists or listeners want to hear more from you, they will ask.

☐ *Stay on the subject.* Resist the temptation to ramble off into extraneous matters.

☐ *Be respectful and considerate of your fellow panelists.* Do not squelch them with sarcasm, with ridicule, or with an overbearing attitude. Do not upstage them by trying to be the one to answer all the questions from the audience.

☐ *Listen carefully to the comments of other panelists and members of the audience.* If any of them disagrees with you, try to understand and appreciate their position instead of hastily launching a counterattack. Then be prepared to follow the next guideline.

☐ *Be willing to alter your position.* If you listen with an open mind, you may see merit in others' views, and you may decide that you need to modify your original position. Though such a shift may seem like an embarrassing loss of face, it actually causes the audience to have greater respect for you. It shows you are a person who possesses intellectual courage, flexibility, and integrity.

Summary

Small groups are important elements in business and professional life, and much of the work of small groups is done in meetings. To lead a meeting, you should establish an agenda and make sure that it is followed; you should encourage all members to participate in group discussions, and you should guide the discussion to make sure that it stays on the subject. When you are a participant in a small-group meeting, you should enter the discussion with a positive attitude and an open mind.

One of the most effective agendas for problem solving is known as the reflective-thinking method. It involves seven steps: defining the problem; analyzing it; establishing criteria for evaluating solutions; suggesting possible solutions; choosing the best solution; deciding how to implement the solution; and deciding how to test the solution.

Sometimes groups appear in public to discuss or debate an issue. Two popular formats for team presentations are the symposium (a series of brief speeches on a common topic) and the panel discussion (an informal presentation involving a moderator and panelists).

Review Questions

1. Why is an agenda necessary for a meeting?
2. Why should a participant speak up, if possible, early in a meeting?
3. If you disagree with what everyone else in the group is saying, what should you do?
4. What is the best way to express objections to an idea?
5. What are the seven steps of the reflective-thinking method?
6. What are the duties of the moderator in a panel discussion?

Tips
FOR YOUR CAREER

Tip 17: Strive to Improve Your Communication Skills throughout Your Career

As you give speeches during your career, I hope that you will try to become better and better as a communicator. Here are three suggestions:

1. Seek opportunities for speaking. The best way to improve your skills is to actually give speeches, so look for opportunities in your career and in your community. An excellent place to practice is in a Toastmasters club, where your speaking skills will be critiqued in a friendly, supportive atmosphere. For the name and phone number of the club nearest you, write Toast-

masters International, P.O. Box 10400, Santa Ana, California 92711.

2. Seek feedback. Some speakers never discover that they have serious flaws in their speechmaking because they fail to seek feedback. I once knew a professor who was brilliant in his field, but he had a strange habit in lecturing. Most of the time he spoke forcefully and clearly, but occasionally—whenever he digressed from his subject—he would look down at his notes, and his voice would disintegrate into a mumble which even students on the first row could not comprehend. It was obvious that his subject matter during the mumble was the oral equivalent of an aside or a footnote in a scholarly paper. If he had looked at his audience at such moments, he would have seen students grin and shake their heads in disbelief.

To find out how your listeners react to you and your message, you should seek feedback, if not for every speech, at least occasionally. Here are three possible methods: (1) Ask several friends or colleagues to critique a speech (be sure to give instructions as suggested on page 272). (2) Pass out evaluation forms to all your listeners, asking them to make comments anonymously and then drop the forms in a box near the exit. (3) Invite a small but representative group of listeners to join you after a meeting to sit down and share their responses to your speech; this is especially useful in finding out whether the listeners understood and accepted your message. Try to listen and learn without being argumentative or defensive.

Also, arrange to have some of your speeches videotaped, and then analyze the tape to spot areas in which you need to improve.

3. Be a lifetime student of public speaking. You can improve your own speaking skills by studying the speechmaking of others. Whenever you listen to a speech, make notes on what works and what doesn't work. Which delivery techniques were effective? Which were ineffective? What speech material seemed to please the listeners? What seemed to bore them? Keep your notes in a file for future reference, so that you can profit from both the successes and failures of others.

Notes and Acknowledgments

Chapter 1

1. "A Spunky Tycoon Turned Superstar," *Time,* April 1, 1985, p. 33.
2. Ibid.
3. Barbara A. Magill, Roger P. Murphy, and Lillian O. Feinberg, "Industrial Administration Survey Shows Need for Communication Study," *American Business Communication Association Bulletin* (1975), 31–33.
4. Teresa L. Thompson, "The Invisible Helping Hand: The Role of Communication in the Health and Social Service Professions," *Communication Quarterly* 32 (Spring 1984), 148–163; Thomas E. Harris and T. Dean Thomlison, "Career-Bound Communication Education: A Needs Analysis," *Central States Speech Journal* 34 (Winter 1983), 260–267.
5. Garda W. Bowman, "What Helps or Harms Promotability?" *Harvard Business Review* (January–February, 1964), 14; Edward Foster et al., *A Market Study for the College of Business Administration, Univversity of Minnesota, Twin Cities* (Minneapolis: College of Business Administration, University of Minnesota, 1978); *Instruction in Communication at Colorado State University* (Fort Collins, CO: College of Engineering, Colorado State University, 1979).
6. William R. Kimel and Melford E. Monsees, "Engineering Graduates: How Good Are They?" *Engineering Education* (November 1979), 210–212.
7. Ibid., p. 211.
8. Foster, op. cit.
9. Frank S. Endicott, *The Endicott Report: Trends in the Employment of College and University Graduates in Business and Industry 1980* (Evanston, IL: Placement Center, Northwestern University, 1980).
10. Stewart L. Tubbs and K. J. Gritzmacher, "Supervisory Communication as a Contributor to Organizational Success." Paper presented at the annual convention of the Speech Communication Association (Minneapolis, MN, November, 1978), p. 6.
11. Jack Valenti, *Speak Up with Confidence* (New York: Morrow, 1982), p. 99.
12. John F. Kikoski, "Communication: Understanding It, Improving It," *Personnel Journal* 59 (February 1980), 126–131.
13. David W. Richardson, professional speaker (see Acknowledgments), in reply to author's survey, November 1984.
14. Nido R. Qubein, *Communicate Like a Pro* (Englewood Cliffs, NJ: Prentice-Hall, 1983), p. 67.
15. James ("Doc") Blakely, professional speaker (see Acknowledgments), in audiotape, "Anatomy of a Bomb, Analysis of Success," copyrighted 1983 by Blakely.
16. Michael McGuire, "The Ethics of Rhetoric: The Morality of Knowledge," *Southern Speech Communication Journal* 45 (Winter 1980), 133–149.
17. Philip D. Steffen, professional speaker (see Acknowledgments), in response to author's survey, November 1984.
18. Ibid.
19. Dorothy Sarnoff, *Never Be Nervous Again* (New York: Crown, 1987), p. 61.
20. Roy Fenstermaker, professional speaker (see Acknowledgments), in response to author's survey, November, 1984.
21. Arnold ("Nick") Carter, professional speaker (see Acknowledgments), in response to author's survey, November 1984.

22. Hope Mihalap, professional speaker (see Acknowledgments), in response to author's survey, November 1984

23. Rosita Perez, professional speaker (see Acknowledgments), in response to author's survey, November 1984.

Chapter 2

1. Paul B. Thornton and Paul J. LeVarge, "Avoid Communication Breakdowns," *Toastmaster* magazine, March 1985, p. 18.

2. D. A. Roach, "State of the Art in Listening Comprehension: A Compendium of Measures." Paper presented at the International Listening Association Convention, Denver, 1981.

3. Lyman K. Steil, "Your Personal Listening Profile," booklet published by Sperry Corporation, undated, p. 5.

4. Lyman K. Steil, interview in *U.S. News & World Report,* May 26, 1980, p. 65.

5. M. Scott Peck, M.D., *The Road Less Traveled* (New York: Simon & Schuster, 1978), p. 128.

6. Roger Ailes, *You Are the Message* (Homewood, IL: Dow Jones-Irwin, 1988), pp. 47–48.

7. Gary T. Hunt, *Communication Skills in the Organization* (Englewood Cliffs, NJ: Prentice-Hall, 1980), p. 63.

8. Robert Bostrom and Carol Bryant, "Factors in the Retention of Information Presented Orally: The Role of Short-Term Listening," *Western Journal of Speech Communication* 44 (Spring 1980), 137–145.

9. Margaret Lane, "Are You Really Listening?" *Reader's Digest,* November 1980, p. 183.

10. M. Scott Peck, M.D., op. cit., p. 122.

11. Ralph G. Nichols, "Listening Is a 10-Part Skill," in James I. Brown, ed., *Efficient Reading* (Boston: D.C. Heath, 1962), p. 101.

12. Ibid., pp. 101–102.

13. Enid S. Waldhart and Robert N. Bostrom, "Notetaking, Listening, and Modes of Retention." Paper presented to the International Listening Association, Washington, D.C.: 1981; Francis J. Divesta and G. Susan Gray, "Listening and Note Taking II: Immediate and Delayed Recall as Functions of Variations in Thematic Continuity, Note Taking, and Length of Listening Review Intervals," *Journal of Educational Psychology* 64 (1973), 278–287.

14. Wayne Austin Shrope, *Speaking & Listening* (New York: Harcourt Brace Jovanovich, 1970), p. 232.

15. Lyman K. Steil, "Ten Ways to Effective Listening," undated pamphlet published by Sperry Corporation, p. 10.

16. Anonymous speaker quoted by Ronald B. Adler, *Communicating at Work,* 2d ed. (New York: Random House, 1986), p. 88.

Chapter 3

1. Stu Schrieberg, "Beyond the Sound and the Fury," *USA Today,* September 12, 1986, p. 2.

2. Cleveland Amory, "The Loves and Hates of George C. Scott," *Parade* magazine, October 27, 1985, p. 4.

3. George C. Scott, interview in *Playboy,* December 1980, p. 126.

4. "What Are Americans Afraid of?" *The Bruskin Report* 53 (July 1973); Susan R. Glaser, "Oral Communication Apprehension and Avoidance: The Current Status of Treatment Research," *Communication Education* (October 1981), 321–341; James C. McCroskey and Lawrence R. Wheeless, *Introduction to Human Communication* (Boston: Allyn & Bacon, 1976).

5. Reggie Jackson, interview during an ABC sports telecast, October 2, 1984.

6. Don Beveridge, professional speaker (see Acknowledgments), in response to author's survey, November 1984.

7. Elayne Snyder, *Speak for Yourself—With Confidence* (New York: New American Library, 1983), p. 113.

8. I. A. R. Wylie, quoted in Bert E. Bradley, *Fundamentals of Speech Communication: The Credibility of Ideas,* 4th ed. (Dubuque, IA: Brown, 1984), p. 385.

9. The term *stage fright* originated in the theater, but it is used today to designate the nervousness or fear experienced by a person before or during an appearance in front of any kind of audience. Other terms sometimes used to describe this condition are *speech fright, speech anxiety,* and *communication apprehension.*

10. Joel Weldon, professional speaker (see Acknowledgments), in response to author's survey, November 1984.

11. Joel Weldon, in audiotape, "Elephants Don't Bite: Joel Weldon Live," copyright 1984 by Joel H. Weldon & Associates, Scottsdale, Arizona.

12. Michael T. Motley, "Taking the Terror out of Talk," *Psychology Today,* January 1988, p. 49.

13. Ali MacGraw, quoted in James Link, "Dealing with Stage Fright," *Cosmopolitan,* October, 1982, p. 112.

14. James ("Doc") Blakely, professional speaker (see Acknowledgments), in response to author's survey, November 1984.

15. Steve Allen, *How to Make a Speech* (New York: McGraw-Hill, 1986), p. 9.

16. Ibid., p. 9.

17. Philip Zimbardo, *Psychology and Life,* 11th ed. (Glenview, IL: Scott, Foresman 1985), p. 448.

18. Joe W. Boyd, professional speaker (see Acknowledgments), in response to author's survey, November 1984.

19. Hugh Downs, quoted in Max D. Isaacson, *How to Conquer the Fear of Public Speaking* (Rockville Center, NY: Farnsworth Publishing, 1984), pp. 70–71.

20. Ralph R. Behnke, Chris R. Sawyer, and Paul E. King, "The Communication of Public Speaking Anxiety," *Communication Education* 36 (April 1987), 138–141; Theodore Clevenger, Jr., "A Synthesis of Experimental Research in Stage Fright," *Quarterly Journal of Speech* 45 (April 1959), 135–136.

21. Dick Cavett, as quoted in Steve Allen, op. cit., pp. 9–10.

22. Dr. Henry Heimlich, professional speaker (see Acknowledgments), in reply to author's survey, November 1984.

23. Danielle Kennedy, professional speaker (see Acknowledgments), in reply to author's survey, November 1984.

24. Maggie Paley, "Modern Image Signal: Voice," *Vogue,* August 1984, p. 412.

25. Associated Press news dispatch, July 31, 1981.

26. Motley, op. cit., p. 49.

Chapter 4

1. Thomas Leech, *How to Prepare, Stage, and Deliver Winning Presentations* (New York: American Management Associations, 1982), p. 253.

2. Carl Sagan, *Cosmos,* (New York: Random House, 1980), p. 196.

3. Janet Elliott, "That's No Lady, That's My Wife," *Toastmaster,* August 1986, p. 15.

4. Karen Carlson and Alan Meyers, *Speaking with Confidence* (Glenview, IL: Scott, Foresman, 1977), p. 73.

5. Fred Ebel, "Know Your Audience," *Toastmaster,* June 1985, p. 20.

6. Paul Gillin, "Sparse Attendance May Turn Out to Be the Kiss of Dearth [sic] for Softcon Shows," *PC Week,* April 9, 1985, p. 18.

7. John Naber, professional speaker (see Acknowledgments), in reply to author's survey, November 1984.

8. Earl Nightingale, *Communicate What You Think* (Chicago: Nightingale-Conant Corp., 1976), Audiocassette #11.

9. Rosita Perez, professional speaker (see Acknowledgments), in response to author's survey, November 1984.

10. Ibid.

Chapter 5

1. Charles Osgood, *Osgood on Speaking* (New York: Morrow, 1988), p. 35.

2. Arnold ("Nick") Carter, professional speaker (see Acknowledgments), in response to author's survey, November 1984.

Chapter 6

1. Stewart Brand, editor in chief, *Whole Earth Software Catalog* (New York: Quantum Press/Doubleday, 1984), p. 143.

2. Thomas Hunter, quoted in "Conducting Interviews," *Speechwriter's Newsletter,* May 2, 1986, p. 3.

Chapter 7

1. Jon M. Shepard, *Sociology,* 2d ed. (St. Paul, MN: West, 1984), p. 164.

2. News article distributed by The Associated Press, July 8, 1984.

3. Report cited by Shepard, op. cit., p. 164.

4. Lewis Thomas, *The Lives of a Cell* (New York: Viking Press, 1974), pp. 11–12.

5. Robert R. Updegraff, "The Conscious Use of the Subconscious Mind," in Barry M. Smith and Betty Hamilton Pryce, *Reading for Power* (Providence, RI: P.A.R., Inc., 1982), p. 241.

6. Joe W. Boyd, professional speaker (see Acknowledgments), in response to author's survey, November 1984.

Chapter 8

1. Anita Taylor, *Speaking in Public* (Englewood Cliffs, NJ: Prentice-Hall, 1984), p. 174.

2. William J. Seiler, "The Effects of Visual Materials on Attitudes, Credibility, and Retention," *Speech Monographs,* 38 (November 1971), pp. 331–334.

3. George L. Gropper, "Learning from Visuals: Some Behavioral Considerations," *AV Communication Review XI* (Summer 1963), pp. 75–95.

4. Hower J. Hsia, "On Channel Effectiveness," *AV Communication Review* (Fall 1968), pp. 248–250.

5. Bill Crider, "Professional Presentations," *PC World* (August 1984), pp. 248–254.

6. "Achieving the Proper Image," *PC Magazine,* September 27, 1988, p. 124.

Chapter 9

1. Shelley Chaiken and Alice Eagly, "Communication Modality as a Determinant of Message Persuasiveness and Message Comprehensibility," *Journal of Personality and Social Psychology* 34 (1976), pp. 605–614.

2. John P. Houston et al., *Essentials of Psychology,* 2d ed. (Orlando, FL: Academic Press, 1985), p. 185.

3. Harry Sharp, Jr., and Thomas McClung, "Effect of Organization on the Speaker's Ethos," *Speech Monographs* (33 (1966), pp. 182–184.

4. Adapted from Donald M. Murray, *Writing to Learn,* 2d ed. (New York: Holt, Rinehart & Winston, 1987), p. 182.

Chapter 10

1. Frye Gaillard, "New Crusade for Chambers," *The Charlotte Observer,* November 12, 1987, p. 12.

2. Ibid.

3. Joel Weldon, in audiotape "Elephants Don't Bite: Joel Weldon Live," copyright 1984 by Joel H. Weldon & Associates, Scottsdale, Arizona.

4. The musical analogy is derived from Michael Adams, *The Writer's Mind* (Glenview, IL: Scott, Foresman, 1984), p. 126.

5. John E. Baird, "The Effects of Speech Summaries upon Audience Comprehension of Expository Speeches of Varying Quality and Complexity," *Central States Speech Journal* 25 (1974), pp. 124–125.

6. Edward L. Friedman, *The Speechmaker's Complete Handbook* (New York: Harper & Row, 1955), p. 16.

7. Martin Luther King, Jr., "I Have a Dream," reproduced in *The World's Great Speeches,* edited by Lewis Copeland and Lawrence W. Lamm (New York: Dover, 1973), p. 754.

8. Introduction and conclusion printed with the permission of Thomas Vandenberg.

Chapter 11

1. Stan Lee, *The Best of the Worst* (New York: Harper & Row, 1979), p. 51.

2. Outline, notes, and classroom speech by Joan Cohen, used with permission.

3. "American Preaching: A Dying Art?" *Time,* December 31, 1979, p. 64.

Chapter 12

1. Julian L. Simon, *How to Start and Operate a Mail-Order Business* (New York: McGraw-Hill, 1981), p. 196.

2. Ibid., p. 216.

3. Janet Elliott, "That's No Lady, That's My Wife," *Toastmaster,* August 1986, p. 15.

4. Kenneth McFarland, *Eloquence in Public Speaking* (Englewood Cliffs, NJ: Prentice-Hall, 1961), p. 186.

5. Roy Fenstermaker, professional speaker, in response to author's survey (see Acknowledgments).

6. Edward T. Thompson, "How to Write Clearly," reprint of advertisement by International Paper Company, undated.

7. William Zinsser, *On Writing Well,* 3rd ed. (New York: Harper & Row, 1985), p. 110.

8. "What Do You Mean by That?" *Decker Communications Report,* July 1985, p. 8.

9. Theodore Solotaroff, quoted in Frederick Crews, *The Random House Handbook,* 4th ed. (New York: Random House, 1984), p. 128.

10. Winston Churchill, as quoted in William Safire and Leonard Safir, *Good Advice* (New York: Times Books, 1982), p. 253.

11. Ibid., p. 294.

12. David Johnson, as quoted in *The Nido Qubein Letter: A Confidential Report for Speakers, Trainers, and Consultants,* PO Box 6008, High Point, NC, 27262, undated, p. 59.

13. Frederick Crews, *The Random House Handbook,* 4th ed. (New York: Random House, 1984), p. 220.

Chapter 13

1. R. T. Kingman, quoted in Thomas Leech, *How to Prepare, Stage, and Deliver Winning Presentations* (New York: American Management Associations, 1982), p. 223.

2. Elayne Snyder, *Speak for Yourself—With Confidence* (New York: New American Library, 1983), p. 69.

3. Waldo W. Braden, "Abraham Lincoln," in *American Orators Before 1900,* edited by Bernard K. Duffy and Halford R. Ryan (New York: Greenwood Press, 1987), p. 267.

4. Steve Allen, *How to Make a Speech* (New York: McGraw-Hill, 1986), p. 12.

5. Arnold ("Nick") Carter, professional speaker (see Acknowledgments), in response to author's survey, November 1984.

6. Roger Ailes, *You Are the Message* (Homewood, IL: Dow Jones-Irwin, 1988), p. 20.

7. Ibid., p. 30.

8. Ibid.; Robert Rosenthal and Bella M. DePaulo, "Expectations, Discrepancies, and Courtesies in Nonverbal Communication," *Western Journal of Speech Communication,* 43 (Spring 1979), pp. 76–95.

9. Janet Stone and Jane Bachner, *Speaking Up* (New York: McGraw-Hill, 1977), p. 55.

10. Jack Valenti, *Speak Up with Confidence* (New York: Morrow, 1982), pp. 74–75.

11. James ("Doc") Blakely, professional speaker (see Acknowledgments), in response to author's survey, November 1984.

12. Danny Cox, professional speaker (see Acknowledgments) in audiotape of speech entitled "Perils of the Platform," delivered to a National Speakers Association convention and provided in response to author's survey, November 1984.

13. Dorothy Sarnoff, *Never Be Nervous Again* (New York: Crown, 1987), p. 43.

14. Adapted from "Be Prepared to Speak," videotape produced by Kantola-Skeie Productions, San Francisco.

15. Rosita Perez, professional speaker (see Acknowledgments), in response to author's survey, November 1984.

16. Sandy Linver, *Speak Easy* (New York: Summit Books, 1978), p. 121.

17. Steve Allen, op. cit., p. 120.

Chapter 14

1. Reprinted with permission from Hoang Pham.

2. Reprinted with permission from Gina Hawkins.

3. Adapted from Stephen E. Lucas, *The Art of Public Speaking,* 2d. ed. (New York: Random House, 1986), p. 278, and Rudolf Flesch, *The Art of Readable Writing* (New York: Harper & Row, 1949), p. 12.

4. "What We Don't Know," Associated Press article in the *Charlotte Observer,* July 28, 1988, p. 1.

5. Dorothy Sarnoff, *Make the Most of Your Best* (New York: Doubleday, 1981), p. 51.

6. The Diagram Group, *Comparisons* (New York: St. Martin's Press, 1980), p. 22.

7. Outline and speech reprinted by permission of Martha Penland.

Chapter 15

1. Douglas Ehninger, Bruce Gronbeck, and Alan Monroe, *Principles of Speech Communication,* 9th brief ed. (Glenview, IL: Scott, Foresman, 1984), pp. 249–259.

2. Lord Chesterfield, quoted by William Safire and Leonard Safir, *Good Advice* (New York: Times Books, 1982), p. 60.

3. Reprinted with permission from Patricia Caldwell.

4. Carol Burnett, as filmed in the video program "Drink, Drank, Drunk," KQED-TV, Pittsburgh, 1974.

5. Eliot Aronson, *The Social Animal,* 4th ed. (New York: Freeman, 1984), p. 87.

6. Ibid.

7. Jeanne Fahnestock and Marie Secor, "Teaching Argument: A Theory of Types," *College Composition and Communication,* 34 (February 1983), pp. 20–30.

8. Aristotle, *Analytica Posteriora,* Book I, in *Introduction to Aristotle* (New York: The Modern Library, 1947), pp. 9–34.

9. Michael Adams, *The Writer's Mind* (Glenview, IL: Scott, Foresman), p. 234.

10. Abraham H. Maslow, *Motivation and Personality* (New York: Harper & Row, 1970).

11. Reprinted with permission from Vanessa Rivers.

12. Aronson, op. cit., p. 83.

13. Ibid., p. 85.

14. Outline and speech reprinted by permission of Jeffrey Cordell.

Chapter 16

1. Representative Jim Courter, speech delivered in the U.S. House of Representatives, June 20, 1988, as printed in the *Congressional Record,* June 20, 1988, p. E2060. Reprinted with permission.

2. Excerpted from Benjamin L. Hooks's speech, "Struggle On," in Owen Peterson, *Representative American Speeches 1983–1984* (New York: Wilson, 1984), pp. 90–91.

3. Hope Mihalap, professional speaker (see Acknowledgments), in response to author's survey, November 1984.

4. John Naber, professional speaker (see Acknowledgments), in response to author's survey, November 1984.

Chapter 17

1. Thomas J. Peters and Robert H. Waterman, Jr., *In Search of Excellence* (New York: Warner Books, 1982), p. 126.

2. Ibid., p. 127.

3. Ibid.

4. Ibid.

5. Letitia Baldridge, *Complete Guide to Executive Manners* (New York: Rawson Associates, 1985), pp. 191–192.

6. Adapted from Harold Tyler, as quoted in *Decker Communications Report,* March 1984, p. 1.

7. John Dewey, *How We Think* (Boston: Heath, 1933), pp. 106–115.

Appendix A

1. "Video Headhunting," *Time,* January 13, 1986, p. 52.

2. John F. Budd, "Video: A Corporate Communications Tool," *Vital Speeches of the Day,* July 15, 1983, p. 593.

3. "The Media and the Message: The Executive on Television," a supplement to *Decker Communications Report* (November 1985), p. 2.

4. Ibid., p. 3.

5. Jack Valenti, *Speak Up with Confidence* (New York: Morrow, 1982), p. 101.

6. Ibid., p. 122.

Acknowledgments

The following professional speakers responded to the author's survey and generously gave advice from their experience on the public platform: Sheila Murray Bethel, 1390 Market St., Suite 908, San Francisco, CA 94102; Don Beveridge Jr., P.O. Box 223, Barrington, IL 60010; Dr. James "Doc" Blakely, 3404 Fairway Dr., Wharton, TX 77488; Joe W. Boyd, 3534 Riley St., Bellingham, WA 98226; Arnold "Nick" Carter, Nightingale-Conant Corp., 7300 N. Lehigh Ave., Chicago, IL 60648; Danny Cox, 17381 Bonner Dr., Tustin, CA 92680; Lyle Crist, 2550 Belleflower, Alliance, OH 44601; Dr. Charles B. Dygert, 6314 Oakhurst Dr., Grove City, OH 43123; Ruth Duskin Feldman, 935 Fairview Rd., Highland Park, IL 60035; Roy Fenstermaker, 4223 Hackett Ave., Lakewood, CA 90713; Bonnie Gordon Flickinger, 31 Nottingham Terrace, Buffalo, NY 14216; Ed Foreman, 2995 LBJ Freeway, Suite 115, Dallas, TX 75234; D. Michael Frank, Box 27225, Columbus, OH 43227; Patricia Fripp, 527 Hugo St., San Francisco, CA 94122; Ira M. Hayes, 326 Meadowlark Court, Marco Island, FL 33937; Christopher Hegarty, P.O. Box 1152, Novato, CA 94948; Henry Heimlich, M.D., Xavier University, Cincinnati, OH 45207; Tom Hopkins, 7531 E. 2nd St., Scottsdale, AZ 85252; Robert William Hunt, 4106 N. State Rd. 269, Bellevue, OH 44811; E. Ray Jerkins, 307 Doctor's Pavilion, 1916 Patterson St., Nashville, TN 37203; Danielle Kennedy, P.O. Box 4382, San Clemente, CA 92672; Hope Mihalap, 1316 Graydon Ave., Norfolk, VA 23507; E. Larry Moles, 1940 Elida Rd., Lima, OH 48505; Bob Murphey, Attorney, P.O. Box 854, Nacogdoches, TX 75961; John Nabor, P.O. Box 50107, Pasadena, CA 91105; Thom Norman, P.O. Box 536, Scottsdale, AZ 85252; Rosita Perez, 756 Fortuna Dr., Brandon, FL 33511; David W. Richardson, 36 Old Redding Rd., Weston, CT 06883; Jeanne Robertson, 2905 Forestdale Dr., Burlington, NC 27215; Dick Semaan, 20214 Lake Sherwood, Katy, TX 77450; Philip D. Steffen, 3217 Fox Tail Ct., N.E., Marietta, GA 30062; Dr. Jim Tunney, P.O. Box 189, Lakewood, CA 90714; Joel Weldon, 7975 N. Hayden Rd., Suite D-261, Scottsdale, AZ 85258, and Dave Yoho, 10803 West Main St., Fairfax, VA 22030.

APPENDIX A

Speaking
in Front
of a
Camera

The next time you go for a job interview, you might find yourself sitting in front of a video camera, because more and more businesses are using videotapes to select their employees. "The video interview has some advantages over the face-to-face chat," says *Time* magazine. "The tape can be passed around to several executives for review, crucial parts of the interview can be watched more than once, and if a candidate looks hopeless in the first 5 minutes, the employer can hit "fast forward" and move to the next applicant."[1]

Once you have a job, you may appear again on television. Many companies communicate by means of teleconferences—video hookups that enable employees in different parts of the country to talk to one another on-screen. Each year almost 1 million business meetings are conducted in the United States by means of teleconferences.[2]

A growing number of firms also use videocassettes for in-house communication and training. For example, Sonoco Corporation sends news to its plants throughout the world by means of a monthly videocassette that features interviews with executives, human interest stories about workers, safety tips from engineers, and footage of new equipment in operation. "The beauty of a videocassette 'newsletter,'" said one Sonoco official, "is that you can show it to every shift and it builds a team spirit. Our people are thrilled to see themselves and their fellow workers on television."

There is also a chance, of course, that you will appear someday on regular television. You might be asked by a local TV station, for example, to give comments related to your job, your club, your church or synagogue, or your neighborhood. Or you might be asked to participate in a debate over some local controversy.

Here are some guidelines:

☐ *Find out in advance the production "rules."* The director or interviewer can tell you how the program will be produced. He or she should explain any hand signals that you need to know—such as the signal for "Fifteen seconds left" or "Stop speaking—time is up." In all programs, the camera that has a red light on is the one operating at the moment.

☐ *Find out in advance whether the program involves direct or indirect TV.* There are two distinct types of television programs.[3] *Direct* TV means that you look straight into the camera and speak directly to the viewers. This kind of program is used for news reports and teleconferences. *Indirect* TV means that you talk with an interviewer or with fellow panel members while the camera looks on. Indirect TV is the more popular type; it is used for talk shows, interviews, and many documentaries. It is important for you to know which type of television program you are on so that you can observe the next two guidelines.

☐ *For direct TV, look at the camera.* If you fail to look steadily at the camera in a direct-TV program, you come across to viewers as evasive, untrustworthy, or unprepared. The only exception to this rule would be glancing down at notes occasionally and briefly. In some cases you may want to look at cue cards or a teleprompter placed next to the camera lens—so that you give the impression you are looking directly into the camera (the newscasters you see on television appear to be talking straight into the camera, but they are actually reading the news from a teleprompter).

Practicing with a video camera
can help you learn to speak
more effectively on camera.
(Ulrike Welsch)

☐ *For indirect TV, never look at the camera.* One of the reasons for the popularity of indirect TV is that it creates the illusion that the viewer is eavesdropping on a conversation. Thus, to avoid destroying this illusion, you must never look into the camera. Give your full attention to the interviewer or other participants.

☐ *If possible, practice in the studio.* Being ushered into a television studio, with its bright lights, massive equipment, and bustling technicians, can be unnerving for the person who has never had television experience. If possible, practice sitting and speaking in a studio a few days before the production. If your program will be a *direct* show, practice looking at the camera lens. If you can rent or borrow a video camera, practice on videotape and watch yourself in playback to correct any problems in your delivery.

☐ *Dress conservatively.* The colors that show up best on television are the medium hues—pink, green, tan, and gray. Avoid extremely bright colors such as red and extremely dark colors such as black. Because it reflects other colors, white is a poor choice. Stay away from fine prints like checks or plaids—they can cause visual distractions. Avoid sparkling or noisy jewelry. Both men and women sometimes need makeup such as powder to cut down on shininess and glare.[4]

☐ *Arrange to have a cup of water handy.* When I appeared on a live TV talk show recently, I found that the heat of the bright lights, plus my nervousness, made my mouth go dry. With envy, I observed that the host of the show had a cup of water underneath her chair; during commercial breaks, she would reach for her cup and take a sip. Learning from her example, I arranged to have a cup of water nearby during my next television appearance.

☐ *Always keep your "real" audience in mind.* Let us say that you take part in a videotaped program about your company's new product. If you are interviewed by a colleague about the product, your real audience is not the colleague but the people who will be watching the program. So while you are ostensibly chatting with your colleague, you need to fashion your remarks to reach your true viewers. What are their needs and interests? How can you entice them into buying the product?

☐ *Speak conversationally.* Jack Valenti, president of the Motion Picture Association of America, makes frequent appearances on television in programs such as the Academy Awards presentations. "The indispensable element of television speaking," he says, "is [to be] conversational, as if you were in a living room talking to a half-dozen people." But how can you be conversational if you are on a *direct* TV program, needing to speak straight into the unblinking gaze of a camera? "I think it useful," says Valenti, "to have someone (preferably two or three people), either friends of yours or studio technicians, stand slightly behind and around the camera. When your cue comes, and the red light [goes on], talk to them. If they are grouped closely around the camera, you will not be diverting your own gaze too far to the left or right of the lens but will be able to talk to living people rather than that robotlike, sterile companion." If no one is available to stand near the camera, says Valenti, "imagine the camera eye to be a window through which you are speaking to the cameraman on the other side of the lens" or "pretend that someone you trust is sitting in front of you. Speak to that imaginary friend."[5]

☐ *Be yourself.* Try to be relaxed and natural. Do not paste a smile on your face and wear it throughout the program; smile only when it is appropriate. Do not feel that you must be an expert on everything discussed. If the interviewer asks a question and you do not know the answer, simply say so.

☐ *Never assume that the eye of the camera is no longer on you.* During interviews, many people assume that because another person on the show is talking, the camera is no longer focused on them, so they scratch their head or look around at the TV studio or grin at someone off camera. Meanwhile, of course, the TV camera is mercilessly broadcasting this rudeness and inattentiveness, because the camera operator has broadened the focus to include all participants. You should always assume that you are being televised—not only to avoid making a fool of yourself, but also to keep from distracting viewers from the content of the program.

☐ *Scale down movement and gestures.* The kind of vigorous movement and powerful gestures that are excellent in a speech to an auditorium of 500 people will make you look like a buffoon if repeated in front of the TV camera. In the language of television, these actions are "too hot" for the medium. Any gestures you make should be small and low-key. Jack Valenti says, "It is fine to express passion in your cause, but without flailing of arms and head. On television, passionate belief is better expressed by a gaze or an emotional inflection of a phrase than by an out-thrust fist or jaw."[6] Avoid sudden, swift movements such as crossing your legs rapidly; this can have a jarring effect on viewers. If you must make such movements, make them very slowly.

☐ *Sit in a relaxed, confident posture.* Neither sit in a rigid position that suggests nervousness and anxiety nor go to the opposite extreme and slouch in a casual position that suggests boredom and lack of interest. Try to make yourself comfortable, yet alert—the way you would sit if you were carrying on an animated conversation with your best friend.

☐ *Use the microphone correctly.* There are two facts about microphones that you need to know: (1) A microphone picks up all sounds, not just your words. Avoid coughing, rustling papers, whispering side comments to someone off camera, and brushing against the microphone. (2) A microphone works best if you do not put your mouth right next to it. Some people think that they must almost eat the mike in order to get their words picked up. In reality, today's microphones are engineered so that they work best when you speak at some distance from them. The best advice is to simply speak in your normal voice and forget all about the microphone. (If, however, you are required to hold a microphone, hold it about one foot below your mouth and speak over it, instead of into it.)

☐ *Ignore distractions.* When the red light goes on, concentrate all your attention on reaching your audience. Ignore the crew members and the machinery.

☐ *Speak briefly.* If you are long-winded, rambling, or tedious, your viewers will tune you out— of their minds or their TV screens. Be brief. Be concise.

APPENDIX B

Sample

Speeches

Outfoxing Mr. Badwrench

Kristin Amondsen

A student at Bradley University, Kristin Amondsen delivered this speech at the 114th annual contest of the Interstate Oratorical Association at College Park, Maryland, in 1987. It is reprinted with permission from *Winning Orations 1987*.

1   For over five years now, after *60 Minutes,* we've seen a kindly man with greying temples in a clean, pressed mechanic's uniform, come into our living rooms and proudly state, "Quality care for your car is what I provide for you." But when we go out—looking for Mr. Goodwrench—we invariably encounter his alter ego and we end up dropping our keys into the hands of someone I'd like to call Mr. Badwrench. Because in America today, according to Lauren Petite, Commissioner of Consumer Services in Chicago, auto repairs are still the biggest consumer complaint. And you know what? I know you're not surprised. Because according to the U.S. Office of Consumer Affairs, auto mechanic fraud is our country's number one consumer problem. So let's take a look at how we're taken. First, let's take a look under the hood: how bad is auto mechanic fraud? Secondly, we'll examine two important parts—two reasons why it exists. Then let's run a safety check: let's check the harms of this problem. And finally, we'll run a major overhaul to stop the breakdown—the breakdown of our consumer-mechanic relationship.

2   Sloppy and needless auto repairs cost us over 30 billion dollars annually. How widespread is mechanic fraud? In a study of 836 major chain store repairs, conducted by diagnostic centers at the University of Alabama in 1985, 25 percent of the repairs were found to be unnecessary. And one firm actually had a 47 percent rate of unnecessary repairs. But the U.S. Department of Transportation uncovered an even more disturbing fact. They found that at least 53 cents out of every dollar paid for auto repairs was spent unnecessarily because of inflated prices or needless work. Are you questioning the ethics of your so-called trusty mechanic yet? Well, the Colorado Public Interest Research Group did. They intentionally loosened a drive belt on a '71 Volkswagen. Then they brought the VW to eight repair shops in Boulder. Only one of the shops solved the problem and charged the appropriate fee. Well, four other shops did fix the problem. But they also did costly and unnecessary tune-ups. Another type of dishonesty that makes us suffer is the overcharging of labor. Take, for example, Roberta Grey of San Francisco. Well, Roberta took her red Datsun into a repair shop for a number of repairs. The shop made it clear that they charged $35 an hour for labor. One might assume, by looking at Roberta's $350 labor bill, that ten hours of hard work was put into her Datsun. However, the shop only put in 6.4 hours. Now, logically speaking, Roberta's bill should have only come to $224; however, she spent an unnecessary $126. This is a perfect example of the auto repair industry's old con game. It's called a Flat Rate Fiddle . . . and it's perfectly legal. Basically, what flat rate manuals do is list various repair operations for a car. Then they state exactly how long a repair should take. Flat rate manuals are published by auto manufacturers for mechanics to follow when doing repair work. Now,

in Roberta's case, the flat rate manual stated that her repairs should have taken ten hours. These manuals give our mechanics written permission to steal from us. And unfortunately, most repair shops do usually take advantage of this opportunity to take. The New York State Consumer Commission found during the investigation of some 408 repair shops, that 56 percent of them were grossly overcharging their labor. The New York State Attorney General's Office has estimated that motorists of that state alone are being overcharged 73 million dollars annually just through the use of flat rate manuals. But the overcharging of labor isn't enough for Mr. Badwrench.

3   It's been discovered that numerous mechanics will go much further. According to the June 18, 1984, issue of *U.S. News and World Report,* some mechanics will go as far as to paint your old automobile parts to look like new, and then proceed to put them back into your car, and better still, squirt fluid on shock absorbers before telling the motorists that they're leaking. Other examples include barbecue sauce being poured on the alternator to cause a burning smell, a seltzer tablet being dropped onto the battery to make it foam, and one mechanic in Colorado went so far as to stick a blade in the toe of his shoe in order to slash tires. But why is this occurring? Well, often the mechanic has the incentive to sell you extra parts because he's receiving a commission and according to Sandy Mitchell, the New York State Assistant Attorney General, auto repair is so ripe for abuse because consumer ignorance is so widespread. Let's face it. How many of you know which gizmo goes where, does what and how much it costs? But current studies show that oftentimes, not only can the consumer be ignorant, but so can the mechanic. According to the National Institute for Automotive Service Excellence, about half of all mechanics in our nation can't even completely diagnose and repair even one area of your car. Now obviously, this symbolizes a bit of incompetence. The organization also stated that out of over 500,000 mechanics in our country, only 28,000 passed all competency tests. That means that less than six percent of our nation's mechanics have passed industry-sponsored competency tests. In comparison to some mechanics, I could probably repair your car better (and believe me, that's not saying much!). Think about this. Auto mechanic fraud has cost us billions of dollar unnecessarily. If we don't take any precautions before allowing our mechanics to work on our cars, chances are that Mr. Badwrench could be repairing your car unnecessarily and/or incorrectly.

4   But there are precautions we can take to run a major overhaul, to stop the breakdown of our consumer-mechanic relationship. The first thing that we can do is to find a competent mechanic. According to Lillian Borgeson, auto repair specialist, this can be achieved by finding a mechanic with credentials from the National Institute for Automotive Service Excellence, dubbed ASE. This is the only nationally accepted organization that tests a mechanic's competence. Now in order to receive a certificate from the ASE, the mechanic must have at least one year of experience with the hardware. And must also have passed a three- to four-hour competency test. And that's not all. In order to assure the ASE that their skills are up to par, ASE mechanics have to pass new updated tests every five years. Secondly, we as consumers must be a lot more careful in not only selecting our mechanic, but selecting our repair shop. There's a similar organization

to ASE that awards accreditation to automotive repair shops; and those shops that pass the tough AAA test are awarded the right to display a red, white, and blue sign with the AAA seal of approval. It would be worth your time and money to look for that seal. And, finally, we can establish a checklist. In order to avoid the Flat Rate Fiddle situation, look for a mechanic or a repair shop that charges by the clock hour instead of the victimizing flat rate manuals. Chances are that your labor will be a lot more down-to-earth. And what can you do to avoid the questionable repair shops? You can check with the Better Business Bureau to learn complaint histories of particular repair shops. That way you can avoid one with a record. And before you have anything done with your car, it's a good idea to write down all of the symptoms in advance and then get a written estimate from more than one repair shop. Larry Coorigan from Atlanta found this to be helpful. Larry was having trouble with his Mustang's electrical system. Taking it to one repair shop, he was told that it would need a new alternator, and that the tab would come to $135. However, seeking a second opinion, the mechanic of the garage found the battery cables were simply corroded and solved the whole problem for just three dollars. And what can you do to prevent your mechanic from painting and selling your own parts back to you? Ask your mechanic to give you back your old parts that are to be replaced before he even does the job.

5   And you know what? You don't have to do any of these things. If you want to have more auto mechanic fraud horror stories to tell . . . by all means don't. But chances are you'll have more in the future. Because with every dollar we spend, we're telling Mr. Badwrench that it's good to be bad. If we close our wallets and start spending some common sense, we can say goodbye to Mr. Badwrench . . . and get the monkey wrench out of our lives.

Blue Beans and Purple Potatoes

Cecelia Miller

One of the things all of us humans have in common, someone once said, is that we grew up in the same faraway village—childhood. As you read the following, you will probably remember some of your own eating habits in that village. This speech, delivered in a class at Asheville-Buncombe Technical Community College in Asheville, North Carolina, is a good example of an entertaining speech, sometimes called an after-dinner speech. Notice that Cecelia Miller's talk is simple and light—a tasty snack rather than a heavy meal. Note, too, that it entertains without resorting to comic one-liners.

1   Imagine that you are visiting with a friend you haven't seen in several years, and you receive a last minute invitation to dinner. Of course you accept and everything is fine until you sit down to eat. There on the plate in front of you are blue beans, purple potatoes, and orange meatloaf. What would your reaction be? Would you think your friend is a color-blind artist who takes our her frustrations in the kitchen? Or would you think she was ready for the loony bin?

2   Maybe the answer is much simpler. She probably has a nine-year-old son

who is into "space food" and the only way she can get him to eat a well-balanced meal is to serve "Martian" cuisine. This is just one of the sneaky, devious tricks parents use to get their finicky children to eat what they should. As the experienced mother of two very picky eaters, I'd like to let you in on some other tricks.

3   When children are small, say between the ages of one and four, getting them to eat is fairly simple. We're all familiar with the old "here comes the train—open the tunnel" game. That takes care of half the problem—it gets the food into their mouths. You'll have to find your own way to get them to swallow it. If your toddler doesn't want to eat eggs, try boiling the eggs and then draw faces on the shell. You can use wax crayons or food colors. If that doesn't work, you can fall back on that old favorite, Dr. Seuss. Put green food coloring into scrambled eggs and pretend they are the green eggs that Dr. Seuss made famous in his children's classic. You can also make bunny-rabbit salads out of cottage cheese. Use carrot sticks for ears and raisins for eyes.

4   For children aged nine or ten you may need a little more imagination. Try dyeing food weird colors and telling the children it's space food—fresh from Pluto this morning. You can also put good wholesome food into a pie shape. I believe this is why quiche is so popular—children will eat anything pie-shaped without argument. On some mornings you will wake up to find several boxes of cereal on the shelf with only one or two inches of cereal left in them. The children will not eat these rejects. One way to dispose of them—other than to just throwing them away—is to pour them all into one big box, cover with aluminum foil, and paint "Venetian Surprise" on the front. it will be gone in no time.

5   Teenagers are sophisticated, cool, and too smart to be fooled by anyone as dumb as a parent. Anyway, that's what they think. But getting teenagers to eat is really not that hard—it just takes a little trickery. I used to save the containers from fast-food places and refill them at home. The food was always eaten and enjoyed, and the kids didn't know the difference. (At least not until they heard me rehearse this speech.) Another trick is to make everything into pizza. Teenagers will eat pizza hot, cold, or even lukewarm. Mine usually eat it cold in the morning for breakfast. If you want them to eat a more conventional breakfast, put tomato sauce and cheese on a tortilla over the top of eggs and sausage. It's just a Mexican omelette upside down. If all else fails, try using the old trick my mother used on us. Tell them it's not good for them. A teenager will decide that spinach is his favorite food if he thinks it isn't good for him to eat much of it.

6   I hope these ideas help you when your own children become picky eaters. But let me inject one word of caution. Unless you can stomach green eggs for breakfast, don't eat with your four-year-old. Whatever you feed him, you'll have to eat, too.

Humans to Mars—Why?

James M. Beggs

Will humans explore Mars within the next 60 years? Yes, predicts James M. Beggs, who was Administrator of NASA (National Aeronautics and Space Administration) when he delivered this speech at the National Air and Space Museum in Washington, D.C., on July 16, 1985. Beggs's speech is primarily *informative* (he tells his listeners what is likely to happen in future space exploration), but it is also *persuasive* (he tries to convince the audience that sending humans to Mars is a sensible idea), and *inspirational* (he challenges the listener to reach for the stars). The speech is reprinted with permission from *Vital Speeches of the Day* (November 1, 1985).

1   Mark Twain once said: "Predictions are very difficult to make, especially when they deal with the future."

2   I won't quarrel with that. But even if the immediate future is uncertain, I have no doubts about the more distant years. So I'll make a prediction. It is that some day human beings will rove the surface of Mars. They will crate up those wonderful Viking machines, return them to earth, and send them here to this museum. And future generations of children will come here and stand before not merely one, but three Viking landers, and imagine their journeys and the adventures of the people that replaced them.

3   It is fitting that we should be discussing the question of human journeys to Mars on this tenth anniversary of the Apollo-Soyuz docking in space. That mission was the last to employ a manned Apollo spacecraft.

4   Apollo opened the floodgates of the human imagination to the exciting possibilities of people exploring the universe. Science fiction became fact because we demonstrated conclusively that humans could, indeed, leave earth, land on another world and return safely to their mother planet.

5   Now that we have opened those gates, humankind will never be the same. We will take many more steps on many more worlds before we're through. And one of those worlds, most likely the first we will go to, will be Mars.

6   Indeed, we could be en route to Mars before the middle of the next century. By then, using as our springboard the Space Station and its infrastructure, which will include an interorbital transportation system, we may very well have established a manned lunar base. Mars would be the next logical niche for human expansion in the universe.

7   Why Mars? Clearly, Mars will have priority in any manned solar system exploration program because it offers the least severe environment for humans. Due to its atmosphere, its accessible surface, its probable availability of water, and its relatively moderate temperatures—they range from $-120°$ C to $+20°$ C—it is the most habitable of all the planets other than earth.

8   Moreover, Mars' resources include materials that could be adapted to support human life, including air, fuels, fertilizers, building materials, and an environment that could grow food.

9   There is a truism, but one that bears repeating, that the universe doesn't care who explores it. It is we who care. And because we do, this epochal step in human exploration to a planet which could become the first self-sufficient home for human beings should be a cooperative international effort.

10   Indeed, given the enormous scope of such an effort, the resources required and its benefits to all mankind, it is tempting to say outright that it should not be done unilaterally. Nevertheless, if the commitment and

the resources were forthcoming, nothing would preclude a technologically sophisticated and dedicated nation from going it alone.

11   But whether a manned Mars mission should turn out to be a unilateral or a multilateral undertaking, one thing is clear. To make any sense, such a program must be viewed as a long-term commitment. It cannot focus merely on landing humans on the planet and returning them safely to earth. A Mars landing must also include planning for subsequent sustaining operations. The first Mars explorers probably will not become permanent residents. Rather, they will set the stage for others to come. For others will come—to build, to live, to work, to learn and above all, to explore with their own hands and eyes and tools this exciting and unknown world.

12   Mars has a special meaning as we look out into the universe to plan our next steps in space in the post-Space Station era. It is attainable. It is livable. And its major mysteries remain unsolved. Space-age exploration of the planet has revealed it as a kind of "halfway world," in part like earth and in part like the moon and Mercury. What caused its climate changes? How did its surface features—the great rifts and huge volcanoes—form? Is the whole planet really lifeless? If so, why, given that next to earth, Mars has the best environment to sustain life in the solar system?

13   Mars has a thin atmosphere, climate, weather, and apparently, huge reservoirs of frozen water. Like the moon and Mercury, the ancient, cratered surface of its southern hemisphere is little changed over billions of years. It probably bears evidence of the solar system's formation.

14   In Mars' northern hemisphere, huge volcanic mountains climb as high as 25 kilometers—three times higher than Mt. Everest and up to six times higher than any volcano on earth. Elsewhere on this younger half of Mars, there is a 2800-mile-long canyon stretching three times deeper and seven times longer than the Grand Canyon of the Colorado. In that canyon is probably locked the whole geological history of Mars, and, perhaps, equally important, clues to the history of our own star, the sun.

15   So Mars is geologically interesting. But we can study planetary geology with unmanned spacecraft. Indeed, we have done so on Mars with several unmanned spacecraft. Some have flown by the planet. Others have orbited it. And two have landed on it. We will continue to explore the planet with unmanned spacecraft.

16   In 1990, for example, we expect to launch the Mars Observer, which will do global mapping of Mars for a full Martian year, which is equal to two earth years. We will focus on geoscience and climatology.

17   Later, unmanned spacecraft will surely focus on other science missions—such as the planet's upper atmosphere, its magnetic field, its seismology. And more ambitious unmanned [craft] would, most likely, return Mars samples to earth. We have already demonstrated the ability to learn about other worlds from the moon rocks, from meteorites and from cosmic dust. We can now apply proven techniques to determine the nature and history of Mars from its own rocks.

18   Indeed, by studying the Martian rocks and soil in a laboratory right here on earth, we may even settle the question of whether there is or ever has been Martian life.

19   If we can learn so much about Mars with our robot spacecraft, why would

we want to go there ourselves?: Would we go for the same reason we climb a mountain—because it is there? I doubt it. We would need broader reasons than that. Consider Bernard Shaw's line from "Methuselah": "Some men see things as they are and say, why; I dream things that never were and say, why not."

20   Why not go to Mars to advance the human presence in space?

21   Why not go to Mars to build a permanent gateway to the Asteroid Belt and the other planets?

22   Why not go to Mars to use human judgment, human abilities, and human intelligence to explore an exciting new world? Why not go there to recognize, to describe, to organize, to correlate, and to solve problems as only humans can solve them, using all our experience and skill?

23   On Mars, we could unleash all the richness and subtlety—all the variety and versatility of the human mind and spirit—to plumb the mysteries of who we are, how we came to be and what our destiny might be. So why not go to Mars to better understand ourselves and our earth, our ice ages, the effects of atmospheric changes on our weather and climate? And, in T. S. Eliot's words: "The end of all our exploring will be to arrive where we started and know the place for the first time."

24   Why not go to Mars to stimulate progress in our own space capabilities, to develop new cutting edge technologies—propulsion, life support, habitation, non-terrestrial resource use? These will not only get us to Mars, but also leave their benefits on earth.

25   And, finally, why not go to Mars to build on the framework for international cooperation the Space Station will have begun and, perhaps, a manned lunar base will have continued?

26   An immensely challenging program such as a manned Mars mission could be a strong force for peace in the world. It could redirect creative human brains from the prospects of dealing with armed conflicts to the prospects of planning and carrying out a peaceful, stimulating and ultimately more valuable program of unprecedented scope and magnitude. Ironically, Mars, the primitive symbol of the God of War, could become a powerful instrument for peace.

27   "Humanity is just a work in progress," wrote Tennessee Williams. Indeed we are. And as we evolve and grow, I believe we will demonstrate that there are no limits to our future in the universe.

28   Shakespeare understood that well. And, as usual, he put it best.

> Man is master of his liberty . . .
> There's nothing situate under heaven's eye
> But hath his bound, in earth, in sea and sky.

29   I believe that. There truly are no limits to what we can do if we have faith in the promise of the future.

30   Humans to Mars? Indeed, why not!

31   Thank you very much.

Index